Between Black and Brown

BORDERLANDS AND TRANSCULTURAL STUDIES

Series Editors:

Rudy Guevarra
Paul Spickard

REBECCA ROMO, G. REGINALD DANIEL, AND J STERPHONE

Between Black and Brown

Blaxicans and Multiraciality in Comparative Historical Perspective

University of Nebraska Press | Lincoln

© 2024 by the Board of Regents of the University of Nebraska

All rights reserved

The University of Nebraska Press is part of a land-grant institution with campuses and programs on the past, present, and future homelands of the Pawnee, Ponca, Otoe-Missouria, Omaha, Dakota, Lakota, Kaw, Cheyenne, and Arapaho Peoples, as well as those of the relocated Ho-Chunk, Sac and Fox, and Iowa Peoples.

Library of Congress Cataloging-in-Publication Data
Names: Romo, Rebecca, author. | Daniel, G. Reginald, 1949–2022, author. | Sterphone, J, author.
Title: Between Black and Brown: Blaxicans and multiraciality in comparative historical perspective / Rebecca Romo, G. Reginald Daniel, and J Sterphone.
Other titles: Blaxicans and multiraciality in comparative historical perspective
Description: Lincoln: University of Nebraska Press, [2024] | Series: Borderlands and transcultural studies | Includes bibliographical references and index.
Identifiers: LCCN 2023057196
ISBN 9780803290181 (hardback)
ISBN 9781496240552 (paperback)
ISBN 9781496240651 (epub)
ISBN 9781496240668 (pdf)
Subjects: LCSH: Racially mixed people—Race identity—United States. | Racially mixed people—United States—History. | African Americans—Race identity—United States. | Hispanic Americans—Race identity—United States. | United States—Race relations—History. | Racism—United States—History. | BISAC: SOCIAL SCIENCE / Biracial & Multiracial Studies | SOCIAL SCIENCE / Ethnic Studies / American / African American & Black Studies
Classification: LCC E184.A1 R66 2024 | DDC 305.800973—dc23/eng/20240403
LC record available at https://lccn.loc.gov/2023057196

Set in Linotype Sabon Next by A. Shahan.

For our mentor and friend G. Reginald Daniel

Contents

List of Tables   ix

Acknowledgments   xi

Introduction: Bringing Blaxicans to the Forefront   1

Part 1. Racial Formation and the Blaxican Borderlands

1. Race and Mixed Race: Multiracial Identities in Academia   15
2. Anglo-America and Latin America   33
3. Louisiana and the Gulf Coast   43
4. Black Identity Construction and the Monoracial Imperative   52
5. California and the Southwest   61
6. Mexican American Identity and Monoraciality   68
7. Multiracial Identities: The Law of the Included Middle   83
8. "Dual Minority" Multiracial Identities: Decentering Whiteness   96

Part 2. Living Race and Identity in Black and Brown

9. Racial Labels as a Self-Designation: Blaxican and Proud!   119
10. Defining Blaxicans: Racial-Cultural Existence in a Borderland Space   149
11. Social Agency and Constraint: Family, School, and Neighborhood   189
12. Race and Cultural Authenticity: You're Not Black or Mexican Enough!   209

13. Black and Brown Relations: Situation and Context Matter   233

Conclusion: Bridging the Borderlands   251

Notes   267
Bibliography   309
Index   353

Tables

1. Race/ethnic background of parents   121
2. Blaxicans raised by an African American single parent   132
3. Blaxicans raised by a Mexican or Mexican American single parent   136
4. Blaxicans raised by Mexican or Mexican American mother and African American father   141
5. Blaxicans raised by African American mother and Mexican or Mexican American father   147

Acknowledgments

Between Black and Brown was many years in the making and born out of collaboration, mutuality, friendship, and respect. Neither time nor space allows us to acknowledge the many individuals who helped bring this book to fruition. It would not have been possible without the stellar editorial assistance provided by Laurie L. Lewis and Basia Nowak. Jennifer Burton of Columbia Indexing Group is a miracle worker in compiling an index. We would like to thank the UC Santa Barbara Chicano Studies Institute, American Sociological Association Minority Fellowship Program, and UC MEXUS for funding, as well as Santa Monica College for a sabbatical, to help complete this project. We would also like to express our appreciation to everyone interviewed for sharing their stories and giving us a deeper understanding. We are grateful for the support of Matthew Bokovoy, senior acquisitions editor at the University of Nebraska Press, and Rudy Guevarra and Paul Spickard, series editors for Borderlands and Transcultural Studies, as well as for the readers recruited by the press.

A special thanks to Manuel Barajas, Elvia Ramirez, Rachel Sarabia Ortiz, Jake Alimahomed-Wilson, Sabrina Alimahomed-Wilson, Shigueru Tsuha, Denise Segura, Sarah Fenstermaker, Leonard Cortana, Jennie Marlow, Spotted Eagle, Victoria Bearden, Jeanne Palmer, Dan Palmer, Liz Monday, Jasmine Kelekay, Alyssa Newman, and Maria P. P. Root, in addition to the many unnamed friends, colleagues, students, and relatives whose support contributed to making this a better book. Rebecca Romo would like to thank her parents, José Antonio Romo and María Elena Romo, and her siblings, Leticia Mendoza, Angelica Ibañez, Antonio Romo, Carlos Romo, Francisco Romo, Raquel Coley, and their partners and kids for their love and support. Her son Emilio Romo was the inspiration for the project, and Miles Romo-McKeever, Michael McKeever, Derrek McKeever, Maya McKever, and Malik McKeever gave her continued motivation to complete it. Rebecca had the great fortune to rely on her brilliant partner James McKeever and his persistent encouragement and belief in the completion of this book. Last, we are eternally grateful for our dissertation advisor, friend, and mentor G. Reginald Daniel, who sadly passed away during the publication of this book. We thank him for sharing his brilliance with the world and for being a pioneer in the field of critical mixed race studies. He will forever be remembered and missed. We would like to dedicate the book in his honor.

Between Black and Brown

Introduction

Bringing Blaxicans to the Forefront

"Aren't we all multiracial?" is a common challenge directed at the topic of multiraciality. The confusion lies in the difference between being multiracial in ancestry and being multiracial in identity. Although we recognize certain physical traits as distinguishing populations from one another, a "mixed" lineage is thought to be the norm, rather than the exception, regardless of identity. If you trace a person's lineage back twenty generations, you will find that each individual has over 1 million ancestors that span the globe.[1] The possibilities of their geographical and "racial" composition are staggering. Indeed, racial intermingling has characterized human history. But that intermingling has been ignored, obscured, and erased by several hundred years of Eurocentric thought about racial (and cultural) purity. This phenomenon was shaped by new ideologies and practices accompanying the colonial expansion of Western Europe beginning in the fifteenth century. While expansion, conquest, exploitation, and enslavement are aspects of human history, they were not supported by ideologies or social systems based on race until the beginning of European colonialism.

Racial Formation and the Concept of Race

Increased competitiveness among European nation-states; the cultural and phenotypic differences between Europeans and the populations of the Americas, Asia, the Pacific Islands, and Africa; and the relative ease with which Europeans were able to dominate those populations influenced European perceptions of all non-Europeans. Over the following centuries, this in turn laid the foundation for the full development of the concept of "race," which classified human populations as discrete, mutually exclusive biological groups. This conceptualization also included notions that these biological characteristics reflected behavioral, intellectual, temperamental, moral, and other qualities, which were inheritable.[2] "Scientific" inquiry based on biological determinism confirmed inequalities between the races in a way that supported Europeans' conviction of their own superiority. White racism and white supremacy were institutionalized by the state as systematic components of social structure. This justified the conquest and colonization of the Americas and the enslavement of Africans there. Moreover, the Americas became the site of an unprecedented blending of Indigenous, European, and African peoples and immigrant diasporas across the globe.

That said, all humans descend from a much earlier diaspora after the first modern humans evolved in Africa as early as 200,000 years ago. These first modern humans moved outside of Africa in several waves between 90,000 and 180,000 years ago. The people of this African diaspora adapted to various environments and evolved into geographical populations displaying differences in various bodily features. Some externally visible ones—skin color, hair, and facial morphology—are commonly referred to as "racial traits." These physical differences (phenotypes) reflect some of the differences in genetic information (genotypes) transmitted through one's ancestors. Yet all humans share 99.9 percent of their genes. Consequently, phenotypical differences among humans reflect only 0.1 percent of the genetic information transmitted through ancestors. Notwithstanding the fact that some phenotypical traits are quite noticeable (e.g., skin color, hair form), they are based on practically "nothing," meaning a miniscule part of the total human genome. Still, they are composed of millions of bits of genetic information and are thus composed of "something."[3]

It should not be assumed, therefore, that people have taken leave of their senses when they make assumptions based on observation about the continental origins of an individual's recent ancestors. Indeed, the concept of "race" is used in an attempt to explain, however fraught with contradictions, observable geno-phenotypical differentiations. There are populations that, taken as aggregates, exhibit higher incidences of genetic and physical traits than others.[4] But while geno-phenotypical diversity of racial traits is a biological fact, the boundaries delineating subgroupings are not discrete or fixed entities and have always eroded through human contact and interaction.

The smaller the proportion of any given ancestry the more probable it is that the number of genes inherited from that ancestry is also proportionately smaller. Yet genes are randomly distributed in individuals. Having one or more ancestors from the West African diaspora associated with the Atlantic slave trade from the sixteenth to nineteenth centuries, for example, does not guarantee that individuals will inherit genetic information from those ancestors or exhibit discernible West African phenotypical traits.[5] Individuals may be of partial West African ancestry and inherit genetic material from those ancestors yet appear completely European American.

This "illusion" of complete "whiteness" is partly attributable to the fact that humans are unable to independently perceive information at the genetic level with the naked eye.[6] Still, racial logics are not developed on the back of genetics. In the United States, the one-drop rule of hypodescent (one drop of African blood) designates as Black anyone with African American ancestry. Similar rules, discussed at length in chapters 2 and 3, also rely on ancestry, not genetics, to arrive at racial designations as well as to enforce racialized hierarchies.

Racial Ancestry and Racial Identities

This book argues that Blaxican identification—African American and Mexican American—signifies changes in how multiracial Americans of African descent express their identities. It is a form of resistance to the one-drop rule, as well as the "monoracial imperative," which precludes identification with more than one racial background.[7] These social devices are "commonsense" ways of defining Blackness.

Monoraciality and hypodescent have become *sine qua non* in the U.S. racial order. They have imbued Blackness with a unique place in U.S. jurisprudence and the national-racial imaginary. Therefore, a contemporary examination of identity formation among multiracials of African descent is particularly meaningful.

Notwithstanding their monoracial designation, African Americans and Mexican Americans are "multigenerational multiracial" because of slavery and European colonization. African Americans have African, Native American, European, and in some cases, Asian ancestries. Similarly, Mexican Americans' backgrounds include European (particularly Spanish) ancestry, as well as Native American, African, and in some cases, Asian ancestry. They display various gradations of skin color and other phenotypical features reflecting each of the parent racial groups as well as all types in between. Yet most, respectively, hold singular African American and Mexican American identities, attributable to the legacy of hypodescent and the monoracial imperative.

The monoracial imperative is itself reflective of a broader "monological" paradigm originating in the modern worldview accompanying Europe's rise to global dominion beginning in the sixteenth century. That mindset perpetuates an either/or mentation based on the "law of the excluded middle," which does not acknowledge shades of gray.[8] It necessitates the study of things, including people, in isolation and in parts and delineates them into mutually exclusive (or dichotomous), oppositional, and hierarchical categories of experience.[9] This paradigm is premised on "the precision of interpretation and on the reduction of ambiguity," complexity, and multiplicity.[10] Singularity is the norm in constructing all categories of difference encompassing race (e.g., white or nonwhite), gender (e.g., masculine or feminine), sexuality (e.g., straight or gay), and even one's stance on morality and politics.[11] Indeed, the monological paradigm is part of the "doxa," that is the sphere of sacrosanct, or unquestioned, social concepts or dogmas that have acquired the force of nature.[12]

Hybridity is unsustainable in this framework. Thus, Blaxican identities interrogate and resist normative constructions of identities and categories underpinned by the monological paradigm as well as the monoracial imperative and hypodescent. Blaxican identities are not anti-Black or anti-Mexican, nor are they a dismissal of monoracial identifications. Rather, along with other multiracial identities, they reject normative constructions of identities that deem other forms of identity as illegitimate.

This study of first-generation Blaxicans examines experiences and identities derived from having one parent who is socially designated and self-identified as African American and one who is socially designated and self-identified as Mexican American, regardless of the actual racial and cultural backgrounds in their parents' histories. Blaxicans differ from their monoracial parents because they identify with both of their backgrounds. They may appear Black or Mexican and are viewed differently depending on the context. Yet they form racial and cultural identities that blend socially constructed meanings attached to Blacks and Mexicans and view themselves as and identify as some blend of both in fluid and situational ways.

Some may consider the term *Afro-Mexican* to encompass the experiences and identities of Blaxicans. Notwithstanding the similarities, which will be discussed at length in chapter 6, the differences between Blaxicans and those considered Afro-Mexican are noteworthy. Blaxicans are first and foremost *Americans*. Their national origins as Americans, along with their first-generation multiracial (or biracial) experiences, immediately grounds them in both the African American and Mexican American experiences even as they simultaneously forge racially (and culturally) hybrid identities that are also neither of those. In contrast, Afro-Mexicans are multigenerational individuals, most of them multiracial people, who are first and foremost *Mexicans* of African descent. Those who migrate to the United States, and particularly their descendants born in the United States (that is, Afro-Mexican Americans) may necessarily navigate identities as Mexican Americans and ostensibly as African Americans. Indeed, Afro-Mexicans and Afro-Mexican Americans are frequently taken for or constructed as African Americans and must also come to terms with what it means to be considered Black in the United States.[13]

Blaxican identities are a case study of the blending of African American and Mexican American backgrounds, experiences, and historical sources. We discuss these phenomena in comparative historical detail to provide a broader context for elucidating the contradictions that can arise when claiming membership in these two groups as a catalyst for the development and declaration of a "dual minority" multiracial (or biracial) identity. Blaxican identities are also shaped by gender, sexuality, class, parental socialization, peer groups, and marginalization vis-à-vis white supremacy and monoraciality.

Blaxican identities signify a borderlands space where the ambiguities and contradictions of being simultaneously both and neither African American and Mexican American are embraced and accepted.[14] As comparative ethnic studies scholars Josh Kun and Laura Pulido maintain, "While we too have approached African Americans and Latinas/os as two distinct populations, this overlooks the possibility of hybrid spaces for those who identify as both Black *and* Brown. . . . In fact, it is precisely that mixed zone that is one of the most dynamic topics within comparative ethnic studies."[15] *Between Black and Brown* exposes readers to that in-between, or liminal, space and allows for an imagining of race and identity outside of the paradigms that dominate U.S. society's thinking about how race is socially constructed.

Racial Formations

According to racial formation theory outlined by Michael Omi and Howard Winant, race is a cultural, political, and legal construct. Racial formation theory therefore seeks to explain the sociopolitical reality of race as a contingent and historical development. Race is also a social construct based on perceived biological characteristics. It thus refers to a range of multifaceted and intersecting social and political discourses that include biological matters. The original tenets of race, particularly those based on scientific racism and biological determinism, were overturned by the middle of the twentieth century. Still, race has been and continues to be inextricably intertwined with wealth, power, privilege, and prestige and is therefore also intertwined with inequality. Despite attempts to propose its neutrality as a biological concept, racial difference has created a chasm of social distance expressed explicitly and implicitly in all kinds of social intercourse.

Because humans construct meanings of race largely dependent on a person's appearance and on conceptions of ancestry, the selection of human features for purposes of racial signification is necessarily a sociohistorical process that groups different geno-phenotypical features for social and ideological purposes. The resulting racial categories are unstable and decentered complexes of meanings that are continuously created, inhabited, contested, destroyed, and transformed. Racial formation theory therefore encourages us to analyze the processes by which a society determines racial meanings and assigns racial identities, categories, and membership in the racial order. The racial order encompasses ideological beliefs, as well as institutional and social practices, establishing racial categories, group boundaries, and membership in which the state has a central role.[16]

David Theo Goldberg argues that race is fundamental to the conceptual, philosophical, and material emergence of the state and to its ongoing management and internal functioning. The state encompasses the political organization of society, or the body politic, and more narrowly, the institutions of government, which establish order and security. This also includes the state's methods; laws and their enforcement thereof; territory, area of jurisdiction, or geographic boundaries; and sovereignty. The state has exercised power not only in the politics of racial exclusion and inclusion but also in enforcing racial definition, classification, and identification in the racial order.[17] The racial order thus has a significant impact on the distribution of resources, wealth, power, privilege, and prestige, which in turn determine groups' social locations and statuses in relation to one another.

The racial state has been characterized by despotism and tyranny, rather than democracy and reform. Because U.S. institutions organize and enforce the racial politics of everyday life and systematically enforce the prevailing racial order, under normal conditions the racial status quo has gone undisturbed for extended periods of time. Correspondingly, legal and political challenges to the racial order are extremely marginalized. Only since the second half of the twentieth century has there been the necessary political space and conceptual flexibility about race to reformulate racial meanings, forge oppositional racial ideologies, and constitute alternative racial institutions.[18]

The racial state and its institutions are the site of the enforcement of inegalitarian privileges and collective demands for egalitarian reforms. The racial policies of the state and opposition to these policies alternate between periods of virtual stasis and rapid change, eras of relative passivity and ones of massive mobilization. At any given moment, the racial order may be characterized by many interpretations of and initiatives surrounding race. In one period, race might be commonsensical by its own "naturalness" and "taken-for-grantedness." In another, race might be highly politicized and the site of significant social mobilization when a critical mass of individuals views state institutions as enforcing an unjust racial order. Here we would expect a high degree of contestation in the form of a national debate about race and a great deal of popular uncertainty about its significance in everyday life. When racially based opposition challenges the equilibrium of the racial order, establishing a new equilibrium becomes paramount and is achieved through a process of conflict and compromise between the racial state and that opposition.[19]

Thinking Racially and Ethnically

Some scholars and members of the public view "ethnicity" as a less problematic concept than race and as a suitable substitution, while also erroneously viewing racial and ethnic lines as critically different from each other.[20] Ethnicity generally refers to a social subset whose members are thought by themselves and by others to share a common culture that sets them apart from other groups. These individuals also purport to share a common ancestry or geographical origin—and thus they may have similar geno-phenotypical traits they use to distinguish themselves. They may also participate to varying degrees in shared activities based on their purported common origin and culture.

While the term *multiethnic*, rather than *multiracial*, might seem to lend itself to a more nuanced discussion of identity, the notion of ethnicity experienced as culture—the "culturalization" of ethnicity—is different from the experience of racial or geno-phenotypical and ancestral differentiation (that is, the "racialization" of ethnicity). This does not mean ethno-cultural differences between groups that are ethno-racially similar have not been the source of prejudice and discrimination. But the overriding structural wedge in the United States has historically been, and continues to be, based primarily on ethno-racial differences and secondarily on ethno-cultural ones.

We use the term *multiracial* to capture ethno-racial difference while also acknowledging that Blaxican identities are informed by both race (geno-phenotype, ancestry) and culture (beliefs, values, customs, artifacts). The paired concepts of race-culture and racial-cultural are used as the equivalents of race-ethnicity and racial-ethnic, which typically appear in studies of race relations. Occasionally, we use the term *multiethnic* to convey both racial and culture phenomena. Finally, unless otherwise indicated, the words *multiracial*, *biracial*, *mixed race*, and similar terminology are used interchangeably to refer to multiracials.

We employ *Chicana/o*, *Latina/o*, and *Hispanic*, interchangeably. *Latina/o* and *Hispanic* are typically used as more encompassing terms that include other Latin American origin groups besides Mexican-descent individuals. *Mexican American*, *Mexican-descent American*, and *Chicana/o* are also used interchangeably. For historical reasons we use *Chicana/o* mainly for the period from the 1960s onward for individuals of Mexican American background. *Mexican American* or *Mexican-descent American* are often used to encompass the period before, as well as after, the 1960s. *Mexican* as a standalone generally refers to Mexican nationals, although for historical purposes, we sometimes use it to encompass the entirety of the period prior to as well as just after U.S. annexation and colonization of Northern Mexico, that is, the U.S. Southwest.

Finally, *Black* and *African American* are used interchangeably to refer to individuals of African descent, unless specified otherwise—for example, when it is meaningful to distinguish between Blacks and multiracials. *African-descent* is often used as an adjective (e.g., *African-descent multiracials*) or a noun (e.g., *multiracials of African descent*). The terms *individuals of African descent* or *African-descent individuals* can include Blacks and all other individuals of African descent, including multiracials. *White, European American*, and *Anglo-American* are used interchangeably in terms of the United States. *White, European-descent individuals*, or *individuals of European descent* are sometimes more encompassing of the United States and elsewhere. In addition, we use the term *Blaxican* to refer to study participants with one African American and one Mexican or Mexican American parent. Most of the participants themselves use the term *Blaxican*, and some used *Black and Mexican*.

Chapter Summaries and an Overview

Chapter 1 examines the investment of U.S. sociology and race studies in dominant binary racial logics characterized by monoraciality and hypodescent. Consequently, scholars failed to comprehend the emergence of multiracial identities during the late 1980s and early 1990s. This omission is examined as part of a long-standing failure of U.S. sociologists to anticipate and map the trajectory of race relations in the United States. We then locate Blaxicans within a critical mixed-race studies framework that centers multiracials as subjects of historical, social, and cultural processes.

Chapter 2 provides a comparative historical analysis of Anglo-America's binary racial order and Latin America's ternary racial order, particularly in Spanish America, since Blaxicans are at the intersection of both. Anglo-America largely assigned African-descent multiracials the same subaltern status as Blacks. Spanish America and the rest of Latin America allotted them an intermediate status lower than whites but more elevated than Blacks.

Chapter 3 analyzes "Latin" North American racial formation in the Spanish and French territories of Louisiana and the Gulf Coast in the U.S. Southeast. The region's ternary racial order situated African descent multiracials in an intermediate location subaltern to whites but higher than Blacks. With Anglo-American rule and the enforcement of a binary racial order in the early nineteenth century, multiracials of African descent lost their elevated status and were recategorized as Blacks. This culminated with Jim Crow segregation in the late nineteenth century.

Chapter 4 explores how Jim Crow segregation perpetuated racial inequality while also helping form and validate a monoracial identity among Blacks. This, in turn, served as the basis of mobilization in response to exclusionary boundaries and racial equality maintained by whites. These strategies ranged from the civil rights movement's integrationist goals in the mid-1950s and early 1960s to the pluralist objectives of Black nationalism, Black Power, and Black pride in the late 1960s and early 1970s.

Chapter 5 turns to "Latin" North American racial formation in the Mexican territory of California and, by extension, the rest of the U.S. Southwest. Mexicans were largely multiracials of Spanish and Indigenous descent, although African ancestry was present throughout the population. Under Anglo-American rule and the implementation of a binary racial order in the mid-nineteenth century, Mexicans were legally categorized as white. But in practice, their whiteness was frequently disregarded, as were their rights as U.S. citizens.

Chapter 6 examines how exclusionary boundaries constructed by whites also galvanized Mexican American resistance that facilitated the formation and legitimization of a monoracial identity. During the first half of the twentieth century, this involved asserting and litigating a white identity. In the late 1960s and early 1970s, continuing racial discrimination impelled a younger generation of Mexican Americans to proclaim a Chicana/o identity based on Brown Power, Brown pride, and Indigeneity.

Chapter 7 discusses the dismantling of Jim Crow segregation, including removal of the last antimiscegenation laws and the passage of civil rights legislation. More fluid race relations led to an increase in racial intermarriage and multiracial offspring. We also highlight the multiracial movement that has challenged the binary racial order, hypodescent, and the monoracial imperative, and contrast post–civil rights multiracial identities with previous ones.

Chapter 8 provides a comparative historical overview of the unique experiences, challenges, and marginality of dual-minority multiracials to provide a context and a theoretical framework for discussing Blaxicans.

Chapter 9 begins part 2 by offering a brief explanation of study methods and sample characteristics. Readers are introduced to forty Blaxican adults living across the United States. Their identities are explored in terms of how they break from defining who is Black or Mexican.

Chapter 10 explains how Blaxicans choose both parents' backgrounds as an egalitarian and nonhierarchical expression of identity and how they use racial and cultural strategies to navigate their social worlds as multiracials.

Chapter 11 observes how the social arenas of family, school, and neighborhood contribute to Blaxican identities and experiences, as participants carve out and claim a unique racial-cultural identity outside of monoraciality and whiteness.

Chapter 12 considers how authenticity policing by African American and Mexican American peers shapes Blaxicans' sense of self. It includes how Blaxicans feel pressure to conform to the racial, cultural, classed, and gendered expectations in the African American and Mexican American communities.

Chapter 13 examines participants' perceptions of the so-called Black-Brown divide that has dominated academic and public discourse on Black-Latina/o relations. Blaxicans view conflicts between African Americans and Mexican Americans as mostly a nonissue. However, conflicts sometimes arise in family attitudes about participants' dating preferences.

Chapter 14 concludes with an analysis of how Blaxican and multiracial identities and experiences, more generally, provide an opportunity to imagine conceptualizing racial formation, as well as cooperation and alliances across racial-cultural differences, revolving around a "both/neither" as opposed to an "either/or" axis.

Part 1

Racial Formation and the Blaxican Borderlands

Chapter One

Race and Mixed Race
Multiracial Identities in Academia

U.S. sociologists' lack of attention to multiracial identity reflects their long-standing failure to anticipate and map the trajectory of race relations in the United States. This is largely attributable to biases in sociologists' own racial subjectivity and lack of self-reflexivity.[1] James B. McKee argues that most U.S. sociologists of race relations did not foresee Blacks as autonomous political actors in the civil rights struggle in the 1950s and 1960s. They believed that Blacks lacked the sociocultural capital to commandeer a movement for their own liberation. This myopia was also attributable to the prevailing order-functionalist paradigm that disregarded and disparaged conflict as a meaningful tool for bringing about social structural change. The order-functionalist framework envisioned the eventual integration of Blacks into the larger society in a manner like that of European immigrants, through gradual, piecemeal, and above all peaceful reform, not through radical transformation.[2] Whites would be at the helm of collaborative initiatives with "sober-minded" Blacks to achieve this goal.[3]

The Failure in Historical Perspective

Robert Blauner, Joyce Ladner, Stephen Steinberg, and others argue that this failure to anticipate the African American civil rights movement is attributable to the white racial subjectivity and standpoint of elite European American male sociologists who dominated the discipline. Racial subjectivity is the specific way individuals are informed by and interact with the racial dynamics of the world they inhabit. This includes the social and cultural processes of race relations and the political economy. Individuals' racial standpoint is affected by their racial group membership and is a product of a group's history in a given society.[4] Sociologists' supposed value-free sociology was, in fact, implicitly and explicitly value-laden with white racist and white supremacist biases of the larger society from its institutionalization in the 1890s well into the 1960s. These biases were so normative and commonsense that they were taken for granted.

Blauner, Steinberg, and Ladner maintain that the sociological establishment was even more blindsided by the radical insurgency of Black Power, Black pride, Black nationalism, and violent urban uprisings in the late 1960s and early 1970s. These developments advocated immediate social transformation, rather than gradual reform, and jettisoned integration as a primary goal. Blacks viewed the United States as a plural society and their culture separate from that of whites. Beginning in the early 1970s Blauner and others addressed these developments with the power-conflict framework. This paradigm emphasizes the historical and contemporary structural obstacles placing Blacks and other groups of color disproportionately at the bottom of society.[5]

Power-conflict theories also indicate that the pursuit or accomplishment of integration among communities of color into the political economy and other public spheres did not necessarily indicate a desire for cultural integration in a manner similar to European immigrants and their descendants. Such integration would include embracing Anglo-American values, behaviors, beliefs, customs, and artifacts to the exclusion of Blacks' own core culture. For instance, Anglo-Americanization would encompass the reification of private property and private enterprise and the embrace of electoral politics, rather than radical and revolutionary insurgency, for political change.[6] Integration also does not necessarily indicate a desire or ability to racially integrate into the larger (and ostensibly white) mainstream, at least as deracinated "others." Taken to its conclusion, racial, along with cultural, integration would erase the particularity of Blacks and other communities of color.[7]

Given that sociologists historically defined the race problem as the "Negro Problem," they were even less attentive to civil rights or nationalist movements and radical insurgency among Latinas/os, Native Americans, and Asian Americans.[8] Juan Perea attributes this omission to the Black white binary. This paradigm not only broadly necessitates identification as either white or nonwhite but also has historically tended to marginalize the experiences of the abovementioned and other nonwhite groups.[9] Their experiences have instead typically been framed and understood by a Black white polarity. Eileen O'Brien refers to these groups as the "racial middle" based on racial and, to some extent, cultural markers that differentiate them from both whites and Blacks.[10]

Borrowing O'Brien's concept, we maintain that U.S. sociologists have largely lacked a meaningful framework for studying the mixed racial middle; that is, experiences informed by identifications with ancestral (and cultural) ties to both white and nonwhite, or to several nonwhite, groups. Much as they failed to anticipate developments in the 1950s and 1960s, sociologists were unprepared for and unable to comprehend the emergence of multiraciality beginning in the late 1980s and early 1990s. This failure is credited to a standpoint informed by hypodescent and the monoracial imperative.[11] These social devices have repressed the articulation and recognition of multiracial identities. Much like the larger society, sociologists took monoraciality and hypodescent for granted, internalizing U.S. racial norms, which blinded them to their own racial subjectivity and positionality. Their assumed objectivity was imbued with monoracial biases that have permeated the discipline since its inception.

Hypodescent and the Monoracial Imperative

English Americans began enforcing hypodescent and the monoracial imperative during the late seventeenth and early eighteenth centuries to maintain dominance over subaltern nonwhite groups. Hypodescent buttressed a binary white or nonwhite racial order and was implemented as part of antimiscegenation legislation regulating interracial intimacy, specifically interracial marriages. It defined as nonwhite any progeny born of these relationships, with Black white relations the most common targets with the most severe restrictions.[12] Hypodescent helped sustain the ideology of white supremacy by preserving white racial "purity" and white economic and political power. These regulations culminated with Jim Crow segregation that legally sanctioned unequal treatment of Blacks and other communities of color in most aspects of social life.

F. James Davis argues that hypodescent applies most stringently to first-generation offspring. It is less applicable to those with Latina/o, Asian American, and Native American ancestry, especially those without connections to reservations.[13] While frequently they have flexibility in terms of self-identifications, particularly in later generations, Winthrop D. Jordan maintained that this flexibility does not encompass individuals of African and European descent, whether first generation or later.[14] Instead, they have experienced the most restrictive rule of hypodescent—the one-drop rule. Unique to the United States, the one-drop rule has precluded self-identification and ensured that all African descendants have been designated and have self-identified as solely Black. Davis points out that this mechanism gained currency as the commonsense definition of Blackness between the seventeenth and nineteenth centuries and became a customary part of the legal apparatus in the early twentieth century (circa 1915).[15]

U.S. attitudes toward dual minority offspring of African Americans and other groups of color have varied. All have generally been subject to the one-drop rule and monoracial formations. Greater ambivalence is displayed toward non-Black dual-minority offspring, such as children born of Asian Indian Americans and Mexican Americans ("Punjabi Mexicans") or children born of Filipino Americans and Mexican Americans ("Mexipinos").[16] These groups occupy a more ambiguous position in the U.S. racial hierarchy with membership less clearly defined in law. Hypodescent still tends to push them toward the less privileged background in the racial hierarchy, though the most subaltern background can vary situationally. Still, in each instance, monoracial norms have disallowed the articulation and recognition of multiracial identities.

Monoraciality and monoracial privilege qua hypodescent has perpetuated macroaggressions involving state agencies, public policy, and institutional practices that ignore or erase multiracials. It has sustained meso-aggressions vis-à-vis organizations, the workplace, community, and schools, ranging from not being able to fill out a form that reflects one's identity to the absence of material on multiracials in the mass media and school curricula. It has also perpetuated microaggressions in the sphere of interpersonal relations.[17] These involve brief and commonplace verbal, behavioral, or environmental indignities that communicate hostile, derogatory, or negative racial slights and insults. These may encompass questioning the legitimacy of and negating identity through erasure, bullying, and so on. Multiracial identities or experiences might be seen as psychologically "abnormal," or the individual might be said to have issues because they are mixed. Multiracials are also often accused of trying to deny their "actual" and appropriate—that is, monoracial—category membership to avoid the racial stigma associated with the less prestigious background of color.[18]

George Lipsitz maintains that the "possessive investment" in whiteness has been critical to maintaining white racism despite increasing repudiation beginning in the 1960s and 1970s.[19] Buttressed by hypodescent and the monoracial imperative, white racism and white racial privilege lead to significantly different life chances and overall quality of life along racial lines, including grossly inequitable access to education, employment, health care, transportation, and housing. Rather than the byproduct of benign neglect, it is the purposeful designs of whites that assign people of different racial groups to differential and inequitable social spaces.[20]

The structures that produce unearned benefits of whiteness also benefit monoracial groups of color ("monoracial privilege") even as these structures are responsible for pervasive and egregious forms of structural oppression against people of color.[21] Though monoracials of color do not experience anything near the advantages of whites, their cultural, social, economic, and political outlets and resources may make it difficult for them to recognize their own monoracial privilege and biases as well as possessive investment in monoraciality. Whether intentional or unintentional, their own discriminatory attitudes and practices form part of what Marc P. Johnston and Kevin L. Nadal refer to as "monoracism."[22]

Although monoraciality and hypodescent go hand in hand, they are not necessarily synonymous. White support of monoraciality and, by extension, hypodescent differs considerably from that of communities of color. Whites formulated hypodescent to sustain white racial exclusivity. The unintended consequence was that exclusionary boundaries constructed by whites also helped forge and legitimate monoracial identities among groups of color. According to Rhett S. Jones, Blacks and other communities of color view hypodescent and monoraciality as necessary for maintaining community and solidarity in the struggle against inequities perpetuated by white racism.[23] They uphold monoraciality and the accompanying dichotomization of racial differences by *rearticulating* rather than *reproducing* hypodescent.[24] This involves the repetition of hypodescent in support of racial difference without hierarchy (that is, difference based on equality). Notwithstanding this critical distinction, the outcome in both cases is the same: individuals reinforce, if only unwittingly, racial designations as if they were mutually exclusive and singular categories of experience as well as objective phenomena.

Multiracial identity formations interrogate monoracial norms supporting European Americans' investment in whiteness and the associated cultural, social, economic, political, and other advantages. They also call into question the investment communities of color have in preserving monoracial identities, a mindset that overlooks, or outright rejects, the possibility of a multiracial identity formulated on egalitarian or antiracist premises. This does not mean monoracial identification is illegitimate. As stated previously, multiracial identity formations instead question the external ascription of monoracial categories as the norm against which all other identities are considered unacceptable.

Studying Mixed-Race Identities

The dismantling of Jim Crow segregation and implementation of civil rights legislation during the 1950s and 1960s dissolved legal racial discrimination and inequality. Subsequently, hypodescent was removed from state laws. The comparatively more fluid social relations in the post–civil rights era led to a growth in interracial marriages.[25] Unlike coercive unions of the past, these marriages involved choice and conferred equal legal status on both parties and, by extension, equal legitimacy on both parents' identities. Nevertheless, there was no immediate social challenge to hypodescent or the monoracial imperative vis-à-vis racial categories and identifications.[26] It was not until the late 1970s and early 1980s that many interracial couples, particularly in Black white unions, began countering the one-drop rule and the monoracial imperative by socializing their children to identify with their multiracial backgrounds.

The Social Sciences and Ethnic Studies

This development was accompanied by a growth in mixed-race individuals' literary narratives, autobiographies, film, and performance pieces, which provided an insider's view of their interior and lived experiences. In the late 1980s and early 1990s these creative expressions, along with contemporary scholarship, made contributions not only to explicating but also to validating and celebrating multiracial identities and mixed-race experiences.[27] Social scientists—specifically psychologists and social psychologists—conducted most of the research on mixed-race identities and multiracial experiences. A few scholars in social work, as well as historians, literary scholars, and philosophers, also made contributions. Sociology and anthropology were conspicuously silent.[28]

In ethnic studies mixed-race identities were largely marginalized, if not ignored. Black studies scholars specifically were ambivalent, if not unreceptive. Such identities were considered incompatible with and inimical to the canonical boundaries of the field and deleterious to the struggles of traditional communities of color and their monoracial imperatives, especially with respect to maintaining racial solidarity in the face of white oppression.[29] Asian American studies was more receptive due, in part, to the high rate of outmarriages among Asian Americans, as well as to the large number of first-generation multiracial offspring of Asian American descent, particularly those of white and Asian or Asian American backgrounds. The same was somewhat true of Native American studies, given that "mixed-blood" is an established, if often debated, social category among Native Americans.[30] Jessie Turner argues that some Chicana/o studies scholars were engaged in the topic of *mestizaje*. But she maintains that there has been a disjuncture between some of those analyses and the conceptualization of "multiraciality" in other disciplines.[31]

Demographers began to grapple with the statistical implications of the growing populations of interracial couples and multiracial children.[32] This became increasingly the case when interracial couples and multiracial-identified individuals formed a nascent grassroots movement in the late 1980s and early 1990s in concert with the growing support of multiculturalism, which espoused an egalitarian ethos valuing racial and cultural diversity related especially to immigration.[33] The increased saliency of "multiracial" as a self-identifier and category also came about through the growth in the population of multiracials, who were sometimes referred to as the "Loving Generation."[34] These individuals were born in the late 1960s and early 1970s following the 1967 *Loving v. Virginia* decision, although some definitions extend the parameters into the early 1980s.

The movement's efforts included educational initiatives addressing the marginalization, erasure, and pathologizing of interracial families and multiracial individuals.[35] Another key initiative targeted the standards for official racial data collection as in the census. Activists targeted the 1990 census so that multiracial-identified individuals could be enumerated instead of being required to select one racial background. While their efforts did not change the 1990 census, the 2000 census, for the first time, allowed multiracial-identified individuals to check more than one box on the race question. During the height of the debate, the multiracial movement included thirty grassroots organizations with about 3,500 active participants.[36] Still, in the late 1980s and early 1990s, the movement was considered marginal. At best, multiracial identities were considered symptomatic of largely isolated and ephemeral psychological concerns with personal identity. Even with increased coverage in the mass media in the wake of the 1990 census, the multiracial phenomenon was located outside the normative terrain of the racial state, the public imagination, and that of most social scientists.

Just as scholars were slow to study multiracial identities, they also failed to examine multiracial political mobilization. Political scientists did not view multiracialism as reflective of wider-ranging sociopolitical questions and failed to meaningfully assess multiraciality within the context of the state, government, political systems, and political behavior.[37] Sociologists were slow to engage in analyses of multiraciality in terms of broader social behavior, social relations, organizations, and institutions. Consequently, they failed to anticipate the intergenerational transfer of multiracial identities or mixed-race collective identity, agency, and political action.[38]

For example, Jack Niemonen examined all racial and ethnic relations articles (677 in total) published over a twenty-seven-year period from January 1969 through December 1995 in the *American Journal of Sociology, American Sociological Review, Social Forces,* and *Social Problems*. He found that the articles borrow from, take for granted, accept, and reify U.S. racial commonsense or U.S. Census definitions of race and ethnicity as opposed to critically evaluating them.[39] That critique would be central to any discussion of multiraciality and mixed-race experiences.

G. Reginald Daniel noted similar patterns in *Sociological Abstracts*. He found that articles investigating race in the United States from 1952 to 1992, the year of publication of Maria P. P Root's *Racially Mixed People in America*, indicate limited attention to mixed-race offspring, multiraciality, and mixed-race experiences.[40] Between 1988 and 1992 there was a noticeable increase, and there was a significant increase from 1992 to 2013.[41] In 1995, and even more so beginning in 1998, papers, roundtables, sections, and regular sessions on multiracial identity increasingly became a component of American Sociological Association (ASA) annual meetings. One cannot, however, consider this exponential growth.[42]

The topic of mixed race was not included in the second edition of the canonical *Racial Formation in the United States* by sociologists Omi and Winant, published in 1994. This edition encompassed changes in U.S. racial formations that had occurred since its initial publication in 1986 yet failed to include a discussion of the census debate that was well under way.[43] That sociologists failed to see what really was there in the late 1980s and early 1990s with respect to multiracial identities and mixed-race experiences reflected their monoracial subjectivity and standpoint.[44] Scholarly interest in multiraciality may, in part, have been dampened by the fact that the actual size of the multiracial population was rarely visible in statistical series and reports produced by state and federal agencies in the late 1980s and early 1990s. The subsequent surge in sociological and other scholarship on multiraciality can be attributed, in part, to the publication of findings from the 2000 and 2010 censuses.[45]

From Marginality to Liminality

Sociologists and psychologists studying multiraciality made important advances by reevaluating the concept of marginality, which focused on the psychological dysfunction purportedly originating in mixed-race experiences.[46] Individuals stood on the margin of two racial or cultural worlds conceptualized as mutually exclusive and hostile. Marginality was deemed pathological and the source of life-long conflict characterized by divided loyalties, ambivalence, and hypersensitivity. Such theories emerged when the United States was significantly more hostile to the affirmation of multiracial identities. They fixated on the supposed genetic inferiority of multiracials, an idea supported by scientific racism and theories of hybrid degeneracy.[47]

By the end of the first half of the twentieth century, these theories had been substituted with theories of marginality but rarely focused on the social forces that made psychological functioning difficult for multiracials. Rather, dysfunctionality reinforced what

Cynthia L. Nakashima calls a "multiracial mythology"—that is, a longstanding, normative yet unsubstantiated belief in the inferiority of multiracials.[48] Studies supported prevailing ideologies prohibiting or discouraging miscegenation and thereby helped to preserve white racial purity and dominance.

Theories of "negative" marginality emphasizing pathology, especially the work of sociologist Everett V. Stonequist (1901–79), overshadowed the nuances of sociologist Robert E. Park's (1864–1944) original "marginal man" thesis in the 1920s. Park did not dismiss the challenges, psychological ambivalence, and conflict that could accompany marginality. However, he believed marginality could also imbue individuals with a broader vision and wider-ranging sympathies. This "positive" marginality might provide them with an ability to help facilitate mutual understanding between individuals from different groups.[49] Park's positive conceptualization of marginality was elaborated on and refined by subsequent sociologists, yet the received wisdom still reified theories of negative marginality emphasizing pathology.[50]

Along with this disregard of positive marginality, prior to the 1980s identity formation of children from interracial marriages had received limited attention from educators, researchers, social scientists, and mental health professionals. The extant research was outdated, contradictory, or based on small-scale case studies of children experiencing "problems" with identity, who were referred for psychological counseling.[51] Rather than being posited as a sign of alienation in response to hypodescent and monoraciality, identity struggles were deemed symptomatic of anomie or temporary deviations in an otherwise functioning racial order. Children with Black and white parentage were taught by most professionals the importance of learning to cope as African Americans because society would view them as such. Their mental health was assessed in terms of how successfully or unsuccessfully they achieved a Black identity.[52]

By the 1980s a new wave of research put to rest theories of negative marginality. These and subsequent studies indicated that multiracials, generally speaking, were just as psychologically and socially well-adjusted as monoracials, notwithstanding the challenges to forming positive identities.[53] The concept of positive marginality (or liminality)—that is, the sense of being "betwixt and between"—in turn gained greater acceptance among mental health professionals.[54] This scholarship acknowledged that the liminality experienced by multiracials may result in ambiguities, strains, and conflicts in a society that views racial identities as mutually exclusive and monoracial. Nevertheless, like Park, it maintained that such potentially negative feelings can be counterbalanced by increased sensitivity to commonalities and appreciation of racial and cultural differences in interpersonal and intergroup situations.[55]

One case in point is former president Barack Obama. The immediacy of Obama's interracial parentage, of his rearing outside the continental United States in Hawai'i and Indonesia by his white mother and her relatives, and of his Indonesian stepfather imbued his consciousness with a broader vision and wider-ranging sensibilities in forming his identity. To some this has enhanced Obama's image as the physical embodiment of the principles of inclusiveness and equity.[56] Yet for all his hybridity, Obama's identity is situated in the Black community and extends outward from that location. This would also be true of Vice President Kamala Harris, whose father is Afro-Jamaican and whose mother is South Asian.[57]

Golfer Tiger Woods, on the other hand, is more aligned with multiracial identities. Woods set off a controversy in the 1990s when he defined himself as "Cablinasian," a term he coined reflecting his white, Black, Native American, and Asian American ancestry.[58] This multiracial identity manifests itself between the boundaries of monoracial groups, extending outward from that liminal location (which is contingent upon an individual's orientation) toward the groups that compose their own backgrounds, although multiracial identities can vary depending on the region and the backgrounds involved.[59] Despite myriad backgrounds, experiences, and identities, multiraciality has become the basis for an emergent collective subjectivity. No matter how porous, fuzzy, and thin the boundary, no matter how soft and illusive the collectivity's center, a shared liminality based on identification with more than one racial background is an integral, fundamental part of the self-conception of multiracial-identifying individuals and a defining component of mixed-race experiences.

Order-Functional and Power-Conflict Paradigms

By 2004 scholarly articles on multiracial identity and mixed-race experiences had appeared in all the flagship and high-impact journals in sociology, psychology, anthropology, political science, history, and literature, as well as in other disciplines and fields. In particular, since 2002 sociological analyses have increased considerably. Yet they continue to be less visible than analyses of other racial groups. Furthermore, sociological scholarship is heavily focused on ethnographic, survey, and quantitative research with less attention to theoretical, comparative historical, and cross-cultural analyses. Also, studies intersecting with gender and sexuality, socioeconomic class, and education, particularly higher education, have been less prominent.[60]

From some of this research, one can draw several key conclusions. Multiracial identifications differ depending on the various backgrounds and identity options available.[61] For example, Sarah S. M. Townsend and her coauthors discovered that Asian American white individuals were more likely than Black white or Latina/o white individuals to identify as multiracial. Jennifer Lee and Frank D. Bean found that white Asian American or white Latina/o multiracials have greater flexibility, institutionally or through social interaction, to identify as Asian American or Latina/o, respectively, as well as multiracial, as white, or simply as deracinated others—that is, as ordinary Americans. Jennifer Lee and Frank Bean, Bruce C. Hoskins, and Michael Miyawaki indicate that many white Asian Americans heavily tilt in the direction of whiteness in terms of marriage partners and multiracial progeny. In fact, individuals with a more European American appearance among white Asian American, white Native American, or white Latina/o multiracials have greater white adjacency in the racial order and are more able to achieve monoracial white identification.[62]

Tomás Jiménez's research illustrates that Latina/o white multiracials and their offspring display considerable identity flexibility and variation, including the option to identify as Latina/o, multiracial, and white.[63] Many are perceived as white, and for some their Latina/o identity is largely "symbolic," without much impact on their daily lives.[64] Whereas whiteness is possible for Latina/o whites, Asian American whites, and Native American whites, this option is not necessarily available for multiracials with African ancestry. It is precluded by the one-drop rule, which still influences identity formation through external imposition and self-ascription.[65]

Jennifer Bratter's study of the intergenerational transfer of multiracial identities in terms of part-Black multiracials highlights this finding. Her data reveal robust evidence of the continuing impact of monoracial categories and boundaries.[66] These can be measured where multiracial-identified parents of African descent did not consistently transfer their multiracial identification to their offspring. Bratter discovered that many formed families with people of similar racial backgrounds (e.g., white Black mother and Black father) and identified their children according to monoracial norms, reproducing single-race families in keeping with the one-drop rule. Lee and Bean reached similar conclusions regarding the strong retention of Black identities among African descent multiracials, who are also more frequently designated and self-identified as Black. Like Bratter, they attribute this retention to the enduring influence of the one-drop rule.

Other analyses indicate that the one-drop rule has less impact on identity formation among some African-descent multiracials.[67] This research shows that some Black white young people who more closely approximate European Americans phenotypically often have access to a white racial identity due to the preponderance of whites in their social milieu or relative lack of contact with Black family members and other African Americans. Moreover, their identity is validated through social interaction, particularly with white peers.[68] While the affirmation and acceptance of multiracial identities partially negates the one-drop rule, for this to become a normative part of U.S. racial common sense would require its complete repudiation.[69] Moreover, Hoskins and Rebecca Romo contend that dual minorities, particularly those who are part Black, do not necessarily have this option.

Their background and physical appearance typically mark them as nonwhite no matter how they identify.[70] Hoskins found that Asian Black participants were treated as Black by whites and as Asian Americans and as "marginalized others" by African Americans.[71]

Notwithstanding the contribution of this research, there has been less engagement with multiraciality regarding the order-functional and power-conflict paradigms of sociological analysis. Yet by virtue of their hybridity and liminal positionality, multiracial identities raise questions about the theoretical assumptions of these paradigms. On the one hand, multiracial identities challenge the power-conflict paradigm that reinforces the notion that multiracials will display monoracial identities of color. Monoracial identities are deemed not only normative but also a means of maintaining community and solidarity in the struggle against white racism, oppression, and privilege.[72] On the other hand, multiracial identities challenge the order-functionalist paradigm, which portends the eventual racial absorption of multiracials into the larger racial (and ostensibly white or not "othered") mainstream due to increased interracial marriage.[73]

Both the power-conflict and order-functional paradigms are refracted through a monoracial lens that ignores, if not dismisses, any longevity to multiracial identities and any societal scaffolding upon which they might take root.[74] Notwithstanding Bratter's findings on the inconsistent intergenerational transferal of mixed-race identities among African-descent multiracials, Miri Song's analysis of multiracial parents—that is, multiracials who are married to other multiracials and have children—in the United Kingdom, indicates a strong retention of multiracial identities among the majority of her respondents and their offspring including those who were part Black.[75] This is an indication that sociologists need to reexamine the theoretical foundations of race and ethnic relations in terms of multiracial identities.

Critical Mixed Race Studies

As previously stated, there has historically been limited research on multiracial identities and mixed-race experiences in the United States. Paul

Spickard's *Mixed Blood: Intermarriage and Ethnic Identity in Twentieth-Century America* (1989) and Maria P. P. Root's award-winning anthology *Racially Mixed People in America* (1992) were groundbreaking in terms of establishing foundational discourses in what is now referred to as mixed race studies, and subsequently, critical mixed race studies. By 2004 academic works on multiraciality and the mixed-race experience across disciplines laid the foundation for further growth and innovation.[76] Initiatives of the multiracial movement had a significant impact on and helped inform these works. Together, scholarly, artistic, and popular discourses composed part of the emerging field of mixed race studies, although scholarship did not yet encompass a formally defined area of inquiry. During the early part of the twenty-first century, many individuals began describing works as being part of the field of mixed race or multiracial studies, which crystallized in Jayne Ifekwunigwe's *"Mixed Race" Studies: A Reader* (2004).

Since then the number of articles, book chapters, and monographs published on mixed-race identities and multiracial experiences across disciplines has grown exponentially. Papers, roundtables, sections, and regular sessions on multiracial identity have increasingly become a component of annual meetings of various academic professional associations. Indeed, the study of this topic has become a distinct interdisciplinary area of scholarly inquiry. These developments, in turn, were instrumental in the 2010 inaugural biannual Critical Mixed Race Studies Conferences subsequently incorporated in 2015 as the Critical Mixed Race Studies Association and founding of the *Journal of Critical Mixed Race Studies* in 2011.

At that point, the number of publications on the topic of multiraciality from various disciplines reached a critical mass, attaining viability as a distinct field. Mixed race studies has possibly been the fastest growing, and one of the most controversial, areas of racial and ethnic studies over the past few decades.[77] There were no academic platforms or journals specifically devoted to the topic until the founding of the biannual Critical Mixed Race Studies conferences in 2010, which eventually incorporated as an association in 2015. The *Journal of Critical Mixed Race Studies* was inaugurated in 2014. Rather than indicating an abrupt shift or change, mixed race studies was formally defined at a time that beckoned scholars to be more *critical*—that is, to be self-reflexive and assess the merit of arguments made over previous decades and their relevance for future research.

Even with the emergence of critical mixed race studies, there has been limited research on dual-minority multiracial identities, particularly Blaxicans. Our study of Blaxicans is located within this critical mixed race studies (CMRS) framework. The word *critical* comes from critical race theory and critical legal studies. The latter developed in the 1970s to address the role of society and culture within a racialized and race-driven legal system. Critical race theory borrows from it, as well as from conventional civil rights scholarship, but it also interrogates both fields. Critical race studies addresses continuing racialized inequities and a lack of representation of marginalized communities of color, particularly in education and public discourses.

CMRS, as an interdisciplinary field that derives from the work of ethnic studies scholars and activists, encompasses interests and scholars from various disciplines. Critical race studies and ethnic studies are therefore key components of CMRS and continue to advance similar inquiries and scholarly discourses about race, culture, and society.

CMRS includes a critical examination of society and culture; the intersection of race, law, and power; racial justice scholarship; and legal practice. CMRS encompasses these areas of analysis with an emphasis on all things "mixed" race, including interracial intimacy, interraciality, multiraciality, transracial adoption, and interethnic alliances, and so on. CMRS places mixedness, hybridity, liminality, and related phenomena at the critical center of analyses in terms of miscegenation and historical "multigenerational multiraciality" that occurred prior to as well as originating at the time of Western European colonial expansion. It also addresses the contemporary "first-generation" experiences of the multiracial progeny of interracial marriages in the United States and elsewhere.

CMRS stresses critical analysis of the institutionalization of social, cultural, and political structures based on dominant conceptions of race. In keeping with racial formation theory, it acknowledges that the concept of race invokes biologically based human characteristics but also that the selection of particular human features for purposes of racial signification has changed over time.[78] Consequently, racial formation is necessarily a sociohistorical process, and CMRS emphasizes the constructed nature of race. CMRS underscores the mutability of race and porosity of racial boundaries to provide a critical examination of local and global systemic injustices. It is attentive to how racial groups and racial hierarchies are constructed through processes of racialization as it interrogates racial essentialism and racial hierarchy.

CMRS also emphasizes the intersection of racial phenomena with gender, sex, sexuality, class, and other categories of difference. As Candice West and Sarah Fenstermaker point out, these are more than individual characteristics or some vaguely defined and performed set of role expectations.[79] Rather, they are ongoing phenomena that must be situated in social situations and institutional structures. The identities associated with these phenomena normalize and naturalize social dynamics, thus legitimizing ways of organizing social life. This in turn reaffirms institutional practice, the social order, and power relations.

The accountability of individuals to categories of difference is key to understanding these dynamics. Situated social action therefore contributes to the reproduction of social structures and systems of domination (by extension) based on race, sex, gender, class, and sexuality, among others, as entrenched ideas, practices, explicit decisions, and procedures that construct social hierarchies that exclude, control, and constrain human agency. Boundaries, hierarchies, and identities associated with social categories of difference are continually constructed in everyday life. But individual agents or collective subjectivities also resist pressures to conform to these social forces, as is the case with Blaxican and other U.S. multiracials.

| Chapter Two

Anglo-America and Latin America

Examining Blaxican identities and experiences is integrally linked not only to racial formations of African Americans, Mexican Americans, and multiracials but also to broader U.S. (or Anglo-American) and Latin American, particularly Spanish American, identities. Consequently, it is useful to provide a comparative historical analysis of the Anglo-American and Spanish American racial orders. Both originated in the Eurocentric paradigm and inherited European norms granting whites privileged status relative to other racial groups. They also stigmatized African ancestry due to the racist ideology used to justify African enslavement and retain individuals of African descent in a subaltern position long after the abolition of slavery. Consequently, Blackness and whiteness have represented the negative and positive designations in a dichotomous hierarchy grounded in African and European racial and cultural differences.

Yet Anglo-America and Spanish America approached multiracials of African ancestry differently. In the racial orders of the Americas and elsewhere, European attitudes toward miscegenation and socially differentiating multiracials, particularly individuals of African descent, were motivated by self-interest. Attitudes were strongly influenced, if not determined, by the ratio of white men to women, the proportion of whites in relation to nonwhites, the extent to which Indigenous labor could be coerced, and the need to use non-European labor in positions, particularly interstitial ones, of importance in the political economy.[1]

Anglo-America and the Binary Racial Order

Large numbers of European settlers in Anglo-America arrived as families, making the gender ratio comparatively balanced throughout the colonial period. Despite the high mortality among some early settlers, due to malnutrition, starvation, and disease, the European American population rapidly increased and became a majority early in the colonial period. European settlers were relatively unsuccessful in coercing Native Americans into labor, although in some parts of the Southeast (e.g., Virginia, South Carolina) they continued to be enslaved into the early eighteenth century.[2] Yet the sheer size of the white population reduced the need to use non-European labor in important positions in the political economy. Whereas France, Spain, and Portugal were plagued by a chronic labor shortage when they began colonizing the New World, Britain had a surplus of individuals. It developed indentured servitude to meet its agricultural labor needs in the colonies. Indenture involved a contractual arrangement of temporary duration between two parties in which the price of passage from Europe was advanced in exchange for usually five to eight years of voluntary labor.[3]

From European Indenture to African Slavery

Throughout the early colonial period the Anglo-American colonies were overwhelmingly composed of white yeomanry, indentures, former indentures, and wage earners. Slavery gradually became established in the 1650s and 1660s. European indentures and African slaves worked under similarly harsh circumstances. Until slave laws were enacted, Africans held in bondage maintained a legal status like that of white indentured servants, but enslaved Africans did not volunteer their labor. Still, European indentures and African slaves shared the same living quarters. Interracial intimacy was not legally prohibited despite strong prejudice. Consequently, a small but not insignificant number of Blacks and whites intermarried or formed common-law unions and had legitimate offspring. More widespread were clandestine and fleeting liaisons resulting in births outside of wedlock, which largely involved the rape and extended concubinage of slave women of African descent by white masters or overseers.[4]

As priorities shifted from European indenture to African slavery in the late seventeenth century, servitude became in perpetuity and the slave's legal status was that of property. By the mid-eighteenth century, the dramatic increase in the number of enslaved Blacks was matched by an equally dramatic reduction in the number of white indentured servants due, in part, to the former being a cheaper labor source.[5] To help further the racial divide and maintain white supremacy, elite whites increasingly impelled indentured servants and former indentured servants to identify with their whiteness as a means of incorporation into the body politic. White labor was promised "a public and psychological wage" affirming their racial superiority to subaltern Blacks, even if socioeconomic rewards did not materialize.[6] As Free Coloreds, multiracials filled interstitial roles in the political economy, yet there were always enough whites, particularly impoverished European immigrants, to fill these roles. Whites had little incentive to socially differentiate mulattoes from Blacks to gain their collaboration against Black slaves.[7]

Yet to preserve the racial divide, barriers to interracial intimacy between Blacks and whites were also maintained and strengthened. To help achieve this objective, English Americans began enforcing hypodescent during the late seventeenth and early eighteenth centuries to maintain inequitable social divisions between themselves as the dominant "white" group and subaltern "nonwhite" groups. Hypodescent was implemented as part of antimiscegenation legislation regulating interracial intimacy, particularly interracial marriages. By defining as nonwhite any progeny born of these relationships, hypodescent enforced a monoracial imperative necessitating identification as either white or nonwhite. More specifically, these devices mandated identification as either Black or white.

Antimiscegenation Legislation and the One-Drop Rule

Black white relations were the most common targets of these statutes and suffered the most severe restrictions. Notably, the first antimiscegenation laws enacted by Virginia in the 1660s and by Maryland in the 1690s were initially concerned with interracial intimacy between European women—particularly indentures—and enslaved men of African descent. The earliest laws did not actually forbid interracial marriages. Rather, they sought to deter them by imposing stiff fines or severe penalties including banishment, whippings, and additional terms of servitude for the women. They also stipulated that the Black white progeny of these unions—that is, mulattoes—would be held in prolonged indenture servitude.[8]

By the mid-eighteenth century Black white marriages in the southern and some northern colonies were stigmatized to the point where they were not legally prohibited. Black male–white female unions, whether casual, common-law, or legalized in marriage, were strictly forbidden. These relationships threatened the sanctity of white womanhood and the integrity of the white family, which were pivotal to preserving white racial "purity." They were also fundamental to the numerical self-perpetuation, as well as the intergenerational transmission of white wealth, power, privilege, and prestige.[9]

The key difference was found in public attitudes, which continued to tolerate sexual assault and extended concubinage involving white men and women of African descent. These unions had no legal standing, posed little threat to the slave-based racial order, and would become the source of most subsequent miscegenation. Moreover, men typically disavowed their multiracial offspring from these relationships. Indeed, white landowners (particularly slaveholders) were exempted from the legal obligation of passing on inheritance and other benefits of paternity to their multiracial children. The Anglo-American patriarchy found the ideal solution to its labor needs: extramarital sexual behavior and obsession with protecting white racial "purity," as well as economic and political power.[10]

Spanish America and the Ternary Racial Order

In colonial Latin America, Spanish settlers were unsuccessful at exploiting Indigenous people as a captive labor force in the sparser semisedentary societies of the Caribbean that were based on farming, fishing, and some hunting—unlike the densely populated agricultural societies of Mexico and Peru. Throughout Latin America, however, Indigenous peoples were decimated by warfare, violence, overwork, and physical abuse, with many resisting enslavement and encroachment on their lands by escaping into the interior. The epidemics nearly annihilated the Indigenous population.[11] This led to a legal ban on their enslavement in 1542.[12] The increased need for laborers produced a dramatic rise in the demand for enslaved Africans. Beginning in the early sixteenth century, enslaved Africans supplemented or replaced Indigenous people as a labor force. Lack of familiarity with the terrain made their escape into the interior more difficult. Nevertheless, they did resist enslavement as indicated by the many runaway slave settlements (*palenques*) scattered throughout Spanish America.[13]

Prior to 1640 Mexico was the second largest slaveholding society in the New World. It is estimated that 100,000 to 200,000 Africans slaves were brought into Mexico. Mexico's national census in 1646 indicates there were 130,000 people of African descent and only 114,000 to 125,000 Spaniards, most of whom were criollos born in Mexico. Yet Afro-Mexicans never constituted more than 2 percent of the total population, which had an Indigenous majority.[14] After 1650 the demographic recovery of the Indigenous population meant that it could again perform the work of Afro-Mexican slaves. Thus, the African slave trade and population declined.[15]

Miscegenation and the Prevailing Moral Code

In contrast to Anglo-America, in Spanish America, as in much of the rest of Latin America, Europeans were small in number and mostly single males. Given the scarcity of European women, white males formed liaisons, initially with Indigenous women and later with women of African descent, setting into motion a pattern of extensive interracial intimacy. Magnus Mörner argues most interracial relationships during the early colonial period were between white men and women of color. According to Sarah Cline, most of those unions, as in Anglo-America, were consummated largely through coercion and violence, such as rape, fleeting extramarital relations, and concubinage.[16]

Whether through coercion or consent, civil and ecclesiastical authorities condemned all concubinage. Yet relationships between social unequals were necessarily restricted to concubinage or consensual unions given that codes mandated by the church insisted on the racial and class equality of marriage partners.[17] Still, even as the church frowned on concubinage, it required supporting evidence, typically through the testimony of witnesses, before pressing charges. Moreover, Spanish authorities were known to pressure interracial couples engaged in concubinage to legally marry rather than "live in sin."[18] Ultimately, the church turned a blind eye to it. The Crown equivocated about intermarriages between whites and individuals of Indigenous descent but ultimately sanctioned them if for no other reason than to expand the colonial population and establish settlements. Attitudes toward marriages of whites with individuals of African descent were vacillating and contradictory but clearly less favorable. Numerous colonial statutes sought to restrict, if not prohibit, these unions through negative sanctions, including jeopardizing social advancement.[19]

The Royal Pragmatic on Marriage (1776–78) allowed parents or civil officials to prevent marriages if they were between social unequals, for example, in terms of class or race, as this was a prime determinant in an individual's status.[20] Steinar A. Saether argues one could conjecture that the law worked in practice to prohibit interracial marriages with individuals of African descent.[21] Still, common-law unions and more informal relations and concubinage involving Spanish males and women of color were prevalent and more or less accepted, if not encouraged.[22] Notwithstanding legal barriers to racial intermarriage, the interracial family was informally legitimized throughout Latin America.[23]

In Spanish America Europeans established ternary racial orders characterized by sizeable multiracial populations and comparatively less restrictive racial boundaries than in Anglo-America. This was due, in part, to Indigenous people and Blacks composing a majority of the population and whites constituting a minority. Multiracials occupied a social location intermediate to whites, Blacks, and Indigenous peoples. During the early colonial period most multiracials were of European and Native American descent (mestizos). When colonists began importing African slaves, there was a significant increase in the numbers of multiracials of African and European, or African, European, and Native American, descent (*mulatos* or *pardos*) and, to a lesser extent, individuals of African and Native American descent (zambos).[24]

Degrees of Multiraciality, Degrees of Freedom

As a reflection of the increasingly miscegenated charter of the racial order, in the seventeenth and eighteenth centuries Spanish America developed the Sociedad de Castas (Society of Castes) or Sistema de Castas (System of Castes), a hierarchical system of racial classification representing the parent racial groups as well as permutations on them. In terms of Mexico and the rest of Spanish America, Españoles (Spaniards or whites) were at the top of the racial hierarchy. White and Indigenous multiracials occupied a more favorable position than other multiracials. Indeed, early colonial society did not ascribe the label *mestizo* to all persons of known or presumed Spanish and Indigenous ancestry. Individuals with property or social connections to elite Spaniards were less likely to be labeled *mestizo*. Individuals with stronger ties to Indigenous society and of lower economic position were more frequently referred to as *mestizos*. Also, given the extent of miscegenation, mestizo identity ceased to have a clear meaning after the sixteenth century. Mestizos were set apart from other *castas* in both law and public esteem long before the end of the eighteenth century. In fact, *castizos* as progeny of mestizos and whites were considered near-white, while the offspring of *castizos* and whites resulted in the restoration of Spanish "racial purity."[25]

Blacks and Indigenous people were at the bottom of the racial hierarchy. Mulattoes and other multiracials of African ancestry were ranked lower than mestizos in terms of prestige, privilege, and the potential for vertical mobility. Indeed, no reduction in the degree of African ancestry in Spanish America made possible a return to Spanish racial purity, since all African-descent individuals were considered impure.[26] Still, casta identities were enforced arbitrarily and inconsistently. They frequently involved assumed ancestry based on perceived phenotype. Culture and socioeconomic standing were also taken into consideration. Consequently, Laura A. Lewis maintains that the caste schema never completely closed off the possibility of vertical mobility.[27] Cline also contends that the myriad terms found in the famous eighteenth-century casta paintings had no legal standing. Casta paintings may have been the white colonial elites' attempt to put into place racial divisions based on hybrid fixity in a social reality characterized by increased race and class fluidity.[28]

Moreover, the caste system existed alongside the social distinction between *gente de razón* (people of reason) and *gente sin razón* (people without reason). Spaniards designated themselves *gente de razón*, capable of making rational decisions. They automatically qualified based on their Christian faith. On the other hand, Spaniards relegated Indigenous people to the status of *gente sin razón*. Since the sixteenth century Indigenous people had been categorized as minors under the protection of the Crown. Yet *gente de razón* standing was granted to Christianized Indigenous people, multiracials, and Blacks.[29]

Indeed, racialized religion (and employing it to maintain class privilege and domination) through laws of purity of blood (*limpieza de sangre*) informed the caste system and attitudes toward miscegenation and intermarriage in the Spanish colonies. Originating in fifteenth-century Spain, the concept of purity of blood reflected an obsession with the belief that the religious "unfaithfulness" of Jewish people not only endured in those who converted to Catholicism but also was transmitted by blood to their descendants, regardless of how sincerely they professed the Christian faith. Old Christians "of pure blood" viewed these New Christians as impure and morally unacceptable as members of their communities. This judgment primarily targeted the influential group of Iberian *conversos* (Catholics of Jewish origins), who wielded considerable political and economic influence but was also extended to *Moriscos* (Catholics of Muslim lineage). Subsequently, civil and ecclesiastical institutions and communities issued discriminatory and segregation laws against Indigenous people and individuals of African descent in the colonial territories.[30]

Still, as slaves, African-descent multiracials were often assigned more exacting tasks and were potentially the recipients of socially tolerated demonstrations of affection, as well as economic and educational protection. Despite the social stigma and liabilities associated with African ancestry in colonial Mexico and the rest of Spanish America, enslaved mistresses and multiracial progeny were often given preferential liberation. This made it possible for African-descent multiracials to enter the free classes in large numbers. Because of the smaller number of whites, they tended to view the disproportionately multiracial class of Free Coloreds as an integral part of the economy. They filled interstitial economic roles (e.g., overseers, seamstresses, washerwomen, street vendors, laundresses, cooks, artisans, and skilled laborers) due to a shortage of European labor and for which slave labor was impractical.

Spanish monarchs also often viewed Free Colored militia, disproportionately composed of multiracials, as a means of expanding the frontier, securing colonial borders against foreigners, and providing a military brake on independence-minded whites. Considering that whites and Free Coloreds shared bonds of ancestry and culture, they also viewed Free Coloreds as natural allies against enslaved Blacks and the Native American majority. This often included suppressing slave uprisings, as well as catching and returning fugitive slaves. Accordingly, both the Crown and the colonists won the loyalty of the Free Coloreds while maintaining white domination and control. Indeed, the inclusion of Free Coloreds in the state's security apparatus contributed as much to their own circumscribed status as to the superordinate position of whites. Free Colored militia could hardly overthrow whites while subordinating slaves: any revolt would bring them into opposition with the Crown and colonial government, resulting in serious reprisals in the event of defeat.[31]

| Chapter Three

Louisiana and the Gulf Coast

During the colonial period the experience of multiracials in the Lower South (or "Latin" North America) differed from that in the North and Upper South (or "Anglo" North America).[1] The early patterns of Spanish and French settlement followed the ternary Latin American model. White settlers were fewer in number and primarily single males, who first formed liaisons with Native American women and, after the introduction of slavery, with African-descent women. As in the rest of the Americas, there were legal barriers to interracial marriages, but rape, temporary extramarital relations, extended concubinage, and common-law unions between white men and women of color were tolerated, if not encouraged. Whites also granted multiracials of African descent an intermediate social location inferior to that of whites but somewhat superior to that of Blacks, who composed a majority of the population.[2]

Louisiana and the Ternary Racial Order

Interracial unions became such an accepted social practice in Louisiana that they developed into an institution called *plaçage*: relationships between white men and free women of color. The white man provided financial support for his multiracial offspring according to an agreement negotiated with the woman's parents. This was an important source for the wealth of some Free Coloreds because mistresses of color and their mulatto offspring often received sizable inheritances from white fathers. Notably, a white man could maintain his interracial family on one side of town while simultaneously maintaining his life in white society, including marriage to a white woman.[3]

This institutionalized concubinage, along with the Quadroon Balls that emerged at the turn of the nineteenth century, enabled white men, particularly those of means, to maintain romantic and sexual liaisons with African-descent and, specifically, multiracial women.[4] These relationships were not, however, between social equals, though some historians have argued that free women of color desired to be the mistresses of white men because it improved their own and their children's statuses and security. The system also gave mistresses the illusion of relative equality with free white women, at least compared to the brutalization and enslavement typical for women of African descent.[5]

The more socially sanctioned miscegenation in Latin North America and the preferential liberation of enslaved mistresses and their multiracial offspring made it easier for multiracials in colonial French Louisiana to enter the free classes. A similar pattern evolved in Spanish Alabama and Florida. Under Franco-Hispanic rule, Louisiana and the Gulf region developed ternary racial orders. As in the rest of Latin America, there were, in effect, overlapping or intersecting ternary hierarchies: one based on race, the other based on civil status as free or slave. Whites were at the top of the racial hierarchy, followed by multiracials, then Blacks. Whites were also at the top of the civil hierarchy, followed by free people of color, then slaves. Multiracials composed a majority of free people of color; Blacks composed the majority of slaves. In fact, free people of color became almost synonymous with multiracial. Yet some Blacks were free, and some multiracials were slaves. Multiracials were racially intermediate to whites and Blacks; as free persons of color, they were intermediate to whites and the masses of Black slaves. Whites granted African-descent multiracials an intermediate social location somewhat superior to that of Blacks but inferior to whites.

As in the rest of Latin America, Free Coloreds became integral to the economy because of an insufficient number of whites. Due to shared bonds of ancestry and culture, whites also viewed Freed Coloreds as natural allies in locales with a Black slave majority, which often entailed suppressing slave uprisings and capturing and returning fugitive slaves. French, as well as Spanish, monarchs saw Free Coloreds as a potential military counterforce against independence-minded whites and necessarily provided some protection of their rights. Again, by granting multiracials privileges superior to those of Blacks but inferior to those of whites, both the Crown and the colonists won the loyalty of multiracials while maintaining white domination and control. In fact, many Louisiana multiracials were slaveholding planters.[6] Some had the means to live in luxury, receive an education in Europe, and most important, "maintain themselves with poise and dignity in a White-dominated world."[7]

Demise of the Ternary Racial Order

Under Spanish rule (1769–1803) the number of free people of color in Louisiana expanded rapidly, both by natural increase and because of comparatively lenient manumission policies. Simultaneously, Spanish authorities attempted to curb the activities of free women of color, responding in part to the growing number of white women who saw them as rivals. In 1785 legislation was passed forbidding them from wearing jewels and feathers and forcing them to bind their hair in a kerchief. Spanish authorities did grant special dispensations for some legalized unions between European American men and African-descent women.[8]

Between the Louisiana Purchase in 1803 and the annexation of Louisiana by Anglo-America in 1810, the number of Free Coloreds increased fourfold to almost eight thousand due to the influx of émigrés fleeing the Haitian revolution. Like their neighbors in the port cities of Savannah and Charleston, whites in New Orleans attempted to prevent their entry through legislation, but lax administration or humane attitudes limited enforcement. They were also concerned about the Black slave majority and tended to see the prosperity of multiracials as hindering any potential alliance. Acutely aware of their rights and interests as well as their fragile position, Free Coloreds acted with considerable cohesiveness. Louisiana became home to the most numerically significant and economically integrated population of Free Coloreds in the South. These same factors also heightened the distinction between multiracial and Black, which further bolstered the dominant position of whites.[9]

The End of Franco-Hispanic Rule

Circumstances changed after France and Spain ceded their southern territories to the United States through the Louisiana Purchase Treaty of 1803 and the Adams-Onís Treaty of 1819. Creoles—that is, individuals of French and Spanish cultural orientation of all racial backgrounds, white, multiracial, and Black—were overwhelmed by an English-speaking majority. They remained aloof from the new arrivals, who they perceived as a threat to their cultural and political survival. They fought to maintain standing civil law, their cultural traditions, the teaching of heritage languages in public schools, and Creole dominance over local and regional governments.[10] Anglo-Americans concentrated on securing dominance by minimizing cultural differences between themselves and their European Creole counterparts to build a united white front against all individuals of African descent.

Creoles of color, particularly residents of New Orleans, expected equal citizenship given that Article III of the Louisiana Purchase treaty entitled all inhabitants of the colony to "the enjoyment of all rights, advantages and immunities of citizens of the United States."[11] Yet their petitions for equal citizenship and civil rights were denied. Moreover, U.S. authorities showed no desire to extend to even the wealthiest and lightest of multiracials a white racial status and identity or any of the privileges associated therewith.[12] Meanwhile, Creoles of color in Mobile and Pensacola became U.S. citizens through the Adams-Onís Treaty. Article VI of the treaty grants incorporation "in the Union of the United States as soon as may be consistent with the principles of the Federal Constitution, and admitted to the enjoyment of all the privileges, rights, and immunities of the citizens of the United States."[13] Consequently, Creoles of color were initially exempted from restrictions.

By the 1840s and 1850s these comparatively more favorable circumstances had changed. Alabama and Florida enacted restrictive laws targeting citizenship and enfranchisement aimed at Free Coloreds that did not yet specifically exclude Creoles of color.[14] Anglo-Americanization saw the ternary racial order gradually replaced with a binary one designating as Black all individuals of African descent. Creoles of color worked to preserve their intermediate status as the ternary racial order polarized into Black and white. By the time of the Civil War the ethnocultural tension between Anglo-Americans and Creoles of European descent abated as both groups united in support of white racial purity. They devised criteria in which Creole was redefined as having only Spanish and French ancestry.

Still, Creoles of color and whites shared legal, economic, cultural, and ancestral ties. Many Creoles of color were apprehensive about the impact that freeing the slaves would have on their own elevated status. Many opposed abolition and supported secession. Indeed, three thousand Free Coloreds joined the Confederate army. Following the Union capture of New Orleans in spring 1862, most Creoles of color switched their loyalties, hoping that racial prejudice would end. Yet since all African-descent individuals were now free, Union victory brought about the feared loss of wealth, property, and deterioration of their intermediate status.[15]

The Louisiana Supreme Court, as late as 1910, continued to distinguish between *negro* and *person of color*, which respectively designated Blacks and multiracials. Yet these distinctions no longer had the same significance as previously.[16] Many Creoles of color resisted this loss of status by denying any similarity or community of interests with ex-slaves and English-speaking Blacks. Others, benefiting from the generational inheritance of social, cultural, and intellectual advantages, provided political leadership of the Black masses, serving as state senators, representatives, and even state officials in the post–Civil War Reconstruction government.

Black Reconstruction, White Redemption

With the enactment of the Thirteenth, Fourteenth, and Fifteenth Amendments, and other legislation during Reconstruction (1865–77), Blacks gained full rights of citizenship and membership in the people's domain based on what Gunnar Myrdal refers to as the "American creed."[17] Yet this accomplishment was undermined by the Hayes-Tilden Compromise of 1877, which ushered in a period generally called "White Redemption." In this compromise the southern Democratic supporters of Samuel Tilden gave the northern Republican supporters of Rutherford B. Hayes the disputed votes in the presidential election of 1876 in exchange for removal of federal troops who had occupied the South to ensure compliance with Reconstruction legislation. This withdrawal allowed the South to handle the "Negro Problem" without interference from the federal government.

This change was felt acutely in Louisiana. Southern whites mounted an aggressive campaign supporting discriminatory laws to undermine the gains of Reconstruction. Some prominent Creoles of color hoped something could be done to rescind these unjust laws, retain the hard-won franchise, and arrest the segregationist tide.[18] In 1891 they formed the Comité des Citoyens (Citizens' Committee), with the goal of mobilizing Creole resistance to state-imposed segregation. One of the committee's first acts was to test the constitutionality of Louisiana's 1890 Separate Car Act that required African-descent individuals to ride in special streetcars and railway carriages.[19]

The committee chose Hommeré A. Plessy, a young Creole artisan and community activist, who was one-eighth Black and thus white by appearance, as the perfect candidate to challenge segregation. Following Plessy's arrest for occupying a whites-only train car, Plessy's attorneys presented a plea containing fourteen objections to the segregation statute. Among these was the argument that "the Statute impairs the right of passengers of the class to which Relator [Plessy] belongs, to wit: Octoroons, to be classed among white persons, although color be not discernible in the complexion, and makes penal their refusal to abide by the decision of a railroad conductor in this respect."[20]

A substantial part of Plessy's case rested on the question of racial definition. The argument was not necessarily that someone with predominantly European ancestry, such as Plessy, was entitled to the rights accorded to whites—although one could arrive at that conclusion given the pursuit of white adjacency, which historically informed Creole of color identity. Rather, this issue was largely raised to interrogate the arbitrary nature of racial classifications and challenge the state's (or anyone's) authority to define Blackness.[21] It targeted the legality of segregation that was based on the absurd notion that a trace of African ancestry could disqualify a person from equal citizenship rights.[22]

After state courts denied Plessy's arguments and the committee appeal, the U.S. Supreme Court upheld the lower courts' decisions but also gave constitutional sanction to the "separate but equal" doctrine based on egalitarian pluralism.[23] The court made no formal judgment on the legal definition of Blackness. Instead, it took informal "judicial notice" of what it assumed to be racial common sense: a Black individual was anyone with any traceable amount of African American ancestry.[24] Thus, *Plessy v. Ferguson* provided a benchmark for future rulings on legal Blackness according to the one-drop rule.

Plessy v. Ferguson enforced legal segregation in the public sphere, so long as separate facilities were equally maintained. This affirmation of de jure equality was meaningless given the de facto inequality endorsed by the decision. To reconcile these grounds with the Reconstruction Amendments, the Supreme Court divided the people's domain into two realms. The "legal-political" realm was a smaller institutional area, to which the Constitution and the American creed applied. The "social" realm was composed of behavior and practice to which the guarantees of they no longer automatically applied. The court gave constitutional sanction to a doctrine based on egalitarian pluralism—"separate but equal"—while giving local and state governments the authority to legalize discriminatory practices based on inegalitarian pluralism—"separate but unequal." In so doing it nullified the effects of the Fourteenth and Fifteenth Amendments.

This also imbued white supremacy with a "status and sanctity" it had previously lacked.[25] Prior to Reconstruction, the legal-normative code of the people was based on the egalitarian principles of the Declaration of Independence and Constitution. White supremacist beliefs and values articulated in law referred to Blacks as not belonging to "the people." The Reconstruction Amendments changed that. Blacks gained formal legal membership in the people's domain, which meant they, too, were governed by these egalitarian principles. Instead, *Plessy* further racialized the legal-normative framework of the people that enshrined anti-Black racism in a new inegalitarian framework. Reconstruction's promise of freedom, opportunity, and equal citizenship was broken in favor of the reconstruction of African American servitude and the redemption of white supremacy.

Throughout the South, Jim Crow laws were extended to nearly every facet of life as the legal rights gained during Reconstruction were circumvented by segregation, the implementation of "understanding clauses," "grandfather clauses," poll taxes, and literacy tests.[26] From 1896 to 1904 the Supreme Court upheld southern strategies to deprive African Americans of their Fifteenth Amendment-derived right to vote. The court also upheld the segregation of all public facilities, including schools and housing. In the North, theaters, restaurants, hotels, housing, and schools were already segregated in practice, even where the law forbade it.

Creoles of color, who prior to the 1890s had enjoyed a status separate from and more elevated than that of Blacks, were dealt the final blow by Jim Crow segregation, which suddenly pushed into the broader African American community. Some joined Blacks in challenging the onslaught of segregationist policies. Many others denied any similarity or community of interests with the masses of ex-slaves and English-speaking Blacks. Instead, they fought to maintain their intermediate status and the privileges they enjoyed under French and Spanish rule as they watched Louisiana's racial order polarize into Black and white. Others left for Mexico and the Caribbean where racial lines were more fluid. Color, rather than ancestry, was the primary criterion used to define race there. Still others moved to Florida,

Kansas, and particularly California, where they crossed the racial divide or formed Creole residential enclaves.[27]

Many Creoles went north and passed for white, which occurred when individuals of a more European American phenotype and cultural orientation made a covert break with the Black community, either temporarily (discontinuous passing) or permanently (continuous passing), to enjoy the privileges of the white community. A smaller number passed for white in Louisiana by destroying the birth records that were the only legal proof of their ancestry. An estimated one hundred to five hundred African-descent Americans in Louisiana crossed the racial divide every year from 1875 to the 1890s. Other Creoles refused to learn English, remained staunchly Catholic, and sought refuge within the confines of their own world in New Orleans north of Canal Street, particularly in the Sixth, Seventh, Eighth, and Ninth Wards.[28] Over time the multiracial clan of Metoyers on Cane River emerged as a rural pluralistic enclave. In both cases this racial seclusion was often accompanied by a rejection of association with whites, as well as Blacks, if not always a complete denial of African ancestry.[29]

| Chapter Four

Black Identity Construction and the Monoracial Imperative

Throughout the South, Jim Crow laws encompassed nearly every aspect of social life. By the first decades of the twentieth century, state after state enacted legislation to void interracial marriages. Seven of the southern states adopted the one-drop rule as the official definition of Blackness. Virginia abandoned its one-fourth rule in 1910 and settled for one-sixteenth on the assumption that lesser amounts could not be detected but ultimately adopted the one-drop rule in 1930. Seven states resorted to the one-eighth rule early in the century, allowing some persons to be classified as white who appeared to be partly Black or who had at least some African forebears and had been known as Black.[1]

One-Drop Rule and Jim Crow

In practice, the differences between words describing varying degrees of African ancestry had little significance beyond the creation of hierarchy among African Americans. They helped perpetuate a pernicious colorism that granted preferential treatment to individuals contingent on European American appearance and cultural norms. Moreover, this phenomenon gave rise to elite social groups known as "blue-vein societies," which sought to distance themselves from common stereotypes associated with Blacks by recreating the dominant

European American image.² At best, these societies created the illusion of having escaped the taint of subaltern status but never achieved actual equality with whites.

That said, the preoccupation with degrees of African ancestry on the 1890 census reflected the white supremacist paranoia about invisible Blackness, which Thomas Matthews refers to as "cryptomelanism," and the possibility of multiracials passing for white and crossing the racial divide and "contaminating" the European American population.³ According to nineteenth-century scientific racism and biological determinism, these notions would lead to the decline of Anglo-American civilization.⁴ In the late nineteenth and early twentieth centuries, these race suicide fears became part of a broader white supremacist mindset that reached extreme proportions with the institutionalization of Jim Crow segregation, which was buttressed by the one-drop rule.

Joel Williamson argues that the cumulative effects of the one-drop rule, along with forced endogamy and "internal miscegenation" between multiracials and Blacks, as a result of Jim Crow segregation laws, reached such a point by the 1920s that most Blacks were becoming multiracial in terms of ancestry.⁵ This was accompanied by a generalized "browning" of African Americans. Indeed, after the 1920s the census ceased to differentiate between Blacks and mulattoes. Officially and informally, mulattoes who displayed more European phenotypical traits, as well as mulattoes generally speaking, came to regard themselves less as multiracial and more as simply light-skinned Blacks.

The New Negro Movement

This shift was demonstrated among the vanguard of the Harlem Renaissance of the 1920s. As part of the "New Negro Movement," it promoted a sense of racial pride, cultural self-expression, economic independence, and progressive politics. Although the Harlem Renaissance attracted both Blacks and multiracials, the descendants of the mulatto elite assumed a leadership role. Henry L. Morehouse, a white patron of liberal arts study for Blacks, and W. E. B. Du Bois, cofounder of the National Association for the Advancement of Colored People (NAACP), which was founded in 1909, and founder of *The Crisis*, saw the Harlem Renaissance's vanguard as made up of people who could speak out for less privileged African Americans. Du Bois and others eventually rejected the notion of an elite vanguard—the "Talented Tenth"—as assimilationism. Still, the use of this multiracial elite constituted, in its distinct historical context, one of the tactics Blacks deployed in the struggle for equality.

The emergence of the Harlem Renaissance was closely tied to New York's emergence as a land of opportunity for Blacks in the first two decades of the twentieth century, much like Washington DC's role during and after Reconstruction. Between 1914 and 1930 there was a significant migration of Blacks from the South to the North. During World War I, the conscription of many white males to the military draft and the reduction in European immigration created a labor shortage in the North that accelerated this migration. Plentiful jobs that paid relatively well—along with the disincentives of Jim Crow laws and virulent racism in the South—drew many Blacks to northern cities.

African Americans were no longer merely a southern rural people but became part of the metropolitan areas that formed the twentieth century's urban ghettos—most famously Chicago's South Side and, especially, Harlem in New York. Although it began in New York, Harlem's Renaissance extended to Chicago, Washington, Atlanta, and other cities with large Black populations. The same job opportunities that attracted African Americans to the North also attracted African-descent populations from Latin America and the Caribbean. The Black American population in New York City increased by 250 percent between 1914 and 1930, when it reached 327,706 residents, who were mostly concentrated in Harlem.[6]

The Harlem Renaissance also attracted European Americans and reflected a mutually beneficial relationship between many whites and Blacks.[7] Yet the ethos forged by Harlem Renaissance leaders such as W. E. B. Du Bois, Jean Toomer, Countee Cullen, Langston Hughes, Zora Neale Hurston, James Weldon Johnson, and others turned for inspiration to the Black experience and engaged with the question of what it meant to be an African American through an appreciation of southern rural African American life, the human dignity of

Black slaves, and early twentieth-century Black urban poverty. They simultaneously fused this vision with their own European American sociocultural traditions. W. E. B. Du Bois's concept of "double consciousness" captures this dynamic most clearly: for him Blacks were products of two warring cultural identities and nations—one American (read white) and the other African American—both of which were necessary in order to live in their communities as well as to navigate dominant white American social norms.[8]

Yet this double consciousness and its accompanying liminality was cultural rather than racial. While many of the Harlem Renaissance had close personal and professional relationships with European Americans and others explored the multiracial experience in their writing, the clear message to multiracials of the Harlem Renaissance was that the only meaningful future was in fully embracing pride in an identity as "Negroes."[9] Multiple racial ancestries were overridden by a monoracial identity and a bicultural experience that challenged racial hierarchy without daring to fully or directly confront those ancestries.[10]

Although the members of the Harlem Renaissance elite set themselves up as spokespeople for the Black masses, this role was contested by members of the pan-Africanist movement, including Marcus Garvey who declared that he spoke for the "untalented ninetieth." Neither movement articulated a social place for a multiracial identity but rather operated within the dominant binary racial order. Shared African-descent, regardless of other ancestry, was posited as the basis for common life and their shared goals. A multiracial identity, which could contest the mutually exclusive nature of racial boundaries and also challenge the hierarchical valuation of racialized difference, was jettisoned in favor of more politically viable efforts organized around hypodescent, monoraciality, and Blackness based on egalitarian premises.[11]

Integration and the Quest for Equality

From the end of Reconstruction through the first half of the twentieth century, the U.S. racial order was rife with tension between the

American and racial creeds. Supporters of the former envisioned the integration of all individuals as equals into the social order. Adherents of the latter enforced a racial contract premised on exclusionary policies. Neither side succeeded in eclipsing the opposing principle. Southern states immediately grasped the import of the Supreme Court decisions supporting the racial creed's "separate but equal" doctrine. They expanded the institutional area of practice and behavior that came under the jurisdiction of this doctrine—the social realm. However, they sought to do this without contravening the institutional area still protected by the American Creed—the legal-political realm.

The Supreme Court delineated a private sector within the people's domain, which gave the North license to pursue discriminatory practices that legally excluded Blacks from whites' places of employment and residential communities. The local courts were placed at the disposal of whites to enforce private exclusionary agreements, such as restrictive covenants in housing. This racial segregation was solidified with the Great Migration of Blacks northward during and after World War I. These dynamics, along with the hardening of racial segregation in the South, generated a national climate of fear. Blacks not only expressed public indignation at the implementation of the "separate but equal" doctrine but also balked at compliance with its mandates. Southern whites responded with repressive legal and extralegal tactics to keep Blacks "in their place." In the North racial tensions exploded in numerous violent urban riots. Yet increasing racial segregation in employment and housing limited direct contact between Blacks and whites, which in turn prevented overt racial conflict from exceeding certain limits.

In midcentury, the United States moved toward official repudiation of Jim Crow segregation. In 1948 President Truman issued a presidential decree ending segregation in the armed forces and the federal civil service. After the end of World War II, the NAACP's Legal Defense and Education Fund, under the leadership of Charles Hamilton Houston and his protégé Thurgood Marshall, set its sights on winning a case that would overturn *Plessy v. Ferguson*. In 1952 a brief was filed with the Supreme Court leading to the Court's

Brown v. Board of Education decision (1954) ending segregation in public schools.[12]

Over the next decade the tensions intensified as the Supreme Court pushed to delegitimize the racial creed into the farthest reaches institutionally, in the social realm and, geographically, in the South. The task that began during the "First Reconstruction" was completed almost one hundred years later in the "Second Reconstruction" in the 1950s and 1960s. This shift was linked to the pressures of the African American civil rights movement and its interracial coalition, as well as the nationwide revulsion against the racial brutality of the Deep South that was influenced by television news coverage of the civil rights struggle.[13]

The early African American civil rights movement had integration as its goal. The NAACP, the National Urban League, and the Southern Christian Leadership Conference (SCLC) sought the integration of all individuals as equals under the tenets of the American creed. The movement initially focused its energies on the Southeast, the region in which whites most viciously opposed integration. At the time, racial injustice was understood to be a matter of prejudiced attitudes or bigotry rather than broader social structural phenomena. In the liberal tradition of Gunnar Myrdal, the solution to the "American Dilemma" was believed to reside in the abolition of discriminatory practices that would involve overcoming such attitudes and the achievement of tolerance, specifically among white Americans.[14] The early civil rights movement reflected these views and sought to overcome racial prejudice by appealing to the nation's moral conscience.

The unique history of racial discrimination in the United States was overt, ratified by law, and buttressed by the one-drop rule, which fostered the development of separate Black organizations in the struggle for legal and political justice. Blacks have had to operate as a cohesive political and social force with a sense of collective identity and history of activism despite internal tensions and cleavages based on color, culture, class, and gender. Prominent African American civil rights leaders who would be considered white in Latin America—such as Adam Clayton Powell, Walter White, May Street Kidd, Whitney

Young, Henrietta Butler, Thurgood Marshall, Julian Bond, Lyman Johnson, and Charlotte McGill—quite possibly had more incentive to identify with the Black masses than they would have if they had been in Latin America, where the "mulatto escape hatch" has functioned as a form of social control to disincentivize that kind of alliance.[15]

Despite the continuing significance of color, the identification of multiracials with the Black community historically increased during the Harlem Renaissance, a time when the one-drop rule was firmly established. African Americans must certainly have been aware that most are multiracial in ancestry and know the one-drop rule emerged during slavery to maintain white domination and the subordination of Blacks and was consolidated to reinforce Jim Crow segregation. This forced all shades of individuals into the Black community. A sense of unity developed among a people with a wide variation in racial characteristics. Whites' original oppressive reasons for implementing the rule have become irrelevant to most Blacks today.

Equal but Separate

The radical insurgency of the Black Power Movement, Black nationalism, and violent urban uprisings in the late 1960s and early 1970s jettisoned integration as a questionable and even futile goal given its likely inegalitarian (that is, assimilationist) outcomes, if not actual intentions. This is because, taken to its conclusion, this would undermine the particularity of the Black community. The Black struggle thus shifted from the primary pursuit of civil rights to encompass Black pride and Black Power. Black people advocated egalitarian pluralism or Black separatism that viewed Blacks as a self-determining society and culture autonomous from and on equal footing with that of whites.[16]

This ideology drew parallels between African Americans (and other communities of color in the United States) and colonized people of the Third World. This colonial analogy emerged in the 1960s as the rallying cry for Malcolm X, Stokely Carmichael (Kwame Touré), and the Black Panther Party. It also caught the attention of such scholars as Robert Blauner, Robert L. Allen, and William K. Tabb. They, along with Latina/o and Black activists, reframed the experiences of people of color in the United States as a form of "internal colonialism."[17] The colonial analogy recognized that racial inequality and injustice were not simply products of individual prejudice and discriminatory behavior. These were embedded in the very structure of society and U.S. capitalism, the products of centuries of systematic exclusion and exploitation of racially defined "minorities." Thus, the combination of prejudice and discrimination, along with the power to enforce it on the institutional level, defined the concept of "racism" at the end of the 1960s. In turn, the term *racism* (which had surfaced occasionally in the past) increasingly became part of the lexicon of racial "common sense."[18]

The emphasis on Black pride as well as Black political and economic power among Black Muslims in the Nation of Islam affirmed Blackness in a manner similar to the Harlem Renaissance. The Nation of Islam's goal of separate institutional development was generally rejected by the Black community. Still, Blacks embraced its emphasis on pride, beauty, achievement, history, and the use of the term *Black*, rather than *Negro* or *Colored*. The movement wielded the term *Black* as a form of self-ascription and self-determination. This involved a process of reclamation and rearticulation of *Black*, which had historically been a stigmatizing and offensive term.

Toward Integrative Pluralism

By the mid-1970s, the central themes of the Harlem Renaissance were also revived and extended, with strong support for building a Black culture on both African and African American foundations. Blacks generally rejected total assimilation, as well as total separation, favoring instead integrative pluralism.[19] They were demanding equal treatment, mutual respect of all racial groups and cultures, the right to voluntary integration into the larger societal institutions as much or as little as desired, and retention of their own group identity. A strong Black identity and pride in African American culture were an expression of group solidarity in the formation of a plural community seeking to deemphasize racial and class diversity and focus on the unifying symbols of Blackness. Black pride and particularly Black Power were often expressed in such strong rhetoric that many whites feared armed revolution. It became clear, however, that most African Americans supported major reforms, not revolution.

The long-standing definition of who is Black, based on the one-drop rule, was not challenged by Black protests or political demands for equal opportunity through civil rights initiatives aimed at integration and supported by largely middle-class organizations such as the NAACP, National Urban League, and SCLC. Black protests and political demands for equal outcome through social engineering such as affirmative action did not include a challenge to the long-standing definition of who is Black.[20]

The overwhelming reality is that Blacks have accepted the one-drop rule as racial common sense and believe they have a strategic and vested interest in maintaining and rallying to its defense when it is challenged. An African American identity is not, therefore, a mindless embrace of the Blackness that whiteness created based on hypodescent and the monoracial imperative. Rather, whites devised and enforced patterns of exclusion based on racial differences, while Blacks maintained a sense of community grounded in a positive affirmation of these differences, that is, pluralism without hierarchy. This involves repetition of hypodescent in support of difference, grounded in the belief that this is necessary for maintaining solidarity, as well as community, in the struggle against the inequities perpetuated by white racism, oppression, and privilege.

| Chapter Five

California and the Southwest

Few Europeans were available to populate the newly conquered region of Northern Mexico in California and the rest of the U.S. Southwest in the seventeenth century.¹ Consequently, Hispanicized Indigenous peoples, multiracials of all kinds, and Blacks came to the region as soldiers with the first expeditions.² They comingled with Spanish settlers, who were allowed and even encouraged to marry Indigenous people due to an initial shortage of Spanish women. Still, many of these relationships were short-lived. Others involved coercion and violence, rather than mutual consent and peaceful means, involving rape or fleeting extramarital relations and extended concubinage. Spanish men also married multiracial and Black women despite legal restrictions.³

The Ternary Racial Order

During the seventeenth century, African-descent individuals lived in New Mexico as colonists or soldiers and were frequently used as *majordomos* (chief stewards) in Spanish missions.⁴ They participated in most or all the early sea expeditions along the Pacific Coast and accompanied the first expeditions that occupied San Diego and Monterey in 1769. California was subdued by multiracial troops. By 1800 Blacks and mulattoes composed approximately 20 percent of

California's population, ranging from 14.7 percent in San Francisco to over 50 percent in Los Angeles.[5]

Interestingly, gente de razón, a largely religious term, was interpreted differently in the northern frontier region than in the areas with a longer Spanish presence. In Alta California, for example, there were only two kinds of people: on the one hand, the gente de razón and on the other, the non-Hispanicized Indigenous people of California, who were ostensibly gente sin razón. Yet at the turn of the nineteenth century the term *gente de razón* collectively designated Hispanicized Native Americans, as well as multiracials, who made up the system of castes. Indigenous converts, Blacks, and all multiracials were included in this special social category in colonial society. Still, the stigma associated with being multiracial was marked enough to justify distancing the castas from whites, thereby reconjuring the meaning of gente de razón. Indeed, in some circles gente de razón became synonymous with elite class status and whiteness. In others gente de razón were stratified into an upper tier (whites) and a variety of lower tiers (multiracials and Blacks).[6]

In keeping with Spanish American racial formations, African or Indigenous ancestry in the Southwest was not a rigid obstacle to social mobility, although society was divided by class and race. Elites (landowners, officers, and missionaries) were lighter-skinned and race conscious, while most individuals were less privileged and darker-skinned. But many African-descent multiracials were able to rise in the social hierarchy, call themselves *Españoles*, and potentially own property. Some darker-skinned men also married lighter-skinned women and had children who eventually married into the white upper class.[7]

In 1824, following the change from Spanish to Mexican rule in 1821, Mexico removed immigration restrictions on foreigners. European and European American immigrants, particularly males, were granted large tracts of land to settle in California with the backing of the Mexican government.[8] California's Spanish-speaking community—that is, Californios—influenced and were influenced by the growing number of these immigrants, who integrated into their society, becoming Mexican citizens. Many of the prominent and well-to-do men married women from elite lighter-skinned Californio families, who owned massive, highly desirable tracts of land, as well as large herds of cattle, sheep, and horses. Anglo-American men who married Californio women gained extensive landholdings while tapping into existing power networks. Rancho ownership was possible for them because, under Spanish-Mexican law, married women could independently hold title to property as Mexican daughters customarily inherited property on a relatively equal basis with sons.[9] With marriage, these assets were transferred from Mexican to European American hands, with Californio families occasionally arranging such marriages to forestall a loss of influence or to enhance their social standing.[10]

Elite children from some of these marriages, born in the 1830s and 1840s, sought to navigate both the Californio and the Anglo-American worlds. After the U.S. conquest over Mexico in 1848, they were incentivized to assimilate into the Anglo-American one. Many remained firmly rooted in their Hispanic culture and sought to ensure that the Spanish language and their Catholic customs endured. Yet they also largely considered themselves white.[11] Also, African ancestry was suppressed or denied and became a distant memory. In fact, in 1829 African slavery had been abolished in Mexico, including in California and other areas of the Southwest. Consequently, in Mexican California there were no longer any African slaves, whose numbers in the region had always been miniscule anyway. Enslavement of Indigenous peoples, on the other hand, persisted outside the law in the Southwest, including in many Indigenous communities.[12] To some extent, the disavowal or suppression of Indigenous ancestry paralleled that of African ancestry. Yet Indigenous peoples were visible as the largest subaltern, subjugated, and exploited population, even after Mexican independence.

Demise of the Ternary Racial Order

After the Mexican American War in 1848, Mexicans who remained in the United States were legally guaranteed "all the rights of citizens of the United States, according to the principles of the Constitution," which were protected by Article IX of the Treaty of Guadalupe Hidalgo and the United States.[13] Yet the social location of Mexicans in California, most of whom were darker-skinned mestizos, was largely unscripted.[14] Moreover, African ancestry and links to African slavery were widely dispersed among all of California's social classes, including the elite.[15] Some Anglo-American observers were aware or suspected that many Mexicans had African ancestry. It is difficult to determine the extent to which this was a more general perception or what impact that had on their attitudes.

Racial Extinction

Still, Anglo-Americans did disparage Mexicans as multiracial and inferior, voicing race suicide fears about miscegenation in the United States. According to nineteenth-century scientific racism and biological determinism, the resulting "mongrelization" would ultimately lead to the decline of Anglo-American civilization.[16] Anglo-Americans also believed that nonwhites would disappear as new European Americans arrived and saw themselves as Americans, not as future Mexicans.

Indeed, as Anglo-Americans spread westward in the nineteenth century, many intending to take more territory from Mexico, "racial extinction" theories and the "manifest destiny" of Anglo-Americans came to justify notions supporting the eventual demise of all people of color.[17] Thomas Jefferson Farnham, an advocate of Anglo-American expansion into California, encapsulated these ideas: "No one acquainted with the indolent, mixed race of California, will ever believe that they will populate, much less, for any length of time, govern the country. The law of Nature which curses the mulatto here with a constitution less robust than that of either race from which he sprang, lays a similar penalty upon the mingling of the Indian and white races in California and Mexico. They must fade away."[18]

The convention delegates at the Monterey Constitutional Convention of 1849 saw considerable debate on these topics. While it did not question Mexicans' American citizenship because of suspicions of African ancestry, the issue of whether California would be admitted as a slave or free state did become a major concern. The

1849 constitution prohibited slavery, but slaveholders were granted legal possession of African American slaves brought into California from 1848 until 1856.[19] Mexican American and European American convention delegates adopted the motion that "Africans, and the descendants of Africans" were to be denied citizenship, as well as the ability to serve on a jury, to homestead public land, or to attend public school.[20] Any African ancestry among Mexicans was disregarded. Still, the final approved version of the new article of the constitution did formally disenfranchise Native Americans.[21]

White by Absence of Definition

Elite Californio families, including multiracials with African ancestry, insisted that they were "untainted" by racial mixture and often claimed to be descended from Spanish nobility. They considered themselves white and were already considered white under Mexican rule. European Americans accepted this narrative, even if they harbored doubts about its accuracy. Ultimately, all Mexicans were extended an official white racial identity, despite not being strictly "white" in the Northern European sense.[22] Ariela Gross maintains that during the years of the Texas Republic (1836–46), some Mexicans were able to purchase and retain their land by virtue of a similar logic—claiming whiteness through assertions of "Spanish blood." Anglo-Texans who married Mexican women called their spouses Spanish.[23]

Mexican women's agency in and the perceived benefits of these interracial marriages should be taken into consideration despite the patriarchal dynamics involved. In such instances, racial distinctions to some extent coincided with class and landholding.[24] Indeed, the primary beneficiaries of white racial privilege in Texas, New Mexico (present-day New Mexico and Arizona), and California were the lighter-skinned Tejano, Hispano, and Californio elite, particularly the landowning classes. Social tolerance was rigidly circumscribed along class lines.[25]

Furthermore, Mexicans were only white by default because the Treaty of Guadalupe Hidalgo ending the war between the United States and Mexico made them eligible for U.S. citizenship as early as

1848. At the time only "white persons" could naturalize. No state or federal court ever sought to clarify this statute or to designate Mexicans as affirmatively "white." Rather, courts invoked the treaty as precedent in cases involving Mexicans, circumventing questions of their racial ancestry. Unlike for "Negroes" or "Mongolians," who were specifically prohibited from intermarrying with whites, antimiscegenation statutes were not applied to Mexican Americans, who were legally defined by the absence of definition. Still, while Mexican Americans were granted full citizenship and legally defined as "white," restrictionists sought their prohibition on racial grounds. In practice Anglo-Americans generally thought of them as nonwhite.[26]

Power relations between Mexican Americans and European Americans were significantly reconfigured during the latter half of the nineteenth century. Initially, Californios outnumbered European Americans in California by about ten to one. But by 1849 there were one hundred thousand Anglo-Americans and only thirteen thousand Mexicans. Dominant in the state legislature, Anglo-Americans enacted laws as well as political and economic restrictions that increasingly viewed and treated Mexicans as a racialized minority. The earlier accommodation in California, followed by the dispossession of Mexican lands, as well as exclusionary racial attitudes and practices, was replicated across the Southwest.[27]

Mexicans found it increasingly difficult to claim their rights, not only as citizens but also as landowners, both of which were guaranteed by the Treaty of Guadalupe Hidalgo. Yet through a variety of complicated and often underhanded legalistic maneuverings courts across the Southwest, dominated by European American legal officials, became ever more successful in contesting Mexican land titles. Unfamiliar with U.S. law and generally lacking English-language skills, many Mexican landholders became prey to European American lawyers. In the end, whether or not they won their claims, large numbers of the great rancheros lost their lands.[28] Between 1848 and 1880, privately held Mexican land in California was thus transferred on a massive scale to European Americans.[29]

Along with more generalized economic setbacks and a loss of

Mexican political influence came increased racism.[30] As the ternary racial order was replaced with a binary one, elite Spanish-speaking Californians accepted Anglo-American binary and monoracial logic but rejected hypodescent. Instead, they embraced hyperdescent wherein they privileged "Europeanness" over indigenous "Mexicanness." This served as a powerful motivation to identify as "Spanish" and lay claim to whiteness.[31] More important, by the end of the nineteenth century, African forebears were a long-lost, if not concealed, memory among lighter-skinned Spanish-identified descendants of California's first families. This erasure of memory served as the basis for the racial mythology of a California devoid of Indigenous and African ancestry on display in the ritual "Old Spanish Days" celebrations.[32]

| Chapter Six

Mexican American Identity and Monoraciality

By the 1900s segregation of African Americans was vigorously enforced in the Southeast and variously in the Southwest. Attempts were also made to segregate Mexican Americans. Enforcement was inconsistent and the results ambiguous. Indeed, the Black press reported that Mexicans Americans were permitted to ride in whites-only streetcars and trains and attend first-class theaters in the white sections, even when highly educated African Americans could not. By the 1920s the segregation of Mexican American children in California public schools and other parts of the Southwest was well established. This was through the assignment of school districts, rather than by state law, and it was not uniformly applied. In California some districts chose not to separate Mexican-descent children.[1] In Texas, discrimination was the most severe. The majority of children of Mexican descent attended segregated schools. Montejano has shown that in Texas, between 1890 and 1910, patterns of Mexican-white segregation coincided with divisions between "ranch counties" and "farm counties."[2] In the former, Mexicans continued to be landholders and commercial farmers. In the latter they were sharecroppers for white landholders.

White by Law, Not Equal

Where Mexicans held land, they were less likely to be excluded from schools and other public accommodations. *Mexican* was less likely to be used as a racialized term for nonwhite identity. This was not a matter of law as was true for Blacks. Still, Mexican Americans were turned away from white-only swimming pools, sometimes denied service at restaurants, and discouraged from moving into white neighborhoods.[3] The sign "No Dogs or Mexicans Allowed" was commonly posted outside restaurants.[4] Although Mexicans were legally designated as white, they were "white but not equal."[5]

League of United Latin American Citizens

In 1929 the mostly urban and middle-class Tejano elite founded the League of United Latin American Citizens (LULAC) to overcome overt forms of segregation.[6] During the repatriation drives of the 1930s, when Mexican Americans and Mexican nationals were routinely deported, Mexicans' consciousness began to change. Those who identified with the United States began to call themselves Mexican American and were determined to gain full inclusion within its racial order.[7] They stressed an ideology of duality: "Mexican in culture and social activity, but American in philosophy and politics."[8] LULAC restricted its membership to U.S. citizens and emphasized English-language skills and loyalty to the United States.

Concerned about the social stigma of being Mexican American, including the taint of multiraciality, LULAC members became vocal about and insistent on their status as whites. Yet this was not necessarily intended to encompass everyone: upwardly mobile Mexican Americans emphasized their whiteness, in part to distinguish themselves from working-class Mexicans, who tended to be darker-skinned with limited English-language proficiency. They believed their class position made them quintessentially American and thus ostensibly white.[9] To claim whiteness, the organization's members constructed identities as "Latin American" and strenuously objected to being labeled as *colored* or being required to share segregated facilities with Blacks. This was part of their strategy to differentiate themselves, psychologically and socially, as well as to distance themselves from African Americans.[10] Some scholars have characterized LULAC members and similar Mexican American activists as unwavering promoters of assimilation and white identity.[11] Others argue that whiteness was not necessarily based on a sense of shame in or dismissal of their multiraciality. Rather, LULAC's chief architects viewed it as a pragmatic strategy to gain legal advantage against extant proscriptions and material benefits within the racial order's limitations. Consequently, some Mexican Americans voiced opposition to this path and its opportunistic implications.[12]

"Another White Race"

Until 1930 Mexican Americans were counted as white on the census. Following increased immigration after the Mexican Revolution in 1910, the 1930 census established a separate racial category for Mexicans, which LULAC members strenuously opposed. The "Mexican" category included instructions to include any person of Mexican descent "who is definitely not white."[13] Enumerators were not, however, given any instructions to determine which ones were white. LULAC, in concert with the Mexican government and the U.S. Department of State, successfully eliminated the category in the 1940 census. Mexican Americans were reclassified as white.[14]

Part of the rationale for this change was that patterns of racial discrimination in Texas conflicted with demands for cheap labor of the Bracero Program in 1942. The Mexican government initially refused to allow *braceros* to work in Texas until the state guaranteed their fair treatment and ended all informal segregation and formal discrimination. Governor Coke Stevenson tried to assure the Mexican government that Mexicans were no longer targets of racial discrimination. He persuaded the Texas state legislature to pass the Caucasian Race Resolution in 1943, designating Mexican Americans officially as white and giving all whites equal rights in public places, business, and amusement.[15]

This resolution sought to reassure Mexican officials that Texas, if not its citizens, recognized Mexicans as whites. With such official recognition, the Mexican government permitted bracero workers to enter Texas in 1947. The blatant hypocrisy of this legislation was that no Texan regarded Mexicans, least of all braceros, as white. This legal construction of Mexican whiteness stood at odds with the prevailing racial common sense in the Southwest. Mexican Americans faced discrimination there similar to that of African Americans in the Southeast, including lynchings (albeit significantly fewer in number). They also faced discrimination in the white primaries and poll taxes, which aimed at disenfranchising them and reducing their political participation.[16]

There were regional differences in the treatment of Mexican Americans, ranging from harsher proscriptions in Texas to the more tolerant attitudes in California and New Mexico. Indeed, northern New Mexico contained perhaps the largest concentration of native-born Hispanics, who were the most successful in arguing they were of Spanish rather than from Mexican origins.[17] Nevertheless, white opinions and attitudes throughout the Southwest and in the national imaginary constructed Mexican Americans as *other* and *nonwhite*. Mexican American identity in the Southwest, like whiteness itself, was refracted through class, nationality, language, and culture. Primarily the lighter-skinned elite worked to construct American identities premised on whiteness. Among the working class, the majority did not necessarily seek to define themselves as white or to achieve racial adjacency with European Americans. They saw themselves as *Mexicanos*.[18]

Litigating Whiteness

Mexican American leadership took advantage of legal whiteness in early desegregation cases. LULAC provided financial assistance in one of the most significant cases regarding school desegregation: *Mendez v. Westminster* (1946).[19] The first successful challenge to school segregation, this case was filed on behalf of more than five thousand Mexican American students in Orange County, California, where segregation was not legal but was normative.[20] The defendant districts in the *Mendez* case justified separate Mexican schools based on language needs, not race.

The plaintiffs alleged that language segregation was a pretense for racial discrimination against students of Mexican ancestry and illegal because Mexican Americans were legally white, and whites could not segregate "other whites."[21] Consequently, it violated the Fourteenth Amendment's equal protection clause. *Mendez v. Westminster* was never appealed to the U.S. Supreme Court and did not reverse *Plessy v. Ferguson*. Yet it was instrumental in helping establish a judicial precedent for the Supreme Court's *Brown v. Board of Education* decision of 1954, which, spearheaded by the NAACP, ended legal segregation of public schools.[22]

During the same year as *Brown*, LULAC attorneys also argued *Hernandez v. Texas* (1954).[23] This case litigated against the exclusion of Mexican Americans from serving on juries, specifically in Jackson County, Texas, where Pete Hernandez was on trial for a shooting. The first Mexican American civil rights case argued before the U.S. Supreme Court, *Hernandez* presented a conundrum similar to *Mendez*: Mexican Americans were white by law. Attorneys for the state of Texas and judges in the state courts contended that the Fourteenth Amendment referred only to race, not to "nationality." Mexican Americans were tried by juries composed of their racial peers: whites. There was no violation of the Fourteenth Amendment. But the arguments in *Hernandez v. Texas* held that "nationality" groups could, in fact, be protected under the Fourteenth Amendment.[24] The Supreme Court held that Hernandez's constitutional rights under the equal protection clause were violated because of the de facto systematic exclusion of Mexican Americans from the pool of potential jurors.

Mexican Americans and African Americans struggled against legalized racial segregation, but the *Mendez* and *Hernandez* decisions rested on assertions of a white identity. The *Brown* decision rested on claims of a Black identity. African Americans located themselves on the Black side of the binary racial divide, while Mexican Americans placed themselves on the white side. Still, in their different yet historically linked antiracist struggles, Mexican Americans and African Americans reinforced, rather than challenged, the monoracial imperative and hypodescent, which require a person's racial identification as either Black or white.

From White to Brown

In the 1940s and 1950s Mexican Americans attempted to assimilate to whiteness. During the 1960s civil rights era continuing discrimination in employment, education, housing, political representation, public services, and so on, as well as intolerance and erasure in white society, impelled a younger generation to construct new identities as nonwhite.[25] They selected the designation *Chicano*, which was generally understood as a derogatory Spanish name for Mexican Americans of lower socioeconomic standing and was most likely associated with darker-skinned mestizos or Indigenous people.[26] *Chicano* was brandished as a form of reclamation, self-ascription, and self-determination, affirming a heritage as proud as a Brown race.

In 1970 the East LA Thirteen and Biltmore Six criminal cases were among the catalysts for the formation of the Chicano movement as Mexican Americans began to reject whiteness and deny assimilation.[27] This also presented a challenge because Mexican Americans had some success in litigating their whiteness. In the East LA Thirteen case *Castro v. Superior Court* (1970), the grand jury indicted thirteen community leaders for, among other misdemeanors, conspiring to encourage school protesters.[28] The Biltmore Six case, *Montez v. Superior Court* (1970), followed a 1969 California state conference on the needs of Mexican American students that resulted in a hotel fire.[29] The defendants focused on race, arguing that the exclusion of Mexican Americans from grand juries was discriminatory and thus an infringement on the equal protection clause.[30]

During the movement's early phase, the concept of *mestizaje* was evoked through the concept of *la Raza*. This was a reminder that Chicanas/os as mestizas/os are the product of colonization and the encounter between Europeans and Indigenous peoples and that they have a historic claim as the rightful heirs of the Southwest.[31] Yet this new identity politics and resistance would ultimately emphasize Indigeneity, which involved embracing Anglo-American binary and monoracial logics, as well as hypodescent. Also, neither the terms *Chicano* nor *la Raza* contained an awareness or recognition of African ancestry. *La Raza* was derived from the title of the early twentieth-century Mexican intellectual José Vasconcelos's book *La raza cósmica* (*The Cosmic Race*) to reflect the mixture (mestizaje) inherent in Latin American populations.[32] In Mexico national unity and integration through mestizaje would be achieved by "whitening" and by the eventual erasure of Indigenous, Asian, and most important to Vasconcelos and similar Latin American thinkers, African elements.[33] *La Raza* or *mestizaje* meant something different to Chicanas/os: it asserted browning rather than seeking to eliminate it.

Chicanismo, Afro-Mexicans, and the "Third Root"

Still, African ancestry was never considered a component of Chicano "Brown" identity. Some Chicana/o activists initially thought of themselves effectively as Black because they admired African Americans and maintained a close political affiliation and a sense of solidarity with them in the struggle for equality.[34] Yet the Chicano movement continued to deny, or at least lacked awareness of, Mexicans' own African ancestry. In addition, the movement's nationalistic, antiracist, and anticolonial strategy around Indigeneity, which was meant to unify all Mexican Americans as a community, tended to demand uniformity, conformity, and sameness. Consequently, as Tanya Katerí Hernández points out, Afro-Mexicans and Afro-Mexican Americans may have repressed their Blackness in the 1960s to seek refuge in the larger Mexican American community.[35] Yet given the centrality of racial discrimination in informing Chicana/o self-identity as nonwhite, Mexicans of African ancestry would have been drawn to Chicana/o nonwhiteness and Chicano movement demands for social justice.[36]

The experience of Afro-Mexicans in the United States in the 1960s was probably similar to Afro-Mexicans currently living in California. They often express a sense of alienation from Mexicans, who do not view them as authentically Mexican in the United States or even in Mexico. Many white and mestizo Mexican migrants are unaware of Afro-Mexican history and ancestry. Many Afro-Mexicans themselves—especially middle-aged ones—have no knowledge of African ancestry or else deny it.[37] In California, the site of early Afro-Mexican immigration, U.S. racial politics may have also influenced an Afro-Mexican adoption of Chicana/o Brown identity and a de-emphasis of African ancestry.[38] Frequently taken for African American, they must also come to terms with what it means to be Black in the United States, even if they do not identify as such.

Hernández maintains that anti-Black sentiments or ambivalence toward African ancestry among Mexican Americans should not be attributed solely to U.S. influence. Mexico's own history also created and perpetuated anti-Blackness.[39] In Mexico there continues to be a pattern of favoring lighter-skinned marriage partners to have lighter-skinned children, who will "improve the race." Many lighter-skinned mestizos simply identify with European and Indigenous ancestry, purposefully omitting any mention of African ancestry.

Mexican national ideology continues to be predicated on the idea of mestizaje as Indigenous-Spanish mixing.[40] Therefore, Mexico's silence about Afro-Mexicans has been a major contributing factor to the lack of recognition of Blackness among Chicanas/os.[41] Furthermore, the ideology of mestizaje has convinced Mexican citizens that they are "raceless," and that Blackness and Mexicanness are mutually exclusive. Sylvia Zamora argues that a raceless mestizaje, which excludes Blackness, is one piece of "racial baggage" Mexican immigrants bring to the United States. This affects how they view the U.S. racial order and themselves within it.[42]

Beginning in 1992 the concept of the third root (*la tercera raíz*) gained momentum when the Mexican government, as part of its commemoration of the five hundredth anniversary of the encounter between Spain and Mexico, acknowledged the African presence. For the first time, individuals were allowed to self-identify as Afro-Mexicans (or Afro-descendants) on the 2020 national census after a protracted struggle on the part of activists.[43] Aside from historical erasure, collecting these data is complicated in terms of racial composition and identification since the majority of Mexico's Afro-descendants are actually *afromestizos* of African, Indigenous, and Spanish ancestry in a nation that is overwhelmingly of Spanish and Indigenous origins. According to census data, there are 2.5 million individuals who self-identify as being of African descent, which represents 2 percent of the national population.[44] The constitution has also officially recognized Afro-Mexicans as a minority, which makes it possible for the state to provide funds for the promotion of their culture and for public health programs.[45]

Mestiza Consciousness and Anti-Essentializing Race

The Chicano movement's ideology, rhetoric, and identity politics were largely based on what Gayatari Spivak calls "strategic essentialism": a tactic that nationalities and ethnic or minority groups can use to achieve certain goals.[46] While strong differences may exist among members of these groups, Spivak argues it is sometimes advantageous for them to "essentialize" themselves and project a reductionist group identity that tends to focus on one axis of experience, identity, and ultimately, oppression.[47] The Chicano movement's nationalistic, antiracist, and anticolonial strategy around Indigeneity was a form of such essentialism.

Strategic essentialism in the Chicano movement crystallized around race, hypodescent, and the monoracial imperative while ignoring other types of difference, notably gender. Movement men articulated Chicano identity through a patriarchal lens excluding Chicana voices and ideas. As defined by some of the movement's dominant male voices, a Chicana's main function was to support Chicanos and maintain the race through bearing and raising Chicana/o children.[48] In response some Chicana feminists articulated an identity that included aspects of race, class, gender, and sexuality.[49] The "strategic antiessentialism" that underpins this perspective maintains that it is advantageous for members of national, ethnic, or minority groups to accommodate the differences that may exist among members *notwithstanding* overarching similarities. The goal is to project a complex identity to address multiple axes of experience and oppression, as well as their interlocking and ambiguous nature.[50]

Gloria Anzaldúa called for a new mestiza consciousness that rejects static notions of the self and essentialist ideas of what it means to be Chicana/o, including notions of skin color and Spanish proficiency. She sought to escape the confines of colonial discourse by emphasizing critical mestizaje that integrates European, Indigenous, African, and other backgrounds to create a postcolonial consciousness.[51] This perspective critiques the anticolonial consciousness that shaped Chicana/o identity in the 1960s, which often spawned a superficial racial and cultural fundamentalism. While anticolonialism operated under stringent binaries, racial and otherwise, the postcolonial consciousness of the new mestiza/o embraces a hybrid or intermediate space that "contest(s) the terms and territories of both" colonialism and anticolonialism.[52] This new mestiza consciousness helped inform what Chela Sandoval defines as "radical mestizaje."[53] This framework maintains that identities, more generally, involve a complex and hybrid negotiation across myriad lines of difference, including epistemological and spatiotemporal ones.

Gregory Rodriguez points out that amid the heated debates during the apex of the Chicano movement in the 1970s, some male Mexican American intellectuals, such as Herman Gallegos, Julian Samora, Carlos G. Vélez-Ibáñez, Ernesto Galarza, Federico A. Sánchez, Manuel A. Machado Jr., and Roberto R. Bacalski-Martínez also voiced reservations about anticolonial initiatives that narrowly defined Chicanismo by emphasizing Indigeneity, leading to the exclusion not only of the Spanish contribution but also, by implication, the African and Asian ones.[54] James Diego Vigil also sought to counter reductionism through the concept of *Chicanozaje*.[55] This term melded notions of Chicanismo with the longstanding and broader understanding of the word *mestizaje* to expand the boundaries of mestizaje and bring a deeper meaning to the term *Chicano*.

Mexican Americans—a Race or Ethnicity?

Notwithstanding this legacy of mestizaje, Chicana/o and Mexican American identity is socially constructed as monoracial. Beginning in the early 1970s the U.S. racial state began to define people from Spanish-speaking origins not as a race but as a "Hispanic" ethnic group. Mexican Americans are officially considered a subethnic group that falls under the all-encompassing Hispanic category. As an ethnic category, *Hispanic* does not appear as an option on the census race question, and Hispanics do not comfortably fit U.S. racial categories. The collection of census race data that emerged from civil rights legislation requires the racial state to track inequalities and discrimination. Classifying Hispanics as an ethnicity, rather than a race, benefits the state and leaves Hispanics vulnerable to data misinterpretation and manipulation.[56]

Officially, *Hispanic* was sanctioned for governmental use and became a substitute for more specific ethnic designations such as *Mexican* in 1968 when, at the request of New Mexican senator Joseph Montoya, President Lyndon Johnson declared the week beginning September 15 as National Hispanic Week. A Congressional Hispanic Caucus had already been developed in 1960 to consolidate a block of congressional votes on issues important to all Hispanics. In New Mexico, *Hispanic* (or *Hispano*) was widely used, as was *Chicano* in California among Mexican Americans. But unlike the term *Chicano*, *Hispanic* was perceived to have a strong connection and identification with a Spanish component rather than with an Indigenous one. Consequently, many individuals have criticized and rejected the term *Hispanic* as Eurocentric.[57]

As mentioned, from 1940 to 1970 the census racially classified Mexican Americans and others of "Latin descent" as "white" unless they were specifically identified by observation to be Negro, Indian, or "some other race." On the 1980 census this practice was dropped for a separate ethnicity question regarding "Hispanic" origins "of any race" chosen out of a limited number of options.[58] Many Latinas/os do not see themselves as fitting any of these options and increasingly count themselves as some other race with write-in responses like "Mexican," "Hispanic," "Latin American," "Puerto Rican," "Latino," and so on.[59]

In 1980, when the Hispanic origin question was first asked of 100 percent of the population, just over half of all Latinas/os identified as white; 44 percent selected "other." On the 1990 census approximately 46 percent of Hispanics identified as racially white and 51 percent as "other race."[60] This 51 percent constituted almost all (95.7 percent) of the approximately 10 million people who responded as "other race."[61] On the 2000 census, while nearly half (48 percent) of Hispanics reported only white, approximately 42 percent reported some other race.[62] On the 2010 census 53 percent reported white and

37 percent reported some other race. This was almost identical to the reporting of Mexican Americans. Latinas/os were the overwhelming majority (97 percent) of the 15.4 million people who reported some other race.[63]

On the 2020 census there was significant reduction in the numbers of Latinas/os who reported white alone (20.3 percent), whereas the numbers in some other race alone indicated a modest increase to 42.2 percent.[64] The number of Latinas/os in some other race dropped from 97 percent in 2010 to 92 percent in 2020. The 2020 census indicates that the majority (67.3 percent) of Latinas/os still identified with one race alone. Yet 32.7 percent checked two-or-more-races, which is a dramatic increase from 6 percent in 2010. Moreover, these data indicate that the largest number of two-or-more-race people, based on ethnicity, are Latinas/os (60 percent), and this is likely an undercount.[65]

Sonya Tafoya examined microdata from the 2000 census, as well as information from survey and focus groups, and found that Hispanics who check "white" have slightly higher incomes, slightly more years of education, and are possibly less likely to speak Spanish.[66] Choosing "white" on the census, however, does not necessarily reflect a desire to be racially white. Some may view "white" as a default identity, particularly given the other available options.[67] In fact, Julie A. Dowling's research on Mexican American respondents in Texas indicates that Mexican Americans who identified as white generally saw this as a means of projecting an "American" identity.[68] Laura Lewis found that, for first- and second-generation Afro-Mexicans living in the United States, "Hispanic" was the typical response to an open question about "race." She interpreted this also as a quintessentially "American" racial identity category but as a nonwhite one.[69]

Notwithstanding the problematic and implied power dynamics in conflating American identity with whiteness, Dowling argues that her respondents espouse a colorblind ideology that is fundamentally different from that of European Americans, who use such an ideology to justify racial privilege.[70] Nellie Tran and Susan E. Paterson found that, for some, *American* is often a proxy for *white* that justifies or even denies racial privilege and racist beliefs and attitudes to hide discussions of race and racial inequality more generally. For most Mexican Americans in Dowling's study, in contrast, a colorblind ideology was a defensive strategy to cope with discrimination. Accordingly, for people of color, *American* as a proxy for *white* might be a protective mechanism delegitimizing racially discriminatory practices that target them and prevent them from being treated as equals with whites.[71]

In the 2000 census 89 percent of Hispanics who reported they were some other race (97 percent of everyone who did) reported only "Hispanic" as their race. Of the multiple-race responses, the most common were some other race and white (72 percent), some other race and Black (10 percent).[72] In 2010, 44 percent of Hispanics wrote "Mexican American" or "Mexico" in the some other race category.[73] These represented the nearly 32 million people of Mexican background, who constitute nearly 63 percent (or two-thirds) of the Latina/o population.[74]

The 2010 census added new instructions stating that "Hispanic" was not a race. It encouraged use of the ethnicity question to enter "Hispanic" rather than writing in "Hispanic" in some other race in the race question. Many disregarded the new instructions.[75] Clearly the census will eventually have to reckon with the growing number of Latinas/os who do not identify with official racial options. Those who choose Hispanic as an ethnicity and also write in their racial identity as some other race are the fastest growing segment of the Hispanic population and are concentrated in the Southwest.[76] The vast majority are Mexicans or Mexican Americans.[77] Adding a Hispanic category to the census race question would have a significant impact on the number of Latinas/os who would otherwise check white or some other race.[78] It would create a significant new racial category in the United States.

The Equality of Difference

Anglo-Americanization of the Southwest, beginning during the latter half of the nineteenth century, led to a shift from the previous ternary racial order under Spanish and Mexican rule and the implementation of a binary racial order. This imposed monoracializing dictates on Mexicans. (Re)negotiating racial categories, identities, and claims about racial status followed. Paradoxically, monoracialism has served as the primary racializing and subordinating process and as a tool for antiracist and anti–white supremacist counter-organizing. For many Mexican Americans, this initially meant an attachment to whiteness and its privileges. Subsequently, Mexican Americans rejected the allure of whiteness, made mostly available to those who were sufficiently light skinned. Instead, they affirmed an identity based on Brownness.

One could argue that, notwithstanding the absence of African and Asian elements, Chicana/o identity initially deployed mestizaje as an interrogation of hypodescent, the monoracial imperative, and binary racial logics, although it eventually crystallized around Indigeneity premised on each of these tenets. Hybridity has been present in some articulations of mestizaje, particularly among feminists.[79] Still, critical engagement with discourses on mestizaje has neither permeated Chicana/o consciousness nor resulted in an essential challenge to monoracial norms.[80] Mexican nationals and Chicanas/os in the United States can *acknowledge* the significance of different cultural backgrounds, as well as the impact of multiple ancestries on physical appearances. Still, they do not necessarily *identify* as multiracial. Indeed, they articulate their racial position as singular, in line with the U.S. binary and monoracial paradigm. Their identities are neither fundamentally posited or constructed on hybridity nor located in the U.S. racial order as multiracial.

African American identity has gone through a parallel process of monoracialization. For several hundred years African American identity has been refracted through the monoracial imperative and hypodescent of the Anglo-American binary racial order. Mexican American identity was informed by the Spanish American ternary racial order and did not intersect with monoraciality and hypodescent until the Anglo-Americanization of the Southwest in the nineteenth century.[81] During the first half of the twentieth century, Mexican American organizations such as LULAC mobilized around a white identity as they launched challenges to Jim Crow segregation. During the same period, African American organizations such as the NAACP mobilized around African American identity, seeking to resist these same restrictions. In their different tactics both had a primary goal of pursuing civil rights as a means of integrating into the racial order as equals.

In the 1960s Mexican American and African American radicals criticized the inegalitarian, that is, assimilationist, outcomes of integration given the unequal power dynamics in the racial order. They shifted from the primary goal of integration to advocate for egalitarian pluralism in the form of Chicano nationalism and Black nationalism based, respectively, on Brown pride and power and Black pride and power. They envisioned African Americans and Mexican Americans as self-determining plural societies and cultures distinct and separate from, but also on equal footing with, European Americans.

Notwithstanding a few exceptions, neither African Americans nor Mexican Americans have conceptualized a multiracial identity within the U.S. binary racial context that can contest its mutually exclusive racial boundaries while challenging the hierarchical valuation of racialized difference. Yet their embrace of monoraciality and hypodescent requires consideration of the historical and contemporary racial orders: put succinctly, by drawing boundaries that excluded them, hypodescent legitimated and forged monoracial Mexican American and African American identities as part of normative U.S. binary racial common sense. Many individuals simply display an unquestioning acceptance of these identities, thus naturalizing, if only unintentionally, racial designations as singular and mutually exclusive as well as objective categories of experience. Others take a more political stance. Support for hypodescent, monoraciality, and binary racial logics is based on the belief that they are necessary for maintaining solidarity and community in the struggle against white racism, oppression, and privilege. Chicana/o and Black identities involve a rearticulation or repetition, rather than reproduction, of hypodescent. They support racial difference based on equality rather than hierarchy.

| Chapter Seven

Multiracial Identities
The Law of the Included Middle

Since the late 1980s discussions on U.S. race relations have increasingly included references to multiracial identities, which are paradoxically an unintended consequence of the one-drop rule. This solidified African Americans' status as a subaltern group, which legitimated and forged Black identity. This identity, in turn, formed the basis for the civil rights movement of the 1950s and 1960s, resulting in the dismantling of Jim Crow segregation and the implementation of civil rights legislation. Ultimately, this legislation led to the 1967 *Loving v. Virginia* decision, which overturned remaining antimiscegenation statutes.[1]

There were several judicial antecedents, if not precedents, to *Loving v. Virginia*.[2] These included *Perez v. Sharp* (1948), which made California the first state to overturn an antimiscegenation statute.[3] The case is particularly important in terms of African American–Mexican American intermarriage. In 1947 the plaintiffs, Andrea Perez (a Mexican American) and Sylvester Davis (an African American) applied for a marriage license with the county clerk of Los Angeles. Under California law individuals of Mexican ancestry were classified as white, and on the application Perez identified her race as "white" and Davis's as "Negro."[4]

The county clerk refused to issue the license based on California Civil Code, Section 60 ("All marriages of white persons with

Negroes, Mongolians, members of the Malay race, or mulattoes are illegal and void") and Section 69 ("No license may be issued authorizing the marriage of a white person with a Negro, mulatto, Mongolian or member of the Malay race").[5] Perez and Davis took their case to the California Supreme Court. In a 4–3 decision, the court ruled that restricting the fundamental right to marry based on race alone violated the constitutional requirements of due process and the Equal Protection Clause of the Fourteenth Amendment. The California legislature did not actually expunge the invalid statutes from the California Civil Code until ten years later.[6]

The Growth of Interracial Marriage

Perez predated *Loving* and the landmark 1954 *Brown v. Board of Education* decision desegregating public schools, from which *Loving* benefited. Indeed, in *Loving* Chief Justice Earl Warren, who presided over *Brown*, cited *Perez* in footnote 5.[7] After the court ruling, Perez and Davis vanished from public sight. They did not consider themselves community leaders or civil rights activists but ordinary people. The 1967 decision in *Loving v. Virginia* is generally considered the key turning point in legalized interracial marriage. Prior to *Loving*, the racial state regarded interracial intimacy as a private rather than a public matter.

Such intimacy became central to the debate on the relationship of private matters to the public sphere as it highlighted the contradictions between the state's espousal of freedom and the realities of Jim Crown segregation. Many civil rights activists wanted interracial intimacy to be a public matter as part of the promotion of equal rights and social justice in the legal system of a nation that declared itself the "arsenal of democracy." They endeavored to achieve this primarily through popular culture and litigation. But miscegenation was a volatile issue, and civil rights organizations tactically decided to remain silent and instead worked to dismantle laws segregating the public sphere.[8]

Consequently, *Loving*, much like *Perez*, did not derive from the civil rights movement itself, although the changing climate it engendered paved the way. Rather, it originated in a lawsuit filed by an interracial couple, Richard Perry Loving (white) and Mildred Delores Jeter (Black).[9] Both of their families lived in Caroline County, Virginia, which adhered to strict Jim Crow segregation laws, although the racial lines in their small hometown of Central Point were considerably more fluid and had been characterized by extensive commingling since the nineteenth century.

The Lovings married in Washington DC to evade Virginia's 1924 Racial Integrity Act, which criminalized marriage between whites and nonwhites.[10] A few weeks after they returned to Central Point, local police raided their home and told them their marriage certificate was invalid in Virginia. Supported by two volunteer attorneys from the American Civil Liberties Union (ACLU), the Lovings brought a class-action suit in the district court for the Eastern District of Virginia in 1958. The court upheld the constitutionality of the state's antimiscegenation statute; so the Lovings took their case to the U.S. Supreme Court. On June 12, 1967, it issued a unanimous 9–0 decision overturning their criminal convictions. The court ruled that the freedom to marry was a fundamental right per the Equal Protection Clause of the Fourteenth Amendment, which could not be deprived solely on an arbitrary basis such as race. The court's opinion, written by Chief Justice Warren, struck down all the remaining antimiscegenation statutes, including Virginia's.[11]

The legalization of interracial marriage, the dismantling of Jim Crow segregation, and the implementation of civil rights legislation dissolved the formal mechanisms maintaining inequality in both the public and private spheres. This process began with *Brown v. Board of Education* (1954), which desegregated public schools. It also included the Civil Rights Act (1964), which prohibited discrimination based on race, color, religion, sex, or national origin. Provisions of this act forbade discrimination based on sex and race in hiring, promoting, and firing. The act banned discrimination in public accommodations and federally funded programs. It also strengthened the enforcement of voting rights and the desegregation of schools.[12] The Voting Rights Act (1965) and the Fair Housing Act (1968), respectively, gained federal oversight and enforcement of voter registration and electoral practices in states or areas with a history of discriminatory practices and ended discrimination in renting or buying housing.[13] Finally, these initiatives included the removal of legal restrictions on immigration through the Immigration and Nationality Act (1965).[14]

The more fluid social relations engendered by these changes helped catalyze the subsequent growth in interracial marriages. However, the statistical significance of *Loving* is limited: antimiscegenation laws primarily targeted Black white interracial marriages, historically the strongest taboo.[15] Moreover, *Loving* did not result in a significant growth in the number of Black white marriages, which are still a relatively small percentage of the nation's interracial marriages. Some observers maintain that increased immigration from Asia and Latin America following the Immigration and Nationality Act of 1965 had a more immediate and significant impact than did *Loving*, due to the higher percentage of outmarriages among these populations.[16] Missionary history, commerce, militarization, and U.S. wars in Asia and the Pacific also played significant roles in the development of interracial intimacy among these demographics.

An examination of Black white interracial marriage trends supports the argument positing the limited statistical impact of *Loving*. Census data indicate that there were 51,000 such marriages out of the nation's 157,000 interracial marriages in 1960. In 1970 there were 65,000 out of a national total of 321,000. By 1980 the number of interracial couples approached 1 million, 3.2 percent of married adults, including 599,000 unions between whites and other races and some 167,000 Black and white unions. The number of interracial couples continued to increase steadily until, by 1990, there were 1.5 million, of which 883,000 were white and other race unions (largely whites and Latina/o) and 246,000 Black and white ones.[17]

By 2010 interracial marriages reached a record 9.5 percent. Whites continued to be the least likely to marry interracially (about 4.7 percent).[18] However, most interracial marriages involve a white and a person of color, given the white demographic majority.[19] In 2010 demographer William Frey found that 13 percent of interracial marriages involved Blacks: 9 percent were Black and white unions, while approximately 1 percent were Black and Asian, and 3 percent were Black and Latina/o.[20] Interracial marriages involving African Americans remained lower compared to interracial marriages involving Asian Americans and Latinos, which was roughly 30 percent for both groups. Latinos were involved in 17.4 percent of all intermarriages while Asian Americans were involved in approximately 16 percent.[21]

By 2017 intermarriages totaled 10 percent of all marriages, although these unions were still few.[22] The overwhelming majority of Americans (90.5 percent) still marry someone of the same racial group. Furthermore, while multiracials of white and Native American or white and Asian American ancestry, for example, overwhelmingly tended to marry whites, this was not true of multiracials of white and Black ancestry. This further complicates notions that decreased barriers to interracial relationships can be generalized across populations of color and further highlights the continued social distance between whites and Blacks and the continued significance of hypodescent for people with Black ancestry.[23]

The Loving Generation

If *Loving* is often thought to be overemphasized by many scholars, activists, and the popular media as a watershed, its significance should still not be diminished. Its power is its positive affectivity or emotional resonance as a landmark in the development of a sense of community, evident, for example, in the annual Lovingday.org celebrations across the United States on June 12. Indeed, all collective subjectivities have a creation mythology, which serves as a framework for the self-identity of its members and which they can present to themselves and the larger world.[24] Moreover, *Loving* led not only to increased interracial marriages but also to the subsequent growth in the population of multiracial offspring. Many interracial couples, in turn, began socializing their offspring to identify multiracially. This population of first-generation multiracials (or biracials), which is sometimes described as the "Loving Generation," compose what Maria P. P. Root has referred to as the "biracial baby boom."[25]

It was not until the late 1970s that individuals who maintained interracial relationships and those who identified as multiracial collectively mobilized resistance to hypodescent and traditional monoracial categories and boundaries.[26] Similar to the Black, Brown, Red, and Yellow Power movements in the late 1960s and early 1970s, which sought to rescue racial identities from their distortion and erasure by the dominant society, those of multiracial identities endeavored to counter the invalidation and constraints originating in hypodescent as well as the monoracial imperative.[27] By the 1990s the multiracial movement had organized educational initiatives addressing the marginalization and pathologization of interracial families and multiracial people. Some of the celebratory, and at times overenthusiastic, images seeking to address and remedy these attitudes have understandably been criticized for espousing a naive egalitarianism reinforcing and perpetuating the notion that interracial marriages would lead to a more tolerant society.[28]

Images of multiracials as "happy hybrids," "racial ambassadors," or "post-racial messiahs" assumed these people were imbued with special temperamental qualities making them ideally suited to solve racism and racial inequality.[29] Ultimately, multiracials would serve as vehicles for a universal humanism leading to a raceless society.[30] This line of reasoning was an important step toward recognizing institutional and everyday forms of discrimination and marginalization originating in hypodescent and monoracial imperatives directed at interracial relationships, multiracials, and mixed-race concerns. Although generally well-intentioned, this idea also risked masking the continuing social pathologies of white racism and its outcomes.

One of the movement's key initiatives was to bring about changes in standards of racial and ethnic data collection, particularly the U.S. Census requirement that individuals identify with only one racial background.[31] The census and other official instruments of data collection are not neutral documents that report only "facts." They are instruments of state and elite control, reflecting the social construction of race via classification, quantification, and identification. By focusing on the census, activists made a direct appeal to the racial state. They were unsuccessful in changing the 1990 census, but their efforts intensified. They founded a national umbrella organization, the Association of MultiEthnic Americans (AMEA), in 1988 and Project RACE (Reclassify All Children Equally) in 1991. Such organizations were instrumental in prompting federal officials to convene the Congressional Hearings on Racial Census Categories (1993–97) to discuss potential changes on the 2000 census.[32]

While the movement lobbied for legislation—particularly at the state level—its campaigns largely consisted of letter writing, phone calls, public appearances in the media, and testimony at hearings.[33] Its relatively "quiet" nature and comparatively small number of participants stood in stark contrast to the public displays of mass mobilization in boycotts, demonstrations, and sit-ins associated with the midcentury civil rights and radical nationalist movements. Indeed, the multiracial movement at its height during the late 1990s had no more than a few thousand active participants, mainly residing on the coasts.[34] But the 2000 census succeeded in making it possible for individuals to express multiracial identities institutionally for the first time by checking more than one box for the census race question.

On the 2000 census, multiracials (or the "Two-or-More-Races" population) totaled 7 million, or 2.4 percent of the population. Based on 2010 census data, their numbers increased to 9 million people, or 2.9 percent of the population. Although multiracials still made up only a fraction of the total population, these numbers reflect a growth rate of about 32 percent since 2000. The two-or-more-races population has grown considerably since 2010. The 2020 census data indicates it is now 33.8 million people, a 276 percent increase. Multiracials are still comparatively small in numbers, composing only 10.2 percent of the total population. Yet the multiracial movement brought about measurable changes in U.S. racial formation.[35]

Data from the 2000, 2010, and 2020 censuses show that the majority of multiracials are "majority-minority," meaning of combined white and nonwhite backgrounds.[36] According to the 2010 data, three of the largest populations of majority-minority multiracials are white and Black (1.8 million), white and some other race (1.7 million), and white–Asian American (1.6 million).[37] The 2020 data indicate that three of the largest populations of majority-minority multiracials are white and some other race (19.3 million), white and American Indian or Alaska Native (4 million), white and Black (3.1 million), white and Asian (2.7 million), and Black and some other race (1 million).[38]

In 2010, among Hispanics classified as some other race in combination with one or more additional races, the most common multiple-race group was some other race and white (72 percent), followed by some other race and Black (10 percent).[39] Given that Hispanics constitute the largest percentage of the some other race category, white and Hispanic individuals compose the second largest multiracial population. The 2010 data indicate that 44.3 percent of Hispanics wrote in "Mexican," "Mexican American," "Mexico," or the equivalent in some other race.[40] Mexican white individuals therefore constitute the largest population of Hispanic white multiracials. Data from the 2010 census show that some other race and Black individuals totaled 314,571. In 2020 Black some other race individuals totaled 1 million.[41] Again, given that Hispanics constitute the largest percentage of the some other race category, these individuals are also largely Hispanic Black. Black Mexican individuals constitute the majority, although they are considerably fewer than white Mexican ones.

From "Either/Or" to "Both/Neither"

Post-*Loving* multiracial identities are expressed by "first-generation" offspring of interracial marriages and by "multigenerational" individuals who have two biracial-identified parents or one is biracial-identified parent and one monoracial-identified parent. This identity is also displayed by individuals who have parents, or even generations of ancestors, who have been socially designated as monoracial despite having multiple racial backgrounds.[42] Data indicate multiracial identities are influenced, but not necessarily determined, by individuals' phenotypical traits, family, peers, and society.[43] These data also indicate multiracial-identifying individuals have multiple and shifting points of reference rather than fixed or predictable parameters. This may change over an individual's lifetime, with different affinities or resonances with specific components and groups of their backgrounds depending on the circumstances.[44]

Various Shades of Gray

Individuals who identify as multiracial do not, however, privilege the intrinsic value or worth of any specific background. Instead, they display a turn away from the either/or hierarchical framework perpetuated by the monoracial paradigm and a shift toward a both/neither framework based on the "law of the included middle." This paradigm deconstructs the hierarchical ranking of differences and their dichotomization by acknowledging shades of gray.

Multiracial identities can be broken down into two basic configurations on this continuum of grays. Individuals embracing an integrative (or "both/and") multiracial identity variously reference themselves vis-à-vis the communities that compose their monoracial backgrounds. They are comfortable in social settings involving those and other monoracial groups and can "shuttle" between them. Some individuals may have a stronger orientation toward some backgrounds more than others depending on circumstances. Individuals exhibiting a pluralistic (both/neither) identity locate themselves primarily in-between or intermediate to the monoracial groups composing their backgrounds and other monoracial groups. They may at times have a stronger orientation toward some backgrounds than others but primarily resonate with other multiracials as part of an emerging collective subjectivity.[45]

Notwithstanding the varied and complex permutations of these two configurations, some individuals experience race in a more immediate sense in everyday encounters. Others view their racial identity as merely one of many factors they share with various groups of people. Their primary sense of self is grounded in a more inclusive, universal, or human self. The "metaracial" (beyond race) identity derived thus seeks to transcend questions of racial, cultural, or any other specificity without denying their value and significance. These multiracial identity formations should not, however, be viewed as mutually exclusive. Individuals may hold complex views drawing from these configurations simultaneously or sequentially over their life course.[46]

The Quest for White Adjacency

Multiracials have often been conflated with anti-Blackness and the desire to evade racial stigma and achieve social advantages in the racial hierarchy.[47] There have been comparisons to previous responses seeking white adjacency (e.g., passing, blue-vein societies, Louisiana Creoles, triracial isolates). The phenomenon of "passing" has typically occurred when individuals of a more European American phenotype and cultural orientation have made a covert break with the African American community. Though commonly viewed as a form of opportunism, passing can be viewed as a tactic that seeks to beat white supremacy and racism at its own game.[48] Passing exposes the political motivations behind racial categories and seeks to turn oppression on its head by subverting the arbitrary line between white and Black.[49]

Individuals unwilling or unable to pass often distanced themselves from the Black masses by forming elite groups known as *blue-vein societies*. These exclusive groups shaped and perpetuated a pernicious colorism among African-descent Americans by giving preferential treatment to individuals who more closely resembled European Americans in terms of consciousness, behavior, and phenotype. Meanwhile, after the U.S. annexation of Louisiana and the Gulf region in the early nineteenth century and the subsequent implementation of the one-drop rule, many mixed-race Creoles of color fought to maintain their racially intermediate status and privileges under Franco-Hispanic rule. Others responded by passing for white.

Still others joined Blacks in challenging the onslaught of segregationist policies in the Jim Crow era. Indeed, in the 1960s younger Creoles felt the heightened pride and consciousness that affected all individuals of African descent. Many realized, like others before them, that it was advantageous to join forces, at least politically, with Blacks in the fight for civil rights if gains for Creoles were to be made as well. Many Creoles have, in the decades since the 1960s, sought to affirm identities in a manner that embraces their multiraciality but eschews the previous anti-Blackness and desire for white adjacency. Nevertheless, they primarily identify as Creole and only secondarily, if at all, as multiracial.[50]

In the nineteenth century multiracials formed separate communities, either on the fringes of villages and towns or in isolated rural enclaves (commonly referred to as "triracial isolates" by social scientists), if not the communities themselves. These communities have been scattered throughout the eastern United States, particularly in the Southeast. They are known to have European, Native American, and African ancestry; historically they have affirmed only their Native American and European American ancestries, and some, such as the Lumbee of North Carolina, have fought for federal recognition as Native Americans, a status that has been recently recognized in the U.S. House of Representatives, with Senate approval pending.[51]

Other groups, including the Melungeons, have begun to affirm their African, along with their Native American and European, ancestry. Since the mid-twentieth century, many individuals from these communities have migrated to the cities. This trend, along with increased intermarriage (generally with European Americans), has led to the extinction of many communities and the loss of collective identity. Still, they again primarily identify as Melungeons and only secondarily, if at all, as multiracial, notwithstanding these changes.[52]

Admittedly, these previous identities were forged under regimes of egregious and legalized white racism and supremacy that culminated in Jim Crow segregation. They were generated by white racist and supremacist pressure that rewarded whiteness and punished Blackness through policies and practices preventing Blacks from having contact as equals with whites. They have been less a reaction to the forced denial of European American ancestry than to the denial of the privileges that have accrued to such ancestry.

Still, at a fundamental level, multiracial identities, historically and currently, are simply reflective of individuals who embrace more than one racial background. Consequently, they are inherently "critical" of the monoracial imperative, as well as of hypodescent. Yet earlier formations were largely grounded in hyperdescent privileging white ancestry and seeking white adjacency. In contrast, post–civil rights multiracial identities do not privilege any ancestry. Indeed, they resist the pursuit of white adjacency. Previous identities interrogated racial categories and perhaps subverted the racial hierarchy between whiteness and Blackness that buttressed those categories. Yet they were not aimed at dismantling the hierarchy. Rather, they were complicit in maintaining and taking advantage of that hierarchy supporting white racism and supremacy.

There is no substantive data to support the notion that post–civil rights multiracial identities are based on the aforementioned premises. Contemporary multiracial identity formations, unlike previous ones, are critical of and contest the mutually exclusive nature of racial boundaries *and* challenge the hierarchical valuation of racial differences that still serve as the basis of social structures that perpetuate social inequality and forms of exclusion. Multiracial identities, like all racial identities, thus continue to function under the constrictions of racist structures of the U.S. racial order.

Multiraciality makes the performance of racial identities more complex and complicated but is not inherently immune to the lingering effects of previous and persistent, though often insidious, toxins in the larger racial ecology. In the post–civil rights era, these social structures, among other things, provide greater opportunities for social mobility through selective inclusion of individuals of color who more closely approximate European Americans in terms of physical appearance as well as in terms of assumed behavioral and attitudinal characteristics.[53] Individuals of color may internalize those biases in terms of their own self-esteem, self-worth, and self-competence.[54] Consequently, some individuals may identify as multiracial out of a desire to evade racial stigma and display anti-Blackness and seek white adjacency because, like all racial identities, multiracial ones continue to function under racist social structures.

This selective inclusion could become all the more important to whites given the increasing decline in the numbers of European Americans in the U.S. population and the concomitant growth in the numbers of people of color. It would serve to create an alliance with new "insiders" to counter their demographic deficit. These social dynamics also indicate a shift from maintaining racial rule primarily through white domination and exclusion—although the latter is not absent—to the increasing juxtaposition with white hegemony, that is, selective inclusion. This fosters the illusion of power sharing while also allowing European Americans to maintain structural control.[55]

Data indicate multiracials are not unaware of these biases. While they are not immune to the larger U.S. racial ecology and are not inherently the solution to racism and racial inequality, they also do not seek to further the larger racial ecology. Aside from embracing multiracial identities, many seek to find other ways of resisting pressures to conform to the existing racial order's inequitable power relations. These can range from informal criticism of everyday manifestations of racist power dynamics to formal engagement in antiracist work, which centers multiracials' role in the struggle for racial justice.[56]

Chapter Eight

"Dual Minority" Multiracial Identities
Decentering Whiteness

Given the dominant white and nonwhite, and particularly the white and Black, binary paradigms, it follows that research on multiraciality has historically focused heavily on Black white multiracials and to a lesser extent on Asian white and Mexican white ones. Less attention has centered on dual minority multiracials with two backgrounds of color.[1] Multiracials do have similar experiences and psychological processes regarding racial identifications. Yet multiraciality is not generalizable. Each combination is a product of specific historical influences, racial hierarchies, and relations in terms of wealth, power, privilege, and prestige. Moreover, their varying histories are also embodied.[2] Consequently, there is a need for more complex theoretical conceptualizations of multiracial identities and experiences.

Dual minority multiracial backgrounds are composed of two subaltern groups with nothing comparable to the wealth, power, privilege, and prestige of whites. Accordingly, their experiences may differ considerably from that of majority-minority multiracials. If their backgrounds are composed of two racial minority groups that have historically been oppositional, identification with one of these groups may present difficulty with acceptance in the other. Embracing a dual-minority multiracial identity that incorporates both groups is not without obstacles and challenges.

Having parents from different minoritized groups means something qualitatively different than having one white parent.[3] This is attributable in part to the fact that whites' identification with their specific European ethnocultural backgrounds is usually tenuous or nonexistent.[4] Of course, this varies depending on the European background and region involved. It is largely due to historical processes of assimilation wherein there has been an exchange of ethnocultural difference for the benefits of ethnoracial white privilege.[5] Whites are not forced to identify with their European backgrounds because they are white first. But many choose to do so.

By virtue of the unstated pervasiveness and dominant status of whiteness, some multiracials with one white parent do not necessarily seek out and learn about that parent's European ethnocultural backgrounds.[6] Privilege also means that whites do not have to confront how race shapes life experiences. Barbara Flagg argues there "is a profound cognitive dimension to the material and social privilege that attaches to whiteness in this society, in that the white person has an everyday option not to think in racial terms at all."[7] Indeed, Flagg contends that the very definition of being "white is not to think about it."[8] Flagg employs the term "transparency phenomenon" to describe the extent to which whites do not think of themselves in racial terms.[9] Importantly, Flagg does not argue that whites do not see race and are unaware of their own racial identities and those of others.[10] Rather, she argues that because whiteness is the racial default, whites can easily and comfortably "relegate [their] own racial specificity to the realm of the subconscious."[11] Still, white parents and important others do teach their children "how to be white" and how to meet expectations incumbent upon that racial category. But this is shaped by how white racial identity often functions in a "hidden" or "transparent" manner.[12] Consequently, this socialization typically takes place in an unintentional and invisible, albeit ubiquitous manner.[13]

Dual-Minority Experiences

The protection provided by whiteness does not extend to dual-minority multiracials.[14] Consequently, analyses of them are understandably celebrated as a long-overdue shift to discussing cases in which whiteness is absent or decentered, at least in terms of personal identity.[15] While the parents of first-generation dual-minority multiracials such as Blaxicans typically have some European ancestry, whiteness is, for the most part, not a salient component of their identity due largely to the monoracial imperative and the multigenerational nature of that European ancestry. Whiteness is absent or decentered in the identity formation of dual-minority multiracials, notwithstanding some European ancestry.[16]

Moreover, dual-minority identities, like all multiracial identities, are also influenced by the monoracial imperative and Black white binary. They are also affected by white racist and supremacist conceptions of race wherein white and Black are viewed, respectively, as the "superior" and "inferior" poles of the racial hierarchy. Research suggests that Black multiracials, whether from majority-minority or dual-minority backgrounds, are further marginalized due to their African ancestry, even among multiracial peers.[17]

To help elucidate Blaxican experiences and identities, a brief overview of dual-minority multiracials highlights and situates differences in experiences and identities within a broader trajectory of multiraciality. We have selected four groups as emblematic of dual-minority experiences and identities based, in part, on their prevalence, the literature examining them, and their usefulness in contextualizing Blaxican experiences and identities, which will be discussed in part 2.

Mexican Asians

In the Imperial Valley of California, Mexicans and Punjabis forged alliances through agricultural labor, immigration policies, citizenship, and shared limited access to resources, leading to many intermarriages and multiracial children. Karen Isaken Leonard found that identity choices among these children varied across generations. Dominant white society's attitudes toward either group also influenced social relations. Indeed, non-Black dual-minority racial formations are affected by white supremacist notions of racial identity, much like the one-drop rule for dual minorities with African ancestry, though it is experienced differently.[18] Rules of hypodescent were less restrictive for Mexican Punjabis, yet they tended to distance themselves from the perceived lower-status group (Mexican or Punjabi), depending on dominant European American attitudes toward either group at the time.[19]

Rudy P. Guevarra Jr. examines the formation of racial and cultural identity among the children of Mexicans and Filipino Americans (*Mexipinos*) in San Diego, California. Immigration, wage labor experiences, formation of community, a shared Spanish colonial past, and segregation provided them with opportunities to forge alliances and romantic relationships that would eventually culminate in the Mexipino experience.[20] Three recurring themes emerged from Guevarra's findings. First, his interviewees expressed a "best of both worlds" sentiment and a positive attachment to both backgrounds. Second, Mexipinos experienced an "ambiguous identity" where physical traits were blurred by their multiplicity. Finally, Mexipinos are often able to intentionally and unintentionally pass and blend into cultures and racial groups that are not necessarily composite parts of their background, which Guevarra calls "multiple passing."[21]

Punjabi Mexicans and Mexipinos live in shared communities in California due to white racist antimiscegenation laws, exploitative employment experiences, and cultural commonalities. Mexipinos seem to experience the least racial conflict and the most cohesiveness because Mexican and Filipina/o cultures share colonial and Catholic heritage. Punjabis and Mexicans, on the other hand, differed in their cultural backgrounds, which has been a primary source of conflict and lack of cohesiveness.

White attitudes toward Mexicans and Punjabis shaped how Punjabi Mexican multiracials chose to self-identify and express themselves racially and culturally. In the Imperial Valley Punjabi Mexicans most often identified as Hindu. The external political context changed as they were presented with new labels and new choices.[22] Mexicans and Asians constitute part of the racial middle as they have historically been located somewhere between white and Black—and are thus also socially located somewhere between white and Black—particularly in California.[23] A dual-minority multiracial identity conveys a different experience, meaning, and social location when it includes a Black parent.

Black Asians

Most studies of dual-minority multiracials explore Black Asian Americans. James W. Loewen's field explorations of whites, Blacks, and Chinese in the Mississippi Delta is a seminal contribution to this topic. The Chinese were recruited to replace African Americans as agricultural labor in Mississippi, working with cotton after the Civil War and the abolition of slavery. The first wave came to the Delta soon after the Civil War. The pace increased by the early 1900s.[24] The Chinese quickly realized that working on a plantation did not further economic mobility. They began opening grocery stores, where they functioned as "middlemen" between Blacks and whites, serving mostly the African American communities where they resided. During the establishment of Jim Crow, the Delta's binary racial hierarchy necessitated they be classified as either Black or white. They initially experienced considerable social distance from whites through their exclusion from organizations, country clubs, fraternal groups, recreational activities, and white public schools. Several Delta cities maintained not only separate schools for Blacks and whites but also for the Chinese.

Since the white upper class controlled the conditions that affected racial minorities, Loewen noted that "any study of the Chinese minority must become at the same time an analysis of the actions and ideology of the white upper class."[25] He found that both race and social class were strong determinants of racial relations and formations in the Delta. Although the Mississippi Chinese had no African ancestry, southern whites originally defined them as closer to Blackness than to whiteness due to the similarity of their social position to that of African Americans and the fact that they were not of European descent. Yet despite their location within the African American community, the Chinese resisted these legal and customary efforts to conflate their status with that of Blacks, and neither whites nor Blacks quite thought of them as Blacks.

By the 1940s the Mississippi Chinese succeeded in moving their racial positioning closer to whiteness. While they did not enjoy full equality with whites, they were accorded white status, affirmed, for example, by the W on their driver's licenses. This transformation resulted from elevating their socioeconomic status and changing their social relations with African Americans. The exceptions were Chinese men who had married Black spouses or had common-law Black spouses. These Black-Chinese marriages were common due to the fact that U.S. immigration laws made it difficult for Chinese women to immigrate and to establish solely Chinese American families. As part of the process of their social elevation, the Chinese community disowned Chinese-Black interracial couples and biracial offspring as soon as entrance into white society became their overriding concern. Some Blacks also ostracized Black women who may have thought they were marrying "up" with Chinese men. Chinese Black families were never fully participating members of either group.[26]

Notwithstanding the significance of studies on Mississippi's Black Chinese, most work on Black Asian research has been on Black Japanese. This includes artistic works by playwright, poet, and scholar Velina Hasu Houston. One of the earliest analyses of dual-minority multiracials was Christine C. I. Hall's research on thirty Black Japanese.[27] She identifies several factors that influenced their identity choices, including the frequency of contact with Black or Japanese neighbors and friends and cultural knowledge. Hall found that most identified as Black or as both Black and Japanese. Only one respondent identified solely as Japanese, and one refused to racially self-identify.

Similarly, Michael C. Thornton interviewed Black Japanese individuals and their parents whose unions were formed through the U.S. military presence in Japan. Thornton found that 51 percent of his respondents identified as Black, 37 percent as biracial, and 12 percent as Japanese. These identities also shifted and were in flux—what Thornton calls "multiethnic." While over half of the respondents identified as Black, they expressed low affinity with Blacks as a group, which points to the continuing power of the one-drop rule.[28]

Mukoyama's survey of thirty-two Black Japanese found that

respondents had parental support and encouragement to explore both racial and ethnic backgrounds, perhaps due to the expectation that dual minorities need to be aware and knowledgeable of both cultures.[29] Mitzi Uehara Carter, a Black Japanese woman, described herself as "Blakanese—a mixture of the two in ways that cannot be divided. My blood and mentality are not split down the middle where half is Black and the other half Japanese, I have taken aspects of both worlds to create my own worldview and identity."[30]

Several studies examine individuals with Vietnamese Black backgrounds. Most of the Vietnamese are immigrants or refugees from Vietnam and the offspring of U.S. soldiers of many different racial backgrounds.[31] Yet they were primarily from working-class backgrounds.[32] Vietnamese multiracials with European, rather than African, features are treated more favorably and are more socially accepted in the Vietnamese community. Vietnamese prejudice toward Blacks is compounded by color prejudice in Vietnam, where dark skin is associated with peasantry and light skin with the wealthy. Such animosity might stem from the French colonial period, when negative ideas about North African soldiers in the French army were ingrained and subsequently combined with negative U.S. stereotypes.[33]

Further work by Maketa Randolph, Janet Stickmon, and Teresa Hodges provides understandings on the experiences of individuals of Black Korean and Black Filipina/o descent.[34] Each scholar challenges notions of racial inauthenticity as well as negative notions of Blackness. Indeed, Root notes that Black Asian multiracials are "often challenged as to whether they are authentically black or black enough."[35] For example, Randolph notes, "For most Black people at Cornell, I am too light. But with Asian people, I am too dark. So, I don't get acknowledged on either side."[36] Stickmon characterized her identity and experience as "the third movement, the blend": "I am 'Blackapina.' Black. Filipino-American. Woman. I am an African American unafraid of identifying as Black because it hearkens back to the Black Power Movement when Black, the color, and the culture, were embraced with pride. I am a second-generation Filipina American, holding my mother's immigrant dreams and sacrifices; as my *utang na loob*, I offer Momma and Daddy the fruits of my work as professor of Filipina(o)-American Heritage and Africana Studies."[37]

Myra S. Washington's *Blasian Invasion* is the most detailed recent study of Black Asians or *Blasians*, a term that first appeared in 2001 in Korean adoptee Zak Heaton's description of his racial identity.[38] Washington addresses individuals ranging from lesser-known video models to highly recognizable stars like Tiger Woods, Kimora Lee Simmons, Hines Ward, and Dwayne "The Rock" Johnson, centering how Blasian identities are mediated by gender and the power of celebrity and play out differently for women. Simmons, for instance, uses her image (and at times her daughters') through her fashion companies, reality shows, and skin-care products to successfully brand her Blasian identity, including its materiality. Depending on the context, that identity is flexible and cognizant of the different ways women of color are perceived.[39]

Washington's discussion of Tiger Woods examines the impact of masculinity in his racial positionings at different moments in his career. Initially defined as a Black athlete who escaped the dangerous characterization of Black masculinity by participating in the "intellectual" sport of golf, Woods's 2009 marital scandal made him dangerous, hyperaggressive, and hypersexualized, the same tropes and stereotypes of earlier Black athletes. Woods's supposedly "true" character was therefore revealed by his infidelity. Washington also finds that "feminizing" discursive strategies were deployed against Woods to target his Asianness. Woods and his team of public relations individuals, managers, and agents used his Blasian identity to navigate public reaction. Woods publicly apologized by emphasizing his continuing rehabilitation for sex addiction, which countered his hypersexualized Black male image. He also invoked Buddhism as a reminder of his Asianness and moral values, which returned to his feminized and nonthreatening Asian masculinity.[40]

Washington illustrates how Blasian identity problematizes the one-drop rule. Blasians are conscientious objectors, so to speak, to the racial comportment line based on that rule. Their identities not only center Black and Asian racial identities but also interrogate the boundaries of both. Borrowing from transgender theory, Washington argues that Blasian identities "transect" race: they do not merely shuttle back and forth between racial Black and Asian but are a transracial synthesis of both.[41] Blasians therefore "shift discussions of multiracialness from being a threat to Whiteness, or being anti-Black, and/or functioning as a racial salve, to strategically using Blackness and Asianness (sometimes in combination, other times singly), to assert a particular subject position that has its own benefits and advantages."[42]

Black Native Americans

In New England and elsewhere in the Northeast, ports, maritime trade, and whaling brought Native Americans and African Americans together with the arrival of the first English colonists and the institution of African enslavement. Some Blacks escaped slavery and found refuge among Native Americans, who were themselves threatened with genocide. Consequently, Black Native Americans were one the first dual-minority multiracial groups in the United States and include figures like Crispus Attucks (1723–70), believed to be the earliest casualty of the American Revolution. Attucks's father was thought to have been an enslaved African, and his mother a Native American. Yet Attucks is typically identified as Black. His Native American background is virtually erased.[43]

Many members of the northeastern Native American nations, including the Pequot of Connecticut, the Nipmuc and Wampanoag of Massachusetts, and the Shinnecock of Long Island, New York, display features indicating varying degrees of African ancestry. Consequently, they do not exhibit physical characteristics associated with normative societal expectations and stereotypes based on Native Americans west of the Mississippi. Because of that, these nations have long fought with federal gatekeepers over who is or is not authentically Native American.[44]

The Rappahannock of Virginia are another example of Native Americans who exhibit these complexities of East Coast Indigenous populations. They maintained communities in Caroline County as well as several other counties. Yet they did not live on a reservation and, like many other Indigenous Virginians, had intermarried with other racial groups, including Blacks.[45] Indeed, during the colonial and antebellum periods, people of African and Native American descent comingled and intermarried, since many shared the common status as slave or free disenfranchised citizen. They also shared racial designations, as Virginia identified its nonwhite population with terms largely associated with people of African descent, such as Black (that is, Negro), mulatto, colored, or free people of color. Individuals of African descent, Native American descent, or African American Native American descent were included in these categories. Definitions of these categories changed over time and were applied inconsistently. Consequently, the line between Native American and African American lacked clarity. This made it difficult for the Rappahannock to establish tribal continuity as required for federal recognition.[46]

These social dynamics had critical implications for the *Loving* decision. Mildred Loving maintained that her mother was a full-blooded Rappahannock and that her father was Rappahannock and white. She stated that, to her knowledge, there were no African American ancestors in her family genealogy.[47] The framed marriage license the Loving's displayed in their bedroom reads: "Richard Perry Loving—White; Mildred Delores Jeter—Indian."[48] Still, Mildred Loving's birth certificate identifies her parents, Theoliver Jeter and Musie Byrd, as colored. Census records indicate that her antecedents, as far back as 1870, were Black, mulatto, or colored.[49] Yet racial designations on government documents have been challenging as many individuals of Native American or part–Native American descent were often designated as mulatto, Negro, Black, colored, or persons of color.

In Virginia the 1924 Racial Integrity Act imposed the one-drop rule. This legislation originated in the obsession with Eugenics, the pseudoscientific doctrine of "good breeding." After this law was implemented, most of the Rappahannock and other Virginia Native Americans lost their records as "Indian." Individuals were classified as "white" or "colored," even requiring changes to vital records to reflect this.[50] Notwithstanding these changes in vital records, Caroline County residents, particularly in Central Point, were aware of a racial hierarchy in which Native Americans were somewhat more advantaged than Blacks but subaltern to whites. Various residents argued that some individuals emphasized their Native American ancestry and denied, or at least did not acknowledge, their African ancestry, to escape the social stigma of Blackness and gain access to some venues (e.g., white hospitals and the white-only section of rail and street cars).[51]

Arica L. Coleman argues that, given these complexities, Mildred Loving's racial composition may have become a concern during court proceedings. In order for her attorneys to build a case for dismantling the last antimiscegenation statutes before a Supreme Court that viewed these issues exclusively in Black and white terms, Mildred Loving would need to maintain she was African American Native American, which in keeping with the one-drop rule, meant she was Black.[52] While Mildred Loving may have accommodated this as a legitimate legal strategy, she primarily identified as Native American. Therefore, viewing the Loving case simply in Black and white terms has obscured the complexities of African American Native American relations in the South.[53]

Other Native American communities in the South, such as the federally recognized five "civilized" tribes—the Cherokees, Seminoles, Creeks, Choctaws, and Chickasaws—were historically acknowledged as citizen individuals without any Native ancestry. These nations embraced U.S. assimilationist policies, which many viewed as a means of survival. More prosperous members copied the southern plantation agricultural model, including the adoption of race-based African chattel slavery and the racial hierarchy that sustained it.[54] But the few who did own slaves were mostly either intermarried with whites or with their multiracial white Native American descendants. Indeed, one goal of U.S. policy was to racially assimilate Native Americans through intermarriage with whites. Similarly, Native Americans were impelled to culturally assimilate by converting to Christianity and learning to speak and read English, including by forcibly sending children to boarding schools.[55]

Local whites wanted (and held they deserved) lands occupied by

Native Americans, particularly in the Southeast, where many maintained profitable plantations. In 1830 President Andrew Jackson pushed through the Indian Removal Act, which gave the federal government the power to negotiate treaties with Native American nations for their land. Native Americans were to give up lands east of the Mississippi in exchange for lands in the west. Those who decided to remain in the East would become citizens of their home state. Notably, the language of these treaties did not permit coercion and provided only for land negotiations based on payment. Several northern tribes peacefully resettled in the West. Yet the Five Nations refused to trade their farms for a permanent title to unfamiliar and largely semiarid or barren land in Indian Territory, now in Oklahoma. They variously resisted, from open revolt to litigation.[56]

Eventually, the federal government forced compliance. Between 1830 and 1850 the Choctaws, Creeks, Chickasaws, Cherokees, and Seminoles were removed from their homelands. Their deadly mass exodus to Oklahoma under military coercion has been called the Trail of Tears, as thousands died along the way with their footprints in the snow resembling teardrops. This relocation involved tens of thousands of Native Americans, as well as several thousand Black slaves, Black spouses, and freedmen of African descent. Remnants of the nations that chose to remain in the Southeast—or as in the case of the Seminoles, to engage in open warfare—were subject to legal conflict, harassment, and intimidation.

The federal government drafted treaties in 1866 requiring Native American nations to free their slaves and grant them and their descendants citizenship, regardless of their ancestry. The Chickasaws did not comply with adopting their former slaves as citizens, and the Choctaws did so grudgingly. But in the Creek, Seminole, and Cherokee nations, former slaves who were referred to as freedmen, were largely accepted as tribal members with the rights inherent to this status, including the right to vote. Yet they faced racial prejudice and were never fully embraced as citizens.[57]

This all changed after Congress passed the General Allotment Act in 1887, commonly referred to as the Dawes Act. Initially, the

Cherokees, Chickasaws, Choctaws, Creeks, and Seminoles in Indian Territory were exempt but were subsumed under the Curtis Act of 1898. These laws were designed to break down traditional Native American communal land ownership and authorized the president to assign allotments to individual, nuclear families, thus dismembering tribal sovereignty, social structure, and governments. The Dawes Commission, established in 1893, further removed sovereignty and distributed land to freedmen and Native citizens on an individual basis. It allowed Native Americans to be incorporated as U.S. citizens and was applauded by those who believed it would convert them into compliant supporters of American progress.[58]

Under the Dawes Act Congress also adopted a blood quantum standard of one-half or more Native American ancestry—eventually reduced to one-quarter—to be legally deemed Native American. But the Dawes Act had a deleterious impact as census takers eyeballed and interviewed applicants to determine eligibility for land parcels: if someone "appeared" Native American, or a combination of white and Native American, they were listed on the Dawes Roll as Native American or part–Native American. Individuals who "appeared" African American, including multiracials of Native American and African descent, were listed as freedmen. In keeping with the one-drop rule, no Native American lineage was noted irrespective of its presence.

The Dawes Act thus erased from official U.S. rolls many tribal members of African descent, even though they had been full citizens for decades.[59] The two rolls also conferred different rights. Freedmen were granted considerably less land than citizens by blood. Each nation eventually made presence on the Dawes Roll necessary for tribal citizenship.[60] In the late nineteenth and early twentieth centuries, the Creek, Seminole, Choctaw, and Cherokee nations extended citizenship to those on the freedmen roll. But freedmen citizenship rights have been repeatedly contested in the courts. In the early twenty-first century this conflict intensified through attempts to implement more restrictive rules to consolidate economic gains or due to the military importance of some reservations.

In 2017, after a thirty-year legal battle, the U.S. District Court in

Washington DC ruled that the descendants of freedmen should be granted full citizenship in the Cherokee Nation, including the right to vote and access to all medical, educational, and housing services provided tribal citizens. Debates among the Chickasaw, Choctaw, Creek, and Seminole nations continue.[61] Some critics contend that discussions of this topic are typically framed as if they are solely a matter of U.S. governmental and public policy. But they are also emblematic of the historical narrative supporting U.S. colonial power in and racial domination over Native America. This has all but disregarded their sovereignty and right to practice their systems of government and law, including the determination of tribal citizenship.[62]

That said, the Cherokee state in the early part of the nineteenth century is a case study of the confluence of racial ideologies and practices of the U.S. state and Native Americans nations in terms of determining tribal citizenship. This is evident, for example, in the 1824 passage of a series of antimiscegenation statutes by the Cherokee Nation that sought to discourage intermarriage between Cherokees and their African American slaves; they were willing, however, to accept intermarriages between themselves and whites.[63] According to James F. Brooks, lineage, rather than race as we understand it, was the determining factor in a person's tribal identity or tribal membership. He states, "A person who appeared 'Black' and had a Native American mother would have been defined and accepted as Indian."[64]

Yet Circe Dawn Strum maintains that subsequent statutes in 1839 indicated the Cherokees' own system of matrilineal descent was increasingly informed by European American racial ideologies of the nineteenth-century based on the one-drop rule.[65] African ancestry from either parent was becoming sufficient to determine one's social standing. This would have fateful consequences for the growing numbers of Black Cherokee offspring who were evidence of interracial intimacy between Black slaves and Cherokee slave owners despite legal prohibitions against interracial marriage with African Americans.[66] Some of these mixed-race individuals spoke Cherokee and lived as Cherokee, yet their experience of being racialized as Black still set them apart.[67] Celia E. Naylor also points out that Blackness informed an individual's status as slave and free. "Cherokee blood," in conjunction with free status, guaranteed limited rights to multiracials of African and Cherokee descent in the antebellum Cherokee Nation. These rights were not granted to free people of African descent with no "Cherokee blood."[68]

Daniel F. Littlefield Jr. suggests that few intermarriages with Blacks occurred within the Five Civilized Tribes, citing harsh laws forbidding them. Yet there was considerable interracial intimacy whether sanctified by marriage or not. The exceptions were the Creeks and Seminoles. Like many Native American nations, the Seminoles historically adopted individuals from other tribes and non-Native people as members, no matter their descent. They had a long history of interacting with Africans in Florida since the colonial period. Runaway slaves from the U.S. South fled there when it was Spanish territory. They blended into the Seminole community, which they joined in an unsuccessful defense against U.S. soldiers in the series of Seminole Wars (1816–58). White settlers introduced the concepts of race and blood quantum, imposing Western concepts of lineage and pedigree on the Seminoles.[69]

Some intermarriage between Seminoles and self-emancipated Africans (maroons) occurred in Florida before removal to reservations in Indian Territory west of the Mississippi. Among the matrilineal Seminoles, the designation of the Black Native American offspring depended on the mother. It was likely that marriage brought increased status for male Black freedmen because their children would be included in Native American bands and clans and considered Seminoles.[70] Band affiliation suggests Seminoles considered some Black Native Americans as Native American and others as freedmen. But regardless of how Black Native Americans were identified and designated within Native American bands, whites portrayed Seminoles as mongrelized and tainted by Black ancestry and characterized them as criminal, lazy, drunken, and backward. Black Native Americans were thought to possess "the worst traits of both groups, resulting in a criminal type more ruthless than any other known."[71]

How Black Native Americans have historically self-identified and to what extent they have embraced both of their backgrounds remains an open question. Most experiences are unknown and reported. Some historical figures of notoriety, such as sculptor Mary Edmonia Lewis (1847–1907), straddled Native American and African American experiences.[72] Sarita Cannon argues that legendary 1960s guitarist Jimi Hendrix sought to resist the rigid contemporary racial essentialism by performing a Black Cherokee American identity. He did this by embracing Black Power and Red Power, reflecting his understanding of himself as a multiracial with European, African, and Indian ancestry. Hendrix is generally known as Black rather than Black Native American.[73]

Contemporary vocalist Radmilla Cody, whose mother is Navajo and whose father is African American, reigned as Miss Navajo Nation in 1997–98. Though most in the community supported her crowning, some found a "mixed-blood" Navajo woman with African ancestry unacceptable to represent the Navajo Nation. Cody rejects essentialist definitions of Navajo and Black identity by asserting her multiraciality. She uses Navajo Nation teachings to imagine ways of rethinking racial and tribal belonging that do not rely solely on legal, biological, or cultural definitions.[74] Similarly, Morgan James Peters, who directs the African and African American studies program at UMass Dartmouth, traces his ancestry to Africans as well as the Mashpee Wampanoag Tribe. He wears locks and carries the single name *Mwalim*, like the Swahili word for teacher, but embraces both parts of his racial background.[75]

Law professor and journalist Kevin Maillard is a member of the Seminole Nation. His father is Black, and his mother is Black Native American. Maillard identifies as Black Native American but typically is accepted only as Black. Still, he describes not being perceived as authentically Black by his African American peers because he did not grow up in the "hood." Neither is he accepted as authentically Native American because he did not grow up on a reservation. Maillard observes that in the Native American community, "If you're part white, then you are a mixed blood. If you are mixed with Black, you're just Black. Black overpowers every other culture you have."[76]

Black Latina/o

Very few studies focus on Black Latina/o multiracials, including Blaxicans. They are first-generation individuals in the United States who are the offspring of parents from two different monoracial groups one of which is African American and the other Latina/o (e.g., Puerto Rican, Dominican, Mexican American, Cuban, etc.).[77] Black Latina/o multiracials differ from Afro-Latin Americans, including Afro-Mexicans. The latter are products of multigenerational racial formations constructed *outside* of the United States, even when they reside in the United States. Black Latinas/os, including the Blaxicans in this research, are typically first-generation multiracials with one African American and one Latina/o parent.[78]

Sandra Smith and Mignon Moore's interviews with Black Latina/o students at a predominately white U.S. university give insight into how parents influence a multiracial, rather than a monoracial, identity.[79] Black Latina/o students were influenced by their non-Black parent to identify with both aspects of their racial background. One such student describes this influence:

> [My first name] is African, West African meaning warrior, and [my middle name] is my mom's maiden name, which is Cuban, and she said it's because she never wants me to forget that side because she knows when I go outside, I won't be seen as Cuban, I'll just be seen as Black, probably. But I always try to enforce that I'm more than just something you can define in one word. And I guess it's important to me to not let other people define me. Because defining is limiting. It creates boundaries you can't go outside of, and I think it's important not to have boundaries. It would be like limiting yourself.[80]

Mia, another student, echoed these sentiments:

> To say I'm Black, my mother would just get upset. She says, "Mia, you are Hispanic, too." But I think there's a lot of things that are rooted in me that are rooted in most Black people that aren't rooted in other people. But then I have to say, well, I am Hispanic, and I've

grown up with a lot of Hispanic ideas, and my mother raised me, so then I have that aspect of my life. But and other people always are asking me, "Well, Mia, what are you?" And when you say, "I don't know," a lot of Black people will feel, "Well look, if you don't know who you are, then you aren't us, because we know who we are, and we don't need that uncertainty with us."[81]

Mia and other Black Latinas/os, as well as Black dual minority multiracials, more generally, must negotiate the one-drop rule. Some define themselves solely as Black while their parents encourage them to embrace other aspects of their racial and cultural identity. This is not simply for the sake of embracing their differences as a harmonious blend. Rather, parents of minority backgrounds encourage their children to learn important skills as members of their racial and ethnic group of color, which is imperative in navigating a highly racialized society.

Dual-minority multiracials with one Black parent must not only navigate white racism but also prejudices from minority peers who do not fully accept them unless they exemplify loyalty and affinity to one racial group. Therefore, although multiracials with Black parentage can be viewed as Black by virtue of the one-drop rule, they are at the same time not always viewed as authentically Black. Monina Diaz, a biracial women of African American and Puerto Rican parentage who identifies as "Blatina," felt that she had to choose to form relationships with either her Black or Puerto Rican friends. She notes, "There's pressure from both sides to almost forsake your other side. My Black and Latino friends acknowledged and knew that I'm Puerto Rican and Black, or Black and Puerto Rican, but while I was with them, I couldn't be both at the same time. I had to affirm the culture they belonged to."[82] Monina eventually made friends with a Blaxican girl at her school and together they were able to express themselves as Blatinas comfortably, without criticism, although they continued to pursue friendships with other Black and Latina/o peers because of the lack of a larger Black Latina/o community available to them.

Marginalization of Black Dual Minorities

Dual-minority multiracials with African ancestry share similar experiences in terms of being held accountable to the racial and cultural authenticity tests required by the respective monoracial groups in their backgrounds. In addition, they must contend with questions of affirming one of those backgrounds over the other. Without exception, they have experienced the consequences of the one-drop rule that socially designates them as Black, even as they actively assert their multiraciality.

Physically resembling one group or the other is a major issue and has consequences for how a person may think and represent themselves as well as be seen. For dual-minorities with African ancestry, class, racial, and cultural signifiers are also melded together in a way that authenticate their identities as urban and working class.[83] Thus John R. Logan found that the socioeconomic profile of Hispanics who marked "Black" as their race on the 2000 census was more similar to non-Hispanic Blacks than to other Hispanics.[84] Raced, classed, and gendered expectations are some of the ways that begin to uncover the multiple layers of oppression that Black Latinas/os experience.

More generally, Kimberly M. DaCosta observes that multiracials of African ancestry have unique challenges in negotiating racial matters, not only in terms of being accepted into the Black community but also in relation to other multiracials. While Black white individuals are the archetypal multiracial, they, along with dual-minority multiracials with Black ancestry, remain marginalized within the multiracial population.[85] For example, *Hapas*—that is, multiracials of partial-Asian Asian American descent who were not half-white—felt that the definition of Hapa did not encompass their nonwhite ancestry.[86] As Elaine Johnson, a Black Japanese woman observed, "Even within the multiracial community there is a problem related to blackness."[87] Political activism around Hapa issues also focuses mostly on white Asian issues. As she further remarked, "If the White-Asians are saying, you know, that our agendas aren't addressed in the organizations that focus on Black-White mixtures, they turn around and they do the same thing. They form an organization, and they don't focus on Afro/Asian issues and Latina/o/Asian issues. They focus on white-Asian issues."[88]

This is attributable to the fact that within the Asian American community, Asian white multiracials tend to be more accepted than Asian Black ones.[89] Bashi Treitler indicates how Blacks are the basis for discrimination and whites are the measure for comparison. In the context of Asian Black multiracials, Black exceptionalism holds weight in relationship to how they experience racism and their position in society relative to whites.[90] As Root points out, Asian Blacks "suffered more rejection, more lack of recognition, and less acceptance by other Asian Americans, particularly first-generation Asians" compared to white Asian multiracials.[91] This is a product of the ruling social relations and the traditional racial hierarchy constructed around monoraciality, in which whites are at the top or in the ruling position of the ladder and Blacks are at the bottom. In their interactions with other multiracials, multiracials with African American ancestry are further marginalized because of it.

Part 2

Living Race and Identity in Black and Brown

| Chapter Nine

Racial Labels as a Self-Designation
Blaxican and Proud!

The following chapters provide a qualitative analysis of Blaxicans with the goal of contributing to the literature on the identities and experiences of dual-minority multiracials of African ancestry. Another objective is to help fill in the gap on analyses of Black Latinas/os. The contradictions that can emerge when claiming membership in the Black or Mexican American communities are central to the formation and assertion of a dual-minority multiracial identity. These identities are also examined in terms of gender, sexuality, class, parental socialization, neighborhood, and peer group.

We explore the marginalization of Blaxican identities and experiences in a monoracial social order that has not only privileged whiteness and stigmatized Blackness but has also prohibited, and indeed repressed, the formation, articulation, and recognition of multiracial identities. Blaxican identities thus signify a *borderlands space* where the ambiguities and contradictions of being both African American and Mexican American, as well as neither, are embraced and accepted. These data have coincided with the emergence of increased public discussions on the topic of racial composition that occurred in the first decade of the 2000s, with the election of Barack Obama, who openly discussed his own multiracial background. They capture the uniqueness of Blaxican experiences, with generalizable significance into the present and beyond.

The Current Study's Methods and Characteristics

Between 2006 and 2010, forty first-generation Blaxican men and women between the ages of eighteen and seventy-one were interviewed. Most participants (80 percent) were between the ages of twenty and forty. Recruitment materials sought out people with one African American and one Mexican or Mexican American parent. Five of the participants' parents also had known Native American, Anglo, or Japanese ancestries and were included in the sample. Of these participants, all indicated that their parents identify as Black or African American, and it was the interviewees who pointed out their parents' mixed ancestry. For example, LaTrice Johnson's father is "African American and Japanese," yet her father identifies as African American. LaTrice identifies as "Blaxican" and is included in this study.

More than half of the interviewees (twenty-seven) resided in California, which has the largest "two or more races" population in the country (1.8 million people).[1] In California most of the participants' residences were within with the "multiracial belt" around the Central Valley and greater Sacramento regions where there is a concentration of counties with higher percentages of multiracial people.[2] The remainder of the participants resided in New Mexico, Delaware, Georgia, Ohio, Indiana, Arizona, Maryland, and New York at the time of our interview. Thirteen of the participants have fathers of Mexican ancestry and African American mothers. Ten fathers are Mexican American, and three fathers are Mexican and born in Mexico. The remaining twenty-seven participants have African American fathers and Mexican or Mexican American mothers. Six of the mothers were born in Mexico. In this study, participants' Black parents were all American born. The racial and gender patterns of participants' parental interracial unions are consistent with current data that shows that African American men outmarry more than their African American female counterparts. In addition, native-born Americans are also more likely to interracially marry than those who are foreign born.[3]

Table 1. Race/ethnic background of parents

Mother: African American Father: Mexican American	10
Mother: African American Father: Mexican	3
Mother: Mexican American Father: African American	21
Mother: Mexican Father: African American	6

Chandra Waring and Bandana Purkayastha found that Black white biracials with an immigrant parent often adopted a half-racial–half-cultural identity (i.e., Black and Swedish or white and Ghanaian).[4] As we discussed in chapter 6, Mexican American identity is viewed as both a culture and race given the long-standing history of racialization in the United States. Therefore, Blaxican identity represents a blending of both racial and cultural elements that are not always easy to compartmentalize.

Many of the participants in this study pursued higher education. Six of the participants had earned bachelor's degrees and ten were in the process of earning a bachelor's degree at the time of our interview. Two participants earned a master's degree and another a PhD. One participant had a law degree, and one was pursuing a law degree. The remaining nineteen participants had high school diplomas. Thirty of the participants (75 percent) stated that they were from working-class backgrounds. One participant identified as "working-middle-class," and eight said that they were from middle-class backgrounds, while the remaining participant reported upper-class social origins. To keep the promise of confidentiality, pseudonyms are used in place of participants' actual names. There were cases in which it was appropriate to convey African American and Mexican or Mexican American names that approximated the participants' actual name. Blaxican names were a significant part of the data and would have otherwise been lost. Personal names are connected to cultural aspects of collective identity. A name may convey religious affiliation, social class, and cultural background.[5] Participants' names announced their racial-cultural ties to others and played a role in the negotiation of their multiracial identities. Names are not given to people strictly based on their racial-cultural backgrounds, nor are they inclusive or exclusive to entire communities. There are patterns and commonalities in names that appear with more frequency in Mexican/Mexican American and African American communities. In cases where participants had names frequently heard in and associated with these two groups of color, a name was used to reflect that dimension (e.g., María, José, Malik, Tameka).

Racial Identities and Racial Designations

There was a range of differences and similarities in the life stories of study participants. Indeed, even though the "mix" was the same, their experiences and identity formations were not. All the men and women that were interviewed identified racially as Blaxican, or Black and Mexican, regardless of how they looked or within which subdominant culture they were raised. Identification as Blaxican signifies a change in how people mixed with African American are claiming and expressing their racial identities. As we discussed in part 1, beginning with North American slavery and continuing beyond Reconstruction, people with any known African ancestry were designated and identified as Black in accordance with the one-drop rule of hypodescent.[6]

Blaxican as a Racial Self-Designation

Blaxican identities symbolize a deconstruction of the one-drop rule, a powerful mechanism used to reinforce a Black white dichotomy and an inegalitarian racial structure. While depending on the context the men and women interviewed would sometimes not correct people when they were perceived to be from one group (African American or Mexican American), they did not deny either on an individual level. Andrea Avila, a woman from Highland Park, California, speculated about the nuances we might find in the experiences of Blaxicans:

We are not all the same, just because we are half-Black and half-Mexican. You're going to find that there are people that either identify more with the Black side because maybe that's where they grew up, or on the Latino side. Or in some cases there is a Latino side that is anti-Black. In my case, my father's side didn't like my mom because she is Mexican, and they believed that he should be with a Black woman. But then you have the opposite. That is why it is important to bring this stuff to the forefront. We are not all the same; we may be mixed the same, but our experiences are completely different. If there would have been a book when I was younger that talked about this, it would have been helpful.

In fact, all study participants expressed a distinction between their racial and cultural identities, dependent on the culture(s) they were exposed to during their upbringing. For example, some participants were raised by both parents and were more likely to view themselves as biculturally African American and Mexican American. Other participants were raised by a single parent and viewed themselves as having a single culture.

Participants were asked, "Given that one of your parents is African American, and the other Mexican or Mexican American, how do you identify?" All the participants in this study identify as Black and Mexican, and many use *Blaxican* as a racial label of choice. Participants viewed themselves as a blending of Mexican American and African American as a mixed racial-cultural identity. People interviewed in their twenties were most likely to use the term *Blaxican*, while participants in their thirties and older either knew of the word and elected not to use it or had never heard of the term. Sometimes participants did not correct people who perceived them as either Black or Mexican depending on the context or situation. Some participants alternated their racial-cultural signifier between Black and Mexican, Blaxican, and a nonracial identity (e.g., human) in public settings depending on the context. Nikki Khanna points out that multiracial people distinguish between public identities (how individuals label themselves to others) and internalized identities (how individuals self-interpret their race). As participants talked about their racial identities, some identified differently over their lifetimes. For multiracial people, identity can change over time and across contexts.[7]

Participants chose a combined Black and Mexican, or Blaxican racial identity, rather than a monoracial label even if their phenotypes and cultural leanings favored one group over the other. The choice to identify internally as Black and Mexican stands in contrast to findings on Black white mixed identities. For instance, most of the Black white participants in Khanna's study internally identified as Black and were influenced by how they thought others viewed them.[8] Even when asked about their racial designations on official forms Blaxicans in this study found monoracial options confusing. On the U.S. Census, Mexican is not considered a racial designation. Therefore, when asked on the census, many participants marked Black as the racial category and Hispanic in the ethnicity question. Blaxicans answered the census in this manner even though many view themselves as two distinct races. Some Blaxicans chose the two-or-more-races option and selected Black and some other race. Since there currently is not a racial option on the census for Mexican, participants choose some other race. Miyawaki found that part-Latinos preferred to express all aspects of their racial identity and desire racial options consistent with a Latino race.[9] Blaxican participants stressed the importance of acknowledging being both Black and Mexican in their self-concepts, as well as having the option to do so on official forms.

Blaxican identities differ from findings of studies on part-white multiracials. Those multiracials identified with their minority parent as a means of associating with a history of oppression, for the simplicity of identifying as monoracial, and because they only had contact with their minority parent.[10] The way multiracials of partial white backgrounds identify is also influenced by phenotype. Part-white multiracials with darker physiognomy perceive more racial discrimination and are more likely to self-identify as a minority race.[11] Blaxicans in this study racially self-identify as Black and Mexican regardless of phenotype or cultural leanings favoring one group over the other.

Blaxicans' phenotypes mark them as racial minorities, and they articulate a connection to two separate histories of racial oppression and cultural heritage. Rather than choose between two racial-cultural minority identities, Blaxicans choose both. As mentioned in part 1, Leonard found that Mexican Punjabi children sometimes distanced themselves from identifying as Mexican American because their social status was perceived to be lower.[12] Blaxicans embraced both groups in their identities and refused to value either hierarchically in terms of intrinsic value or worth for reasons discussed in the next section.

Using Blaxican as a Designation of Choice

Interviewees use the term *Blaxican* to define their racial-cultural experience and identity. Blaxican combines two familiar terms, *Black* and *Mexican*, into one designation. Blaxican can be spelled *Blacksican* and there are other terms used to describe Blaxican individuals including: *AfroMex*, *MexiBlack*, *Black Chicana*, and *Afro-Mexican*. However, most participants used *Blaxican* as the appropriate spelling for this designation and noted that it sounded phonetically easier than the other terms. Participants also pointed out that using the term *Blaxican* with *B-l-a* in the beginning was not meant to privilege Black identity over Mexican identity; rather, this pronunciation sounded smoother than the other related terms. Participants noted that they were aware of several derogatory words in use to describe Blaxicans, such as *spigger* and *wetblack*, and that these are often used by non-Blaxicans.

The experience of Desire Campbell, a twenty-year-old woman raised in Las Cruces, New Mexico, by her Mexican American mother and African American father, shows how the use of language can be liberating in defining one's own experience. Desire switched from using *Blaxican* to *Blaxicana* as a self-label. Desire explains, "I said Blaxican for a long time; I couldn't even tell you when I started. Blaxicana came when I went to Spain after I graduated high school. When I was in Spain I was like, Blaxican? That's in English I'm going to say it in Spanish!" Desire used *Blaxican*, for a period of time, symbolizing her strong sense of a blended identity. She translated the hybrid English word *Blaxican* to the Spanglish word *Blaxicana* to represent her gender identity and bilingual background. The way multiracial individuals claim and interpret their multiracial identities can have positive psychological benefits.[13]

Some interviewees began to call themselves *Blaxican* as early as elementary school, while the majority began in either junior high or high school. One participant began to call himself *Blaxican* in college. Young adulthood and adolescence are typically when the development of racial self-identification occurs.[14] Adolescence is a critical time when multiracial youth are attempting to make sense of their identities.[15] Two participants first heard the term *Blaxican* on the radio. In 1996 a hip-hop group called Delinquent Habits, featuring rap artist Kemo the Blaxican, emerged on mainstream radio stations with their hit single "Tres Delinquentes," selling over a million copies worldwide. Kemo is a self-labeled Blaxican who is biracial Black and Mexican.[16] Some participants picked up the term *Blaxican* after hearing it in the group's music. Kemo made references to both Mexican and African ancestors with lyrics, "Hittin' hard like an Aztec, swift like a Zulu."

The other participants were either called *Blaxican* by others or believed at one time they were the originators of the term. Gaby Porter, a college student living in Fresno, California, and her brother who is also Blaxican believed that they invented the term together.

> GABY: I don't remember necessarily when [I started calling myself *Blaxican*] exactly, but I know that we were together, like, under some bleachers or something. We just had to figure it out because we knew that we had to register for school. And we did not want to be "others" anymore. It had to have been before we went to middle school. It was a big transition period between elementary and middle school; that is where all the big dogs were, and we had to make a game plan and talk to our parents and grandparents. That was a big change.
>
> REBECCA: Did you tell your parents and your grandparents that you were going to identify as Blaxican?
>
> GABY: I remember telling my mom's mom, and she laughed. She

thought it was funny, and she said, "Go ahead." She didn't like us being called "others" either.

Gaby's grandmother was amused by her decision to identify as Blaxican, but ultimately, her African American mother, Mexican American father, and grandparents supported this label of choice. Laughter was the most common reaction elicited from outsiders when participants used the term *Blaxican* to identify. Mostly people laughed because they found the term unique and amusing. Producing laughter may indicate people's reluctance to accept Blaxican as a legitimate mode of identity and experience after being accustomed to monoraciality as the dominant narrative of racial experience. For Gaby and her brother, creating a term to define their racial-cultural identity was important. It was also part of their resistance to the way larger society labels people that do not fit into traditional racial categories as "other."

The category *other* signifies that a person is not designated or identified with traditional and normative monoracial categories. While the label *other* acknowledges multiracials, it does so in a derogatory way. The *other* category can be viewed as derogatory because it implies a casting aside of a group of people that are nonnormative without fully acknowledging their existence. The fact that Gaby did not want to check off "other" is a form of resistance to being monoracialized, as well as an important assertion that she is Blaxican.

Similarly, Julia Miramar, an eighteen-year-old from Sacramento, California, believed that she and her mother came up with the term. Julia and her mother were combining words and after they arrived at *Blaxican*, her mother decided that was what Julia should use as a racial-cultural identifier. Likewise, twenty-one-year-old fraternal twin brothers Eduardo and Antonio Tijerina believed that they created the term by playing with existing language. Antonio said,

> Me and my brother thought we created that word. We thought we had came up with it. We must have put that together when we were like ten or eleven. And it is so funny to see that people did the same thing. I was like, what? But of course, it is not that hard to see how someone could come up with that, but still. I remember my

brother used to play and come up with other things like, *Afro-Mex* was the other one we were playing around with, but we decided on *Blaxican*. It sounds a lot better.

Interestingly, many participants did not know that Afro-Mexicans exist in Mexico, and the blending of the terms *Afro* and *Mexican* seemed novel. Eduardo, a student attending college in Sacramento, describes using *Blaxican* as his label of choice: "I usually say I am Blaxican because I don't want to deny both of them so I always say Blaxican. Off [the] top, people already know what I am talking about." Eduardo suggests that the term *Blaxican* includes both Black and Mexican American backgrounds and, at the same time, helps to avoid a lengthy explanation of his multiracial heritage.

In some contexts, the term is used to describe an interracial union between a Black American and Mexican American or someone who does not identify as mixed-race yet views themselves as ascribing to a fusion of African American and Mexican American culture. For example, people have called themselves *Blaxican* if they identify as Mexican American and listen to hip-hop music and are influenced by African American culture. *Blaxican* can also refer to a characterization of a neighborhood made up of African Americans and Mexicans/Mexican Americans.

In his study of Black and Latino boys in Oakland, California, sociologist Victor Rios calls Blaxican neighborhoods ones where Black and Mexican/Mexican American cultures continually meet and mesh: "The close proximity of Black and Latina/o youth has created common subcultures, interracial relationships, and common institutional experiences, including similar punitive interactions with schools, police, and community members."[17] Rios argues that African Americans and Mexican Americans' close social proximity sets the stage for Latinos to be incorporated into communities and institutions similar to the ways African Americans are treated and incorporated.

For Erica Donald, a twenty-three-year-old Blaxican woman from Indiana, the term Blaxican designates a person with one African American and one Mexican American parent. Erica said, "It [*Blaxican*] means to be Black and Mexican American. To me that means one parent is Black, one parent is Mexican. It's not like one parent is Black and white and one parent is Mexican. To me, *Blaxican* is strictly half-Black and half-Mexican. But some people vary it, but to me you have half-and-half blood. I consider it different from *Afro-Mexican*, but *Blaxican* is just like that, one parent is Black, and one parent is Mexican."

While some people may define Blaxicans as multigenerational multiracials, for Erica, Blaxicans are strictly first-generation mixed people who do not have any other known background. Indeed, Blaxicans in this study are distinguishable from Afro-Mexicans who may trace their origins to Mexico and whose lineage includes a longer process of miscegenation and cultural mixing stemming from Spanish colonization and slavery. Blaxican implies a new category of identity produced by the blending of racial-cultural aspects of African Americans and Mexican Americans in the United States. Blaxicans are "first-generation" individuals in the post–civil rights era in which one parent is African American and the other Mexican American. This differs from the long history of multigenerational blending and internal miscegenation discussed in part I that has characterized both the African American and Mexican experiences.

Some interviewees indeed have parents who are multiracial in ancestry, although their parents identified monoracially. LaTrice's father is Black-Japanese, and Antonio and Eduardo's mother is Black Native; all these participants identify as Blaxican even though their known ancestral background is more extensive. In these cases, the parent with known ancestry from more than one racial-cultural group including African American identifies as Black, not multiracial. Study participants acknowledged the contradiction that their parents have mixed-race ancestry yet identify as Black. The decisions made by these parents to self-designate in monoracial terms are consistent with the historical primacy of the one-drop rule.

Antonio pointed out the contradiction between the one-drop rule and multiraciality when articulating what he thought *Blaxican* meant: "It is funny, two things that seem like distinct identities: Latino and African American and putting those together just encompasses a lot.

It encompasses two cultures. Two massive cultures being brought together. When I think of African American or Mexican it is already mixed, it is already a culture that is mixed, so it is interesting to be another mix. A mix of a mix. A mix of two mixes. Out of that comes this new form. I really believe this."

Illuminating the complexity of the often-overlooked mixed racial middle, Antonio is aware of his identity—and of other identities—as socially constructed products. He is fascinated that Blaxican identities are viewed as the combining of two distinct categories, while the identity joins two groups that are themselves diverse and include mixed racial-cultural ancestries. Antonio expresses the view that each respective group, Mexican Americans and African Americans, could be considered multiracial if multiraciality was widely accepted and defined through ancestry rather than by how one identifies. That is, Mexicans are *mestizas/os* combining largely European, Indigenous, African, and sometimes Asian ancestries, which is similar to ancestries included in African American heritage. Paradoxically, Mexican Americans and African Americans have been systematically constructed as monoracial despite their multiracial ancestry, and yet the offspring of the two produces what Antonio calls a "new form" of racial-cultural identity. Blaxicans indeed view themselves as a novel form of person in a physical and cultural sense. Gaby succinctly summarizes the general feeling of Blaxican identity:

> When I say it [*Blaxican*] I am trying to let people know that this is a whole other race of people. There doesn't just need to be one whole race like just Black or just Mexican. You can mix two people together and create a new race, I do have two legs and a heart and a brain, I am walking around, and I do exist. So, I am trying to let people know that this does exist. It is a new type of person. And it is not just the body that is there, it is a whole new culture. By mixing them both together I think it creates a whole new culture.

Gaby argues that the term *Blaxican* refers to a "new type of person" not just in a racial sense but in a cultural sense as well. By discussing Blaxicans as "a whole other race of people," she also implies that there are Blaxicans who share a sense of collective cultural community, or a group of people who share goals, beliefs, and a racial-cultural identity. However, at the time of our interview, Gaby only knew one other Blaxican, her brother. It can be inferred that Gaby was assuming that more Blaxicans exist, and that Blaxicans thought about their racial-cultural identities in similar ways. In fact, very few participants knew more than three Blaxicans in their immediate social circle, and some knew none on a close and personal level. Nonetheless, Blaxicans express a distinct awareness as Blaxican and seem to imagine a larger Blaxican community during our conversations. As discussed in chapter 10, some participants search for a sense of a Blaxican community on the internet in social media groups.

Parental Influence on Racial Identities

Race and culture, for participants, are separate aspects of identity that intertwine. Racial identity refers to the visual representation of physical characteristics that are often associated with groups of people and is not exclusive because individuals can identify with more than one race. Important persons, such as parents, teach their children about racial identities through racial socialization. Racial socialization refers to the means through which "parents shape children's learning about their own race and about relations between ethnic groups."[18] On the other hand, cultural identity refers to the strength of one's identification with a particular culture in terms of values, customs, beliefs, and artifacts, and it need not be exclusive to one culture.[19]

Many multiracials live their lives negotiating between an "insider" and "outsider" status as they navigate rigid conceptions of racial and cultural categories that leave little room for individuals who do not fit neatly.[20] As is discussed in chapter 12, the act of constantly navigating the contradictions between the often-inflexible conceptions of race and culture as African American or Mexican American sets the stage for participants to identify as Blaxican. On the surface, multiracial identification as Blaxican may suggest that having one African American parent and one Mexican American parent designates participants as bicultural; however, interviews demonstrate otherwise.

Rather, the racial and cultural socialization provided by their parent(s) has a major influence on how participants view themselves racially and how they behave culturally.

In analyzing participants' experiences with racial socialization in single-parent vis-à-vis two-parent households all participants racially identify as Blaxican, some refer to being bicultural (African American *and* Mexican American) and others monocultural (African American *or* Mexican American). Participants raised by both parents are more likely than those raised in single-parent families to report being bicultural.

Raised by an African American Parent

For participants reared by a single parent, we focused on understanding their experiences regarding culture and exploring why they identified as multiracial when only one parent was present. In table 2 we report how participants raised by an African American single parent identify culturally. We also include the race that participants reported they are most often perceived as by others.

Table 2. Blaxicans raised by an African American single parent

Participant's name	Parent raised by	Culture	Perceived as
Albert Bennett	Father	African American	Indian (India)
Claudio Holmes	Mother	African American	Black
Eliza Montes	Mother	African American	Black
Jesus Sanchez	Mother	African American	Afro-Latino
Sabrina Johnston	Mother	African American	Mixed
Selena Fernandez	Mother	African American	Black

A little more than half (twenty-two) of the respondents were raised in a single-parent household. Six of the participants were raised by an African American single parent. Three of the participants were most often perceived as Black, while the remaining three were viewed as Indian, Afro-Latino, and mixed. Despite the differences in how they were commonly perceived racially, all reported identifying more with an African

American cultural experience than a Mexican American one. Participants who were raised by an African American single parent expressed a monocultural affinity as African American yet identified as Blaxican.

Sabrina Johnston, a twenty-three-year-old woman raised by her African American mother in Fresno and later in Salinas, California, describes her physical features as "ambiguous" and believes that people perceive her as "mixed," but not mixed with African American and Mexican American. Rather, people often view Sabrina as Hapa, and she internally identifies as Blaxican. Sabrina's is an example of someone who navigates what it means to be viewed racially as something other than Blaxican while feeling closely connected to African American culture. Sabrina said, "I was raised with my Black family so I feel comfortable—or I wouldn't say comfortable cause you know I feel attached to both, but I was mainly raised by my Black side. I didn't have to go out on my own and find out about Black, you know that side of myself, like I did the other side."

Sabrina explains that Blackness comes naturally to her because she was enculturated to African American culture through her mother. Sabrina's Mexican American father disappeared from her life at a young age, and she was not in contact with her extended Mexican American family. Throughout her childhood, Sabrina's mother had encouraged her to claim a mixed identity that acknowledged her Mexican heritage.

Sabrina's personal journey to seek out her "Mexican side" began in earnest while in college. She aligned her desire to know more about Mexican culture with her extracurricular activities. Sabrina enrolled in Chicana/o studies classes, joined a Chicana/o theater group, and contributed service specifically in Mexican American communities, which strengthened her sense of connection to her Mexican side. The encouragement from her African American mother to embrace a Mexican racial-cultural identity in addition to a Black one facilitated Sabrina's desire to learn about and incorporate Mexican American culture into her sense of self.

Gina Miranda Samuels's study on transracial (Black white) adoptees adopted by white parents found that participants claimed whiteness culturally but not racially.[21] That is, participants identified culturally as white and racially as biracial or Black. Interestingly, most participants who were reared by single parents and are monocultural sought out the other culture in their background in an effort to aspire to, or achieve, a multicultural sense of self. Many believed that having a multiracial and multicultural identity signifies an authentic and ideal Blaxican identity.

Two participants were raised by an African American single parent, are perceived as Black, and identify more with African American culture. Although others interpret these two participants' phenotypes as Black, they chose to racially identify as mixed. The eldest participant interviewed was Claudio Holmes, a seventy-one-year-old man who was raised by his African American single mother in Texas. Claudio's Mexican American father abandoned the family when he was a baby.

In fact, because interracial sexual contact was socially taboo during the time of Claudio's birth, his mother hesitated to reveal that his father was Mexican American until later in his life. Claudio's mother chose to raise him as African American and never encouraged a mixed-race identity. Claudio learned of his Mexican ancestry during adulthood and began to think of himself as African American and Mexican American from that point on. Claudio's discovery and later acknowledgment of a Mexican ancestral background facilitated his desire to identify as "Black and Mexican," although he was not enculturated as Mexican or even aware of his Mexican lineage until later in life.

Likewise, Eliza Montes, a twenty-year-old woman from Culver City, California, was raised by her African American mother and has a Mexican American father who was in and out of prison for most of her life. Consequently, Eliza never developed a relationship with her father or extended Mexican American family and views herself as culturally African American. Eliza believes that she is most often perceived as African American. However, she also feels that she does not "fit in" with the larger African American community.

ELIZA: I was raised by my mom, and I feel like I identify more with the African American culture, but then at the same time I don't really feel like I fit in that culture as well. Even now, a lot of my friends are very religious; they go to church every Sunday, and church is a large part of their life. I don't have that. For a lot of African Americans, church is a very important part of their lives, so sometimes I feel like I don't fit in. Or dancing-wise. I know not all African Americans are good dancers, and I know that's more of a stereotype than a fact—but not knowing how to dance that well, I feel like kinda left out.

REBECCA: Do people tell you that, or how do you know?

ELIZA: I get questioned, but not in a mean way. One time my friend—I don't know how it exactly happened—but I'm not sure if I can explain like a 2-step, but basically, she was like "Let me see," as a joke. . . . "Let me see you do that," like dancing or something. It was more of a show for her to put me through for her to laugh at.

Eliza demonstrates that although she is perceived as African American, and is African American culturally, she does not feel completely accepted as African American by her peers because she lacks what she views as some of the important cultural components of an African American identity. Some of these components are religion and knowing how to perform certain hip-hop dances. Appearing racially ambiguous, using multiracial identity labels, and having non-Black parents significantly compromises abilities to be fully accepted as a cultural insider.[22] Church is not a significant aspect of Eliza's life; moreover, she also feels she lacks the dancing skills of her African American peers. The realization that she is not fully accepted as African American because she does not conform to a complete monoracial image of Blackness in a cultural sense spurred Eliza's development of a Blaxican identity.

Raised by a Mexican or Mexican American

For participants who grew up in a Mexican or Mexican American single-parent household, many also experienced a monocultural upbringing. The majority identified as monocultural and reported being perceived as Black. Participants themselves, however, identified as Black and Mexican. All the Mexican parents born in Mexico spoke Spanish, and many Mexican American parents also spoke Spanish. However, Spanish did not always transmit to the children.

Table 3. Blaxicans raised by a Mexican or Mexican American single parent

Participant's name	Parent raised by	Culture	Perceived as
Andrea Avila	Mother	Mexican American	Black
Erica Donald	Mother	Mexican American	Black
Eli Maciel	Mother	Mexican American	Black
Lewis Cole	Mother	Mexican American	Black
Loraine Fisher	Mother	Mexican American	Black
LaTrice Johnson	Mother	Mexican American	Black
Nicole Hodges	Mother	Mexican American	Black
Monica Bell	Mother	Mexican American	Black
Jackie Jones	Mother	Mexican American	Dominican
Suzanna Williams	Mother	Mexican American	Black & white
Terrance Williams	Mother	Mexican American	Mexican American
Curtis Sandoval	Mother	Mexican American	Puerto Rican
Sheila Ramirez	Mother	Mexican American & African American	Puerto Rican
Sebastiano Flores	Mother	Mexican American & African American	Middle Eastern
Talia Ramos	Mother	Mexican American & African American	Black
Margery Samson	Father	Mexican American & African American	Black

LaTrice, a twenty-three-year-old college student from Redding, California, navigates what it means to be perceived as Black based on looks, while feeling more connected to Mexican American culture. LaTrice explains, "When I was younger it was harder because my dad wasn't really a part of my life. My mom was a single parent, and it was harder because when I was younger, I looked a lot more African American than I think I do now, but then I spoke Spanish. It was different, because I looked one thing then I identified with more of the Mexican culture because that was the way that I was raised."

During her childhood, LaTrice was viewed as African American and at the same time, she was raised within Mexican culture and spoke Spanish fluently. By making culture salient and by providing instruction about cultural practices and the achievements of group members, family builds pride and knowledge of cultural traditions and values that underlie an individual's cultural identity; children may also model their family's identification with their cultural group.[23] LaTrice related to her mother and grandparents culturally but identifies as Blaxican because her appearance marks her as Black.

LaTrice's cultural experiences and physical appearance did not match up to monoracial expectations and created space for her to identify as Blaxican. In college LaTrice joined a sorority and made friends with many African American women. LaTrice relied on her friendships to foster a closer connection to African American culture and share meaning with others over a Black experience. Although LaTrice recognized that she was not enculturated as African American, it was extremely important for her in adulthood to try to be closely connected to both African American and Mexican American cultures.

Another participant, Eli Maciel, was raised by his Mexican American single father. He identified culturally as Mexican American and believed that he was most often perceived as Mexican American. He grew up in a heavily immigrant Latino, African American, and Mexican American neighborhood in Fresno, California. Eli attended gifted and talented classes, and his father sent him to predominately white schools outside of his residential area. Eli racially identifies as "Black and Mexican," yet he does not use the term *Blaxican* as a self-designation. Because Eli appears Mexican to most people with whom he interacts and because he speaks fluent Spanish, he often is perceived as a non-Black Mexican. However, Eli argues that there is something different about him that others recognize upon meeting him. Eli said,

"The thing about me, and I'm not trying to toot my own horn, but within the first five to ten minutes of meeting me, I think that people assume that I am Mexican or of Hispanic origin, but they realize that there is more to me than some stereotype. I wouldn't say that you would look at me and instantly just say, oh Mexican [snaps fingers]. You might, but I doubt it."

Eli chooses to identify as Black and Mexican and explains that because he is not a "stereotypical" Mexican American he is often questioned about his authenticity. Eli's high academic achievement and attendance at high-ranking white schools further served to mark him as "different." Furthermore, Eli enjoys that his high academic achievements challenge people's race-based assumptions and the stereotypes that African Americans and Mexican Americans are not intelligent people. Although Eli does not identify with African American culture, he chooses a Black and Mexican racial identity to acknowledge his mother's African American ancestry.

Four participants who were raised by a Mexican American single parent said they identified multiculturally as Black and Mexican. They culturally identified differently than the other participants in this group mainly because of the extent of contact they had with other African American and Mexican American kin in their extended families or with peers in the communities in which they lived. Talia Ramos, a forty-year-old woman born in Oakland, California, and living in Sacramento at the time of our interview, was raised by her Mexican American single mother. Talia's mother has ten siblings, five of whom (including Talia's mother) are Mexican American and the remaining of whom are mixed African American and Mexican American. Talia, therefore, was socialized around extended family members who are racially mixed. Talia feels that her mother's cultural identity influenced how she views her own cultural identity. Talia describes her mother as identifying as culturally more African American than Mexican American. Talia said, "The thing is if a person was to talk to my mother on the phone, they would not know that my mother wasn't Black because my mother was raised with Black brothers and sisters. So maybe she did talk different; you could tell something different in her voice. People didn't think she was not Black until they met her in person. Because you couldn't talk to her on the phone and think that she wasn't [Black]."

Talia explained that her Mexican American mother "sounded" Black because she was raised around her brothers and sisters who are half-Black. Talia's mother was very light skinned, yet if others solely talked to her mother on the phone without viewing her, they would assume by her dialect that she was African American.

Another participant, Sebastiano Flores, was raised by a Mexican American single mother and viewed his cultural identity as both Black and Mexican. Sebastiano is a twenty-five-year-old man living in Indiana. He experienced a mostly white neighborhood and school setting growing up. His mother is a working-class woman who struggled financially to raise him and his younger sister. Sebastiano and his family lived in Indiana most of his life, except for a year when they moved to Atlanta, Georgia. Sebastiano's father was absent from his life, and he never had an opportunity to meet or get involved with any African American family members from his father's side. On his mother's side of the family he has two cousins who are Blaxican, and he remains in close contact with these cousins. Sebastiano feels comfortable with Mexican American culture because his Mexican American mother raised him, yet he feels slightly less of a connection at times because he does not speak Spanish. Sebastiano has many social networks with African American colleagues through his activist work as an underground hip-hop artist. Sebastiano was asked about the degree of his connection to Mexican American culture:

REBECCA: Culturally do you identify more as Mexican?
SEBASTIANO: No. I would say [not] culturally, just because I'm not fluent in Spanish, you know what I'm sayin'? And I look the way that I look. You can't tell. People don't really know: people kinda think I'm from Afghanistan or something. Know what I'm sayin'? But I fit right into the Black community, the Black crowd, the Black people. I'm part of the liberation movement that's going on here in North America to free oppressed people here, Black and

Brown. I'm down with Black Power and Brown pride. I identify with both, but I find myself actively participating more ... with the oppressed Black people of America.

Unlike most of the other participants raised by a Mexican American single parent, Sebastiano does not default to his mother's cultural heritage. Research shows that mothers are more involved in culturally socializing their children.[24] Sebastiano stated that his mother worked a lot, was not home very much, and did not teach him and his sister Spanish. However, when Sebastiano's sister was interviewed, she claimed a monocultural identity as Mexican American. The differences in how this brother and sister felt about their cultural identity can be attributed to findings on African American families, which suggest that boys and girls receive different messages through socialization.

Boys are taught more about racial discrimination, while girls receive more messages about cultural pride.[25] Sebastiano finds himself participating more with the struggles of Black people partly because of the integral part that performing hip-hop music and culture has on his life. By participating in an activist movement through hip-hop music, Sebastiano affirms his connection to Black culture. The Mexican American cultural connection is a part of his experience that is taken for granted, and the incorporation of Black culture into his identity comes from his involvement with hip-hop music. Not being fluent in Spanish is a barrier to feeling more culturally Mexican American, yet Sebastiano expresses "Brown pride" or a sense of pride for being part-Mexican.

In sum, Blaxicans raised in a single-parent family were socialized either with African American or Mexican American culture and identity, and therefore most were monoculturally aligned to one group over the other. Despite being monocultural because of their upbringing in single-parent households, many participants were intentional about incorporating both African American and Mexican American racial-cultural aspects into their own sense of self-consciousness. Many participants believed that an authentic Blaxican identity represented a racial-cultural blend of African American and Mexican

American expressions. Most of the time, participants did not choose to identify and participate as monoracial, regardless of phenotype and even as they viewed themselves as monocultural. A few participants raised in Mexican American single-parent households believed they were multiculturally African American and Mexican, and this is attributed to the degree to which they were exposed to both cultures through extended family and peers.

Blaxicans Raised by Both Parents

The remaining study participants (seventeen) were socialized in coparenting families. Coparenting refers to the extent to which mothers and fathers, who often live in the same household (but not always), work together in the tasks of childrearing, including supporting one another in their parenting roles, backing one another up in their childrearing decisions and disciplinary practices, and conveying consistent socialization messages to their offspring.[26] Thirteen participants were raised with a Mexican American mother and African American father. Participants reported being perceived as Black, Mexican, Afro-Latina/o, Filipina/o, or Italian. Of these thirteen participants, five said they are culturally Mexican American, and the remaining eight participants reported viewing themselves as multiculturally African American and Mexican American. In table 4 we describe participants who were raised by a Mexican American mother and African American father. We include how participants view themselves culturally, as well as how they are commonly perceived by others based on their physical appearances. We explore whether Mexican American mothers had a greater influence on racial-cultural identity than fathers.

Table 4. Blaxicans raised by Mexican or Mexican American mother and African American father

Participant's name	Culture	Perceived as
Debra Gibbons	Mexican American	Black
Desire Campbell	Mexican American	Mexican American
Rachel Mabley	Mexican American	Black

Participant's name	Culture	Perceived as
Zahira Davis	Mexican American	Afro-Latina
James Ramsey	Mexican American	Mexican American
Dan Gonzales	Mexican American & African American	Afro-Latino
Fernando Thomas	Mexican American & African American	Filipino
Gerardo Jones	Black & Mexican	Italian
John Jackson	Mexican American & African American	Black
Vanessa Solis	Mexican American & African American	Black or Mexican American
Jenny Griffin	Mexican American & African American	Black
Demitrius Hunter	Mexican American & African American	Mexican American
Jermaine Wallace	Mexican American & African American	Black

Consistent with research indicating that mothers have a greater impact on cultural socialization than fathers, Debra, Desire, Rachel, Zahira, and James all viewed themselves as monoculturally Mexican American and were influenced by their mothers.[27] For forty-five-year-old Debra Gibbons, her mother was more invested in passing on her cultural knowledge than was her father during her upbringing. Her mother is a Mexican Catholic and took her to catechism until the age of twelve; she frequently spoke Spanish to Debra in the home, and they engaged in Mexican cultural traditions, such as Día de los Muertos and Posadas at Christmas time. Debra's father was agnostic and indifferent to his daughter's religious affiliation. As a Black Native American, Debra's father distanced himself from the reservation, and consequently, Debra visited the reservation on her own as an adult and learned of her father's ancestral heritage.

James Ramsey, raised by both parents, identified more with Mexican

American culture. His appearance marked him as Mexican American and that influenced the sense of closeness he felt with that culture, although he identified as both Black and Mexican American. James grew up in Sacramento, California, and attended high school in the Del Paso Heights neighborhood, a racially diverse area of concentrated poverty, made up of 31 percent whites, 24 percent Blacks, 27 percent Hispanics, 15 percent Asians, and 3 percent other.[28] During high school in the 1990s, racial conflicts between Mexican Americans and African Americans were a serious issue. The pressure to choose between African American and Mexican American friends was a matter of personal safety. James explained that the unspoken rule at his high school was that interracial friendships were acceptable while in class, but once in common spaces during passing periods and at lunch, friendly contact between African Americans and Mexican Americans was strictly limited.

James says he felt that his high school experience "was like prison; I had to choose." Because James appears to be Mexican American, he chose to associate with Mexican American friends. Despite his close relationship with his African American father, he feels more comfortable around Mexican Americans and with Mexican American culture. Even among his Mexican American peers in high school, there was pressure to choose between associating with Norteños or Sureños, Mexican American gangs from northern or southern California, respectively. In California Black and Mexican or Mexican American inmates are segregated in prisons due to conflicts, which tend to spill out on the streets.[29] Chapter 13 delves further into how Black and Brown relations contribute to Blaxicans' feelings of pressure to choose one identity over the other.

Patrick Lopez-Aguado examines how the practice of segregating male inmates in California prisons influences the identities of criminalized Latino youth outside of prison in communities. Sureño and Norteño are what he calls carceral identities, or identities that connect prison and communities where incarceration is commonplace.[30] Choosing a carceral identity is a survival strategy that structures and defines youth interactions and expectations at school and in their communities. Youth, even if they are not involved in gangs, often discover how they would fit into carceral identities based on the experiences of family and peers.

> REBECCA: So, there was no in-between? You couldn't have Black and Mexican friends, and Sureño and Norteño friends?
> JAMES: No, you had to be one thing or another. To be in-between was a dangerous thing.
> REBECCA: What would happen?
> JAMES: Let me put it to you this way: if a Black or a Mexican fought, you can guarantee that at lunch or after school there was going to be a riot. And you had to choose; if you don't choose then you were just a nerd. If you didn't choose you were just a nobody.

James's appearance that marked him as Mexican American, combined with the "prison-like" environment at his high school, forced him to publicly choose one racial-cultural group over another, and one Mexican American affiliation, Sureño or Norteño, over another. Choosing to be in-between placed James at the risk of losing social status and compromising his sense of safety in his highly racialized school environment. Choosing a side allowed James to establish and maintain a safe and comfortable status among his peers. Such experiences contributed to James's feelings of being closely connected to Mexican American culture and people, despite being raised by both of his parents.

Desire from Las Cruces was raised by her African American father and Mexican American mother. Both parents had a deep involvement in her life. However, Desire was enculturated as Mexican American. Like other participants, Desire negotiates appearing Black while feeling culturally Mexican American:

> I would say that I was brought up mostly Mexican, like culturally. I do speak Spanish; I understand Spanish a lot better than I speak it, but I can communicate . . . and there's words that I don't know, so I just avoid them, and I explain what I am trying to say rather than trying to find the words, but I do speak Spanish. When I first meet people, I look more Black than Mexican, but I was brought

up more Mexican so in that sense it is kind of a conflict as far as what people expect from me. As far as looks, I feel more Black, but as far as culture, I feel more Mexican.

Desire explained that she is perceived as Black but culturally identifies as Mexican; at the same time she embraces an identity as Blaxican. Desire speaks some Spanish and was raised in New Mexico, where many people in her community speak Spanish and, additionally, Mexican American culture is more dominant than African American culture. However, Desire perceives that there is an expectation placed on her by her African American peers to behave in specific ways. Desire said,

> When they first see me, they expect me to talk a certain way or act a certain way, or move a certain way, then after that gets past, I get comfortable, and they get comfortable with me, and then we'll get along. As far as me meeting Black people, sometimes I feel like they are judging and kinda like upset with me for not acting or speaking or moving a certain way. Then, after that gets past and it's understood that this is a little Blaxican girl that is more Mexican, then everybody is cool.

Not fulfilling monoracial or monocultural expectations reinforces a Blaxican identity for Desire. She describes herself as a "Blaxican girl that is more Mexican," and that is what she is comfortable with. One's racial-cultural group is considered an extended kin network linked through shared cultural and racial origins.[31] The belief in race as an extended kin network prompts social expectations that people within a group should relate to one another in family-like ways and behave similarly.[32] Desire argues that her African American peers place social expectations on her to talk and act in ways that are viewed as specific to African Americans. Upon further reflection of the closeness she feels to Mexican culture, Desire notices,

> I would like to add that, when all factors are considered, I think that my dad wasn't necessarily raised Black either. Because he grew up in New Mexico and there aren't a lot of Black people around, and so I would say a lot of my *Blaxicananess*, feeling more Mexican, is because my dad probably feels more Mexican, if that makes any

sense, just because that is also his culture. My dad cooks menudo.[33] I think I have a different kind of family as far as culture goes. And we are a very liberal family, and in this area of New Mexico there are more Mexicans, so you are going to be more influenced by that more. And if my family lived somewhere else, then I would be influenced in a different way. So, I think it's my area that I grew up in that influenced me culturally and my family too, but not just my family, I think it has to do totally with the area.

Like Talia who was raised by her Mexican American single mother whom she considered culturally African American, Desire believes that her African American father is conversant with Mexican American culture because of the influence Mexican people have in New Mexico. Desire places an emphasis not only on the influence her family has had on her but also on the racial make-up and dynamics of different spaces. The degree of contact with other minority groups within neighborhoods may influence the degree of felt closeness to one's racial reference group.[34] Mexican American culture is woven into her African American father's experiences, modeling that it is possible for a Black person to feel an affinity toward Mexican American cultural ways of being. The contradictions between being perceived as Black and associating with Mexican American culture opens space for people like Desire to identify as Blaxican.

The remaining eight Blaxican participants who were coparented by a Mexican American mother and African American father expressed a bicultural affiliation. Dan Gonzales, a twenty-one-year man from El Paso, Texas, believes that the blending of music contributes to his bicultural identity as Blaxican. His Mexican mother and African American father raised Dan, and he describes blending the cultures of his parents in the music he listens to. Dan said, "The music that I listen to has been influenced by both my mom and my dad. My mom's music is Spanish, and I listen to more mainstream, but I do tend to have a liking for music in Spanish, like a variety of different genres in Spanish. My dad, he listens to a lot of Blues and Jazz and hip-hop and R&B, so I gotten both influences. On my iPod I got a mixture of both."

Likewise, Vanessa Solis, a twenty-year-old woman from Georgia who was raised by her Mexican American mother and African American father, considers herself biculturally Black and Mexican American. Vanessa lives in closer proximity to her father's side of the family and has less contact with her extended Mexican American family. Vanessa was asked if she felt closer to one culture or the other, given that she didn't have much contact with her extended Mexican American side of the family or many Mexican people in Georgia. She replied, "I think it's equal because my mom listens to Mexican music and celebrates the holidays. My dad's side we listen to hip-hop and pop. I grew up with that culturally."

In addition, Vanessa explained that she made efforts to get in touch with her Mexican culture when she went to college: "When I went off to college, I wanted to explore the Mexican side and culture. I think college is a learning experience, so I'm not sure but for me it made me want to grow closer to my Mexican culture and want to minor in Spanish." In addition, Vanessa mentioned that the employment opportunities at a recently opened IKEA plant have brought an influx of Mexican people to her town in Georgia. She expressed being excited about having more regular interaction with Mexican people and culture because she constantly wants to learn more about her Mexican side.

Interestingly, all the participants brought up by an African American mother and Mexican American father expressed that they are biculturally African American and Mexican, and none expressed a monocultural affinity toward one group over the other. However, given that there were only five participants in this group, perhaps a larger sample would yield different conclusions.

Table 5. Blaxicans raised by African American mother and Mexican or Mexican American father

Participant's name	Culture	Perceived as
Eduardo Tijerina	African American & Mexican American	Mexican American
Julia Miramar	African American & Mexican American	Mexican American

Participant's name	Culture	Perceived as
Antonio Tijerina	African American & Mexican American	Afro-Latino
Gaby Porter	African American & Mexican American	African American
Ron Salazar	African American & Mexican American	Filipino or Native American

For most participants who grew up in two-parent households, the blending of African American and Mexican American culture was a predominant and normalized part of their cultural experiences. Mothers had a slightly higher impact in the role of transferring cultural knowledge in some of the Mexican American mother and African American father households. Overwhelmingly, both parents contributed to the sense of blending both African American and Mexican American cultures. In most cases, the main difference between participants raised by single parents and those raised with both parents was a monocultural versus a bicultural affinity as African American or Mexican American. Participants raised by both parents were likely to have a bicultural identity.

It can be concluded that all participants in this study internally identify as Black and Mexican, although some perceive themselves as either monocultural or bicultural. The monocultural participants make efforts to identify with and learn the culture that is absent from their familial cultural socialization. Seeking out the culture of the absent parent for dual-minority multiracials is different from findings on multiracials with white backgrounds. Many tend to identify with their minority parent and may not seek out their white parent's culture. The lack of commitment to seek out the white side may be due to the invisibility or normativity of whiteness and the loss of European American ethnocultural specificity associated with that parent's background.[35]

Chapter Ten

Defining Blaxicans
Racial-Cultural Existence in a Borderland Space

Blaxicans reported that their peers often do not view them as Black or Mexican "enough," implying they are not authentic. Aside from how their peers view them, how do participants view what constitutes an "authentic" Blaxican? Our interviewees had their own interpretations, and some shared understandings about what is considered a Blaxican identity. The overwhelming majority of participants either knew no or only a few other Blaxicans beyond their own siblings. Therefore, participants determined what made up an authentic Blaxican based on personal experiences, siblings' experiences, and an understanding of race and identity in the larger context of multiracial identities in the United States and globally.

The Authentic Blaxican

All the participants agreed that Blaxicans are first-generation persons with one African American and one Mexican or Mexican American parent. This is consistent with the Loving Generation, or the population of first-generation multiracials born since *Loving*. The first-generation experience involves identifying with more than one racial-cultural reference group and usually involves direct experiences with those backgrounds in the home or family experiences.[1] *First generation* refers to being mixed with African American and Mexican American heritage with no other known ancestry. One participant views her child's identity as Blaxican (the child's father is also Blaxican), but since many other participants do not have children, the way they view the second generation remains an open question. In addition, the generation of the Mexican-descent parent living in the United States is not considered significant. In other words, whether a Blaxican's parent was born in Mexico or the United States, they still considered their multiracial identities first generation and novel. Furthermore, it was widely acknowledged among participants that African Americans and Mexican Americans are multiracial in ancestry, this did not factor into the "generation of family that is mixed" distinction, because these two groups are generally accepted as monoracial.

Another shared idea about what characterizes Blaxican identity is claiming both of their parents' backgrounds. It is important to this group to identify, on an intrapersonal level, as both African American and Mexican American. This is true regardless of how they appear phenotypically or how they were socialized in their families culturally. Even though Blaxicans identify as both on an intrapersonal level, that is not to say that there was not space for them to shift from Black or Mexican depending on the situation or context. For example, James from Sacramento was raised by both parents and is perceived as Mexican based on his appearance. His hair is straight, and he has lighter skin. He identifies as both Black and Mexican, but in high school his peers assumed he was Mexican, and that is how he navigated that social setting.

On the other hand, some Blaxicans are perceived as Black based on their hair, facial features, and skin tone and are sometimes not questioned about whether they are mixed race. In this context Blaxicans may not actively assert that they are both. This is not a denial or distancing from one group or the other but rather signals the in-between nature of Blaxican identities. In other words, some Blaxicans can shift between Black or Mexican, or blend both depending on the situation. In addition, some Blaxicans may not constantly assert that they are both in every single social interaction. This extra work is exhausting and is not typically asked of monoracial people.

While Blaxican identities are viewed as claiming both parents' racial backgrounds, participants expressed that they may not be attached to both cultures. Some Blaxicans view their cultural identities as both Black and Mexican, while some had an attachment to one more than the other dependent on their upbringing and exposure. Over half of the respondents had an absent parent and, in those cases, many expressed that they missed out on learning about one of their cultural backgrounds. Even for participants raised in single-parent households, there was an expectation that they find ways to learn about and incorporate their other culture into their life experiences and sense of self.

The expectation that Blaxicans are bicultural, in addition to biracial, was encouraged by their parent and perhaps influenced by societal ideas about multiraciality. Expectations imposed by African American and Mexican American peers through authenticity policing may also have had the effect of spurring the development of a bicultural identity. Aside from the encouragement from parents and pressure from peers, Blaxicans expressed deep curiosity about their parents' cultural backgrounds (whether exposed or not) and actively explored that through racial and cultural strategies discussed below.

To convey their chosen identity as Blaxican, participants revealed some of the strategies they used to express their mixed identities. Strategy implies an intentional tactic, and in some cases Blaxicans viewed these expressions as intentional ways to represent being multiracial. But more often how Blaxicans choose to express their identities is not viewed as a strategy but rather an unconscious way of being. Again, Blaxicans make a distinction between racial and cultural identity. Racial identity is a frame of reference represented by physical representations associated with groups of people who often share similar experiences and circumstances. Cultural identity is acquired through interactions with family and the broader environment that occurs by learning the values and behaviors that are appropriate or necessary in that culture.[2]

Some Blaxicans engage in "multiracial balancing" to ensure that people know they are both Black and Mexican. Multiracial balancing involves using racial and cultural expressions to convey an egalitarian mixed identity that borrows from and blends more than one racial-cultural group in a nonhierarchical way. Since whiteness is not a consideration in the formation of dual-minority multiracial identities, representing a balance between two minority backgrounds is important and is a way that Blaxican identities dismantle racial hierarchical thinking. Below we highlight the racial and cultural strategies used to express their Blaxican identities.

Racial Strategies

Some participants view their appearance as conveying a "mixed" look; however, often they are not perceived as mixed with Black and Mexican as a combination. Others are perceived as belonging to various monoracial groups. Participants have varying skin shades from light to dark. All the participants have brown eyes and their natural hair is either curly, wavy, or straight. The tightness of the curl and texture of their hair varied, which was, participants believed, a significant aspect of their appearance that others used to determine their racial perceptions of them and also contributed to participants' perceptions of themselves. Some participants had more visible African American features, such as thicker lips, broader noses, and tightly coiled hair. However, sometimes the participants' darker skin and thicker lips were inherited from their Mexican American parent, according to some respondents.

For example, Julia's Mexican American father is darker than her African American mother, and she points out that she inherited her skin color and features from her father. The respondents interviewed reported that they have never manipulated their skin colors by intentionally tanning, bleaching, or whitening their skin. However, Blaxicans spoke about how their skin has the potential to change dramatically from light to dark depending on seasonal sun exposure and about how that affects the way others perceive them. Some participants viewed their skin tone and hair as effortlessly conveying their mixedness. While others sometimes used multiracial balancing strategies to equalize their appearance to represent both their Blackness and Mexicanness.

Several participants felt that their hair in its natural form conveyed to others that they are mixed. When Andrea was asked to describe her hair she said, "My hair is mixed." Mixed hair is often described as hair that is in-between tightly coiled and straight hair, with variable textures. Skin color and facial features can also add to the perception of having mixed hair. For example, a light-skinned Mexican American woman with curly hair is not likely described as having mixed hair. However, in comparison, a medium- or darker-skinned Blaxican woman with the same texture is more likely to be perceived as having mixed hair. Albert Bennett, from Compton, explained that his hair did the talking for him in terms of letting people know he is mixed. He said,

> I had big curls when I was younger. My mom has a picture of me as a baby, and I had different afros, like a white guy's afro. It's not curly, and it's not straight. It's kinda in-between, and you can't do nothing with it. I kept my hair for a long time because it better helped explain the mix. For a long time, I was getting, "You're just Mexican." So now I'm getting older, and the hair doesn't stay around. I don't want to be like my dad and hang on to whatever piece is left, so I shave everything, and people think, "Oh you are definitely just Mexican."

Albert's discussion of his hair shows that mixed hair is viewed as a self-explanatory expression that is useful in reducing the amount of explaining people ask him to do about his identity. Also, Albert's experience demonstrates that racial and cultural strategies are not always viewed as necessary. At the same time, hair changes just like skin color does, and therefore the use of racial and cultural strategies to express mixedness is not constant.

Often light-skinned Blaxicans resented that people did not view them as Black in addition to Mexican. One racial strategy used to balance their light skin to represent a Blaxican identity was to style their hair in recognizably Afro-centric ways. On the other hand, a few darker-skinned Blaxicans sometimes straightened their hair and felt they appeared Mexican in addition to Black. The role of hair in conveying Blaxican identity was important to both men and women. Hair worn in different styles or in different lengths conveyed the mixed aspect of participants' identities. For instance, Gerardo Jones describes himself as having "Black-straight-Indian" hair and an olive skin tone. When Gerardo wears his hair in locks, he notices that he receives fewer questions by Black people about his racial identity and that he is representing both. In his view, his otherwise straight hair is not an ideal representation of his Blaxican identity.

Other men intentionally styled their hair in ways to ensure that people read them as Blaxican rather than monoracially. For example, Antonio, a twenty-two-year-old man, looked Mexican when he was younger and felt that he looked more like he was both Black and Mexican when he grew his hair longer. He said, "I always looked Mexican, and I look Mexican. I think that was part of the need to identify with my African American side, because it was something that was there but not as overt sometimes. Only when my hair grew out, because it is thick, that I feel like I look Black and Mexican." Antonio engaged in multiracial balancing by growing his hair out to communicate to others that he is both Mexican American and Black. Part of the need to identify with his African American side was related to the fact that he was never perceived as such. Adopting hairstyles, when skin color calls Blackness into question, demonstrates how important it is for Blaxicans to represent both in their appearance.

Furthermore, some lighter-skinned Blaxican men could not manipulate their hair to convey a mixed identity even though desired. James Ramsey a light skinned Blaxican resented the combination of his light skin and straight hair. He said,

> It's tough sometimes because as I was growing up, I was the one with the straighter hair. I was the one that looked different, and I wanted to look Black, bad; I really did. Because I looked up to my dad, and he is like really tall, really big and he's really Black. And I was totally the opposite. I'm not short, but he is like 6'4". So, I am just average height, and he is really big; he was Black and had curly hair and I didn't have that, so I used to always wear a ball

cap. I used to always hide who I was. It is like a total identity crisis; it's like who am I? I talked to other people who are mixed, and they felt the same way. They either went one way or the other. I got a friend who is Black and Asian, and he goes more toward the Black side. I noticed that if you are mixed with Black, you mainly lean more towards the Black side because it is more dominant, like in the physical.

If it was possible, light-skin Blaxicans manipulated their hair to convey a mixed racial identity. It was important to them to look like they were mixed with African American. Many Blaxican men grew their hair out and wore curly or wavy afros or locked their hair. A few of the light-skinned Blaxican men resented their light skin, especially if they had straight hair. These participants always compared themselves to siblings or cousins who looked "more" Blaxican, and they desired a racially mixed aesthetic. For example, James feels that his brother appears mixed with Black and Mexican and wished, as an adolescent, that he looked like him. At the same time, James's brother wanted to look more like James. He said, "It's funny because my brother wished he could look like me. He wishes he had straighter hair. I think he takes his identity a whole different way where he wants to be something else. He shaved his head, moved to Arizona, and he has a baldhead. I think he shaved his head because he wanted to look more Mexican."

This contradictory sense of self between James and his brother is a unique marker of Blaxicanness because it illuminates that Blaxicans have racial options and not all necessarily participate in multiracial balancing. It is important to note that none of the Blaxicans that were interviewed expressed the desire to look less Black overall, only to look more Mexican in addition to Black. Only one interviewee admittedly wanted to look less Black the first time she straightened her hair, which she came to immediately regret. This can be attributed to our sampling strategy, whereby participating in a study about individuals with a Black and Mexican parent may preclude those who may identify monoracially.

In addition to the men in this study, Blaxican women also manipulated their hair in ways to convey a mixed-race identity. Some Blaxican women said that straightening their hair made them feel that they looked more Mexican. Desire, who has a medium complexion, said, "I straighten my hair occasionally; it takes too long so I don't do it a lot, but whenever I do straighten my hair, I feel like I look more Mexican. I feel different when I have straight hair, so inadvertently my hair is a big part of my identity." Wearing their hair in straight or curly styles had the potential of making some women feel different racially. When wearing straight hairstyles, women like Desire recognized themselves in the mirror as Mexican, an affirmation of their mixed identity when they otherwise are perceived as Black due to the pervasiveness of the one-drop rule.

On the other hand, some women felt they looked mixed when they straightened their hair. Erica said, "My hair is not nappy enough to put a perm in it because it will fall out. I've permed it before and it went straight; and I couldn't get it to go back curly, and then it thinned out. It's a weird texture; it's not really nappy, but it's not pretty curls that just hang. When I wear it straight, it's really long. So, when I wear it straight, you can tell then that I'm mixed." Participants' skin color and facial features interacted with the length, texture, style, and tightness of curl in their hair in different ways to convey their mixedness. Manipulation of hair and hairstyles is a strategy used in multiracial balancing to convey a Blaxican identity that equally represents both African Americans and Mexican Americans. Equilibrium is not always achieved but is an expressed ideal.

Cultural Strategies

In addition to expressing their mixedness through their physical appearance, many participants engaged in cultural strategies to demonstrate their Blaxican identity. Style of communication, speaking Spanish, music, dance, cooking and eating ethnic foods, celebrating cultural traditions, symbolic tattoos, religious practices, engaging in travel, taking ethnic studies courses, and joining ethnic-based sororities or fraternities were the most common cultural strategies used.

English and Spanish Code-Switching

Another way Blaxicans express their mixedness is through language alteration in the form of code-switching. In linguistics, code-switching is when a speaker alternates between two or more language varieties in one conversation. Code-switching also occurs when bilingual speakers switch languages between words or within sentences and phrases.[3] In the context of sociology, code-switching is also when a person behaves by a different set of rules, which includes how people speak, depending on the situation.[4]

Blaxicans use mainstream English, African American vernacular English, Spanish, and Spanglish.[5] Spanglish is an informal language mixing Spanish and English and depends on "loan words" or borrowing words from one language and taking it into another.[6] Depending on the audience, Blaxicans switch between using different languages or variations of language as a way of demonstrating their multiraciality and affirming their connection to different communities. For instance, some Blaxicans use Spanish or Spanglish with their Mexican American peers, and at other times they use African American vernacular English around their African American peers to affirm their connection.

For some Blaxicans who are viewed as Black based on appearance, use of Spanish or Spanglish around Mexicans or Mexican Americans demonstrates their connection but also conveys their mixed racial-cultural identities. Depending on the context, Blaxicans use both reproductive and resistant agency regarding cultural norms to either affirm their connections to African Americans and Mexican Americans or resist them. Reproductive agency is replicating norms associated with cultural groups, and resistant agency is defying group norms. Indeed, reproducing cultural social norms was often an ingrained self-expression, but sometimes it was not. Reproduction of cultural norms that required more work was evident in how participants used cultural norms they weren't necessarily comfortable with to "fit in."

Rachel Mabley said,

> I do things in different ways, like speak Spanglish. I wouldn't do that if I was with a group of Black people. I would use different

terms, like what is considered slang. If I'm with a group of Black people, there's some pressure to not seem like I don't want to identify as being Black. Because then it's like, "Oh, you don't want to claim us, then you want to act white." I think that they don't always assume that I'm Mexican, so they'll say that I want to act white because I'm acting different. I don't want that. I don't want them to think that I don't appreciate being Black, so I rather just try to fit in and sometimes those things help me fit in if I am speaking a little different. With Mexican people, I just assume that they see me as someone else anyway because I don't look Mexican, so I will speak more Spanish.

Depending on the audience, Rachel uses the skill of code-switching where she alters her use of language to navigate different social contexts. She uses reproductive agency around her African American friends where she does not speak Spanglish or Spanish but rather "slang" to signal she is not distancing herself from Blackness. In the presence of her Mexican American peers, she speaks Spanglish-Spanish, which could be considered reproductive agency to show her connection to them. However, because she is viewed as Black, it is also resistant agency to affirm her mixedness and rejection of monoracial norms. This is another example of how the Blaxicans that were interviewed do not desire to distance themselves from being Black but rather use racial and cultural strategies to solidify an identity that is Black in addition to Mexican.

While both resistant and reproductive agency is used to express different objectives (i.e., connection, showing that they are not distancing from Blackness, or conveying a mixed identity), some Blaxicans are more engaged with using resistant agency. Using resistant agency shows less concern with fitting in culturally with each group. Rather, by defying norms, Blaxicans stretch group boundaries and create in-between spaces accommodating to people that do not "fit in." For instance, Andrea, a thirty-two-year-old woman from Los Angeles, looks Black to most people and speaks Spanish fluently. Speaking Spanish is a strategy she uses to convey to others that she is Blaxican.

Andrea grew up in a bilingual Spanish-English home. She watched *telenovelas*, or Spanish-language soap operas, and spoke Spanish forty hours per week at her job. The first reaction she gets from Latinas/os who see her speaking Spanish is that they stare at her and try to recall if they said anything negative about her or about Black people in her presence. The next reaction is that they ask her where she is from and inquire about how she learned to speak Spanish so well. Andrea said,

> Looking at me, most people wouldn't think I'm Latina anyway. So, there is no expectation that I am supposed to speak Spanish. What is interesting is that I get the opposite. They'll be people that come up to me and they'll think because I'm Black that they need to talk to me a certain way. Like 'What's up girl?' I don't even talk like that. But because I'm Black, what you see on TV, WB, UPN, and everyone is cussing or whatever, slang, they think that is how I'm going to talk.[7]

Andrea instead speaks Spanish at times to reflect that she is Blaxican and outside of the expectations others have of her. Because people assume she is Black, Andrea uses her agency to resist cultural expectations that she speak in a specific way.

Overall, Blaxicans use their agency to both reproduce and resist cultural norms, and often stereotypes associated with Mexican Americans and African Americans depending on the context. Reproductive and resistant agency is used to accomplish expressions of identity related to being Blaxican. Sometimes these cultural strategies are used to affirm their connections to both communities, and often they are used to assert their multiracial identities as Blaxican.

Dance and Music

One of the indicators of how participants identified with African American and Mexican American cultures and how they expressed their Blaxican identities was through music, dance, and arts. For instance, LaTrice attended Mexican *bailes*, or large-scale dances featuring live bands playing *banda* music. Gaby joined recreational centers in her youth that taught African dance. Talia participated in African

Brazilian dance and Spanish dance. Monica Bell danced ballet *folklórico* throughout her childhood. Participating in these cultural dances allows some Blaxicans to learn more about the culture and provides them an outlet of expressing their mixed culture.

Rachel found that enrolling in capoeira, a Brazilian martial art, was a way to engage her African ancestry. Rachel said, "You know what's interesting? I started playing capoeira, it's a Brazilian martial art and that culture has a lot of African influence. It is really interesting because I found myself relating to a lot of Black Brazilians in that culture because a lot of them are a mixture of African and indigenous people." Some Blaxicans found commonality when exposed to Afro-Brazilian and other Afro-Latina/o cultures, even though not their own because of the mixture. Capoeira, for example, is a martial art originally developed by enslaved Africans in Brazil and has since come to represent the national identity as mixed people or mestiços.[8]

Participants also discussed how music gave them an outlet to express their Blaxican identities and how they were influenced by their parents' musical preferences. Vanessa, from Georgia, recalled that her Mexican American mother and African American father listened to Spanish-language music and hip-hop growing up: "I think the blending of music is equal because my mom listens to Mexican music on the holidays. My dad's side we listen to hip-hop and pop. I grew up with that culturally." Dan's choice in music was also influenced by his Mexican mother and African American father.

> DAN: That's one thing that people notice about me at school—that I listen to all kinds of different music. They say that I can be in a study area listening to music and they pass by me a couple of times, and they say one time I am listening to hip-hop and the next minute they come around and it's something in Spanish.
> REBECCA: How do people react to your preference in music?
> DAN: They think it's cool that I listen to a variety of music. I don't get too much of a big response from Mexican people because a lot of them grew up here in the U.S., and they also listen to the mainstream and Spanish music. Blacks, most of them don't listen

to music in Spanish, so sometimes they act surprised, or they say that my Mexican side is coming out.

Dan's example illustrates how his preference for music associated with his parents' cultures reinforces the bicultural aspect of his identity.

Similarly, Fernando Thomas, a thirty-seven-year-old nurse from San Jose, California, blended both of his parents' cultures through music. His parents were divorced and while residing with his African American father, Fernando listened to R&B and Spanish music on the weekends with his Mexican American mother. Likewise, Zahira Davis's Mexican mother introduced her to regional Mexican music in Spanish. Now as an adult Zahira somedays belts out the lyrics to Selena, the late Mexican American Tejana pop star, and on other days she listens to neo soul and R&B depending on her mood. LaTrice watches popular Spanish-language telenovelas and prefers music in Spanish. LaTrice listens to Spanish-language rock and pop and enjoys dancing to salsa and merengue. Salsa and merengue originate from Puerto Rico, Cuba, and the Dominican Republic, respectively, and are musical forms that are popular among many Latinas/os in the United States regardless of origin.

Like all musical genres, different types of Mexican music in Spanish reflect various class dimensions. Eduardo's Mexican father exposed him to music in Spanish from Latin America and Spanish-language music from Mexico that is considered more urban rather than country. On the other hand, his Mexican American fraternity brothers exposed Eduardo to Mexican music from the northern regions of Mexico that is influenced by *el rancho*, akin to poor people's country music. Eduardo said, "My fraternity brothers and I would take road trips to Fresno and Chico, and they would always play Banda El Recodo and force me to listen to it. I really didn't like it at first, but then it grew on me. You go to parties and that is all you would hear so it grew on me. So, I remember singing, 'Y Llegaste Tú' and, like, all these other songs."

On the other hand, Eduardo's father, from Mexico City, disliked and did not identify with some of the popular music from the northern and border regions of Mexico. Eduardo said, "Growing up my dad hated all that music; he hates that style. We listen to, like, modernized Spanish music. It was not like the country style, country Mexican. It was really more modern I guess." Not only did Eduardo view Spanish music as a cultural expression of his identity but he also contemplated the class and regional meanings that Spanish music had for him as a Blaxican living in Northern California as opposed to his father, a native of Mexico City.

James also used music as an expression of his Blaxican identity. James is an aspiring artist who records music. He said, "When I first got into the music business, I did a song where I mixed my culture into it, you know fifty-fifty on the Black and the Brown side and stuff. I have done that and that is how you are as a Blaxican, you know?" As an artist James expresses his African American and Mexican American sides by incorporating both influences into his music. Kun analyzes Mexican African American fusion of music in Los Angeles by the Mexican musical group Akwid, who rap over sampled banda music beats. He argues that hybrid African American Mexican forms of music in Los Angeles signal a changing racial and ethnic landscape, which constitute artists as "cultural crossfaders."

Kun states, "The ability of the DJ working in an African American art form to scratch over Mexican music is the ability to be a cultural crossfader, a DJ who can cut between the cultures he or she lives in, a DJ who understands cultural exchange and cultural collision well enough to make music out of it."[9] The above examples show that Blaxicans use music as an expression affirming their connection to their parents' cultures; they bring their parents' cultures together in their musical preferences or sometimes "crossfade" them into their own musical creations. Musical preferences or creations are cultural strategies used to affirm connections to or resist monoracial cultural norms.

Enchiladas and Gumbo

Food is one of the tangible forms of connection with culture in everyday life. African American and Mexican American cuisine were often on the dinner menu for our participants, and sometimes meals were a combination of the two. Rachel said, "We'll have enchiladas for dinner one day, then gumbo the next day. It's kinda seamless because that is just the way I grew up." Talia said, "I eat Mexican food, but I don't eat it every single day. If I go to my grandmother's house, I would be eating soul food. I pretty much learned how to cook both." Blaxicans reinforced their racial-culture mixtures through the foods they cook and eat. Foods such as posole, collard greens, menudo, barbecue, tacos, and black-eyed peas are examples of dishes prepared and enjoyed.

Mexican and soul food are hybridized cuisines that have in common African, Native, and European influences that share some similarities in histories and ingredients. For example, both cuisines are influenced by ingredients and methods used by indigenous peoples of the Americas. Maize, or ground corn, is used to make cornbread, grits, hush puppies, hominy, and masa used to make tortillas and tamales. Animal fat (lard or *manteca*) is used to bake or fry such foods as biscuits or carnitas. Mexican and soul food also take after Indigenous tradition in that, when cooking meat, the entire animal is used in cuisine. It is common to use organ meats, such as brain, liver, and intestines in food dishes like chitlins and *tripas*. Mexican cuisine also has African influence evident in its use of peanuts, plantain, cassava (yuca), malanga, taro, and sweet potatoes. In addition, *arroz Mexicana*, *agua de Jamaica*, mole, and barbecued goat have West African influence.[10] Interestingly, traditional Mexican cuisines often represent a blending of cultures but are viewed as monolithic. Making the two types of cuisines staples on the dinner table represents an affirmation of Blaxican identity, a new kind of racial-cultural mixture.

Cooking and eating soul food or Mexican food was not generally viewed as an intentionally strategic means of "proving" Blaxicanness; rather, enjoying these cuisines is viewed as a normal part of Blaxican upbringing that is taken for granted and contributes to a sense of identity. In fact, the blending of African American and Mexican American food practices occurs in the privacy of their homes and sharing it with family. Most participants were exposed to the foods of their backgrounds by parents and family members. For example, although Fernando's parents were divorced, he ate Mexican food and African American food, depending on which parent he was staying with. At the same time, the extent and fluidity of cultural exchanges between African Americans and Mexican Americans were apparent in how Blaxicans described their parents' borrowing and blending of cooking practices. Some Blaxicans' Mexican American parents cooked soul food, while African American parents cooked and regularly consumed Mexican food. In Oakland, California, Talia's Mexican American single mother cooked soul food and Mexican food, and Talia was raised consuming both styles of food. She said, "My mother could cook soul food, Mexican food, and the whole works. She has brothers and sisters mixed with Black. Christmas Eve it was always separate, Christmas Eve we would have Mexican food: tamales, mole, everything. Christmas day, everybody would go to their own house and have turkey, ham, dressing, and greens. I eat tamales, chorizo, and mole. So, I have always been exposed to it all, even the pastries. So, I never missed out, and I love that part of my culture."

Talia's mother acquired knowledge about cooking soul food and Mexican food through her Mexican American grandmother who was from San Antonio, Texas. Talia's mother and grandmother adopted many African American cultural practices in addition to cooking soul food. This can be attributed to the fact that Talia's grandmother was exposed to African American culture through her past relationships. Talia's grandmother has ten children, five of whom are part-African American. When she initially moved to Oakland from San Antonio, Talia's grandmother was embraced and mentored by an elderly African American woman who taught her a great deal about cooking and about life. Witnessing family members engage in this type of cultural exchange through food was a powerful affirmation of participants' mixed identities.

Indeed, Blaxicans are exposed to food from both sides of their culture by their parent(s), who learned to cook these foods in places where the cultural exchange between African Americans and Mexican Americans seemed to be a built-in part of the social landscape. In places such as Los Angeles and Oakland, California, participants' parents could easily access foods, ingredients, and grocery stores catering to each cooking style. Many times, sharing knowledge about cooking practices was also facilitated through their parents' personal connections fostered across racial lines in the form of friendships or intimate relationships. These cross-racial-cultural connections modeled the blending and blurring of lines and boundaries and informed Blaxican identity formations.

For instance, some participants who grew up in relatively segregated areas that were predominately Mexican American and immigrant shared that their African American parent adopted Mexican cultural food practices. Zahira's African American father from El Paso, Texas, cooked and regularly ate tacos, flautas, carnitas, and other Mexican foods. Zahira's father was also able to communicate in Spanish and even had a Spanish accent. Likewise, Desire's African American father, from New Mexico, cooks *menudo*, and she believes that he is culturally Mexican. Desire said, "My dad was constantly surrounded by Mexican people when he grew up in Deming, and so my dad cooks *menudo*." These are a few examples of how African Americans who live in predominately Mexican or Mexican American spaces meld and mesh with Mexican culture, marry into Mexican American families, and influence Blaxican identities. Learning from their parents' modeling in the adoption of Mexican American or African American culture through food as one form of expression became part of how Blaxicans understand their cultural mixedness.

While food was an affirmation of their own racial-cultural mixedness, the conversations centering on the topic of food often went back to people's questioning of their racial-cultural identities. Eating certain ethnic foods in public sometimes drew unwanted attention to their identities by outsiders. For example, Erica's Mexican American mother packed her tamales for lunch when she attended the third grade in Indiana. One of her Latina classmates saw her eating and decided to interrogate her about her identity. Erica said,

> My mom had packed me tamales for lunch, and I was like, "Alright, no big deal, I love tamales, whatever." I wasn't even thinking about it; I got my lunch, and this Venezuelan girl was like, "Where did you get those?" I was like, "My mom, she made them for me." And

because I'm dark, really don't look mixed either, she was like, "What is your mom?" I'm like, "She's Mexican." She was like, "No she's not, you're Black." I'm like, "Well my mom is Mexican." And she was like, "No, she's not you're Black. Why are you trying to claim something you're not?" I remember just thinking that it struck me right there that how did I look? My hair is Black, I have Black hair, it's not nappy, nappy, but I don't really look very mixed. I just remember thinking how do I look right here eating this tamale? Do I look weird? And the Venezuelan girl was telling me, basically to my face, that it was weird and didn't look right and what the hell was I doing?

Eating tamales for lunch at school as a Blaxican girl was an experience Erica took for granted during her childhood. Because she appeared Black to her Latina peer, she was questioned for eating Mexican food and told she was "claiming something" she is not. These types of interactions simply informed Blaxicans of how they are perceived by outsiders but did not persuade them into following monoracial norms or cultural expectations.

Religion and Traditions

The majority of Blaxicans interviewed had one religious belief system they followed or were not religious at all. Most of the one-faith participants were Mexican Catholic. When asked about specific religious traditions they engaged in, many identified Mexican American traditions particularly practiced around Christmas. For example, Dan said the way that he and his family celebrated Christmas was heavily connected to Mexican-style Catholicism. Dan exchanges gifts with his family on January 6, celebrating the day of the arrival of the Three Wise Men to Jesus's birth site. Likewise, LaTrice celebrates Las Posadas, a nine-day celebration from December 16 until December 24 that involves a reenactment of Joseph and the expectant mother Mary's procession in search of a home to birth Jesus. Las Posadas is a chiefly Mexican Catholic ritual also celebrated in parts of Latin America. These are important religious traditions passed down through generations.

In addition, a few of the Blaxican women had quinceañeras, a coming-of-age ceremony, replete with rituals, for young girls turning fifteen. Quinceañeras are celebrated in Mexico and among Mexican Americans in the United States and are a blend of pre-Columbian and Spanish traditions.[11] Interestingly, a few Blaxican women said they chose not to have quinceañeras because they are not religious and are racially mixed. Quinceañeras are regarded as extensions of Catholic sacraments, as rites of passage, and as a practice representing historical continuation of tradition.[12]

While these celebrations are secular coming-of-age ceremonies, they have strong religious overtones and usually involve a mass dedicated in the fifteen-year-old's honor. For some of the women in our study, having a quinceañera was viewed as reserved only for monoracial Mexican American girls, not racially mixed ones. For instance, Rachel said, "I never had a quinceañera because I'm mixed and that would be weird. But I do identify a lot with Mexican culture." The quinceañera publicly enacts a culturally specific identity as a Mexican woman. The meanings tied to these ceremonies are replete with ideas about essential group identities.[13] This very visible display of a rite of passage to cultural group identity is better avoided for a Blaxican woman. Having a quinceañera would have been an invitation to interrogate her claims to Mexican authenticity.

A few participants were exposed to and navigated dual faith families but ultimately only practiced one faith. Talia Ramos navigated a dual-faith family where some of her family members are Catholic while others are Baptist. Talia's Mexican American mother was Catholic and converted to Baptist. Talia said, "My mom was Catholic as a child. Then in Oakland, this Black lady had raised them. So, then they started taking them to church with them, and she became Baptist. Then that is how I grew up, as Baptist." Talia grew up Baptist, a faith encouraged by her Mexican American mother, but has extended family members on her mother's side who are practicing Catholics. Talia said,

> When I was younger and I went to a Black church, it wasn't anybody that was white or any other color except my mother. That was a little different. When my grandmother died and family came for

the funeral, they were all Catholic. So things that we did that were different to them they were so not used to, and things that they did we were not used to. Because when I was younger, you didn't wear pants to church. They were Catholic, and they wore pants to church. OK, we were like that is not something you do.

Talia's Mexican American mother converted to the Baptist religion through the influence of her African American friend and mentor. Talia's mother was the only non-African American person at their church in Oakland. When Talia's extended Mexican American family attended her grandmother's funeral, there were notable differences in religious norms and mores. Although Talia was exposed to more than one religious option, she practices her mother's Baptist faith.

Several Blaxican participants noted that they were taught more than one religion in their socialization through their parents and extended family members and chose both. For instance, Sabrina has two faiths, "Christian" and "Catholic." She said, "I was raised Christian and Catholic, so I would go to Christian church, and I would go to the Spanish Catholic church with my friend's family." Sabrina navigates being both Christian and Catholic, and while there are significant differences between them, Catholicism is a form of Christianity, so there is enough similarity to easily navigate both. On the other hand, a few participants chose neither of their parents' religions. For example, Gaby was raised as Baptist and Catholic and navigated both religions all her life. She said,

> My mom's side they are Baptist and my dad's side they are Catholic. So the grandmothers never came together because whenever they did, they would start arguing about religion; so it was really weird. I would go from one church to another, and it was odd. So now it made me agnostic, and I say agnostic because I really don't know, because I really am confused; so I don't claim anything. But if and when I do go to church, I go to Catholic church. I got confused, like I didn't belong to any of the churches, like I was a visitor at each one of them.

Gaby decided as an adult to be agnostic and didn't feel at home in either church. In addition, Gaby forwent baptism into either religion, explaining that doing so would symbolize disloyalty and insincerity. Instead of choosing one religion, Gaby chose neither. This is an example of how some Blaxicans, when presented with the expectation to choose an either/or aspect of their identities, choose both or neither. Gaby chooses neither of her parents' religions and decided to be agnostic. Altogether, the majority of participants were Catholic or nonreligious. A few participants were introduced to multiple faiths by their parents and either practiced one, both, or none. In Gaby's case the conflicting belief systems of her African American and Mexican American family members caused her to choose neither as a way of symbolizing her unwillingness to choose one.

Blaxican Identities and Collective Subjectivities

A few Blaxicans that were interviewed traveled outside of the United States, and some ventured out of the country not in a physical sense but by researching and reading about people in different places. Physical and imaginative travel allowed these participants to gain a global perspective on Blackness and *Latinidad*. In other words, they were able to understand, through direct experience or by learning about the experiences of others, what it meant to be Latina/o and Black in other countries. Imagining how people who look like them are treated and perceived on a global scale broadened their ideas of what their identities mean outside of the restrictions placed on them in the United States.

Gaining a Global Perspective on Race

In the United States many Blaxicans are viewed and treated as Black in accordance with the one-drop rule. Exploring people mixed with African, Indigenous, and European ancestry outside the United States, some Blaxicans discovered that the one-drop rule does not apply in the same way and that in some places mixed people are the hegemonic norm, albeit politically, socially, and economically marginal.

For example, Antonio sometimes travels to Mexico to reconnect with his father's side but always feels that Brazil or Puerto Rico are more fitting places for him, even though he has never visited. Antonio said, "When I would see places like Puerto Rico or Brazil, for the longest time Brazil became this home to me because of what it represents. It represents a place, an identity where you are Brazilian. You say that it means that you are African, Native, European mixed and you are also everything."

Imagined communities are popularized in the media via print capitalism and allow people to identify with a group using images and vernacular.[14] Even though Antonio has not visited Puerto Rico or Brazil, the images he has seen of these countries allow him to envision himself as part of those communities. He imagines Brazil as "home" because of its perceived inclusivity for multiracial people. Indeed, Brazil has an extensive history of miscegenation, and the population is differentiated into a ternary racial project of whites, multiracials, and Blacks.[15] Compared to the U.S. Black white dichotomous thinking about race, Brazil offers a space for more flexibility.

Comparably, Debra travels a lot to other countries and has noticed the different ways people perceive her. In the United States people assume she is Black, and in other countries she is perceived as something other than Black. She said,

> In the United States people perceived me as Black. I've asked them. Sometimes when they ask me that question [what are you?], I ask them "Well what do you think?" And they always say, I just assumed you were Black. Some people, it depends upon the time of the year, which makes a difference because of the sun. When I am whiter a lot of people will say, well maybe we thought you were from Bermuda, some island. The minute I get off the plane in Mexico, nobody will speak English to me, they know I am Mexican from jump. They have no problem with it. In other countries they tend to think I am from the islands; they don't think I am Black. But in America they assume I am Black. I travel a lot in other countries. I have always found it interesting that Americans will tend to not

only assume but take actions and make judgments based upon their faulty assumptions in the first place.

Traveling to other countries has shown Debra the pervasiveness of the one-drop rule in demarcating people as Black. In other countries, such as Mexico, Debra finds that her racial-cultural identity is less restrictive, which she appreciates while traveling. Experiencing or imagining places like Puerto Rico, Brazil, and Mexico as spaces where multiracial people are considered normative is validating. These spaces outside of the U.S. Black white binary and its accompanying one-drop rule offers the impression of belonging. They are also a respite from the questioning, as well as invalidating, experiences that typically accompany the microaggressions mentioned in chapter 12.

Ethnic Studies and Social Organizations

Since over half the study participants had at least some college experience, many pursued ethnic studies courses to learn more about African Americans and Mexican Americans. Studying the social, political, and economic histories of these two groups in the United States resulted in a deeper understanding of their dual-minority multiracial identities. Participation in these types of courses facilitated a comparative understanding of the contributions and oppression of Mexican American and African Americans, in addition to an examination of racial hierarchies. Ethnic studies courses enabled Blaxicans to make connections between the similarities that Mexican Americans and African Americans share in terms of colonization, low and unpaid labor, institutional and individual racism, and prejudice. Participation in these courses deepened an understanding of their connection to African Americans and Mexican Americans.

For the Blaxicans who enrolled in ethnic studies courses, some took classes in both Black studies and Chicana/o studies. On the other hand, some selected to take courses in the area they were most familiar with because of their cultural upbringing, while others took courses in the area with which they were least familiar. For example, Selena Fernandez was raised by her African American mother in

Santa Barbara, California, and as a college student in Northern California she enrolled in Black studies courses. She said,

> My friend's mom is really ethnocentric and is always pushing me to take some Chicano studies classes and get in touch with my Mexican half. It's like OK, I will maybe eventually, but I mean I don't know, my Mexican half of the family puts me down all the time for not knowing Spanish and stuff, and I don't really have a good relationship with my dad, and I am more in touch with my Black half. There is not really an incentive to want to learn about my Mexican half. I know stuff, I am not culturally ignorant on my Mexican half, but as far as doing studies to further my knowledge about the culture [the motivation] is not really there. It is there for my Black half because I did take a Black studies class this year.

Although Selena knows about Mexican American culture, she is more inclined to take courses in Black studies. Her Mexican American side of the family shames her for not being fluent in Spanish, which turns her off to the idea of taking a Chicana/o studies class.

Some Blaxicans joined race-based clubs, sororities, or fraternities while in high school or college. Most Blaxicans joined multicultural organizations, while a few joined Latina/o-based clubs with multicultural memberships. Multicultural fraternities or sororities were chosen because participants wanted to express and represent both their Mexican American and African American heritages. LaTrice was involved in a multicultural and Spanish club in high school, and in college she joined a multicultural sorority. In Spanish club LaTrice's peers viewed her as Mexican because she was able to speak Spanish fluently and identified as culturally Mexican.

LaTrice's multicultural sorority was a space where she represented her Blaxicanness by code-switching. The sorority was a space where racial-cultural differences were recognized, validated, and respected. She said,

> We are all different ethnicities. We have workshops where we invite the public and have discussions about race. All of our discussions

are about the difference between African American–based organizations and about respecting other organizations. We educate each other on our ethnicities. I have a sorority sister who is half-Nicaragüense and Colombian, and she told us about that. I have one who is Black and Irish, and she tells us about that. Socially we tell each other, and then we have seminars where we open up to the public and people come and discuss race.

Multicultural college organizations are spaces where Blaxicans educate others about their identities and experiences. Being involved in such organizations is a cultural strategy to show others that they are Black and Mexican. Multiracial college students educate others about multiracial issues and use support networks' coping strategies to combat prejudice and discrimination.[16] LaTrice's participation in her multicultural sorority gave her a network of other multiracial women as support and a place to engage in education with others about mixed-race experiences.

Comparably, Eduardo was involved in a multicultural fraternity at his college, and he joined because he is Black and Mexican. Eduardo explained why he chose a multicultural fraternity as opposed to a Black fraternity. He said,

> I probably could have been in a Black fraternity, because like I said I relate to them more, but like, I am going to represent both my cultures. But just because I am Black and Mexican that is pretty much why I joined a multicultural fraternity because it represents what I stand for and believe in. I believe in other people's cultures like everybody has the right to their own cultures and beliefs so I will always respect their cultures to learn more about them. Not to be ignorant, so not be one sided, but that is pretty much why I didn't join another fraternity.

Some of Eduardo's fraternity brothers are Filipino, Indian, Japanese, white, and Nigerian Pakistani, but the majority are Latino. Eduardo said, "Well it is funny because right now we say we are multicultural, but most of the members are Latino. That is the reason that when I have to be around my brothers, I tend to represent more of my African American side to get more new members because all you see is Latino. So, if I want to recruit different people of different cultures and colors, I have to represent my other side too." To recruit non-Latino members, Eduardo "represents" his African American side. He said, "I know there is no such thing as really acting Black, but I guess I tend to relate or pit myself with Black people." Eduardo is most often perceived as Mexican American based on his appearance and feels the need to represent his African American side. Eduardo engages in demonstrating his African American side by talking in a way that conveys that he is aligned with Black people ideologically and socially.

In addition, Erica, Sabrina, and Zahira chose to join Latina-based sororities, but ones that accepted a multicultural membership. Sabrina, who was raised by her African American mother, also joined the Chicano theater program at her college that did a lot of organizing. For example, during César Chávez Day and Mexican Independence Day her group organized campus rallies. Sabrina's sorority was involved in the local Mexican community and volunteered service hours by visiting elderly homes.

Sabrina viewed her community service work as a way to learn more about the Mexican aspect that is missing from her cultural upbringing and did not feel the need to get involved with her African American side for that purpose. This is another example of multiracial balancing and one of the strategies that Blaxicans engaged in to learn, understand, and represent both of their racial-cultural backgrounds. Sabrina participated in a Latina-based sorority because she wanted to learn more about her Mexican American side and Latinas/os in general.

On the other hand, Erica was raised by her Mexican American mother and missed out on learning about Black culture in her upbringing. Erica desired knowing about both sides of her racial-cultural background and believed that was the true expression of a Blaxican identity. One of the strategies she used to learn about her Black side was to join her sorority. She said,

> The sorority is about promoting cultural awareness and finding out about yourself—taking a moment to find out who you are so that you can help other people and other women. I joined the sorority, and I went to some convention, and I didn't see any other Blaxicans that I know of. But it's a multicultural membership, and I saw other women embracing their culture. They knew everything about themselves. My sorority sister knew everything about her culture, and she knew all her stuff, and I just wanted to know all my stuff. I wanted to know, and I wish I knew more about my African heritage. I learned more about my African American self, and I was just scared to embrace it. I started researching, and I became so fired up; I started meeting other Blaxicans.

Joining a sorority encouraged Erica to start researching, learning about, and embracing her African American culture and heritage. It also gave her the courage to embrace her African American heritage as part of her identity. The reason it took courage to embrace her African American side was because she was raised by a Mexican American single parent, grew up in a predominately white area, and didn't feel comfortable in her cultural competence about African Americans until she went to college.

Overall, college experiences, including taking ethnic studies classes and joining multicultural and Latina-based Greek life, served as spaces for Blaxicans to learn more about aspects of their dual-minority multiracial identities. Some enrolled in classes in both Black and Chicana/o studies, while others enrolled in just one subfield. For those who chose one subfield, their decision was based on desiring a stronger understanding of one or the other. And sometimes that decision was based on obtaining knowledge they viewed was absent from their upbringing as a way of connecting to authentic Blaxican identity. In addition, the Blaxicans who participated in Greek life all selected fraternities or sororities that accepted a multicultural membership, even if the participants were mainly Latina/o. These spaces gave them an outlet in college to represent "both sides" through recruitment and engagement. Community service and educational workshops and events gave them the opportunity to learn more about Mexican Americans and African Americans and were places to educate the public about being Blaxican. Fraternities and sororities offered a space to network with diverse groups of students that they found to be accepting and supportive of their Blaxican identities.

Blaxican Invisibility

One common theme that emerged in interviews was the sense of the invisibility of Blaxican identities and experiences in the dominant culture. Indeed, dual-minority multiracials, and Blaxicans in particular, are not represented in television or other mass media. Mass media plays an important role in how people view themselves and how others perceive them. Other groups, such as Native Americans, also experience invisibility, which has had the effect of limiting how people understand themselves and how they fit into contemporary social life.[17] Many participants grappled with the experience of invisibility. On the one hand, invisibility was described as isolating because of the lack of a social script that could be followed. On the other hand, invisibility invites a sense of freedom to construct a script as one goes through life, one that is less confined to norms based on race and culture.

Even as multiracials have become more visible in the media and popular imagination some participants recognized that most dual-minority multiracials are ignored and erased from the popular imagination. Andrea said,

> I never seen anything by anybody that talks about growing up with these two cultures. It is always Black and white, or Amerasian. You don't hear about Black and Brown; you don't hear about Brown and Asian. Uniquely, Black and white. I think because that white is in there, it is more accepted because it is more of the norm. For some people you are supposed to aspire to want to be white; that's like a step-up. Whereas Black and Brown, there is some of that, I

don't believe that, but there is that mentality. But it is a little more accepted to be mixed with white. Then the lighter you are, the better.

When multiracial people are visible and have representation, they almost always have white parentage. Andrea recognizes that white multiracials are the most accepted and visible because of their adjacency to whiteness and presumably because they have lighter skin. Andrea asserts that Black Brown or Asian Brown dual-minority multiracials are less visible and accepted because it is more accepted be mixed with white. Indeed, if academia is one indication, most writing and teaching on multiraciality focuses on people who are part white.[18] Erica, from the Midwest, is also convinced that Blaxican identity is marginalized because the white component is removed. Both Andrea and Erica, like other participants, recognize that their ancestry, which includes European heritage, is a product of colonization. Nonetheless, they recognize that ancestry is not the same as having white parentage as a first-generation mixed-race person.

Interestingly, Erica compares Blaxican identities to that of Afro-Latinos. She said, "Blaxicans hang out in the background because you're not mixed Black and white, and you're not Puerto Rican, and you're not Dominican. They got their whole Afrocentric side, the Dominicans, and the Puerto Ricans. They could embrace the part of them that is influenced by their African heritage, or whatever, but Blaxicans, not really. Most Blaxicans don't know that there are such things as Afro-Mexicans and most Mexicans don't even know that, and most Black people definitely don't know that."

Erica feels that Blaxicans "hang out in the background" or are not visible and accepted because they are not mixed with white and are different from Afro-Latinos. She correctly points out that some Blaxicans, Mexican Americans, and African Americans are not aware of the history and presence of Afro-Mexicans in Mexico. This speaks to the fact that, unlike some other Latin American countries where an African presence is more visible, and therefore virtually impossible to ignore, Mexico often negates African influence and ancestry. Offering a national ideology of mestizaje that proposes that all Mexicans are the same, that is, of Spanish and Indigenous ancestry, "worked as an ideology to help keep race below the social radar and better safeguard white power."[19] The erasure and invisibility of knowledge about African ancestry among Mexicans and Mexican Americans makes it challenging for Erica to carve a space as Blaxican within Mexican American and African American communities.

Erica reasons that, because Afro-Latinos have a common group history that includes miscegenation in the colonial era tied to a national history, it is easier for them to embrace and be accepted as Black and Latina/o and have an "Afro-centric side." On the other hand, Blaxicans do not have a script or a collective narrative informing them of who they are as a historical or social group apart from multiracials as a group. Yet within multiracial groups they are invisible and not thought about. Rather, Blaxicans draw from two seemingly separate racial-cultural group histories and from the struggles of African Americans and Mexican Americans in a postcolonial era. Furthermore, Blaxican culture is not visible or as defined as Afro-Latino cultures and visibility in the Midwest or East Coast of the United States. Again, this experience of invisibility is perceived as isolating but at the same time an invitational opportunity to create and build community with other Blaxicans.

Blaxican Community

In addition to not seeing themselves reflected in the media or existing in the general public's imagination, participants also sense a lack of community with other Blaxicans. While it is almost a guarantee that monoracial people will live near one another, largely because of segregation, and can find a physical community, Blaxicans often do not have that experience. As previously mentioned, most participants knew fewer than three Blaxicans outside of their own siblings. There was indeed a lack of community or a feeling of affinity with other Blaxicans who share common interests, especially in a physical space. In the face of invisibility and the lack of a physical community, how then do Blaxicans experience community or try to create one?

Only one participant articulated having regular interaction with and a physical community of a relatively larger group of Blaxicans, and her experience gives insight to the significance of a Blaxican community. Erica from the Midwest has five close Blaxican friends, in addition to a Blaxican brother and three Blaxican cousins, all of whom live in her hometown.

> ERICA: Where I used to live there were five other Blaxicans that were not related to me. I know all of them, and one of them I am mentoring; she's an undergrad, and another one is my mentor in law school; she's Blaxican. It is really rare because it is such a small town in Indiana to come across so many Blaxicans. This is the most there has ever been in this town.
>
> REBECCA: Why were there so many Blaxicans in that town?
>
> ERICA: It's because northern Indiana, Gary, and Chicago have Black neighborhoods and Mexican neighborhoods. In northern Indiana because a lot of Black people went there for industrial work a long time ago for the steel mills, and a lot of Mexican people went there as well. That is a really poor area right now, but people just mixed and then children end up coming to IU [Indiana University] Bloomington, so I think that is why there is at least ten people who are Blaxican. I guess we could be considered a little community because we all know each other. When we're together we're like 'Oh, Blaxican!' We are proud of it.

Erica explains in that in northern Indiana, African American and Mexican American communities were drawn to work in the industrial sector and had the same class status. African Americans and Mexican Americans worked in proximity to one another and had interracial relationships resulting in Blaxican children. In college Erica built community with the other Blaxican undergraduates she knew. While it is rare to find physical community with other Blaxicans, Erica gives us an account of a space where she finds a sense of belonging.

She continued:

> There is definitely a much stronger bond with my Blaxican friends. I feel like my mentor, she's Blaxican, and the girl that I mentor, she's

Blaxican, and when we hang out it's just incredible. I don't have to worry about them saying, "Oh, you not shaking your hips right" or, "You're not 2-steppin' right." Or I don't have to worry about them saying, "Oh, your Spanish sucks," any of that. I don't have to worry about them thinking that I talk white, or I don't have to worry about them thinking that I dress white, or that I'm not hip-hop enough to them, or that I'm not Mexican enough one day or the next. . . . I love hanging out with my Blaxican friends because there is not judgment there. They don't look at you funny like, "Oh, you're not doing this right." Or "You look silly when you do it like that." Pretty much when it comes to dancing that's where you get a lot of shit for how we dance. We can never dance good enough that's for sure.

Erica is at ease when she is around her Blaxican friends and is confident they will not judge her for not being "Black or Mexican enough." Erica can talk, dress, dance, and act how she is comfortable. In her Blaxican circle she does not feel pressured to choose one group over the other. There is a mutual standpoint and understanding of affirming both African American and Mexican American aspects of identity and the ambiguities and contradictions that emerge for doing so. One contradiction may be that Erica is half-Mexican and doesn't speak Spanish fluently, or that she is half-Black and doesn't know how to dance a particular hip-hop dance.

Scholar Gloria Anzaldúa calls for a consciousness of the borderlands, or an in-between state, where there is tolerance for contradictions and ambiguity.[20] From this borderlands space, Erica and her Blaxican peers can appreciate the idea of multiple identities, not from a single source but from many historical sources at the same time, and accept the contradictions that arise. Erica describes her experience of having a Blaxican community as "incredible"; it is a place where she is not invisible and can commune with others that share a Blaxican experience and identity.

The lack of Blaxican community, in a physical sense, prompted some Blaxicans to search for a virtual one on the internet. Even Erica, who had the largest physical community, attempted to build community via the internet when she was in college. She said,

> I search out other Blaxicans, so I have Blaxican friends that I have met online or who I have met living in other places like when I lived in California. The Blaxicans that I meet online, and a lot of Blaxicans, have a unique feeling about ourselves. It's a good feeling and at the same time it's a bitter feeling. I don't think that we come together enough; I think there are so many Blaxicans out there, and I think that we can come together. I seek them out. We need to get together more; we need to do this. I think we should have a conference or something. I really want to promote Blaxican [identity]; I really want to make people start talking to each other and knowing that we share similar experiences and making more of a community even nation-wide.

Erica used the advantages of the internet to search for people throughout the United States who share her same racial-cultural background. She describes the Blaxicans she meets online as having a bittersweet, "unique feeling" about themselves. Erica feels that there is a need for Blaxicans to build community nationwide. Some Blaxicans expressed the same desire and need for collective organizing along these racial lines simply to build a sense of community, and some expressed a desire that had more political reasons.

For example, Andrea, a participant from Los Angeles, found a group on the internet that tried to connect Black Latinas/os with one another and contemplated collective organizing around a Blaxican identity for political purposes. Andrea pondered her own question. She said, "Can you imagine if there was a huge movement of Blaxicans? People that were just mixed Blacktinos/Black Latinos. We wouldn't have this whole thing about Black-Brown issues because everyone would be Black and Brown. There wouldn't be an issue because either way, how are you going to have an issue with yourself? We need to probably come together and be able to know that we exist. I think that's powerful."

Andrea gets excited about the prospect of bringing mixed Black Latinas/os together to acknowledge and validate their existence. She believes that a movement of mixed Blacktinos has the potential to ameliorate Black-Brown issues. Both Erica and Andrea propose a way of transitioning from Blaxican invisibility to community by collectively organizing along racial-cultural lines. Strategies to create a Blaxican community could be by having a conference or organizing a social movement. Indeed, organizing around racial-cultural commonalities are ways other groups have brought their existence and therefore social, economic, and political issues to the forefront.

Dan, an interviewee from El Paso, Texas, created a Facebook group for Blaxicans to create community. Users of Facebook can create groups that are "open," meaning anyone can join, and some groups are by invitation only. Facebook groups allow users to create a webpage where members can write messages, post blog entries, and post pictures. Of the four groups on Facebook dedicated to Blaxicans, Dan's group had the largest membership, with 196 members. The description of the group is as follows: "This is the GLOBAL Blaxican Group!!! This group is for those of you who love Blaxicans (people mixed w/ Black & Mexican), think Blaxican is an Awesome word, are Mixed yourself (any Mixture), Love Mixed people, or if you wish you were Blaxican, whether it's for the ironic combination of the two races/ethnicities or if you'd like to be referred to by an awesome word."

As the description indicates, the group's membership does not consist entirely of Blaxicans. Members of the group also include some people of other racial-cultural groups and African American and Mexican American parents of Blaxican children. During the time of our fieldwork, activity on the group site was regular, with a new post at least once per week. Members usually uploaded pictures of themselves or their children or posed a general question to the rest of the group. For example, a question posted by a Blaxican member was, "So tell me, how do the holidays usually work out? Do you guys cook Mexican food, or soul food, or is it a mixture?" Dan was asked about his motivations to create the online group. He said,

I only had one friend that I know of that was mixed like me, and I wanted to see how many other people out there identified like me. A lot of them have the same response: that they don't know anyone else that is like them, and they like the group. I noticed that a lot of people from California and from different campuses were joining it. I kinda figured that there was more like me from California just because there is a larger Hispanic population and there is also a larger Black population. It kinda did surprise me, and I have seen a lot of interesting discussions on there in terms of what you put down as your race and identity.

Dan created the group because he wanted to meet more people that identified as Blaxican, because at the time he only knew one other person. He noticed that much of the membership originated from California, which did not surprise him given the larger Mexican American and African American populations living together compared to his experience in El Paso, Texas. Dan views the discussions online as informative and validating. He talked more about what he gains from talking to other Blaxicans online. He said, "The Blaxicans I talk to sometimes have gone through similar [struggles with] identity, not knowing which one to choose or how to identify with both. They kinda have gone through the same struggles and still feel a sense of uniqueness. I guess everyone wants to identify and find other people similar to them. Especially when there aren't as many, or you don't know too many, especially depending on what part of the country you are from."

To know that other Blaxicans share similar experiences is validating. Also, this internet group fulfills the desire to identify with a group of people, particularly for those who have limited contact with others who share a common mixed racial-cultural background. Since our fieldwork, Dan's Facebook group has declined in membership. Still, content creators post information on TikTok and Instagram about being Blaxican. These are more individual postings that are somewhat different from Dan's Facebook group. They are, nonetheless, other meaningful platforms for creators to express entertaining or educational material on Blaxican identities and experiences that can serve as the basis for a sense of connection and collective subjectivity. Indeed, engaging with the internet and social media groups based on Blaxican identity are strategies that Blaxicans seek out to create community and escape from being made invisible in U.S. society.

In sum, this chapter began with explaining how Blaxican participants describe authentic Blaxican identities. Blaxicans are largely viewed as first-generation individuals with one African American and one Mexican or Mexican American parent. The Blaxicans in this study choose both of their parents' backgrounds in an egalitarian and nonhierarchical fashion. They use both racial and cultural strategies to navigate and negotiate a "multiracial balancing" to represent their African American and Mexican American aspects of self equally. These strategies involve making conscious, deliberate choices about things like hairstyles, code-switching, food, dance, music, religion, traditions, taking ethnic studies classes, and joining fraternities and sororities in college.

The majority of Blaxicans who participated in this study did not personally know many Blaxicans besides their own siblings or family members. Some participants described the invisibility of their Blaxican experiences as very isolating. Therefore, Blaxicans use social networking sites such as Facebook to attempt to make connections with other Blaxicans. A Blaxican neighborhood community does not exist in a physical sense, for example, one that is recognizable by physical boundaries such as freeways, railroad tracks, or bridges.[21] However, we argue that a Blaxican community does exist for some as an imagined community.

Anderson asserts that the concept of community is not always grounded in a physical or spatial sense but can also be imagined. Communities are imagined because members may never see, know, or hear of other members, yet each member shares an image of their communion. Indeed, larger communities are imagined and not based on face-to-face interactions between their members.[22] During interviews with participants, it was apparent that Blaxicans had an image of sharing communion with others, despite not hearing of, meeting, or knowing Blaxicans outside of their own immediate families. The Blaxican group on Facebook offers some evidence that face-to-face interactions are not necessary for people to have a sense of community with others who are Blaxican.

Blaxicans and Multiracial Collective Subjectivity

More than half of the Blaxican interviewees (twenty-seven) resided in California, which has the largest two or more races population in the country (1.8 million people in 2010, 5.8 million in 2020).[23] California also has a higher percentage of individuals who were two or more races (4.7 percent in 2010 and 14.6 percent in 2020), compared to the rest of the United States (2.4 percent in 2020 and 10.2 percent in 2020).[24] Indeed, the multiracial phenomenon as a racial project has had an immediate impact on patterns of race relations on the West Coast. California in particular has been a major center of multiracial activism, as well as of academic research and university-level study about multiracial identity.[25]

Most of the participants' residences were consistent with the "multiracial belt" around California's Central Valley and greater Sacramento regions, where there is a concentration of counties with higher percentages of multiracials.[26] In fact, Alyssa Newman and G. Reginald Daniel found that adolescents in Northern California living in the "multiracial belt" are more accepted and expected to identify as multiracial.[27] Based on 2000 census data, in California "there is a 'multiracial belt' with a concentration of the highest percent [of] multiracial[s] in the center of the state."[28] While researchers Park, Meyers, and Wei found the distinction between multiracial-belt and nonmultiracial-belt counties may have been minimal (the seven counties they identified ranged from 5.2 percent multiracial to 6.4 percent multiracial) as other counties also exceeded the state average, but this pattern was notable for the interconnectedness of these counties with the highest percentages of multiracial residents.

Interestingly, given this confluence of factors, Newman found that a multiracial identification is a normative part of the racial landscape in Northern California. Our data do not make it possible to provide any definitive or meaningful judgments about the Norteño (northern) and Sureño (southern) regional differences in California as it relates to Blaxican experiences and identities in this regard and more generally. However, based on the more general state data, we can surmise that the pattern in Northern California does not appear to be duplicated elsewhere in California. The greater receptivity of Northern California has had a significant impact on the general population's comfort with Blaxican identities compared to the cultural landscape in Southern California.[29] Moreover, the needle appears to be moving more slowly in terms of general societal norms and racial common sense of the larger society, notwithstanding regional variations.[30]

Still, multiraciality has become the basis for an emergent collective subjectivity, notwithstanding these societal attitudes. No matter how porous, fuzzy, and thin the boundary, no matter how soft and illusive the collectivity's center, a shared liminality based on identification with more than one racial background is an integral, fundamental part of the self-conception of multiracial-identifying individuals, and it is a defining component of mixed-race experiences. Despite numerous backgrounds, experiences, and identities, a shared liminality grounded in identification with more than one racial background can become an integral component of multiracials' self-conception.

Yet to date there are few surveys on group identity among multiracials in the United States, which is hampered by the lack of instruments of measurement.[31] Some insight appears in the Pew Research report "Multiracial in America," whose data was gathered from an online survey of a nationally representative sample of 1,555 multiracials ages eighteen and older. The sample of multiracial adults was identified after contacting and collecting basic demographic information on more than 21,000 adults nationwide. For comparative purposes, an additional 1,495 adults from the public were surveyed. This included an oversample of Black-non-Hispanic adults in addition to those who reported Asian and no race.[32]

The data indicate multiracials variously experience the boundaries of their individual identities as "thick" (comprehensive) or "thin" (less comprehensive) and the centers as "soft" (more diffuse) or "hard" (less diffuse).³³ The boundaries and centers of a multiracial collective subjectivity are currently much closer, respectively, to the thin and soft end of the spectrum.³⁴ Only about a third of all multiracials surveyed believed they have a lot in common with other multiracials who share their racial backgrounds. Only half as many believed they share a lot with multiracials with different racial backgrounds.³⁵

These findings suggest that currently a sense of groupness among multiracials is present but not robust. To some extent this can be attributed to the fact that multiracial identities are still an emerging phenomenon. Because of the aforementioned constraints prohibiting their development, multiracial people have lacked social spaces for the formation of multiracial identities. This has been exacerbated by the social structural separation perpetuated by monoracialized spaces embedded in the larger society. This could change if multiracial identities gain sufficient force to organize social and cultural life around a sense of groupness.³⁶ Indeed, some basic ingredients supporting a sense of groupness are apparent in numerous social spaces that have emerged around collective multiracial concerns. These include websites, social media, student groups, college courses, support and educational organizations, socials, festivals, and conferences.³⁷

Notwithstanding an embryonic sense of groupness among multiracials, multiracial designators currently function more as individual rather than as group identifiers and are porous, multiple, and overlapping.³⁸ Because multiracials have myriad backgrounds and experiences, which are themselves multidimensional, there may always be an intrinsic permeability to any sense of their groupness.³⁹ Indeed, the specific racial components of individuals' backgrounds matter for this sense of groupness, which would link individual well-being to the well-being of one's racial group. Survey research by Pew, as well as by Davenport and others, suggests there is an uneven degree to which subpopulations of multiracials of similar backgrounds identify with a broader multiracial collective subjectivity. Subgroup differences may, for them, impede the development of the sense of linked fate and shared experience that unites many Blacks and other groups of color.⁴⁰

Scholar Song's research indicates that the absence of a sense of groupness does not preclude the intergenerational transfer or longevity of individual multiracial identities. Yet given that Blaxican identity is largely restricted to individuals with one Mexican American and one African American parent, it is unlikely to have much longevity as a particularity beyond the first-generation or biracial identity. The offspring of a marriage between two Blaxican parents or of a marriage involving one Blaxican parent could develop a multigenerational Blaxican identity, depending on their socialization. But at some point, Blaxican identity would likely become part of a larger collective subjectivity composed of an array of multiracial identities encompassing myriad backgrounds.

| Chapter Eleven

Social Agency and Constraint
Family, School, and Neighborhood

Encouragement of a multiracial and multiethnic identity by parents and family members was a major influence on participants' choices to identify as Blaxican. Parents were a main source of socialization to the participants racial-cultural reference groups. Parental lessons provided the foundation for how participants understand their racial subjectivities or how they have been informed by and have interacted with the racial dynamics they inhabit. In addition, parents of dual-minority multiracial children are tasked with teaching their children about race and culture differently than parents of white multiracial children.[1]

It is necessary for parents of Blaxican children to address issues of race, racism, and culture in both their Mexican and Black backgrounds, which is not to say that parents are always skilled, prepared, or knowledgeable in how to do that. Nonetheless, we found in this study that parents of Blaxicans taught (or encourage their children to learn on their own) the cultures from both of their backgrounds. In addition, parents attempted to address issues of race and racism that affect both African Americans and Mexican Americans. However, parents did not always have the language to address their child's multiraciality. Indeed, minority parents in multiracial families may teach their children what they know about being a minority without knowing how to teach them about being multiracial.[2]

We asked interviewees how their parent(s) taught them about race. Overwhelmingly, parents taught participants that they belonged to two racial-cultural groups and talked to them about African American and Mexican American culture and often about issues around race and racism. Jesus, a twenty-seven-year-old man from Washington DC, remembers that his African American single mother would constantly remind him he was also Mexican American. "Growing up she was like, 'Yeah you have another heritage, another rich cultural heritage.' But clearly, she is not Mexican, but she was like, 'I am Black,' but, you know I knew that. And I was raised Black, that's how I identify, but at the same time mother always lets me know, she's like, 'You know, your father is Latino.'"

Although Jesus was enculturated as African American because he grew up with his mother, he was encouraged to embrace his Mexican American background. Named after his Mexican American father, who was absent from his life, Jesus's mother explained to him the origin of his first and last names and told him to be proud of all his heritages. Jesus's example illustrates that even without the presence of both parents' extended families, it was significant to instill a sense of both backgrounds.

Most coparenting families also intentionally taught their children about some African American and Mexican American history and cultural traditions. For example, John, a twenty-one-year-old man living in San Diego, California, was the only respondent born outside of the United States. Born and raised in Tijuana, Baja California, Mexico, until he was thirteen years old, John learned Mexican history from his mother and African American history from his father while in Mexico. John's parents were very involved in his studies and took the opportunity to teach him about his culture. John, who is often perceived as Black based on his appearance, identifies as both Black and Mexican.

The parental lessons instilling a dual-minority multiracial subjectivity as Blaxican, in one case, was extended to the second generation. Talia, a woman from Sacramento teaches her second-generation Blaxican daughter (father is also Blaxican) from the historical sources of African Americans and Mexican Americans. She said,

Here my child is Mexican and Black also, and I am trying to explain to my child why it is important to do well in school. Because now I am going to the Black heritage, because there was a time when we couldn't go to school; they didn't want Black people to learn or want you to have anything. That's why now that she has the opportunity to go to school, you need to go for it. Do the best you can because there was a time when you couldn't do it. I have to teach her both heritages. I have to teach her about her Black heritage, I have to teach her about Hispanics.

Talia imparts in her daughter the importance of obtaining an education, referencing the historical discrimination in education of African Americans. Like many of the other participants' parents, Talia encourages her daughter to consider the racial group history of both African Americans and Mexican Americans when formulating her own self-concept. Teaching their children from the standpoint of each group is one of the important ways that shaped their racial subjectivities as dual-minority multiracial Blaxicans.

Parental teachings about African Americans and Mexican Americans were laced with lessons about racism and prejudices. Blaxicans developed a sense of their racialized identity through an awareness of racism and inequality through the viewpoint of their monoracial minority parent. Parents explained to their children that they likely would experience racism and prejudice directed toward African Americans and Mexican Americans. For instance, Sabrina, a twenty-three-year-old woman from Fresno, California, remembers that her African American single mother instilled in her a great pride in being both African American and Mexican American. Sabrina's family regularly talked to her about racism to ensure that she would be prepared to respond to any prejudice or racist acts. Sabrina's family discouraged the internalization of negative associations given to Mexican Americans and African Americans and provided her the tools to understand the historical and social circumstances of racist behavior.

Sabrina's parents explained to her that she would encounter racist attitudes because she was both Black and Mexican. They discussed with her the idea that she should remain proud, despite any negative remarks she may encounter in life. Likewise, Julia, who was raised by her Mexican American father and African American mother, was taught at an early age about racism directed specifically toward both African Americans and Mexican Americans. Her parents explained to her what racial epithets were and told her that if anyone ever called her a "wetback" or a "n——" she should notify them immediately. As racial-cultural minorities who have experienced racism first-hand, Julia's parents equipped her as best as they could to deal with how others might respond to her as a Blaxican girl.

Parents of dual-minority multiracials often address white racism and prejudice, in addition to race relations between communities of color that often include intragroup marginalization.[3] For instance, one participant recalled an incident where her mother confronted prejudiced behavior in her presence. Nicole, an eighteen-year-old woman from Albuquerque, New Mexico, recalls that her mother began talking to her about being "half" at a very young age. Nicole's mother made sure she knew that people would treat her differently because she was African American and Mexican American. On one of their many trips to Ciudad Juárez, Chihuahua, a border city adjacent to El Paso, Texas, Nicole's mother was pulled over by a Mexican border authority, the same agent she had been stopped by a few times prior. The Mexican agent looked at Nicole in the car and asked her mother, "You slept with a Black guy? You have a Black child?" Enraged that this Mexican man had the effrontery to disparage her Blaxican daughter, Nicole's mother drove off and explained that a lot of Mexican people were prejudiced toward Blacks.

The Mexican agent's questioning of Nicole's mother about having a part-Black child was insulting on many levels. For one, this question reinforces the sexist idea that Mexican women's bodies belong to Mexican men and that having a child outside of that context suggests disloyalty. Second, this question was explicitly anti-Black. In Mexico there is an adage, *"mejorar la raza"* or literally "to improve the race," which still holds currency in Mexican circles today. Indeed, preference for whitening Mexican people by intermarriage with lighter-skinned

Spanish-looking spouses is a notion woven into Mexico's racial fabric.[4] The interaction between Nicole's mother and the border agent was a teaching opportunity used to discuss anti-Blackness among Mexicans.

This example shows how parents of dual-minority multiracials often need to address intergroup prejudice between groups of color that make up their children's backgrounds. Witnessing anti-Blackness among Mexicans did not inspire Blaxicans to adopt a singular Mexican identity or a singular Black identity. Rather, Blaxicans embraced both and had an above average understanding of the nuances of their identities, owed to some degree to their conversations with their parents about white racism and intergroup prejudices.

LaTrice's experiences further illustrate how racism and prejudice from whites and Mexicans alike were often present and how parents addressed this. The first time LaTrice's mother spoke to her about racism was while she was attending a predominantly white elementary school in a working-class neighborhood in Redding, California. She said, "The first time [I thought about my race] was when a girl called me the N-word in elementary school. I don't think I understood, and I went crying to my mom, 'What does this mean?' I knew what it meant, but I didn't understand the concept. My mom wanted to know who she was. And I said, 'Mom, calm down!'" LaTrice asserted that her Mexican American single mother had done her best to instill knowledge and pride about both of her heritages despite the absence of her father.

Being one of the only children of color in most of her Redding, California, public schools, LaTrice knew that her identity was unlike the rest of her peers: "My mom always made it clear to talk to me about why I was different from other people. My grandparents helped raise me and they didn't speak English. I had episodes of kids calling me names, calling me the N-word in elementary school and even junior high. I had my grandpa who told me that I was not Black, but Mexican. So, I never really had a place because I grew up in a predominately white high school and city."[5] LaTrice's story illustrates how Blaxicans encounter racism by white people and may also be caught between intergroup prejudices between African Americans and Mexican or

Mexican Americans. LaTrice's mother tried to resolve this issue by consistently reinforcing positive messages about her Blackness. These familial contradictions are informative, albeit ambivalent, experiences because they present options, which may not be typical in monoracial identity formations.

Jackie Jones, a thirty-year-old from Los Angeles, experienced similar contradictory messages about her racial-cultural identity. At an early age, Jackie remembers children taunting her at school. Through these experiences, she learned to associate Blackness with negativity. Her Mexican immigrant single mother diligently reinforced, however, positive messages about African American women. Jackie recalls,

> When kids at school found out I was half-Black, the first taunts, the first things that would come out of anybody's mouth was, "What, so you're just a n——?" So, I come to associate my Blackness with it being bad. My mom tried really hard to make up for it. She would constantly make me watch the *Cosby Show*; she would tell about my African American history; she would constantly tell me that African American women were beautiful, and that I was an African American woman as well and I should be proud of my features and my hair.

Jackie perceived that her Mexican immigrant mother, from Jalisco, attempted to "make up" for the negative messaging around her Blackness by fostering a positive image of African American women. She taught Jackie about African American history and encouraged her to watch television shows featuring African American families in a positive light. From a woman of color standpoint, Jackie's mother, and other parents in this study, understood the importance of fostering in their children a positive self-image to combat negative controlling images.[6]

Controlling images are stereotypical symbols created by elite groups in an exercise of power to manipulate ideas about Blackness. These controlling images are designed to make racism, sexism, poverty, and other forms of social injustice appear normal and natural.[7] Parental teachings responding to racism evince strategies of resistance to dominant and oppressive notions about gender, class, sexuality, and race. Mexican American parents' teaching their Blaxican children positive Blackness and self-love had a significant impact on shaping their self-concepts. By disavowing anti-Blackness, Mexican American parents send a strong message to their children that they accept and embrace their Blackness and support their multiracial identities.

Overall, participants' racial subjectivities were influenced by the racial and cultural socialization provided by their parents and families. Racial subjectivities involve understanding oneself as products of a racial group's history. Parents taught their children about the social, historical, and political implications of being African American and Mexican American through their own monoracial perspective as minorities. By actively encouraging their children to embrace two monoracial ancestries and histories, parents gave their children options to identify as multiracial Blaxicans. While the ultimate choice to identify as multiracial came from the participants themselves, active encouragement from parents to embrace two monoracial identities was the vehicle that made the development of a Blaxican multiracial identity possible.

Blaxicans' parental teachings are different from white and nonwhite mixed experiences with maybe the exception of Black white mixed people. In many white and nonwhite mixed experiences, there is often an option to choose whiteness. Warren and Twine argue that whiteness is constructed in relation to Blackness; therefore, whiteness is only possible for non-Black groups.[8] Parents of white nonwhite children do not necessarily encourage the embracement of the "other side" of their racial identities because whiteness is the hegemonic norm, and the rules of hypodescent typically associate white nonwhite offspring with the lower status parent group.

For dual-minority Blaxicans, parental encouragement to embrace both African American and Mexican American aspects of their identities occurs because the issue of whiteness is not critical, nor is it factored into Blaxican identity. In other words, there is not an implication that supporting a Blaxican identity is moving toward whiteness. In addition, there is often a need for dual-minority multiracials to address white racism and intergroup prejudice between communities of color that make up their children's backgrounds.

What Are You?

Moving outside of parental influences, we consider how Blaxicans confront the factors they face outside their homes, particularly in everyday face-to-face peer interactions. As early as elementary school and no later than high school, study informants realized that their racial-cultural identities were positioned outside of what is considered monoracial or "normative." The school context for mixed-race adolescents is a critical time where their friendships are perceived to signify their authentic self.[9] One significant way Blaxicans learned that their racial identities were outside the norm was through the ubiquitous What are you? question. The What are you? questions from strangers act as a reflected appraisal of mixed-race identity.[10] The questioning of Blaxicans' racial identities is chronic and, in some cases, occurs daily, particularly when they meet someone for the first time. Challenging Blaxican racial-cultural identities serves as a constant reminder that Blaxicans do not fit into traditional categories and reinforces their status as multiracial and subordinate in a society that privileges monoracials.

We juxtapose these interactions to racial microaggressions, applied to African American experiences and to the experiences of Latinas/os, and later to multiracials. Racial microaggressions refer to subtle or obvious social interactions that are offensive mechanisms designed to convey messages of inferiority and subordination. Microaggressions send messages that people of color are unintelligent, criminal, foreign, and deserving of socially marginal status.[11] Multiracials experience potentially as many microaggressions as monoracial people of color. Mixed people feel they are exoticized, treated as foreigners and second-class citizens, excluded within their own families, and complimented for being a "racialized ideal."[12] The racial microaggressions directed toward Blaxicans are from white people and monoracial people of color alike.

Eduardo, a twenty-two-year-old living in Northern California who describes himself as being "lighter-skinned," said, "They ask me [what I am] all the time. All the time, because when people meet me at first, they are not really sure what I am. Some people think I am white; some people think I am Mexican; some people think I am Black and Mexican. Off the top some people can tell. Some people don't think I am Black at all. Some people think I am Puerto Rican, so they always want to know what I am, so I get that all the time." By asking Eduardo about his racial background, people are trying to figure out if he is monoracial (i.e., white or Black) or multiracial (i.e., Black Mexican, Black and white).

Eduardo's appearance is viewed as ambiguous, which prompts people to ask him about his race. In some ways, questions about his race reinforce his position as a multiracial person, because outsiders constantly read him as nonnormative. From another perspective, this type of question can be viewed as a constant reminder of the possibility of having a multiracial option. As previously mentioned, Newman and Daniel found that adolescents in Northern California, living in the "multiracial belt," are more accepted and expected to identify as multiracial.[13]

Blaxican participants routinely responded to incessant prodding to claim and perform single-race identities. Gaby, a twenty-three-year-old woman from San Jose, California, raised by her Mexican American father and African American mother, noticed that monoracial individuals most often ask about her racial identity. "I notice who tends not to ask [about my race] more often is mixed kids. Usually, kids who are mixed with Black and anything else usually can tell what I am." Multiracial individuals were least likely to ask about a participant's race, while monoracials asked about their racial-cultural identity most often.

The steady and daily questioning about a person's racial designation and identity reinforces the idea that Blaxicans fall outside the norms established by the dominant society and serves as a reminder that they deviate from preestablished conceptions of racial-cultural categories. Participants sometimes perceived the question What are you? as a verbal insult. Asking participants What are you? can be construed as reinforcing and maintaining racial boundaries and hierarchies. Some of the participants felt offended when people asked them about their identities.

For example, Talia, who works in an office setting for the public sector, is often the only woman of color at her workplace: "The most annoying time [people ask about my race] is when it is a whole group of white folks. That is the most annoying time. I'm like, I am not your party favor, move on to something else." When white people ask Talia about her racial identity, she feels as though she is a "party favor" or something that strikes people as entertaining, mysterious, bizarre, or exotic.

This type of questioning creates discomfort because, although quite subtle, it is a mechanism of asserting racial power. These types of interactions are significant in Blaxican identity formations because they remind the receiver that they are mixed, that they are viewed as nonnormative (i.e., not monoracial), and that people are trying to place them within an established racialized hierarchy and order. Being asked to self-define, regardless of who is doing the asking, is about asserting racial power.

An aspect of monoracial privilege is that monoracial people can often take their racial identities for granted and are not constantly expected to explain their legitimacy within established conceptions of racial categories. Although these interactions are about power, there is a difference when white people ask questions about their identity, as compared to when nonwhites ask. Because whiteness symbolizes dominance and is the invisible referent point on which everything else is othered, there is a power displayed in asking a Blaxican person what race they are that is offensive and insulting.

When nonwhite monoracial persons asked this question, these dynamics are also reflective of power, but to a lesser degree. People of color who did the asking displayed a monoracial privilege. However, this was only perceived as offensive when the Blaxican participants thought they were being asked to measure up to African American and Mexican American standards of authenticity. The interactions Blaxicans had with nonwhite monoracials were informative, particularly because it forced the receiver to think about the multiple and layered aspects of their racial-cultural identities from an insider and outsider perspective. While Blaxicans considered African Americans and Mexican Americans their racial-cultural reference groups, they knew their mixedness made them outsiders.

Interactions surrounding a participant's racial background can also serve as a positive reinforcement, and the question What are you? can be viewed as a validation of their difference. For example, it was acceptable to Debra, a forty-five-year-old woman from Sacramento, when an African American security guard at her work asked about her race:

> Now I appreciate the way different people ask it [her race]. There was a security guard where I work, and he is Black. And he came up one day and I was outside, and he goes, "OK, I just got to know," he said, "I keep seeing you and I'm going, that woman isn't Black; what is she?" I said, "I appreciate you asking that way." He's sharp; he said, "Well, it's pretty obvious if you pay attention." I said, "OK, thank you." That happens every once in a while, and I tell them the whole deal.

Debra appreciated how the security guard at her job asked about her race because he did not assume firsthand that she was Black. The security guard recognized that she was something in addition to Black, and Debra was pleased he acknowledged her as such. Debra then felt comfortable telling the security guard that her mother is Mexican American, and her father is Black Native American. The security guard recognized and validated her in-betweenness.

Khanna found that Black people often invoked the one-drop rule in their interactions with Black white mixed people, even while they recognize they are more than Black. The type of interaction described above affirmatively informs a Blaxican identity because it shows that among some Black people, there is a recognition that not all Black people identify in accordance with the one-drop rule with a singular Black identity. The mere acknowledgment that someone is more in addition to Black is significant because it symbolizes the possibility of identifying as something other than Black in accordance with the one-drop rule.[14]

Encountering questions by others about their racial identities evokes a multiracial Blaxican consciousness because informants cannot take their racial identities for granted and are constantly being asked to define who they are. Simultaneously, the constant questioning presents possibilities and affirmations of participants' multiracial identities. Blaxican participants also frequently experience multiracial microaggressions, or subtle insults that reinforce power relationships. Blaxicans are reminded that they not only are subordinate as people of color but also are nonnormative because of their multiraciality.

Questioning serves as a reminder that Blaxicans are outside of normative monoracial boundaries, and this can be validating or offensive depending on the context. By asking the question What are you? most people are asking about what they are seeing visually and want to know about the participant's racial background. The underlying question that people want to know is about how participants racially identify, and this brings to the surface deeper internal questions of racial authenticity, loyalty, and racial orders in the United States and Latin America discussed in part 1 of this book.

School and Neighborhood Influences

Schools and neighborhoods are critical sites for Blaxicans' multiracial identity development and transformations. School is a place where many children learn about the meanings and consequences of race and is a space where youth begin to form their racial, class, and gender identities.[15] The racial make-up of neighborhoods also influences racial identities, particularly for multiracial youth. Melissa Herman found that neighborhood composition was strongly associated with racial identification for white Hispanic multiracials. The social class composition of a neighborhood also has a strong influence on white Hispanics; that is, the wealthier the neighborhood, the more likely they identified as white.[16]

In this analysis, we explore how school and neighborhood contexts influenced participants' choices of racial identification. We find that living in a working-class or middle-class neighborhood further solidified participants' identification as both African American and Mexican American for different reasons. In working-class neighborhoods, participants were more likely to live around other African Americans and Mexican Americans, therefore, giving them more exposure to each community. For participants who lived in white middle-class neighborhoods, an identity as nonwhite and "other" was made even more apparent such that they were made aware of their difference. Not having as much contact with many African Americans and Mexican Americans in white middle-class neighborhoods did not dissuade a Blaxican racial identity. Participants who lived in these types of neighborhoods received instructions from their parents about their racial differences and were encouraged to embrace a dual-minority multiracial identity.

Many informants discussed the importance of school experiences and neighborhood environments in shaping their ideas about being Blaxican. Instructions about race were given within the school setting in which peers and teachers presented racial differences and similarities in both obvious and hidden ways. The neighborhood racial politics also played an important role in shaping Blaxican identities. Antonio, a twenty-two-year-old man from the San Francisco Bay Area, shared his thoughts about the role of racial identities in people's lives. He said,

> What happens is when there are people around you, everybody wants to define you and wants you to be defined. And that is really the insecurity. They create that insecurity. They create the need to want to fit in. And when you try to be yourself, and you don't try to fit in, you stand out, you are isolated, you feel outcasted, and you feel different. You realize that the whole process of going to high school is a way to get conditioned to our identities and ideas and our roles and everything like that. Everybody is just reinforcing everything. Your friends, your family, and the people you are surrounding yourself by, and you know in some ways they are just reinforcing the recipe of identity.

Reflecting on his experience in high school, Antonio explained how most of the push to identify in certain ways derived from the social pressure placed on him by other people based on their perceptions of who he was. Antonio refers to the socialization that happens in family, school, peer settings, and neighborhood environments that produce and reproduce dominant discourses about racial and other identity constructions. Antonio discusses high school as a space where people get "conditioned" to their identities and the roles they are expected to play. Developing an ethnic identity requires the ability to categorize, make inter-group comparisons, and hold a self-concept.[17]

Like other participants, Antonio expresses an understanding of race as essential, rather than an aspect of one's identity that is taken for granted. In general, multiracial people tend to challenge the validity of biological race itself and tend to view race as a social construction more than monoracials.[18] Viewing race as a social construction places multiracial people at an advantage because racial stereotypes lose their meaning and may not affect the way multiracials choose to behave in accordance to race.[19]

Antonio, like other Blaxicans, was aware of the stereotypes associated with African Americans and Mexican Americans and recognized them as generalizations. When a person is multiracial, it is less likely they are going to accept generalized racial characterizations because they are constantly forced to think about the nuances and contradictions of race. Because there are many negative stereotypes, and just as many positive stereotypes, associated with Blaxicans' racial-cultural reference groups, this served as an additional tool used to reject dominant notions of race.

For Talia a consciousness-altering incident occurred while she was attending her Monterey, California, junior high school, where she experienced frequent multiracial microaggressions. Talia's Black peers let her know she was not one of them: "I never associated myself as being anything different than Black, because you would look at me and think that I am Black, until I was in junior high school. And then some friends met my mother, and they were saying, 'Your mom's not

Black?' and I said no." Up to that point, Talia normalized her racial identity as Black, in concurrence with the one-drop rule. It was not until Talia's peers confronted her about her Mexican American mother and subsequently discouraged her from claiming a Black identity that she began to internalize a multiracial identity.

The first time Sabrina thought about her race was after she was called a racial slur as she walked through her Salinas, California, neighborhood: "I remember this one time when I was walking home from school and somebody drove up next to me and called me a n——, and I told my mom and I said someone called me a n—— what does that mean? Then she was pissed off. I have been called wetback. You know I've been called a lot of names, a lot of them by adults, sadly enough." At a young age, Sabrina learned about the negative connotations associated with African Americans and Mexican Americans. Sabrina spoke about a racist schoolteacher. She said,

> I have come across teachers that are very racist, people very ignorant, kids just mean. I remember I was at school and a teacher knew that I was Black and Mexican, and she kinda called me out in the middle of class and I was in awe. Everybody in that class were all Mexican, and she called me out in class and told me that I had to leave; I couldn't be there anymore because I was Black. So immediately right there the students kind of separated me, once she said that, because I had no problems until then. Then when she called me out right there, I noticed that a lot of them started saying things to me.

In this Salinas public school classroom, a white teacher announced to the students that Sabrina was Black and did not belong in the class. Afterward, Sabrina's Mexican American classmates abruptly excluded her. Sabrina's teacher made certain that everyone in the classroom viewed her in the "correct" way. Accordingly, she was not accepted as Mexican American but rather rejected as Black, which therefore meant the other children should not accept her as their equal. As an authority figure, the teacher validated the Mexican American students and sanctioned behaviors that would "other" Sabrina in relation not only to whites but to Mexican Americans as well. The interaction described above is informative to a formation of Blaxican identity because the receiver of this anti-Black message was being taught that if you have one Black parent, you are not Mexican. At the same time this presents a contradiction; Sabrina's father is Mexican, and she was perceived as being Mexican American as a child.

The racial composition of different school contexts and residential living spaces also awakened a racial consciousness in Sabrina. She noticed the differences in how she was perceived and understood by others when she and her African American single mother moved from one town to another in central California. After living in a predominately African American neighborhood in Fresno, the two moved to a Mexican barrio in Salinas:

> Me and my mother, we lived in Fresno with my family for a while, and I grew up in an all-Black neighborhood, and we moved from there when I was really young, probably about three or four, and we came to Salinas, California. We moved to the east side, which is basically like little Mexico. Everyone was Mexican in just that area. When I was a kid, I looked Mexican. My skin tone was very, very light, and my mother was a single parent so she was the only Black woman in that area and so I knew something was up when people would look at us funny, and definitely look at her funny, like what'cha doing with this little Mexican baby?

Sabrina had lighter skin than her mother did, and the neighbors questioned their relationship as mother and daughter with looks of curiosity, disapproval, and disbelief. As a light-skinned baby, Sabrina was viewed as Mexican American, yet her mother was marked as not belonging because she was the only African American woman in the barrio.

Similarly, Eduardo became aware of his racial identity after his family moved around the country. Eduardo, his African American mother, Mexican father, and two Blaxican siblings moved from state to state and finally settled in a working-class neighborhood in the San Francisco Bay Area.

I remember when I moved to California, I didn't know what I was. I moved around a lot when I was younger. I was in New Orleans; I was living in Seattle, Washington, and I lived in Richmond, Virginia. And I would go to just different types of regions, and everywhere I went there would either be white or Black [people]; there wouldn't be no Mexicans. So, I didn't know what I was; I pretty much thought I was white, I guess. When I moved to California it was like a wake-up call. I woke up, and it made me realize because there was Mexicans and they spoke Spanish and all that stuff, and I didn't speak no Spanish. And there were different types of cultures in the Bay Area. So, it is like Filipinos and all these other cultures. So, it was really a rude awakening and that is when I started really, really embracing my culture. And I was about—I was in the fourth grade. I was only like, eleven.

Eduardo's first contact with Mexican Americans outside of his family occurred when they moved to the Bay Area. Although his Mexican father and African American mother raised him, he was not fully aware of Mexican Americans as a group. Despite being around both African American and white people before he moved to California, as a child he thought he was white. It was not until he encountered a critical mass of Mexican Americans and other people of color in a working-class Bay Area neighborhood that he began to embrace being Blaxican. Eduardo's exposure to Mexican Americans who spoke Spanish is an example of how language, particularly the Spanish language, aided in constructing a Blaxican identity. The use of the Spanish language among Mexican Americans in the Bay Area shaped Eduardo's view of Mexican Americans as a distinct group, which prompted him to begin to embrace those aspects as part of his identity. Exposure to Mexican Americans who spoke Spanish exposed Eduardo to the possibility of viewing his racial-cultural identity as both Black and Mexican. The palpable ethnic visibility of Mexican Americans in the Bay Area presented the option to identify with them as an ethnic/racial group.

Like Sabrina and Eduardo, Gaby also felt that the demographic aspects of her neighborhood influenced how she came to see herself early on. Gaby lived in a middle-income, mostly white neighborhood in San Jose, California. Her parents met each other living on the same street. Her parents' families were the only people of color in that San Jose neighborhood: "I lived in a predominately white neighborhood. Then there was only two other colored families, and it was both of my grandmas. My dad's mom [Mexican] and my mom's mom [African American], they lived on the same block. So, by noticing that we were the only—we were the 'other' in the neighborhood, I became aware of racial differences and skin color differences." Gaby's family was "othered" by the residents in her neighborhood not only because they were nonwhite but also because the people in her neighborhood had higher incomes compared to other neighborhoods in San Jose. Parental income or socioeconomic status sometimes influences how multiracials view themselves in relation to their racial reference groups.[20] African American and Mexican American families often are stereotyped as low income and not able to afford middle-class lifestyles and homes. Gaby had to negotiate race and class identities that are socially constructed in a contradictory manner in relationship to one another. Indeed, class and racial meanings are bonded together so that "authentic" Black and Brown identity is imagined as lower class.[21]

The race and class composition of a neighborhood were important factors that influenced Blaxican identity formations. Being the only nonwhite people in a residential area heightens awareness of how multiracials are viewed as "other." The class dynamic also played a role in the feelings of marginalization, particularly because African Americans and Mexican Americans are perceived as being lower class. Blaxicans who grew up in white middle-class neighborhoods experienced different stressors in comparison to Blaxicans who lived in working-class environments. Not only were their racial identities suspect but so were their class backgrounds.

John coped with the meaning of his identity in a transnational context. He was born in the United States to a Mexican mother but was raised most of his life in Mexico. John spoke about his experience being Blaxican and crossing international borders:

I grew up in Tijuana, so after I was born [in San Diego], immediately after I moved to Tijuana. I pretty much grew up there until I was about thirteen, so at that time I knew very little of the African American culture, so the only exposure I had was through my dad, and his brother and his family who are also half-Black and half-Mexican. That was my first exposure, and then when I was thirteen, I moved to the U.S. and that was in the seventh grade. That is when I first had a more formal exposure to the African American culture since the middle school that I started at was very diverse. Most of my friends were African American. That is when I started identifying with and seeing my roots a lot more.

Growing up in Mexico, John learned from his father what it meant to be African American and only knew what it meant to be Blaxican within a Mexican national context. Once he moved to the United States, the ethnically diverse junior high school gave him exposure to other African Americans and provided him with opportunities to find out what his Blaxican identity meant specifically within San Diego, California. In Mexico John was perceived as being darker than his classmates but felt he blended into the environment in a way where his Mexican peers did not make an issue of his difference.

However, regarding his parents' marriage in Mexico, John said, "Initially there was a big problem, especially in Mexico. They are a homogeneous country. You have the Mexican population, then you have the indigenous. The indigenous are alienated and marginalized, so it creates an issue of pigmentocracy that is vivid. So, there was a big clash between my dad and my mom's family. In fact, my grandpa kicked her out of the house when he found out that she had a Black boyfriend." While his Mexican peers in Mexico and African American peers in the United States accepted John, the main difference was that in Mexico there was a greater stigmatization against his dark skin color because it is associated with the indigenous population which is viewed and treated as inferior.

Interestingly, John felt that his dark skin color was viewed as less stigmatizing in the United States, especially by his African American peers. Unlike other Blaxican participants raised in the United States, John did not have negative experiences with African American peers who expected him to conform to "authentic" displays of Blackness. Perhaps his Mexican transnational status eliminated any expectation that John behave and talk in ways defined by an African American as authentic. In fact, in San Diego and other cities with large Mexican American populations, African Americans who speak some Spanish and participate in some Mexican culture may be considered usual and acceptable, particularly considering that they live side-by-side in many neighborhoods.

In California cities, such as San Diego, Los Angeles, Oakland, and Sacramento, cross-pollination of African American and Mexican American cultures can be perceived as normative. Blaxicans growing up in these contexts may view their African American and Mexican American cultures as to some extent seamless and reinforced through the local culture. For example, a Mexican American parent was perceived as speaking Black English vernacular, and an African American parent frequently cooked traditional Mexican food.

Moving to and living in different residential settings provoked a sense of awareness in how the participants racially self-defined. Blaxican identities are relational and gain meaning in relation to other race, gender, and class categories.[22] Living in an all-white neighborhood amplified LaTrice's and Gaby's differences from the rest of their neighbors and peers, which gave them a sense that they did not fit into the dominant white norms of appearance. Similarly, living in an all-Mexican neighborhood with an African American mother marked Sabrina and her mother as questionable. Moving to racially diverse locations and schools, such as San Diego and the San Francisco Bay Area, John and Eduardo were provided with opportunities to connect with Mexican American and African American communities. Previously, they had not had exposure to many Mexican Americans and African Americans other than their immediate family members. For John and Eduardo, contact with the "other side" provided an option to identify as Blaxican.

| Chapter Twelve

Race and Cultural Authenticity
You're Not Black or Mexican Enough!

In her personal reflection María Rosario Jackson recalls her experiences growing up with an African American father and Mexican mother living in a Black neighborhood in Los Angeles.[1] "In my youth and early adulthood, I wanted to be clear that I was both—I felt a compulsion to identify as both African American and Mexican. As I have grown older, I have felt less need to explain myself, and that has been liberating for me. If they care, let them figure it out, or not."[2] Jackson's reflection highlights the navigation in asserting an identity as both African American and Mexican American. Her journey shows that over time the need to "explain oneself" may become less significant.

In this chapter we discuss how interpersonal interactions with African American and Mexican American peers impress on Blaxicans that they are not "enough" to be authentic and how these interactions influence and shape their identities. We pay attention to how African American and Mexican American peers and family often require Blaxicans to "prove" and demonstrate their cultural and racial authenticity, which is ultimately about interrogating their loyalties to one nonwhite group and limiting a multiracial claim. Authenticity policing reveals the mental and emotional effort that goes into claiming a dual-minority multiracial identity. Asking Blaxicans to prove that they are either authentically African American or Mexican

American prompts Blaxicans to develop a self-consciousness of how they are both.

King O'Riain asserts that "race is work" and mixed-race people may work harder at racial claims than whites and monoracial people of color. Race work is the effort that is exerted to maintain and reinforce the idea that race is biological and connected to notions of culture.[3] Whiteness is the default category in which all other experiences are referenced, and because of its pervasiveness it is a muted and unmarked category of experience. On the other hand, monoracial people of color are acknowledged to have culture and many are racialized. Therefore, for dual-minority multiracials, particularly those who have African ancestry because of the one-drop rule, asserting a both/neither identity takes an exceptional amount of effort. Mexican Americans and African Americans seem to suggest that Blaxicans prove their racial-cultural claims to either yet ultimately reject their claims. This opens space for the development of a new identity that is neither and both.

One common experience revealed during our interviews with Blaxican individuals is that their African American and Mexican American friends and family constantly remind them that they are not Black or Mexican "enough." By asking in-depth questions regarding authenticity, we found that Blaxicans' African American and Mexican American peers police the boundaries around what is considered an authentic "half-Black" or "half-Mexican" identity. This policing of boundaries illustrates what is considered normative for these racial and cultural categories. It was evident that African American and Mexican American identities are largely understood as monoracial, monocultural, working class, and heteronormative. An intersecting multicultural, multiracial, queer, or upper-class status violates what is considered authentically Mexican American or African American.

Authenticity policing involves intentional interactions by African Americans and Mexican Americans to enforce racial and cultural categories as impermeable and rigid. These interactions are important factors that shape Blaxican identities. Racial authenticity policing included notions around phenotype, such as hair texture and skin color. Cultural authenticity policing included speech, language fluency, dancing, and more. These social interactions occur in obvious or subtle ways through behaviors, such as body language, gestures, and speech, and they involve power.

Authenticity policing indicates intragroup power dynamics such that the person being challenged to prove their authenticity is viewed as tentative or marginal. Expectations of authenticity are enacted to limit boundary crossing and Blaxicans represent boundaries that have been crossed.[4] Not being viewed as culturally or racially authentic for mixed-race people can be insulting. In this view, authenticity can be juxtaposed to microaggressions, which are offensive mechanisms that are designed to reduce, dilute, atomize, and encase the hapless into place.[5] Studies of microaggressions examine the marginalized experiences of socially devalued groups in our society under a framework of oppression.[6] Indeed, multiracials experience racial microaggressions in similar ways to monoracials yet in unique ways due to their multiraciality.[7] Often the enactors of racial microaggressions are monoracial people of color.

Scholars studying mixed-race experiences have used different terms to describe the interactional power dynamics between monoracial people of color and mixed-race people, such as monoracism, multiracial microaggressions, borderism, and interethnic and intraracial discrimination.[8] Policing racial-cultural authenticity is at the core of many of these conflicting interactions. Authenticity policing is a form of what Heather Dalmage calls "border patrolling" enacted by racial actors, Black and white alike. Individuals invested in maintaining the color line have patrolled the line on both sides. African Americans have policed the line for liberation, and whites have done so to protect white privilege: "Borders created to protect resources such as goods and power are kept in place by laws, language, cultural norms, images, and individual actions as well as by interlocking with other borders."[9] Whites created the color line and are the only ones who have the institutional means to maintain the power granted in its maintenance. However, monoracial people of color continue to monitor the color line to the exclusion of multiracials of color.

It is precisely these types of interactional power dynamics that are present in authenticity policing that contributes to the development of "new" (post–civil rights era) hybrid racial-cultural identities that reject hierarchical valuation. Blaxican identities exist in a borderlands space in-between what it means for them to be African American and Mexican American and emerge out of the contradictions that arise when claiming authenticity to both racial-cultural groups. It is important to highlight the interactional dynamics that show Blaxicans they are not Black or Mexican enough to better understand how these exchanges shape their identities. Being told that they are not authentically Black or Mexican or that they should choose one is a form of exclusion and isolation to which mixed-race people are often subjected.[10] It is also important to note that the way mixed-race people experience interpersonal interactions around their identity formations are gendered. Research focusing specifically on Black multiracials finds that women often experience more invalidation from Black monoracial women, and Black monoracial men are more accepting of Black mixed-race men.[11] We found that while Blaxican men and women are both subjected to racial-cultural authenticity policing, women experience it more. Women were questioned more by their peers and were sometimes objectified by men who judged them using stereotypical assumptions of both African American and Mexican or Mexican American women.

Policing Mexican Authenticity

Interviews reveal that some of the most salient markers of Mexican authenticity included fluency in Mexican or Chicana/o Spanish and phenotype. Research suggests that among Mexican Americans darker skin and Spanish-language ability are key identifiers of racial-cultural identity.[12] Light skin and English monolingualism are associated with Anglo assimilation and devalued by some Mexican Americans.[13] In fact, Mexican Americans report using Spanish as a way to reestablish their Mexican identity when light skin calls it into question.[14] Although Mexicans display an array of phenotypes, the quintessential phenotype represents a mestiza/o aesthetic with brown skin, hair, and eyes, which do not appear European adjacent, African, or Asian. In addition, knowledge of Mexican culture and having a working-class background are also signifiers of authenticity. Indeed, class, racial, and cultural signifiers are melded together in a way that authentic Black and Brown identities are imagined as urban and lower class.[15]

We found that, most importantly, not appearing mixed with African ancestry, as determined by skin color or hair, was a phenotypical determinant of Mexican authenticity. If Blaxicans appeared to be mixed with African ancestry, they were viewed as Black, and many of their Mexican peers assumed they were not Mexican or knowledgeable of Mexican culture. Black appearance often undermined their claims to a half-Mexican identity, even if they demonstrated cultural aptitude. At the same time, demonstrating Mexican cultural markers, such as speaking Spanish, sometimes strengthened their claims to a half-Mexican identity, even if they appeared Black.

Viewing Blaxicans as an inauthentic Mexican can be attributed to perceptions of Blackness that are influenced by racial attitudes and ideas transmitted from Mexico and the United States.[16] In Mexico mixed-race (Spanish and indigenous) mestizos constitute the dominant group. Consequently, they enjoy "mestizo privilege," which involves a sense of belonging and the embodiment of an ideal Mexican.[17] Mestizo privilege is one piece of "racial baggage" Mexican immigrants use to inform their understanding of race in the United States.[18] Mexican-descent people have African ancestry and African influenced cultures. Yet African ancestry is often denied and ignored given that the national rhetoric of mestizaje or process of miscegenation has convinced many that they are all mestizos of one race.[19] This is also generally accompanied by a failure to address the historical role of ethnocide, genocide, and rape in the emergence of mestizaje and being attentive to the unequal power relations the implied conviviality of mestizaje can easily obscure.[20]

As we discussed in chapter 6, Mexican American identity has undergone a process of monoracialization that was exacerbated during the Chicano movement solidifying identification with a distinct Brown race.[21] Evincing the long-standing erasure of Afro-Mexicans in Mexico,

2020 was the first year in which Afro-Mexicans were officially counted in the population despite being present at least since Spanish colonization.[22] The one-drop rule in the United States further exacerbates the view among Mexican Americans that Black-appearing people are not considered Mexican or even part-Mexican.

Rebecca Romo's Blaxican son's experience during his first year of college illustrates this idea anecdotally: He casually used the term *Latino* in a classroom discussion. One Mexican American student, who knows he is Blaxican and has met his blended family, turned to him and said, "We don't use the term *Latino*." He then responded, "What do you mean 'we'? I am Mexican, too." He later told us that he felt shut down and uncomfortable contributing anymore in that mostly Latina/o classroom. These types of interactions can be exclusionary and alienating but are also the kinds of interactions that move people to a borderlands consciousness beyond the U.S. binary racial order way of thinking and imagining oneself.

Indeed, Mexican authenticity is an important factor shaping Blaxican identities for all participants, however, experienced in different ways depending on gender and racial make-up of their environment. Blaxican women and men had similar experiences in terms of how their Mexican American peers policed racial-cultural authenticity, such as expecting them to know Spanish or practice Catholicism. However, Blaxican women perceived that claiming a Mexican identity presented different challenges for women than for Blaxican men. For instance, Blaxican women reported being exoticized by men in general, by Latino and African American men specifically. Eliza, a woman from Culver City, said, "I have had experiences where Latino men would talk to me, and it would be like they are talking to me just regular; they have no interest. Then once it comes up that I am Chicana it's like a heightened level of interest comes out. If I am just Black then I am not interesting to you; however, if I then I say I am Black and Chicana then this whole world of possibility then opens up."

Blaxican women's experiences with some men were such that their mixedness made them more exotic and sexually desirable. Exotification of multiracial women is well documented in the literature on mixed-race experiences.[23] Eliza believes that for Latino men, being half-Chicana made it more interesting for them to pursue her romantically. This type of objectification and exoticization is a multiracial microaggression that occurs when a person is made to feel dehumanized or like an object based on their mixed race.[24]

Latino men may find Blaxican women interesting because they have cultural similarities. It is also possible that Blaxican women's mixed-race bodies represent social and racial boundaries that have been crossed and are therefore intriguing. Indeed, it is documented that in Latin America and Mexico, specifically, the mulatta, or mixed-race Black woman, is an icon of sexual desire and a symbol of the danger of racial contamination through miscegenation.[25]

The nature of Mexican authenticity policing is also dependent on region. Blaxicans living in such places as New York, Washington DC, and Maryland knew few Mexicans or Mexican Americans outside of their own immediate families. Instead, Blaxicans on the East Coast were mistaken for Puerto Rican, Afro-Cuban, or Dominican, and many felt an affinity with these cultural groups. Some Blaxicans lived in regions where there are many Mexican immigrants and Mexican Americans, and others in regions where a Mexican population was virtually nonexistent. Mexican authenticity policing occurred more for participants who lived in areas with a higher concentration of immigrant Mexicans and Mexican Americans. In places with heavy concentrations of Mexicans, Mexican culture is more visible and present and there exists a greater expectation to reproduce and adhere to standards of racial or cultural authenticity, which include not appearing Black. Blaxicans living in cities with a significant Mexican population, even when experiencing authenticity policing, did not adopt a singular identity but a multiracial-multiethnic one.

Not appearing mixed with African ancestry and knowing Spanish were the two most important factors in determining Mexican American racial-cultural authenticity. Desire, whose mother is Mexican and whose father is African American, explained that she feels culturally Mexican yet appears Black. "As far as looks, I feel more Black, but as far as culture, I feel more Mexican." Desire understands and speaks some Spanish. She said,

> I feel more comfortable in a room full of Mexicans speaking Spanish with mariachi music and corridos in the background rather than in a room full of Black people where I felt awkward.[26] I worked at a restaurant where a lot of families only spoke Spanish. I was the only one in the night crew that spoke Spanish, so whenever there was a question, they always directed them to me. I would talk to these people, and they would be really confused. They would be like, "How do you know Spanish?" Or "Where did you learn Spanish?" Then I would have to say from my mom's side of the family, and then I would tell them I'm a Blaxican. Then they would eventually be accepting and think it's really cool I speak Spanish.

Mexican and Mexican Americans had more positive reactions to Blaxicans if they demonstrated the ability to speak Spanish, even if they appeared Black. Speaking and understanding Spanish also made Blaxicans feel more connected to Mexican culture than Blaxicans who were not fluent in the language and resulted in less authenticity policing by their Mexican American peers.

Policing Black Authenticity

The policing of Black authenticity was also prevalent in Blaxicans' experiences, sometimes depending on the region they lived in. Black authenticity was less questioned in all-white contexts (they were assumed to be Black) and more questioned in contexts with Black people (they were asked to prove it). These interactional dynamics are also common for monoracial Black people; however, Blaxicans experience authenticity policing in both Black and Mexican contexts. The list of markers that determined Black authenticity was farther-reaching than for Mexican authenticity. This could be because Mexican Americans occupy a more ambiguous position in the U.S. racial hierarchy (i.e., historically, and presently, having a fuzzier social definition because they have not been held to restrictive one-drop rules). In addition, there may be higher stakes in policing Black authenticity because it is equated with loyalty to Black liberation.[27] Put another way, claiming a mixed-race identity may be viewed as distancing oneself from Blackness and antithetical to Black struggle and therefore questioned.

Some of the markers of authenticity for African Americans include style of dress; talk; hip-hop culture; knowledge of African American history; dancing; "kinky," "afro," or tightly coiled hair; darker skin color; and working-class status. When Blaxicans did not act Black, according to their peers, their behavior was equated with acting white. If their hair was loosely curly or straight and long, they received double-sided compliments about having "good hair"; their hair was complimented but their African ancestry was devalued. Dominant standards of beauty in the form of hair, skin color, and phenotype are one way that controlling images depreciate African American women.[28]

Controlling images are often used to define authentic Black womanhood and reflect the dominant groups' interests in maintaining the subordination of Black women. They are powerful influences on Black women's relationships with one another. Blaxicans, like monoracial Black people, negotiate and are held accountable for controlling images that are diminishing and emerge out of a white supremacist discourse. An additional layer to their subordination involves multiracial microaggressions by whites and monoracial people of color alike based on their mixedness. Marc P. Johnston-Guerrero and Kevin L. Nadal argue that two of the main cornerstones of multiracial microaggressions are exclusion based on one's mixed race identity and denial of one's multiracial reality through invalidation by monoracial people.[29] Blaxicans experienced exclusion and invalidation by both their African American and Mexican American family and peers.

For instance, Talia, a forty-year-old woman living in Sacramento, believes that her physical appearance has caused her Mexican American and African American peers to question her authenticity as a member of both groups. Talia is connected to both African American and Mexican American cultures, and most of her extended family is Blaxican, including her sisters and aunts. Mexican Americans mostly question her authenticity when she is noticed attending Mexican cultural celebrations, such as a quinceañera celebration. Black people seem to notice her authenticity in everyday life, not just at cultural functions. She said,

> Even though I am Black, I am not Black to Black people. A lot of Black people can tell. They know that something is different about you. They know Black people. If my hair is kinky or the same texture as theirs or I am not as dark as them, it doesn't matter how much I am in the sun I am never going to be dark-dark. I'll be a golden color. I'll be something different that they know I'm not just full Black. They know that I am something else. There is prejudice against that.

Talia is recognized as mixed by Black people, which is an acknowledgment but with prejudice. At the same time, her Mexican American peers do not consider her Mexican because they perceive her as Black. In essence, Talia's appearance is not "right" for either group and is rejected despite the fact that she was socialized in each culture. Consequently, she experiences monoracism, or oppression on an interpersonal level of people who do not fit monoracial categories grounded in assumptions about singular and discrete racial categories.[30]

Living Up to Both Standards

Blaxicans are held to the cultural-racial standards of African Americans and Mexican Americans, both separately and at the same time, depending on the context. For instance, Erica, whose father is African American and whose mother is Mexican American, illuminates the phenomena of being expected to live up to both. Erica traces her Mexican side of the family, who labored as migrant farm workers, to Ciudad Juárez, a city bordering El Paso, Texas. After one season of picking strawberries, Erica's mother ended up settling down in Indiana. Erica's mother eventually attended college in Indiana, where her parents met. Erica was raised by her mother and has lived in Indiana most of her life, except for a short time during her teenage years when she lived in Atlanta, Georgia. Erica ponders the greatest challenge of identifying as Blaxican. She said,

I think the hardest thing about being Blaxican is trying to live up to both standards. The hardest thing about it was my mom was a single mom, so she didn't have a lot of time to teach me Spanish as well as I would have liked to learn. She was working all the time. I understand Spanish, and I can speak Spanish, but it sounds bad, and you can tell that I get past tense and future tense off. Being Black is really hard because my dad wasn't really around; so I didn't learn about African American culture the way I would have liked to. My mom always listened to Spanish music. We didn't have cable; so I didn't have MTV or BET to teach me.[31] I grew up in Indiana, and I grew up in Bloomington, which is a really small town with mostly white people. So I didn't have to face any of those [African American] expectations until I moved to Atlanta.

Erica believes that the biggest challenge of being Blaxican is the social expectation that she is knowledgeable about both cultures. Erica was held accountable for speaking Spanish and regrets that her mother did not teach her the language. With the absence of her father and her mother single-handedly raising her, she did not, in her view, receive much instruction from her parents on how "to be" Black or Mexican. Furthermore, Erica feels that she would have been more oriented to Black mainstream culture if her family had had cable television. She claims she would have viewed MTV and BET, corporate television media stations that have been the principal venues to market Black culture, bodies, and aesthetics to a global consumer audience.[32] Additionally, in Indiana Erica was surrounded by white people who viewed her as Black in accordance with the one-drop rule. It wasn't until she moved to Atlanta that her peers began to question her Black authenticity. Erica described her experience in Atlanta:

I went to a school in Atlanta that was all Black with a lot of Mexicans, and it was really segregated. I was from Indiana; I was from the Midwest, and they would be like, "Where are you from?" My name is Erica, and they would be like, "Your name is Erica? You're from Indiana. You talk like a white girl. You don't speak Spanish good, you're not down with any of the Black people because you don't know how to dance, or you dance funny, you dancing like a certain way or whatever and it's not the right way." They doing the "two-step," "walk it out" or some shit, and I'm like trying to figure out who I am, and I had a lot of negativity from both sides. I was never Black enough, and I was definitely never Mexican enough, ever.

In Indiana white people did not seem to question her Blackness. But when Erica moved to Atlanta and attended a high school that was predominately Black and Mexican American yet segregated, she realized she was being held accountable to Black and Mexican American racial-cultural expectations. Erica's Mexican American peers expected her to know Spanish. At the same time, her African American peers accused her of having a white-sounding name and "sounding white." Accusing Erica of not knowing hip-hop dances is laced with assumptions that she is not Black enough, particularly since Blackness has become synonymous with hip-hop culture.[33]

She was not Black enough for Black people and not Mexican enough for Mexicans. Interestingly, Blaxican women are questioned about their dancing skills by their Black peers, while Blaxican men are not. Blaxican men are expected to listen to hip-hop music, but their dancing skills are never brought up. One of the reasons Blaxican women (and not men) are expected to dance hip-hop may be related to how the music industry commodifies Black women's bodies in music videos.[34]

While Erica was expected to know hip-hop dance as a way of proving that she was authentically Black, knowing cultural dances didn't seem to be enough to prove Mexican cultural authenticity if participants appeared Black. Monica, a twenty-five-year-old woman from Tucson, Arizona, whose mother is Mexican American and father is African American, is an example. Monica's parents divorced when she was very young, and she did not have contact with her father or his family growing up. Monica feels very connected to Mexican culture and traditions. As a young girl she danced folklórico with a group at her Catholic church. Monica was socialized around many of her Mexican American cousins, and for a long while she never thought of herself as anything other than Mexican. It was not until the girls in her folklórico group excluded her because of her dark skin that she began to understand that people viewed her as Black. She recalls a story:

> One time in third grade I was in folklórico, and I went to Santa Rosa; it was a very Mexican church, and the girls there were mean to me; they picked on me. I was on a folklórico team, and I thought I was good, and my mom said I was good, and I performed, and I was in it for a couple years. One day I had to miss practice for a day, and they told me, "Oh you can't perform in the next performance because you missed practice." Then my friend that was on the team told me that they really did not want me to be on the performance because I was Black. And that was the first time that I was ever like, "What? I'm Black?" And I got picked on, and it was really weird for me to get picked on because I was always comfortable wherever I was, and so it was really weird for me to feel so picked on because I wasn't Mexican enough for them.

Monica's story illustrates the many monoracial microaggressions Blaxicans encounter. The Mexican girls in the folklórico group excluded her from the performance because she appeared Black. This experience was informative, because it was the first time she realized people perceived her as Black and showed her that her appearance marked her as inauthentic, despite her being competent in folklórico dance. Ironically, ballet folklórico consists of several dances and costumes that reflect the different regions of Mexico. Many dances are a representation of Mexico's history and people and reflect the influence that Arab, African, German, Dutch, and other European cultures had on Mexican people.

For example, dances from the region of Nayarit are inspired by Moorish influence of the Spanish originating from when the Moors conquered Spain. In addition, the African peoples who were enslaved during the Spanish colonization heavily influenced rhythms used for dances in the Veracruz region.[35] Rather than using ballet folklórico as a teaching opportunity to highlight Mexico's diversity, the group decided to alienate Monica. Reflecting on this moment in her life, Monica acknowledges that she was perceived as Black because she looked more Black than Mexican, even though she felt more culturally Mexican. She said,

> I just looked more Black. I think people viewed me more as a Black person than as a Mexican person. And . . . I feel more comfortable [viewed as a Black woman] because it was really awkward trying to hang out with Mexicans, and you can't talk with them, and they look at you funny if you try to act Mexican, you know what I mean? There's a certain way that you need to act, and I was never good at acting either way. Act Mexican or act Black. Black people always say, "You act white," [and] "Oh she's a white girl in a Black girl's body." They would always say that.

Monica's Mexican American peers viewed her as Black and picked on her. Simultaneously, her Black peers accused her of being "a white girl in a Black girl's body." Perhaps a more accurate description would be that she is a "Blaxican in a Black woman's body" since she feels that she looks Black and is comfortable being perceived that way. Like other participants in this study, not "acting" Black in the eyes of their Black peers was automatically equated with "acting white." Even though Monica is perceived as Black visually, this did not signify her acceptance as Black by her Black peers because of her connection to Mexican culture, which they interpreted as "acting white." Paradoxically, Monica's proficiency in folklórico and her involvement with the Catholic church did not translate into acceptance by her Mexican American peers who did not consider her culturally authentic. Her Black phenotype trumped her Mexican cultural knowledge and engagement.

Consequently, Monica expressed her Blaxicanness as a woman who appears Black, is Mexican culturally, and experienced alienation from both Mexican Americans and African Americans. She said, "I'm Blaxican; that's what I am. I am not more Black than I am Mexican. This is who I am—Black and Mexican—and I love both sides the same. I went to school, and I was the only Black person, and I was half-Mexican too, but that side is only like at family life. Whenever I told people that I was half-Mexican, they would be like, 'Yeah' [sarcastically]. They never look at me like I'm half-Mexican; so sometimes I don't feel comfortable being around Mexican people."

Monica's experience demonstrates mixed-race peoples' individual negotiation of identity that is constricted within existing racial-cultural frameworks (i.e., being self-reflexive about what race and culture they identify with but unable to choose without restriction).[36] She claims a Blaxican identity and feels connected to Mexican culture but sometimes feels uncomfortable around Mexican people. Although she individually identifies as Blaxican, she is comfortable living in the world perceived as Black. At the same time she faces marginalization there as well.

Interestingly, Monica viewed herself as Mexican, until her Mexican American peers excluded her for appearing Black. These intrapersonal interactions can be juxtaposed to "intragroup marginalization," which is the diminishing and discriminatory attitudes that more privileged group members have toward other less privileged group members.[37] An example could be African American heterosexuals discriminating against queer African Americans. While Blaxicans are not necessarily "intragroup," in a monoracial sense, with African Americans and Mexican Americans, they do view themselves as half. These two racial-cultural groups serve as a reference to what is (or should be) blended in Blaxican identities.

The ways Blaxicans do not fit neatly into these racial-cultural categories in part shapes their sense of self. The in-between spaces underscored by authenticity checks exemplifies the relevance of Anzaldúa's "borderlands" thesis calling for a political and social in-between space that allows for contradictions and ambiguity in the bringing together of different cultures.[38] Blaxican identities signify a borderland terrain through which claiming both identities without valuation of the other (i.e., "I am not more Black than I am Mexican . . . I love both sides the same") challenges traditional hierarchies based on race and culture.

Participants experienced authenticity checks by their peers in various ways, such as questioning their language proficiencies, speech patterns, or dancing skills. This was particularly the case if their physical features or cultural competencies did not match the monoracial and conventional images of African Americans and Mexican Americans. My interview with twenty-three-year-old LaTrice demonstrates the expectation that she act either as Black or as Mexican. She said, "People will be like, 'Why are you acting so Black? Why are you acting so Mexican?' I am Mexican! I am Black! One minute I will be talking fast English and one minute I'll be talking in Spanish. I don't do it on purpose; that is just who I am."

LaTrice switches between speaking English fast and then talking in Spanish, she considers that a Blaxican behavior. The questions Why are you acting so Black? or So Mexican? imply that LaTrice compartmentalizes herself in ways that privilege one racial identity over another because of the monoracial imperative that claims she cannot be both. LaTrice, however, resists the expectation to choose and asserts that she is both even if she appears more Black than Mexican to most people and was raised by her Mexican American mother.

The way LaTrice expresses her Blaxican identity reflects her upbringing. She said, "My mom, she made sure that I was aware that I was Black, like those are my roots, but she didn't educate me about the culture. I wasn't culturally aware of African American traditions and food. I knew that I was Black, but I never really embraced it; I grew up in a Spanish speaking home and that was all I grew up with. Mom didn't really know anything about it [Black culture] besides that little time she was with my dad."

LaTrice describes the cultural traditions practiced in her family. "We celebrated posadas; we did the whole piñatas [thing], and I had a quinceañera. No Black traditions though." Her immigrant Mexican grandparents raised LaTrice: "My grandpa worked in the fields; then he worked in a mill. My grandma worked in the fields for a little bit. She was the traditional Mexican grandmother that would wake up at five in the morning and make her husband breakfast and lunch."

Although LaTrice's appearance marks her as Black, she feels closer to Mexicans culturally. LaTrice claims that her fluency in Spanish gives her an affinity to Mexican culture. Indeed, we found that fluency in the Spanish language garnered less questioning of authenticity in Mexican American social spaces. She said, "I think that Black people reject me the most. Mexicans reject me at first; then I start speaking to them in Spanish, and they start seeing that they relate to me. They see how I was brought up; then they start accepting me little by little and feeling comfortable around me. With Black people, once they get to know me, I get rejected a lot more by them because of the fact that I don't know a lot of Black traditions or culture."

Both African Americans and Mexicans reject her at first. The more they get to know her, Mexican Americans accept her more and African Americans accept her less, due to her affinity to Mexican culture. LaTrice is perceived visually as Black. While this allows her flexibility in choosing a Black identity based on her appearance, she doesn't feel accepted because she is not culturally Black. She said, "My Black friends would hear me speaking Spanish and be like, 'OK, what are you?' I don't just think that it is me being half-Mexican; people who are full-blooded Black and light skin are accused of being not Black enough [too]." Indeed, skin color is a significant concern in authenticity policing, for multiracials and monoracials alike. However, because she appears Black to her Mexican peers, that fact limits her acceptance as a cultural insider until she can "prove" her competence by speaking Spanish.

The above examples illustrate the extra mental and emotional work it takes to "live up to both standards." Blaxicans navigate the Black white binary *and* the mixed-racial middle as dual-minority multiracials with African ancestry. In white contexts Blaxicans are unquestioned as Black because of the one-drop rule. In another context, they are questioned by their Black peers on claims to a half-Black identity despite the one-drop rule and are asked to prove that they are *really* Black. Then their Mexican identity is often rejected if they appear Black, until and sometimes despite of their demonstration of Mexican American culture.

Authenticity policing exhausts the psyche and reveals the need to create a space for a less tiresome, more liberating expression of identity outside of rigid boundaries. Authenticity policing is about making

Blaxicans do the extra work of proving that they belong and therefore limiting the choice for a multiracial expression. Policing the authenticity of Blaxicans interrogates their loyalty to one nonwhite group and implies that they value one over the other. However, authenticity policing seems to have the opposite effect, and Blaxicans choose to rather blend both and refuse to participate in hierarchical valuation of their racial-cultural reference groups.

Phenotype and Racial-Cultural Authenticity

Across all interviews, hair was the second-most frequent topic of discussion.[39] The significance of hair among African Americans has been documented through literature in its relationship to Africa, enslavement, constructions of race, self-esteem, images of beauty, politics, identity, and the intersection of race and gender.[40] The issue of hair and skin color among African Americans is significant because these characteristics have historically been held as symbols denoting enslavement. Orlando Patterson argues that hair, more so than skin color, became the powerful marker that symbolized servitude during slavery in North America and the Caribbean. Patterson notes that "hair type rapidly became the real symbolic badge of slavery, although like many powerful symbols it was disguised, in this case by the linguistic device using the term 'black,' which nominally threw the emphasis to color."[41]

Ingrid Banks interviewed sixty-one Black girls and women on why hair matters. She found that hair is tied to constructions of gender and sexuality and that Black women's politics and authenticity can be read through their hair.[42] Furthermore, women are held to gender ideals in terms of beauty more than men, and hair is used as a medium to understand complex identity politics that intersect along the lines of race, gender, class, sexuality, power, and beauty. Hair is also important to Blaxicans for these same reasons; however, hair is also viewed as an arbiter to communicate loyalty to one nonwhite group as dual-minority mixed-race persons. As we show in chapter 10, in addition to being judged by their hair as a way of interrogating their loyalties, Blaxicans themselves use hair as a strategy to proclaim how they blend their identities in an egalitarian way.

In addition, both hair and skin color intersect when determining authenticity. Margaret L. Hunter's interviews with African American and Mexican American women about skin color demonstrate that darker skin signifies a presumption of having a deeper connection to non-European ancestors and validates racial authenticity. While light-skinned Mexican American and African American women enjoy more structural privileges and advantages, dark-skinned women appear to be authentic racial beings such that they are less likely to be questioned about their racial authenticity. Skin tone becomes a source of intragroup power, such that darker-skinned members may use their skin color to their advantage within their community. In other words, they use the fact of their darker skin as a means of asserting authenticity and as a source of racial privilege over lighter members.[43]

While light-skinned monoracial people of color may have structural advantages because of colorism, darker-skinned monoracial people of color have an intragroup advantage of making racial-cultural claims to authentic group membership. This is especially true if they "fit" within what Stanford M. Lyman and William A. Douglass term "ethnic cues."[44] Ethnic cues are phenotypic aspects of appearance and behaviors associated with an ethnic group that are readily recognized. Taking this into account, monoracial privilege, or the advantages of being recognized in the U.S. racial order that excludes mixed-race people, is further complicated by colorism. Blaxicans navigate the meanings of skin color, much like the meaning of hair, and present unique challenges because they are dual-minority multiracials with African ancestry.

Obviously, how Blaxicans navigate skin color meanings is dependent on phenotype. Blaxicans can sometimes be too light to be recognized as Black, and while they may benefit from colorism, they are often rejected from claiming group membership as Black. At the same time, Blaxicans with darker skin, in combination with their facial features and hair texture, are read as Black and therefore rejected as Mexican American. In those cases, they do not benefit from colorism and are often rejected from claiming group membership as Mexican American. In addition to phenotypic concerns regarding hair and skin color, culture also plays a role in how Blaxicans are viewed as "not enough" of either, regardless of how they look.

Blaxican women particularly dealt with Mexican American and African American authenticity policing regarding hair and skin color; they also had to grapple with how they measured up to Eurocentric beauty standards. Erica from Indiana highlighted the significance of hair regarding authenticity and Eurocentric beauty standards. She said,

> Hair has always been an issue for me my whole life. That is probably one of my biggest issues being Blaxican. For example, I was dating this Mexican guy, and he was in a white fraternity, and he took me to a big formal dance. I remember I went and straightened my hair because it was a big dance and I wanted to feel pretty. Went there, I don't even know why I did this, but I permed it, looked really nice, really long, and beautiful. Not that curly isn't beautiful as well, but at that moment in my life I thought that it would be prettier if I wore it straight. Everyone told me how beautiful I was, and I was so upset that I had straightened my hair to be prettier, to what I felt would be pretty in their eyes, socially. I was the prettiest girl there, and I came home, and I shaved my head . . . ; I shaved all my hair off. I was so upset with myself that I allowed society to influence me like that. I came home and my brother was giving me all this shit. He was like, "Man, you are so vain! I can't believe that you straightened your hair just to go to this formal dance because you felt like it would make you prettier." Which it did, it made me feel prettier because I looked more something else other than Black; that's why. I felt bad. My brother was like, "You're so shallow; you should have just wore it in braids; you should have just wore your hair curly." I got so mad at him that I shaved it off and everybody freaked out.

The first time Erica decided to straighten her hair was when she attended a formal dance at a white fraternity. Upset that she received many compliments on her hair, as well as with her brother's criticism of her choice to straighten it, Erica shaved all her hair off. Erica reflected on the idea that straight hair is viewed as socially acceptable, beautiful, and closer to appearing "something else other than Black." Indeed, the dominant interpretation of the practice of hair straightening among African American women has been that it expresses identification with a white hair aesthetic.[45]

By shaving her hair off, Erica exercised her agency to reject Eurocentric and patriarchal notions of beauty. This example shows that regarding hair, Blaxican women deal with beauty ideals established in the white world (both locally and globally Eurocentric) and in the racial middle (among African Americans and Mexican Americans). Erica recognized that she felt prettier because she looked something other than Black, received compliments, and was questioned by her brother ("you should have just worn it in braids or curly"). The pressure to reflect beauty standards—standards that please and conform to a range of cultural tastes—through her hair resulted in Erica shaving it all off. This act was a symbolic affirmation that Erica rejects conforming to other people's expectations of her, especially the kind that place her within rigid boundaries around her choice of expression.

Rachel, a twenty-three-year-old participant from Bellflower, California, further teased out the significance of hair and power dynamics. She said,

> There are times when people were trying to compliment me. Like, "Oh, your hair is so nice; what are you mixed with?" As if I weren't mixed with something my hair would be bad. That is a conversation that happens a lot in the Black community: "good hair" and "bad hair." People would say that I was pretty for a Black girl. I think they are commenting on certain features, skin color, and hair. There are some that are considered more desirable. I am not even that light skin, but I am lighter skin, and my hair is curly which is considered "good hair." I don't believe in that, good hair, and bad hair, but I noticed that is a response that I get—that I have good hair. But people have talked about my hair for as long as I can remember and have made comments about that.

Patricia Hill Collins argues that Black women's ideas about beauty are shaped by understandings of racial hierarchies based on skin color and hair. In the above excerpt, Rachel discusses light skin and "good" and "bad" hair attributes.[46] "Bad" hair speaks to the texture of tightly coiled Black hair as juxtaposed with straighter hair, otherwise known as "good" hair.[47] There is an expectation that Rachel should be flattered by compliments of her "good" hair; however, she interprets these comments to mean that kinkier-textured hair is not beautiful. Rachel understands that the compliments she receives are a validation of her ancestry that is non-African. She continues, "Someone was surprised that my hair was soft. Something like because of their experience with other Black people they were surprised that my hair was soft. It was like a compliment, like, 'Oh, your hair is not as bad as I thought it would be.' When I hear it, I don't take it as a compliment because I understand why they are saying that. [It's about] the different value that is placed on different types of hair."

Like Erica, who shaved her hair off after realizing she was receiving compliments for appearing less Black, Rachel also interpreted comments about her "good" hair as an insult to African ancestry, phenotype, and beauty aesthetics. Both Erica and Rachel resented any devaluation of their African ancestry in the interactions about their hair.

Authenticity policing around these markers was certainly an issue for Andrea from Los Angeles, especially at her high school, which had a large African American student body. Andrea said, "When I went to school in Pasadena, it was the reverse of what I experienced with Latinos in Highland Park. So it was like, 'You think you're better?' 'Why do you talk like that?' 'Why do you have that accent?' The hair thing came up. 'You think you're better because you have good hair.' So, I got that. So, I always experienced that type of racism or behavior from my own people." Black racism would require a widely accepted racist ideology directed at whites with the power to systematically exclude others.[48] Andrea experienced multiracial microaggressions in the form of authenticity policing. Andrea was invalidated by her Black peers for her hair texture and Spanish accent and experienced exclusion when her peers decided she felt she was better than them for being mixed.

The significance of hair for Blaxicans is further complicated because family members and peers often read their hair as being a symbolic representation of favoritism or loyalty to one racial or cultural group over another. Symbolic loyalty expressed through hair can also be interpreted as favoritism toward one side of the family over the other. For instance, Andrea had conflicts about her hair within her own family. She said, "My hair is mixed. When I was little, I had an afro. Then when I got to a certain age my mother and my grandmother would fight about my hair. My mom wanted my hair to be braided like a Black girl, [but] my grandma wanted my hair to be like a Latina girl; so there was always that conflict there in my family."

Kevin L. Nadal and his coauthors calls this "recruitment," or when monoracial family members try to influence their kin to favor one cultural practice over another.[49] Andrea's hair became the battleground between her Mexican American mother, who wanted her to have a Black hairstyle, and her Mexican American grandmother, who desired a non-Black Latina aesthetic. While Andrea's mother supported a mixed-race identity in her daughter, Andrea's grandmother seemed to want her to wear a style that would not signify her as a Black girl. Interfamilial issues regarding racial-cultural authenticity were common among Blaxicans' experiences and sometimes resulted in estrangement from one's family.

In this chapter we discussed the interpersonal interactions around African American and Mexican American authenticity policing. These interpersonal interactions reflect intragroup power dynamics and are a way of maintaining boundaries around traditional racial-cultural categories and limit claims to multiraciality. Examples from interviews exhibit that it is precisely authenticity policing and interactions like it that contribute to the development of new hybrid racial-cultural identities that embrace a borderlands space between what it means for respondents to be African American and Mexican American.

Interactions around authenticity policing also give insight into how Blaxicans choose a both/neither formulation of identity without hierarchical valuation of Mexican Americans or African Americans. By asking Blaxicans to exhibit loyalty to one nonwhite group, they instead assert that they value both groups and seek to embody that in their expressions of identity. This chapter mainly focused on Blaxicans' interpersonal interactions that resulted in not being viewed as culturally or racially aligned enough with African Americans and Mexican Americans and how these interactions informed their identities.

| Chapter Thirteen

Black and Brown Relations
Situation and Context Matter

The relationships between African Americans and Latinas/os in the United States have recently become a significant topic of interdisciplinary study, prompted by the growth of the Latino population. Latinas/os now outnumber African Americans in the United States and are projected to make up 25 percent of the population by 2050.[1] Scholars have expectedly studied African American and Latina/o political contentions or alliances, their intergroup perceptions, and their attitudes with an emphasis on the impact of immigration, conflicts, or coalitions within Los Angeles and in the United States more broadly.[2]

While most of the research on Black and Brown relations focuses on either conflict or cooperation as a dichotomous outcome, recent scholarship suggests that Black and Brown relations are neither.[3] For instance, Cid G. Martinez and Victor M. Rios, in their study on African American and Latino gangs in California, argue that African Americans and Latinos that live in the same neighborhoods often avoid interacting with one another.[4] In our interviews, we found that participants brought up narratives surrounding Black and Latino conflict more than narratives about Black and Latino cooperation. These narratives impacted Blaxicans' experiences and identity formations.

When Blaxican participants were talking about their observations of African American and Mexican American relations they referenced the media and specifically discussed conflicts that they witnessed between the two groups in their communities and within their own families. However, many perceived that the media overemphasized the cleavages between Blacks and Latinos in general, and that these real or imagined conflicts did not influence them to choose one group over the other. Black and Latino relations more broadly, and African American–Mexican American relations specifically, are part of the symbolic imaginative narrative about Blaxican origins and identities. For instance, African Americans and Mexican Americans are viewed as separate communities who find solidarity along cultural and racial lines by reinforcing monoracial and monocultural norms and who are perceived to not "get along."

Yet Blaxicans are living proof that the social norms that maintain the boundaries around these two groups can be broken, blurred, and blended. The so-called Black-Brown divide informs their understanding of where they fit into the larger racial context and sense of community. Blaxicans represent a crossing of racial-cultural boundaries between African Americans and Mexican Americans and consequently embody the contradictions that arise when they claim membership to both groups. An example of such a contradiction would be appearing Black and speaking Spanish or being perceived as Mexican or Mexican American physically and also having a deep kinship to African American language, music, food, and shared history.

Black-Brown Divisions and the Media

The mainstream news media is a powerful institution that reinforces a Black-Latino divide. The typical media narratives about Black-Latina/o relations include Latino anti-Black racism, gang violence, and African American anti-immigrant sentiments.[5] For instance, media stories in Southern California create the appearance of steadily increasing tension between Mexicans and African Americans.[6] In addition, the media's depictions of Black-Latino relations suggest to consumers that the issues of each community is mutually exclusive. Obviously, there is an overlap in Black-Latino social, economic, and political concerns due to the existence of Black immigrants, Afro-Latinas/os,

Black-Latino interracial or interethnic families, Blaxicans, and more. Gaby believes that the media exaggerates the division between African Americans and Mexican Americans. She dislikes reading the news because of the monoracial imperative that presents issues as "Black or white" and forces people to choose an either/or state of mind.[7] During our interview, which occurred in 2006 during the immigrant rights marches, Gaby observed that the news media intentionally found African Americans to speak against immigrant rights. She said,

> It doesn't make sense to me for any Black person at all to not be on the sidelines for minorities fighting for anything. That is why I don't like reading the news because I know that they don't want you to be in the gray; they want you to either have a black or a white opinion and be swayed to make a decision. And I have a feeling that they have to find people that say those things. Because my mom's mom [African American] . . . was even for immigrant rights. It makes sense, and though she is not always on good terms with my dad's mom [Mexican], in her mind she is fighting for her too.

Gaby notices the monoracial imperative in news media reporting and negotiates this either/or narrative with an account of the relationship between her African American and Mexican grandmothers. She disrupts the dichotomizing narrative of Black-Brown relations by interjecting that her own African American grandmother fights for immigrant rights, acknowledging that shades in-between do exist. Black-Brown divisions addressed in the media are part of the symbolic imaginative narrative that informs Blaxican identities that must be negotiated. Blaxicans like Gaby are aware that intermediary areas beyond the either/or way of thinking about Black-Brown relations and issues exist. Blaxicans turn away from the either/or mentation and embrace the both/neither law of the included middle.[8] Embodying the contradictions that arise when claiming a both/neither Blaxican orientation shapes their sense of identity and community.

Another interviewee, Eduardo, a twenty-two-year-old college student from New Orleans, Louisiana, was an organizer for an immigrant rights protest that took place in Sacramento in 2006. He expressed some of his frustrations with how the media represented the march: "I was mad because it was mostly Latinos at the march, and I am like no other cultures? It's called immigration rights. It should be more about every culture, not just the Mexicans. The media also made it a Mexican thing, and I think it should be everyone who is going to be enforced by the law." Eduardo was also frustrated that the media discourse pitted African American struggles against immigrant rights struggles. He said,

> And another thing that pissed me off was I think that the media was trying to make it seem like it was a civil rights type of thing, to get Blacks mad at Mexicans. Because now there is like this division between Blacks and Mexicans because they got mad that some Mexicans were comparing it [immigrant rights] to civil rights, but I don't believe they really were. And now it is like, "Well what about our causes? What about our rights? What about our things?" So now it is like this big ol' thing and being Black and Mexican is kinda hard because you want to represent both, so it was really hard for me.

During the marches that took place around immigration reform in 2006, Eduardo noticed that immigrant rights was being juxtaposed to African Americans rights. Indeed, while many African Americans supported immigrant rights struggles, still others expressed resentment that these marches were being touted as the "next civil rights struggle." Indeed, some African Americans are reluctant to extend policy benefits that they themselves enjoy to Latinas/os and view African American and Latina/o economic and political interests as incompatible.[9]

On the other hand, many African Americans are sympathetic to the plight of the poor and know that attacks on immigrants can readily turn into attacks against African Americans.[10] Nonetheless, Eduardo's overall perception was that this type of dividing rhetoric by the media was meant to disunite two historically marginal groups to dissolve a potentially powerful coalition. Presenting the two as separate erases the commonalities and once again reinforces Black and Latino issues as unrelated. Eduardo takes this separation personally in his own activism because, as he said, "being Black and Mexican is kinda hard because you want to represent both." Eduardo rejects the media's divisive narrative that seems to symbolically separate and erase his own Blaxican identity.

Andrea Avila from Los Angeles thought the discourse on Black-Brown divisions in Los Angeles has been blown out of proportion by the media. "In terms of the division, the media plays it more than what it is. There is obviously going to be division because there has been a shift in demographics in South LA, you have more Latinos than African Americans, when there is a demographic shift there is a power shift."

James Diego Vigil argues that conflict between Black and Brown people in inner-city gang neighborhoods in Los Angeles does not stem from racial hostility as portrayed by the media but from ethnic succession, or newer groups moving into areas that create demographic changes and transformations in neighborhoods.[11] Andrea references the demographic shift in South Los Angeles in which more Mexicans and Central Americans began moving into the area, their numbers soon outnumbering African Americans, particularly during the 1990s when many fled Latin America to seek refuge in the United States. Andrea understands that the dynamics between Blacks and Latinas/os change when there is a demographic shift but views the media as responsible for perpetuating the myth of widespread Black-Brown division.

Indeed, intergroup relationships between African Americans and Latinas/os in the media often portray a negative relationship and are used to illustrate opposing sides of controversial issues or political debates, such as immigration. Seeking a conflict-based storyline, the mainstream media has fixated on Black-immigrant tension in particular, fed by conservative anti-immigrant groups with the intention of driving a wedge between the two communities.[12] For example, Sylvia Zamora and Chinyere Osuji found that immigrant rights groups in Los Angeles confronted challenges when trying to mobilize African Americans due in part to the mainstream media's portrayals of interracial conflict and framing that pits immigrant rights against native workers' economic well-being.[13]

Recently, the story of Jamiel Shaw Jr., a seventeen-year-old African American boy murdered by Pedro Espinoza, a Mexican-born undocumented immigrant, sparked controversy over Los Angeles's status as a sanctuary city and the LAPD's order not to cooperate with Immigration and Customs Enforcement.[14] Subsequently, Shaw's father was featured in a presidential campaign ad for Donald Trump, spoke at the Republican National Convention and Trump campaign rallies, was invited to Donald Trump's first address to a joint session of Congress, and was lauded for his stance against sanctuary cities.[15] Indeed, a number of African Americans in California previously joined anti-immigrant groups stating positions against Latinas/os.[16] The mainstream media's framing of the relationships between African Americans and Latina/o immigrants, in particular, advances a monoracial imperative that consistently reinforces Black and Brown issues, communities, and relationships as a mutually exclusive either/or choice.

Aside from using Black-Brown relations to highlight political divides, the news media also uses incidents simply to sensationalize violence, which has the effect of maintaining racialized stereotypes. Reinforcing stereotypes about Blacks and Latinas/os further divides these communities and is the basis for conflict between the groups.[17] Barry Glassner posits that the media uses antidotes as trends to depict entire categories of people as inherently dangerous.[18]

For instance, in 2016 the local news media in Los Angeles covered a fight at a high school located in the northeast San Fernando Valley. A twenty-minute brawl resulting from a dispute at a prom after-party the weekend before involved forty African American and Latino students during school hours.[19] Some of the youth recorded the fight and posted it to YouTube and were subsequently contacted by the local news media for permission to broadcast their video as a news story. The next morning, news helicopters and TV crews were present at the high school, and newscasters attempted to interview the children about the fight on their way onto the campus. The local news presence exacerbated the problem by bringing unproductive visibility to the fight without contributing to positive solutions. Airing a video of Latino youth being violently assaulted by African American youth and vice versa brings public shame and glorifies violence, and it has the potential to create more violence, as some of the students involved may feel the need to save face. An unsubstantiated rumor spread among the youth that a "green-light," which in gang culture makes a person or a group fair game to shoot and kill, was issued against African Americans.[20] After attending a community meeting at the school with students, parents, school administrators, and the Los Angeles Unified police chief, we learned that many of the Latina/o and African American parents had concerns for their children's safety.

The actor Danny Trejo, who has roots in the neighborhood, was also in attendance at the community meeting. The superintendent and police chief used most of the time at the meeting, until Danny Trejo interrupted and demanded that the school listen to the students for a solution. Urging unity, Trejo stated, "The first time African Americans and Mexican Americans got together, we got a Black president. So good things can really happen when we get together."[21] Students in an open microphone commentary interpreted the fight as a gang issue, rather than as a result of ethnic conflicts. The students explained that Black-Latina/o friendships existed at the school but could not be engaged in openly. With resentment, Black and Latina/o students perceived that the neighborhood Latino gang imposed informal but strict social rules that erected boundaries around their interracial social interactions.

Students came up with the solution to hold a walkout and unity rally seeking to challenge the media's depiction of a "race war." Some students criticized the news media for showing up for the negative, rather than positive, aspects to report about their student body.[22] Ultimately, many of the 72 Black students (out of 2,157 Latino students) ended up leaving the school after that incident, a decidedly different solution.[23] Manuel Pastor contends that Black-Latino conflicts are exaggerated, are only part of the story, and miss the daily accommodations and negotiations that happen within neighborhoods. He argues that this lack of nuance in reporting has the detrimental effect of distancing groups in marginal communities.[24] To add, media portrayals of Black-Latina/o relations never seem to take into consideration the multiracial and multiethnic families who live in these communities. How Blaxicans navigate an antagonistic narrative about African American–Mexican American relations is certainly invisible in the discourse.

Black-Brown Relations

The tale surrounding Black and Latina/o relations and supported by media accounts assumes that these two groups are in constant conflict, which reinforces racialized stereotypes and sustains the either/or monoracial imperative. How does this narrative play into the everyday experiences and identity formations of Blaxicans? Participants discussed examples of the common interactions in which they deal with the real or imagined dichotomization of their ethno-racial reference groups in various contexts. Black-Latino relations vary based on region, gender, class, and other factors.[25] Indeed, the relations between African Americans and Mexican Americans may not visibly factor into Blaxicans' day-to-day experiences depending on the racial demographics of their neighborhood or city. For instance, Desire Campbell said: "About Black-Brown tension, I guess you can't have too much because Mexican here is totally the majority. It outnumbers white; it outnumbers everything. It is the obvious majority. I would say as far as the Black-Brown tension I kinda think it doesn't too much exist, at least not in this area; I think the media tries to build it up sometimes. But by the same token, it goes by area."

Indeed, Las Cruces's population is predominately Latino; it is 61 percent Latino, 33 percent white, and 2 percent African American.[26] In other southwestern cities and towns, race relationships between African Americans and Mexican Americans may not be viewed as an everyday issue that Blaxicans encounter. On the other hand, in places where African Americans and Mexican Americans share space, the symbolic narrative of race relations between the two groups is more apparent. Indeed, current trends show an increase of Black-Latino residential integration, particularly in such places as Los Angeles, Houston, and San Antonio, where Latinas/os account for between one and three of the neighbors of a typical African American resident.[27] Albert, a thirty-four year old man, explained his experiences in the Los Angeles metro area, which is very diverse yet remains the seventh most racially segregated metro region in the nation.[28] Navigating a multiracial identity in racially segregated spaces is the norm. Albert said,

> There is a lot of tension between the predominantly Black community and the Mexican community. I had friends and family on both sides; so if I was hanging around some of my cousins that are mostly Black, and we went through a Black community, there would always be a person that was eyeballing the wrong way or had something to say about why I was there or why I was in that area. The same thing on the other [Mexican] side. I'm with them and we are at a BBQ or some kind of a house party function, and I don't think that it's easily noticeable, but some people can pick out that there is a mixture there, and [they'll say], "How come you have reddish brownish hair?" "Why are you here? Go back to the other side." It's kinda a flip back and forth, and you have to pay attention to where you are at, who you are around, and who is paying a lot of attention to you.

Albert describes scenarios in which he is with his Black friends or family or with his Mexican American side and needs to constantly read body language to catch signals indicating that he is not welcome in that space based on his gender and his appearance as mixed. Jessica M. Vasquez argues that men are racialized based on stringent racial and gendered stereotypes stemming from the perception that they are a threat to safety.[29] Albert was highly conscious of who was staring at him in both Black and Mexican neighborhoods and believed his mixedness signaled that he did not belong. Albert was cognizant about whether he was being viewed as a threat in both settings by noticing how he was being "eyeballed" or questioned based on his mixed-race appearance.

This extra awareness is a unique key element in Blaxican racial formation. Being sized up as "familiar or different" translates into being perceived as "safe or a threat" in monoracial communities and makes one conscious of both/neither orientation of identification.

There are many instances that prompt Blaxicans to think about their identities in the shadows of the perceived Black-Brown relations that frame the two groups as inherently dichotomous. These interactions inform their racial identity formations and sense of self by prompting awareness around how they fit in as both/neither in the face of constant messaging around the either/or mentality.

Andrea further illustrates how the very real displays of prejudice between Mexican Americans and African Americans played into her experience and identity. Andrea discussed some of the daily interactions she had while in different racially segregated neighborhoods in the Los Angeles area:

> It's interesting when people talk about racism and "the white man is keeping us down" and all that kind of stuff. Because my experience has been Latinos growing up would call me "n———" and stuff like that, "*mayate*."[30] Then when I went to high school. I went to Pasadena, and Pasadena was more Black people. So when I went there, it was the reverse. . . . Then my mom would come out, and they wouldn't know that's my mom because she looks like that [lighter-skinned]. So I always experienced that type of racism or behavior from my own people. There was no white people that lived here at the time; now it's more gentrified, but back in the day it was Latinos, and in Pasadena, Black.

In Andrea's experience, whites were not the people she perceived to be racist toward her; rather it was her Black and Latina/o peers. The phrase "white man is keeping us down" refers to a structural disadvantage stemming from race, class, and gender exploitation in a capitalist society, which is distinguishable from intergroup acts of prejudice between nonwhite people of color. Manifestations of racial prejudice can operate among and between communities of color, and the same stereotypes that whites have of Blacks and Latinos are also shared about each other.[31] Andrea's overall assessment is that she has experienced oppressive behavior from her "own people" more than from whites on an interactional level, admittedly in racially segregated spaces. These interactions illustrate how monoracism, or discriminatory attitudes and practice directed toward Blaxicans by their monoracial reference groups, brings awareness to the many contradictions that arise when choosing both.[32]

Jenny Griffin, a thirty-year-old woman from Inglewood, California, went through high school witnessing fights between African Americans and Mexican Americans, as well as fights where students from both groups would unite and fight against white students, a form of cooperation not often discussed. Jenny thinks that the antagonism between African Americans and Mexican Americans is the product of the racial hierarchy. Jenny was asked how she felt when African Americans and Mexican Americans fought at her high school. She said,

> It was almost part of your everyday; it was part of going to high school. I guess I didn't have a feeling toward it because it was so normalized to me. I felt like that's the way it is. Mexican people in my family don't like me because I'm Black; these people don't like Black people because they are Black. Or some Black people get irritated because they don't understand Spanish. I was just like, "I am both, and I'm not fighting." I had a friend in high school who asked me, "When it comes down, we are going to be fighting, and are you going to choose the Mexican side or the Black side?" It was like well I'm not choosing any side.

Unfortunately, fights between some African American and Mexican American students at her school were almost an everyday occurrence, to the point of normalization. The conflict narrative about Black-Mexican relations was common sense, particularly since Jenny's Mexican side of the family often ostracized her and her African American father. Jenny also noticed that some of her Black peers expressed irritation that they could not understand Spanish. In Los Angeles, Latinas/os make up nearly 49 percent of the population, and many residents speak Spanish.[33] Tatcho Mindiola Jr. and his coauthors argue that language changes brought on by immigration contribute to social divides between African Americans and Latinas/os and that Spanish-language barriers are viewed by African Americans as an additional barrier to economic mobility.[34]

In addition, when Jenny was asked by a friend to choose sides when the fighting at her high school took place, she refused, proclaiming, "I'm both" and, "I am not choosing any side." Navigating the conflicts and tensions around two mutually exclusive racial and cultural groups is common for multiracial people and not unique to Blaxican experience. However, in some settings such as the ones described in Los Angeles, there is a blatant, almost daily reckoning of African American and Mexican American relations that is impossible to ignore. This kind of navigation impacts Blaxican racial identity formation because respondents are quite literally asked to choose an either/or identification, considering the constant dichotomization of African Americans and Mexican Americans as mutually exclusive groups in competition and conflict with each other. What the above example demonstrates is that Blaxicans choose a both/neither group affiliation, rejecting a hierarchical ranking of African Americans and Mexican Americans. In concurrence with the law of the included middle, which was discussed in chapter 7, Blaxican identities deconstruct and challenge hierarchical valuations and dichotomization by acknowledging shades of gray and rejecting unequal power relationships.

Unequal power relationships were apparent to respondents in their observations of interactions between Mexican Americans and African Americans. My interview with thirty-one-year-old Eli was illuminating. Eli was raised by his Mexican American single father in Fresno, California, and witnessed anti-Black attitudes and behaviors toward African Americans in his neighborhood. He said, "I would say at face, I would think that there's some core deep-seated issues with one culture to the next. But I would say that it would seem that the Mexicans have a little more hatred toward the Blacks than vice versa. Like, 'This fuckin' *mayate, este pinche* fuckin' *negro*.' I would always hear the Black guys they would be all, 'This Mexican motherfucker.' It was always, 'He's Mexican' and, 'This José' and, 'This Julio over here.' That doesn't seem quite as bad as *'Este pinche mayate.'*"

Eli observes that Mexican Americans seem more prejudiced toward African Americans based on their insults toward African Americans. Mexican men in his community refer to African American men in

Spanish as *mayate*, which literally translates to "black dung beetle." *Mayate* is a derogatory word referring to African Americans or a dark-skinned person, which arguably has the same power connotations as the N-word in English. He also heard Mexican Americans refer to African Americans as *negro*, Spanish for "Black person." There are disagreements in Latina/o circles about whether the term *negra/o* is intended to be derogatory or a term of endearment. It seems to depend on the context.[35]

Tatcho Mindiola found in his research on Black-Brown relations in Houston that African Americans had more positive views of Latinas/os than vice versa.[36] Latino perceptions of African Americans are influenced by racial ideologies of their country of origin, in addition to anti-Black xenophobia in the United States.[37] Oddly, African Americans and Latinas/os have little sense of the historical or cultural connections between their two communities.[38] In this research, we found that there were more accounts of Mexican Americans expressing prejudiced attitudes and behaviors toward African Americans and Blaxicans than vice versa. Blaxicans are aware of the perception that Mexican Americans have a higher status than African Americans on the racial-cultural hierarchy, nonetheless, they reject choosing one.

Black-Brown Dichotomy

In addition to navigating some of the negative aspects that may characterize African American and Mexican American relations in the media and daily interactions with peers, participants reported experiencing and witnessing these prejudices within their families. When participants discussed conflict in their families regarding their parents' interracial unions, more often than not they referenced anti-Blackness in their Mexican families. However, in a few cases there was what could be interpreted as anti-Mexican sentiment expressed by African American families. For example, Gaby talked about how in junior high school her Spanish-sounding name was changed to a more Anglo-sounding one. The decision to change Gaby's name was influenced by her African American grandmother, who pressured Gaby's mother into making the name change: "When I was going into middle school, they changed my name from my name that was on the birth certificate to the name that I use right now. My name is Gabriella Marina Porter, but they changed it to just Gaby Porter. She said it was because when I got older, I would have more opportunities because even if they don't see me and they see my name they might discriminate against me, as a scapegoat. It was bad, and I am going to change the name back."

Gaby's grandmother convinced her mother to change her name as a strategy that would protect her from possible housing or employment discrimination when she filled out applications in the future. Interestingly, each side of Gaby's family calls her by a different name, "My whole family on that side [Mexican], they just call me Gabriella. Then on my Black side they call me Gaby." Admittedly, changing Gaby's name from a Spanish one to an Anglo-sounding one is not necessarily anti-Mexican, but Gaby certainly perceived this action as a denial of her Mexican ancestry and Blaxican identity. Gaby represents one of the most extreme examples of how family members force Blaxicans to separate and monoracialize their identities. Most participants witnessed a narrative in the media that reinforces this separation, or experienced interactions with their peers or families that maintain it, but to legally change a name of a minor child while in middle school is a special kind of denial, violation, and erasure.

Conversations around boundary crossing in the form of dating are another way that the hostile dichotomization around Black-Brown relations gets reinforced. Some participants discussed social interactions around how Mexican American families often disapprove of interracial dating with Black partners and how this affected their sense of self. Disapproval of interracial dating between Mexican daughters and Black men can be tied to anti-Blackness in American culture, and Mexico's historic prejudice toward the Indigenous, African-descent Mexicans and dark-skinned people in general. Talia, a respondent from Sacramento, was socialized in a family where there were many Black and Mexican interracial unions. While she did not directly experience anti-Blackness in her own family, she witnessed her Mexican American best friend's father disparage her for dating a Black man. She said,

My best friend since the ninth grade, she is Mexican, and she likes Black guys. Her dad would kick her out of the house all the time because he was against it. He was really strict; so she would spend more time at my house. I guess somebody has done something bad to her dad that was Black, maybe when he was younger, and when that happened, he stereotyped everybody that was Black. I remember him telling her, "When you finish school, you'll never come see her [Talia] again, you won't be friends with her." I would come and pick her and her baby up, and her child was mixed with Black. Her dad had kicked her out, and she went to live with the baby's dad and his parents.

Talia and her interracial extended family were a refuge for her Mexican best friend and mixed-race baby daughter after they were rejected by her prejudiced father. The forbidden boundary crossing in the form of interracial dating or love between African Americans and Mexican Americans contours Blaxican identity and experiences. Witnessing prejudice against interracial love is an insult to their own creation narratives—what it is that makes Blaxicans even possible. This type of prejudice can be viewed as erasure. In many instances, whether through the media or social interactions with peers and family, Blaxicans receive the message that African Americans and Mexican Americans are hostile enemies that harm, rather than compliment, one another. Owning a Blaxican identity is a form of resistance to monoraciality. Monoraciality prescribes an essentialist either/or identity with rigid boundaries that even dictate who a person can love based on their culture or race.

Engaging in an interracial relationship and bringing a multiracial child into a family often disrupts family members' basic worldviews about culture and race. Some Mexican American and African American families change their prejudiced attitudes toward interracial dating and multiracial kin, particularly after couples marry or have children. Dan from El Paso talked with me about how his parents' marriage changed his Mexican grandfather's attitudes toward African Americans:

When I have told people that I am Black and Mexican, a lot of them say, "That is ironic," because I guess they thought that they didn't like each other. Which I don't know how true that is, or how big of a theory that is or not. But I know that my mom said that her father was racist against Blacks, and once she got married that that changed him. If one of your children ends up with someone from another ethnic group, you may have no choice but to accept them and change your views.

When his parents were married, Dan's Mexican grandfather was forced to confront his anti-Blackness and chose to behave differently for the sake of his daughter and future grandchildren. Grappling with family histories of anti-Blackness in Mexican American families in addition to the Black-Brown divide narrative that frames African Americans and Mexican Americans as contentious is something that Blaxicans must deal with in negotiating their identities. Blaxicans are painfully aware of how the relationship between African Americans and Mexican Americans is perceived, and sometimes articulated, as antagonistic. Yet Blaxicans cut through this narrative by pointing out each time the hypocrisies, contradictions, and nuances reveal the borderland, or area of overlap between two things. The borderlands between what it means to be African American and Mexican American are a place Blaxicans inhabit.

Race matters in the marriage and dating market, not only for single race people but also for multiracial people.[39] Remarkably, a few Blaxican participants in this study reported that some of their Mexican American family members discouraged them from dating Black partners. Ironically, two Mexican immigrant parents frowned on the choice their Blaxican daughters made to date a Black partner and made it clear that a Mexican partner was preferable. Although the Mexican parent had crossed these racial boundaries, they seem to now reinforce the same racial divide enforced by the larger society. For instance, Jenny discussed her experiences dating a Mexican American man. Jenny understood that her Mexican immigrant mother preferred that she date a Mexican.

I only one time dated a Chicano guy, and I can say in my family it made a difference. Particularly for my [Mexican] grandmother; she just really loved him, and he did speak Spanish. It was someone that she could talk with, and even now that we have broke up for four years, she still asks about him. She liked that we would go to Mexico together and do all these things, like I had pride in being Mexican, and that was a big deal. There were times when people would ask him if he had a girlfriend and he would say, "Yes." Then they would ask if she was Mexican or Chicana, and he would say, "Yes, and she's Black." Then people would ask, "Well are your parents OK with this?" So, it was a big deal if his parents were OK with him bringing home a Black person, and they were, but I think part of the novelty was that I was also Mexican and I could speak Spanish. If I was just plain Black and didn't speak Spanish, I don't know if it would have been horribly OK. I mean it wouldn't have been horrible, but I definitely did get extra points.

Jenny felt that her Mexican side of the family thought it was more desirable for her to date a Mexican, particularly because her ex-boyfriend spoke fluent Spanish and could communicate with her Mexican grandmother. Her family enjoyed the cultural familiarity, and it didn't seem as if they were anti-Black. Disapproval of Black-Mexican interracial romance is not necessarily rooted in anti-Blackness or deep-seated prejudices (though it can be) but may also be about reinforcing monocultural norms that are more comfortable, safe, and familiar. For mixed-race people, dating choices are symbolic of loyalty to one cultural or racial group. For instance, Jenny's family felt that her relationship with a Chicano affirmed her pride and loyalty in being half-Mexican, and they were pleased that she was exploring her Mexican roots by traveling to Mexico. Furthermore, Jenny's fluency in Spanish and her identity as half-Mexican deemed her acceptable to his Mexican American family, despite appearing Black.

Similarly, Jackie, an attorney from Los Angeles, reflected on the way her Mexican family felt about her dating a Black man. Living and working in New York City, Jackie is commonly mistaken for

Dominican or Puerto Rican. She was raised by her Mexican immigrant mother, speaks fluent Spanish, and considers herself culturally Mexican. She reflected on her family's response when she decided to date a Jamaican man. She said, "I'm now dating a Black man. He is Jamaican American, and they make comments, like my Mexican family seems to think that I have betrayed them in a sense. Like, 'Our culture is not good enough for you?' And, 'Your children will have no Mexican experience because of your choices.' Which is funny to me because anyone who meets me is like, 'You are so Mexican!' It happens I grew up around Mexicans! So, it is impossible for me to believe that my children will not have that."

Again, dating choices of multiracial offspring are seen as indicating loyalty to one group. Jackie, however, illustrates that the race or culture of a dating partner does not indicate the choice of one group over the other. Certainly her Mexican family feels seemingly betrayed by her choice to be with a Black man. Jackie's family assumes that cultural transmission of Mexican culture will not take place if she has children with a Black man. In addition, her family seems to deny that Jackie is culturally Mexican based on her appearance as Black. Presumably, a Mexican spouse is the only way that Jackie would be able to transmit Mexican culture through her mixed-race body. The above example illustrates that the conversations around dating taboos that cross racial and cultural barriers between Blacks and Mexicans and Blacks and Blaxicans are not always explained as the devaluation of Blackness but rather the fear of losing Mexican culture. Certainly, racial hierarchies and colorism relating to power are a concern, but it is not always expressed as such. Jordan explains that while the one-drop rule did not develop in the Caribbean and Latin America, in Latin-dominated cultures as well as in the United States, lighter has been understood as better.[40] One ponders if Jenny's and Jackie's Mexican immigrant mothers and extended family would have had concerns about the cultural transmission of Mexican culture if they had, respectively, dated an Afro-Mexican partner. In other words, were the concerns about dating Black men more about the ability to transmit Mexican culture to their future children, or about race?

Conclusion

Bridging the Borderlands

The first part of this book, titled "Racial Formation and the Blaxican Borderlands," examined broad macro- and meso-discursive structuring of the categories contributing to the formation of the Blaxican borderlands as the simultaneous blending of African American and Mexican American backgrounds, experiences, and historical sources. In doing so, we provide a broader comparative historical context for elucidating the contradictions that can arise when claiming membership in these two groups as a catalyst for the development and declaration of a Blaxican identity. The second part, titled "Living Race and Identity in Black and Brown," moved to the micro-level analyses that encompass the qualitative study of Blaxicans. Here, we engage Blaxican identities and experiences as an opportunity to reimagine not only racial formations but also new possibilities of conceptualizing cooperation and alliances across racial-cultural differences, particularly between African Americans and Mexican Americans, and by extension, Blacks and Latinas/os.

Migration and settlement patterns of people from Mexico and other Latin American countries contribute to the changing racial dynamics and demographics of race in the United States. Often, housing segregation and labor experiences group African Americans, Latinas/os, and other groups of color in common spaces, increasing possibilities for intercultural and interracial exchanges and unions. Blacks and Latinas/os—and in this case, Mexican Americans—have tended to compete for the lowest-paying employment in the formal labor market.[1] Correspondingly, Blacks and Mexicans at times experience racially driven violence against one another on the streets and in prison institutions.

Certainly, the commonsensical and academic characterization of relations between Blacks and Latinas/os has been, more often than not, one of conflict and being "at odds" with each other. Of course, there is considerable evidence that African Americans and Mexicans American have historically coexisted harmoniously. Blaxican identity is, to some degree, a direct reflection of how these material relations, like Mexican migration, housing, and labor experiences, intermesh with the life experiences of African Americans. Still, this dominant narrative is also significant in understanding Blaxicans' sense of self-acceptance (or lack thereof) and the limitations placed on their choices of identity. Identification with one of these groups may cause, or be understood as causing, difficulty with acceptance by the other one.[2] But what of Black-Brown solidarity and its relationship to and possibilities for Blaxican identity?

An Alternative Perspective

Nicolás Vaca and others astutely point out that one cannot presume that African Americans or Mexican Americans, and Latinas/os more broadly, automatically have a natural alliance with interests that override these areas of conflict. It is no surprise, then, that the master narrative regarding Black-Brown relations, particularly in the mainstream media, has been solely, or at least primarily, focused on conflict.[3] Consequently, in the popular imagination conflicting interests among African Americans and Mexican Americans override any possibility for the consideration of mutuality and coalitions. Yet scholarship in the past two decades on Black-Brown relations has emphasized counternarratives that highlight intersecting Black-Brown experiences and cooperation. Counternarratives are an important tool to advance the power of storytelling, to challenge cultural stereotypes,

CONCLUSION

and to create new ways of perceiving. Therefore, it is imperative to examine cross racial unions and experiences in Black and Mexican communities.

Los Angeles is a perfect city in which to examine these social dynamics and counternarratives. South Los Angeles, traditionally considered the heart of Black Los Angeles, has undergone a significant demographic transformation over the last five decades. Approximately 80 percent African American in 1970, the area is now about two-thirds Latina/o. The iconic neighborhood of Watts—the center of the 1965 rebellion against policing that eventually gave rise to momentum for a Black mayor and a new cross racial politics—is now 70 percent Latina/o. Historic South Central, an area along the Central Avenue corridor that gave rise to Los Angeles's most important Black cultural and religious centers of the twentieth century, is now nearly 90 percent Latina/o.[4]

There have been several recent scholarly contributions examining these dynamics and providing a counternarrative. For example, Gaye Theresa Johnson's *Spaces of Conflict, Sounds of Solidarity* (2013) covers nearly eight decades of Black-Brown relations in Los Angeles and interrogates the concept of "spatial entitlement," examining the histories of deindustrialization, displacement, and other injustices shared by African Americans and Mexican Americans. These spatial entitlements refer to the ways that marginalized groups creatively construct collectivities together with other marginalized groups to reclaim space. They are achieved through activism and "soundscapes," or shared sonic spaces of mutual recognition and belonging.[5] Johnson illustrates the interracial connections in R&B, hip-hop, and punk music and the parallels to political mobilization in Black and Mexican American communities.

Relatedly, Josh Kun's and Laura Pulido's edited volume *Black and Brown in Los Angeles* (2014) examines the historical and contemporary relationship between Blacks and Latinas/os, particularly Mexican Americans, in Los Angeles. It highlights the intersecting histories, fates, and shared struggles of Black and Brown communities by examining politics, art, history, culture and more. The volume's essays provide an analysis of how Black and Latina/o lives are intricately linked through politics, car culture, policy, and music. Some examples, corroborated by one interviewee (Eduardo) below, include stories of unification between the Black Panthers and Brown Berets in the late 1960s and early 1970s and the blending and borrowing of each other's cultural expressions in lowrider culture. In recounting examples of coalition building and the creation of new cultural expressions that blend and borrow and cut across racial lines, the authors move away from the narrative of conflict and highlight acts of both groups relating to each other in everyday moments.

South Central Dreams, edited by Pierrette Hondagneu-Sotelo and Manuel Pastor (2021), is another excellent example of this counternarrative research that moves beyond the fraught relationship between Blacks and Latinas/os. The book examines the lives of first- and second-generation Latina/o immigrants and how they make a home alongside their African American neighbors in South Central Los Angeles. Drawing on testimonies from residents who have experienced this community's transformation, as well as on quantitative data, Hondagneu-Sotelo and Pastor offer a penetrating examination of social change and adaptation by tracing the evolution of South Central from a predominately African American community to one that is mostly Latina/o.

Although South Central Los Angeles continues to have its economic and social challenges, the everyday reality is one in which Black and Latina/o neighbors are mostly cordial and where political organizers frequently take into consideration the "linked fate"—namely, the shared realities and issues for Black and Brown people.[6] Cultural fusion is commonplace. For example, Black taco trucks have become an increasing phenomenon. The authors describe how many Latina/o youth have forged a new political identity that is shaped by Blackness. Latina/o youth draw from and are informed by insights of their immigrant elders and African American peers in their neighborhoods and schools. These are some of the insightful ways the book complicates and interrogates notions about Black-Brown relations.

Black and Brown Lives Matter

The preceding discussion points outs how the narrative around Black-Brown relations (and African American and Mexican American communities, specifically) arises. It is not only framed as divisive by the media and broader public imagination but also is (re)articulated in a variety of social interactions with family and peers. Throughout this book, we have explained how choosing a both/neither identity as Blaxican is a form of resistance to monoraciality and the daily interactions that reinforce the two as inherently separate and conflicting. This section further reiterates how the Black-Brown divide is negotiated in a distinctly Blaxican way, which we synthesize around a series of three "resolutions."

The first resolution is that Blaxicans resist monoracial and monocultural norms asserted by the Black-Brown divide by not choosing a side. This might be conceptualized around a language of both/neither, whereby Blaxicans embrace all aspects of themselves, including the contradictions that arise when the larger society tries to separate their biracial backgrounds. For example, the dominant narrative of Black-Brown relations is that Mexican Americans and African Americans are intrinsically harmful to one another. Blaxican identities exist despite these contradictions and overlap regarding what it means for them to be African American and Mexican American simultaneously. Consequently, by simply choosing to identify as Blaxican, rather than as either Black or Mexican, individuals are opting for a critique of monoracial (and monocultural) norms. Specifically, the choice makes its critique in a manner reflective of a borderlands logic, whereby being Blaxican is constitutive of and requires being *both* Black *and* Mexican, while at the same time being *neither* Black *nor* Mexican. That is, we can understand this first resolution as encompassing the premise of "mixedness" altogether.

The second resolution is that Blaxicans take an interest in both African American and Mexican American communities without hierarchical valuation and similarly find ways to connect them in their own consciousness and sense of self. In contrast to the first resolution, which is organized around an articulation of the both/neither of the borderlands, this second resolution more closely maps onto a both/and formulation. Indeed, here we see a reflection and articulation of consciousness more in line with positive marginality or liminality, whereby individuals consider themselves as being members in *both* communities simultaneously—that is, they hold a mutual interest and belonging in both—without hierarchically valuing these memberships. Much like the above, the second resolution is also an articulation of resistance to the U.S. racial hierarchical order.

The third resolution, then, can be understood as having to do with the internal (mindful) and in some cases external (engagement) work individuals do to dismantle racially hierarchical valuations. This mindful work is done by choosing a both/neither identification, much like in resolution one, and subsequently challenging media messages *and people* when they try to devalue one group over the other. The engagement work is done by advocating and supporting others when they cross the Black-Brown divide (i.e., Talia taking in her Mexican best friend and mixed-race baby when she was kicked out). Engagement in dismantling racial hierarchical valuations is also done through social justice organizing and activism for both Black and Brown issues, as well as by articulating the linkages between the two.

In an example of how Blaxicans overcome the Black-Brown divide by choosing both, Andrea from Los Angeles said,

> I think it's about trying to keep people down by having to pick a side. If we were all to come together, I couldn't even imagine what kind of power we would have. When you have two identities together and you are mixed, people try to force you to choose as a way of trying to keep people apart again. And that explains the whole mentality of "pick a side." You are either one or the other. You have to pledge allegiance to one or the other. That is another way of keeping us separate. You stay on your side, and I'll stay on my side. The more separate you are, the more ignorant you are of each other, and you don't realize similarity.

The need to choose loyalty to African Americans or Mexican Americans is an articulation of the monoracial imperative that presents identity options for Blaxicans as an either/or choice. Once again, Blaxicans interviewed for this research reject the either/or formulation of monoraciality and choose a both/neither one. Andrea believes that similarities between African Americans and Mexican Americans are not recognized because of psychological and physical separation, and she ponders the potential power of their unification.

Eduardo from New Orleans also articulated choosing both and overlapped the two groups in his identity. Eduardo is an example of an interviewee who has done social justice organizing and activist work addressing issues for Black and Brown people. Eduardo recounted a transformative experience he had while discussing a current event. At the time, a significant news story involved incidents of street violence in Southern California between Blacks and Latinas/os that stemmed from prison issues. During that period, Eduardo went to a talk on his college campus where public intellectual Dr. Cornel West presented. He said,

> I was supposed to go down there [Southern California]. And I didn't go, but there was a Black and Brown rally with the Black Panthers and the Brown Berets, and they were supposed to have a peace conference because there was a lot of stuff going on in the jails. So Blacks and Mexicans were killing each other. Around this time I actually had the opportunity to meet Cornel West. Cornel West came to our school, and I had the opportunity to talk with him because he was talking about Black and Brown relations and the importance of Black and Brown people getting together, and I told him that I was Black and Mexican, and he pulled me aside and told me [I had] "the opportunity, . . . the responsibility" to make sure, that I always take an interest in both and to find a way to connect the two together and not divide them. And I was like hecka motivated and changed by it. Because I never really looked at it like that. I never looked at it as a responsibility and as a—I have an opportunity to make a difference, so it kinda, like, woke me up when he came, and he talked about what's going on and stuff.

This is one example of how Blaxicans resolve the Black-Brown divide narrative by taking an interest in both the African American and Mexican American communities without valuing one over the other. Blaxicans find ways to connect the groups in their identities and grasp the linkages and similarities between them. For Eduardo, this came when he was involved in activist work on immigrant rights and Black and Brown unity. Dr. Cornel West pulled him aside and pointed out his unique positionality as Blaxican, empowering Eduardo to see his identity as an opportunity to unify rather than divide.

Erica Donald, a twenty-three-year-old woman from Gary, Indiana, resonates with the sentiment that Blaxican identity represents an opportunity for unity rather than division between African Americans and Mexican Americans. She said,

> I feel that I have a duty, and I feel that it is a very special gift to be Blaxican. Because right now Black people, Latinos—Mexicans specifically—we need to come together more, I think. I think that oppression is a big deal for us. I think that we need to help bring our people together more because as long as we stay divided in certain areas, we are divided. And as long as we stay like that, we're never going to be able to overcome the oppression that we face.

Erica articulates a view that Blacks and Mexicans are divided and that they need to unify to overcome oppression that both groups encounter. In fact, she states that it is her duty to work toward uniting these groups. She points out that together, Blacks and Mexicans are in a better position to resist oppression than they could be separately. This example shows that Blaxicans reject choosing sides, take an interest in both African American and Mexican American communities, and through critical analysis and action, dismantle hierarchies by viewing both groups equally. Blaxicans make connections between the struggles of both groups and view them as equally valid, and they represent them in their articulation of self. Erica's brother, Sebastiano Flores, talked about how the idea of "dual oppression" manifests itself in his hip-hop music and in the way he thinks about his Blaxican identity, which further illustrates this idea of Blaxican articulation of self. Sebastiano said,

What is the dual oppression? I got twice the fire burning inside me. I got both of them. This is how I look at it, I communicate with my ancestors. It is easy to ignore ancestors, and it's easier to ignore ancestor's voices whispering in your ear when you have one whole cultural oppression and genocide whispering in your ear. But when you got two completely separate, cultural, ancestral, genocidal, conversations going on—one in each ear—it's going to move you to action. Both of our ancestors are suffering from the genocidal oppression, both talking at the same time, and I'm going to turn the heat up even that much more. The heat is going to be turned up that much more. I am going to reiterate it to other people, that dual culture.

In his own words, Sebastiano describes how he draws from Mexican American and African American histories of oppression in the United States and how these histories inform his social and political consciousness and self-awareness. Sebastiano "communicates" with his ancestors, both African American and Mexican American. He takes an interest in both histories of genocide and oppression and does not choose sides; rather, he articulates a "dual oppression." Overlapping both histories move him into action. Sebastiano engages in dismantling racial hierarchies that place one group above another in his music and his social justice activist work. He feels motivated to spread the message of "dual oppression" or "dual culture" through his music as a way of impressing the idea of unification among Black and Brown people.

Indeed, a 2020 poll by the *New York Times* and Siena College indicated that 21 percent of Latinas/os said they marched in support of Black Lives Matter protests in response to the May 25, 2020, death of George Floyd, an African American murdered by a white police officer; that number was nearly identical to the 22 percent of Blacks who said they participated as well.[7] Still, during the same period when George Floyd and other African Americans, including Breonna Taylor, Mario Woods, Eric Garner, Michael Brown, and Tamir Rice, were murdered by law enforcement, Latino boys and men, such as Sean Monterrosa, Erik Salgado, Andrés Guardado, Antonio Valenzuela,

Manuel Diaz, Santos Rodriguez, and Adam Toledo, among others, were also killed at the hands of law enforcement. Their murders provide the occasion to emphasize that Brown lives have been the target of racist attitudes and practices comparable to those endured by African Americans, including police brutality and other abuses. Yet there was no similar national media coverage. Also, there was practically no local or national support or community mobilization against these wrongful killings.[8]

Such dynamics have import for Blaxicans, given their dual ties to both Black and Mexican communities. Indeed, many Blaxicans are seeking ways to convey that their Mexican background matters just as much as their Black background. This becomes especially important given that Mexican Americans face hostile responses from law enforcement, including police brutality, that are similar to what Black Americans endure. Some mixed-race individuals say the lifetime effort to bridge the gap between their two halves has intensified with the Black Lives Matter movement, particularly in terms of helping the Latina/o side understand what it is like to be Black. With the new focus on racial accountability, they are also more determined to address the anti-Blackness coming from friends and relatives.

Geron McKinley, who grew up multiracial in the mostly Black and Latina/o neighborhood of Willowbrook, near Compton, California, recognized a common thread in both of his cultures, which have been oppressed but remained proud. McKinley, a twenty-five-year-old model, is founder of a clothing brand and nonprofit called Concreet, which offers sports, arts, music, and entrepreneurship programs for children. McKinley is now even more determined to support both Black and Latino causes. He stated, "Now more than ever, even if I've felt like I'm not Black enough to be Black or I'm not Mexican enough to be Mexican, if either side needs me to ride, then I'm riding."[9]

Black and Brown Faces in High Places

These Black and Brown matters are a clear indication that racial differences continue to perpetuate social inequality and forms of exclusion of Blacks and Latinas/os, notwithstanding the significant gains that have been made in the post–civil rights era due to the dismantling of Jim Crow segregation, as well as the achievement of historic civil rights and other legislation in the 1950s and 1960s. The growth, prosperity, and increased integration of some individuals of color, which is one of the achievements of the post–civil rights era, does not, therefore, mean racism has abated. Racial differences continue to perpetuate systemic social inequality and forms of exclusion. Rather, some of the most egregious forms of legalized racial inequality have been eradicated. Pervasive formal exclusion and coercion have been replaced with more informal dynamics, which are increasingly juxtaposed with patterns of selective and inequitable inclusion.

Consequently, the inclusion of "Black [and Brown] faces in high places" is not, in and of itself, equivalent to equality.[10] These individuals and their integration into the white power structure merely further the illusion of equality. They conveniently deflect attention away from the overrepresentation of communities of color, particularly Blacks and Latinas/os, in the secondary labor force and among the ranks of the underemployed and unemployed. This has led to the emergence of colorblind ideology, or what Eduardo Bonilla-Silva refers to as "colorblind racism," which has prevailed since the last decades of twentieth century.[11]

The colorblind mindset fosters the ideology of individualism and meritocracy. It maintains that social outcomes are based not on ascribed characteristics such as race but rather on acquired economic and cultural characteristics, which can be altered by individual merit, effort, and achievement. Individual deficit behavior, rather than systemic structural racism, is the explanation for continuing social inequality. Even worse, it espouses the belief that the excluded masses of color could surmount their difficulties if only they had the character and drive to do so. This ideology also obscures selective integration wherein some individuals of color gain increased access to wealth, power, and prestige, but those who more closely approximate European Americans are favored. For Blacks, phenotype has partially replaced the one-drop rule because "racial capital" is now increasingly based on physical appearance, as well as on white cultural, behavioral, and socioeconomic attributes.[12]

From White Domination to White Hegemony

Drawing on Antonio Gramsci, Omi and Winant encapsulate the partial nature of this form of selective integration as "hegemony."[13] It effectively allows whites to maintain a hierarchy of power sharing without requiring them to give up structural control. This does not preclude the existence of more egalitarian patterns of integration based on equality. However, it follows that integration (inclusiveness) would continue to be deeply marked by more inegalitarian—that is, assimilationist—dynamics given that the larger social order is still underpinned by racial hierarchy. White hegemony thus indicates the United States has largely shifted away from white domination supporting and supported by explicit and overt white racism and supremacy. Yet hegemony disguises the fact that the social structure in the post–civil rights era remains fundamentally grounded in racial inequality.[14]

White domination, although diminished, is not absent.[15] This trend was reinvigorated during the Obama administration (2009–17) as indicated by the white anxiety, resentment, and rage that underpinned the backlash against Obama's presidency as the first African-descent American to be elected to the Oval Office. This includes the Tea Party and Alt-Right movements, as well as other far-right initiatives. Moreover, Tesler argues that since Obama's presidency there has been a resurgence of "old-fashioned racism" espousing white supremacy that was long thought to have disappeared from the United States. Among other things, this form of racism is characterized by a belief in the biological inferiority of Blacks, Latinas/os, and other communities of color and support for racial segregation and discrimination. The Obama phenomenon also tapped into the "new racism," which is characterized by a moral sense that Blacks violate traditional U.S. values like individualism, self-reliance, work ethic, obedience, and discipline.[16]

In 2013 further evidence of this backlash was displayed in the June 24 and June 25 Supreme Court decisions that respectively undermined the enforcement of affirmative action initiatives and sections of the

1965 Voting Rights Act.[17] The latter were originally intended to prevent certain jurisdictions, primarily among the southern (and some western) states, from enforcing historical practices (e.g., white primaries, poll taxes, literacy tests, and grandfather clauses) designed to disenfranchise "racial minorities," particularly Blacks and Latinas/os. These provisions have also targeted contemporary discriminatory practices, including voter ID laws and gerrymandering (or redistricting), designed to achieve similar objectives.[18] Subsequent to the 2013 Supreme Court decision, and increasingly so in the wake of the 2020 election of Democratic president Joe Biden, there has been a dramatic increase in these developments. Under the guise of protecting voter integrity, Republican-led legislatures have passed draconian voter registration ID requirements and gerrymandered, and they have taken similar measures designed to suppress the votes of people of color, particularly Blacks and, to some extent, Latinas/os, who have historically tended to lean Democratic.[19]

If Black Lives Matter protests in response to the murder of George Floyd have been described as a "racial reckoning," there has also been an unsurprising white backlash against those protests.[20] Yet this merely represents the latest phase of the most recent cycle of white supremacist reaction that extends back to the Obama administration. It escalated during the Trump administration (2017–21), and since Trump's defeat, culminated in the January 6, 2021, siege on the nation's capital. This social unrest was in response to claims, which have been thoroughly discredited, that Democratic candidate Biden purportedly won the 2020 presidential election through massive voter fraud, ostensibly involving people of color. Correspondingly, the claims also suggested that Democrats supported an invasion of illegal immigrants to replace white American voters and undercut white working-class jobs. This historically racist exhortation, known as the Great Replacement theory, has become a mantra among some Republican lawmakers and candidates across the nation, used to retain or gain power.[21]

Republican-led legislative initiatives have banned critical thinking about race and racial inequality from school curricula and distorted it into a right-wing talking point. This legislation endeavors to bolster a "positive"—that is, sanitized—sense of national pride by ignoring or glossing over an accurate history of colonialism, slavery, segregation, the civil rights movements, and other manifestations of or responses to white supremacy and systemic white racism.[22] Other developments aim to monitor faculty and students on some university campuses for similar "biases" that undermine "intellectual diversity."[23] These and other advances, including the banning of books from schools and libraries, are principally articulated to incite the Republican base, which is largely composed of whites.[24] This tactic was on display in the days of racist and disrespectful attacks on exceptionally qualified African American Judge Ketanji Brown Jackson during the March 2022 Supreme Court confirmation hearings determining whether she would be appointed as a new justice.[25]

Multiracial Identities and Multiracial Knowledge

A response to these initiatives is increasingly urgent given that the Trump administration exacerbated the extant racial and political polarization. Keith Boykin argues that the core of this crisis is the fear of a darkening America wherein whites will no longer be a numerical majority given the growing numbers of people of color. Instead of seeking to advance a platform that could speak to a broader constituency, the Republican leadership and party are engaged in a self-destructive "last-ditch race against time" to maintain the party's power by inciting white Americans, suppressing voting rights, promoting falsehoods and conspiracy theories, and so on.[26]

The aforementioned developments indicate that white racism, white supremacy, and anti-Blackness (and anti-Brownness), however much attenuated, still underpin the U.S. racial order. Challenging these inequities necessitates attention to power relations and exploitation, which the implied conviviality of multiraciality can conceal. Indeed, some celebratory popular images perpetuate the notion that interracial marriage will lead to a more tolerant society. There have also been imaginings that multiracials are automatically imbued with temperamental qualities ideally suited to solve racism and racial inequality.[27] Even if well-intentioned, this naive egalitarianism can easily fall prey to the assimilationist erasure of racial (and cultural) distinctions under the guise of transcending difference through more egalitarian forms of integration that mask subtle forms of selective and inequitable inclusion or inegalitarian integration. They also divert public attention and state policy from tackling continuing racial inequities and patterns of exclusion based on inegalitarian pluralism.

If the post–civil rights era provides an opportunity to conceptualize mixed race and multiracial identities on egalitarian premises, they must be refracted through a critical lens that scrutinizes and interrogates their potentially problematic agency and implications. Studies indicate that many present-day individuals who identify as multiracial do indeed display this criticality. They informally speak out against everyday racism and racist power dynamics and formally engage in antiracist work. These identities have the potential to, and often do, challenge white racism, white supremacy, anti-Blackness, and inequitable power relations. Survey findings also suggest multiracials may be more open and understanding in terms of people of other races and cultures.[28]

This study of Blaxicans supports those observations by seeking to provide a fresh and unique way of looking not only at racial formations but also at new possibilities of conceptualizing cooperation and alliances across racial and cultural differences. Yet it would be dangerous and naive to suggest that Blaxicans or Blaxican identities, multiracials or multiracial identities, more generally, are the solution to intergroup tensions between African Americans and Mexican Americans or to racism and racial inequality.[29] Rather, they hold the possibility of conceptualizing multiraciality based on egalitarian (i.e., "critical") premises as an additional tool in the antiracist struggle.[30] Critical multiraciality posits what Marc Johnston-Guerrero and Charmaine L. Wijeyesinghe refer to as "multiracial knowledge."[31] This involves engaging in a social praxis that critiques racial essentialism and racial hierarchy while advocating for inclusive collective subjectivities across the racial spectrum, including multiracials.

More broadly, this includes social and intellectual stances that are "betwixt and between"—that is, inhabit the borderlands—as a framework that is open to nuance and ambiguity. It seeks social justice that revolves around a both/neither as opposed to an either/or axis. These can help avoid defensive-aggressive binarisms and polarizations bound in an irresolvable stalemate between inclusion and exclusion, which may be counterproductive in terms of collaborating on other issue-based concerns. The politics involved adapt to contingency and provisionality and proceeds pragmatically without capitulating to pragmatism as an overriding guide to action. Instead, this mindset is driven by broader goals that can offer a basis for advancing thinking and policies seeking to foster social justice. Consequently, the betwixt and between framework is an important contribution to civic engagement, with implications not only for Black-Brown relations but also race relations more generally.

Notes

Introduction

1. Tobias, "Meaning of Race," 19–43; Olson, *Mapping Human History*, 32–48.
2. Smedley, *Race in North America*, 14–16, 27–29; Wilson, *Racism*, 37–47.
3. Gunz et al., "Early Modern," 6094, 6097. Although there is general agreement that the earliest modern humans evolved in Africa, there is considerable debate about where in Africa they first emerged. Forbes, "Manipulation of Race," 37–38.
4. Banton, *Racial Theories*, 1.
5. Davis, *Who Is Black?*, 19–23.
6. It would be necessary to discern this information through genomic technology.
7. Daniel, "Sociology of Multiracial Identity," 106, 108; Daniel and Sterphone, "Hypodescent."
8. Sheldon Teitelbaum, "Making Everything Perfectly Fuzzy," *Los Angeles Times Magazine*, April 1, 2017, https://www.latimes.com/archives/la-xpm-1990-04-01-tm-633-story.html.
9. Wilber, *Integral Psychology*, 278.
10. Simone, *About Face*, 141.
11. Nagle, "Framing Radical Bisexuality," 305–12; Colker, *Hybrid*, 1–10.
12. Bourdieu, *Outline*, 164, 166.
13. Lewis, "Little Mexican Part," 7, 14.
14. Anzaldúa, *Borderlands*, 2.
15. Kun and Pulido, *Black and Brown*, 19.
16. Omi and Winant, *Racial Formation*, 10, 16, 18, 69.
17. Goldberg, *Racial State*, 9–10.
18. Omi and Winant, *Racial Formation*, 77–91.
19. Omi and Winant, *Racial Formation*, 77–91.
20. This distinction dates back to the 1920s and 1930s and is one of the many problematic outcomes of the Black-white paradigm in sociology. The term *ethnic* differentiated the experience of European immigrants from that of

African Americans. This originated in two assumptions about the U.S. social order: that Black Americans were fully Anglo-Americanized and possessed no unique culture and that European immigrants carried distinctive cultures, supposedly different from Anglo-Protestant Americans. When paired with race, *ethnic* soon became the accepted terminology in a developing vocabulary of race relations and the study of subaltern groups. But this ignored the fact that Africans Americans also displayed a unique culture, while European immigrants displayed a white racial affinity with Anglo-Protestant Americans. Consequently, the distinction between race and ethnicity never accurately described Black and white relations. It certainly would not be applicable to Mexican Americans and other groups of color that differ from European Americans and African Americans in terms of both ethnoracial and ethnocultural characteristics. McKee, *Sociology and Race Problem*, 130–31, 146.

1. Race and Mixed Race

1. This chapter borrows from Daniel et al., "Emerging Paradigms," 7–62; and Daniel, "Sociology of Multiracial Identity," 106–25.
2. Feagin and Feagin, *Racial and Ethnic Relations*, 26, 34–48
3. McKee, *Sociology and Race Problem*, 6, 11, 136–38, 146.
4. Blauner, *Racial Oppression*, 11–14; Ladner, *Death of White Sociology*, xix–xxix; Steinberg, *Race Relations*, 9–39; Kinefuchi and Orbe, "Situating Oneself," 70–90.
5. Blauner, *Racial Oppression*, 11–14; Ladner, *Death of White Sociology*, xix–xxix; Steinberg, *Race Relations*, 9–39; Feagin and Feagin, *Racial and Ethnic Relations*, 26, 34–48.
6. Rodríguez-García, "Intermarriage," 9, 11–14; Song, "Is Intermarriage?," 333, 337–42; Telles and Sue, *Durable Ethnicity*, 25, 28; Cheeseboro, "Conflict and Continuity," 151.
7. Alba, *Blurring of the Color Line*, 43, 45–46; Alba, *Great Demographic Illusion*, 5–10; Gans, "Symbolic Ethnicity," 2; Gans, "'Whitening,'" 267–79; Newman, "Revisiting Marginal Man," 30; Rodríguez-García, "Intermarriage," 11; Song, "Is Intermarriage?," 334, 338–39; Telles and Sue, *Durable Ethnicity*, 25, 28.
8. Omi and Winant, *Racial Formation*, 101–4.
9. Perea, "Black/White Binary," 128, 133, 134.
10. O'Brien, *Racial Middle*, 1; Alcoff, *Visible Identities*, 121–24; Gines, "Introduction," 28–37; Kim, "Racial Triangulation," 105–38.
11. Mavin Harris coined the term *hypodescent* in 1964, referring to the one-drop

rule, which designates as Black anyone with "one-drop of African blood." M. Harris, *Patterns of Race*, 56–57. In principle, hypodescent is applicable to degrees of ancestry less restrictive than the one-drop rule in terms of Blackness, as well as to all mixed-race combinations.

12. A few antimiscegenation statutes restricted intermarriage with Native Americans. Yet legal prohibitions against such marriages were not uniform. In places where there were no formal restrictions against Native American intermarriages, legal allowances often contradicted social practice. Moreover, permeable racial boundaries did not overcome a longstanding history of racial tension and genocidal destruction. By the nineteenth century, these laws included Asian Americans but not Mexican Americans, who were legally white. Murray, *States' Laws*, 5–8, 19; Maillard, "Pocahontas Exception," 355; Pascoe, *What Comes Naturally*, 5; Moran, *Interracial*, 17–28.
13. Davis, *Who Is Black?*, 12, 55, 58, 77; Wilson, "Blood Quantum," 109, 122.
14. Jordan and Spickard, "Historical Origins," 101.
15. Davis, *Who Is Black?*, 12, 55, 58, 77.
16. Davis, *Who Is Black?*, 12; Forbes, "Black Africans and Native Americans," 1–6, 190–220; Loewen, *Mississippi Chinese*, 58–153. Leonard, *Making Ethnic Choices*, 174–76, 185–219; Guevarra, *Becoming Mexipino*, 1–12, 41–61, 63–69, 79–83, 131–55, 169.
17. Parker et al., "Multiracial in America," 5–9; Johnston and Nadal, "Multiracial Microaggressions," 123–44.
18. J. Harris, "Multiracial Campus," 1–15; Johnston and Nadal, "Multiracial Microaggressions," 125; Christophe et al., "Examining Multiracial Pride," 22–38; Nadal et al., "Microaggressions and the Multiracial Experience," 43.
19. Lipsitz, *Possessive Investment*, 2.
20. Lipsitz, *How Racism Takes Place*, 2–21.
21. Nadal et al., "Microaggressions and the Multiracial Experience," 43.
22. Johnston and Nadal, "Multiracial Microaggressions," 125.
23. Jones, "End of Africanity?," 201–10.
24. Omi and Winant, *Racial Formation*, 103.
25. The post–civil rights era encompasses the period since the official dismantling of Jim Crow segregation, beginning with *Brown v. Board of Education* (1954), which desegregated public schools, the Civil Rights Act (1964), the Voting Rights Act (1965), and the Fair Housing Act (1968), which gained federal oversight and enforcement of voter registration and electoral practices in states or areas with a history of discriminatory practices and ended discrimination in renting or buying housing. This legislation also included *Loving v. Virginia* (1967), which eliminated the remaining statutes against

racial intermarriage, as well as the removal of legal restrictions on immigration through the Immigration and Nationality Act (1965), also known as the Hart-Celler Act.

26. Roberts, "Black-White Intermarriage," 57–74.
27. Ifekwunigwe, *"Mixed Race" Studies*, 8–9.
28. Domínguez's *White by Definition* is a rare exception among anthropologists.
29. Jones, "End of Africanity?," 201–10; R. Spencer, *Spurious Issues*, 29–85; J. Spencer, *New Colored People*, 2–5; Itabari Njeri, "Mixed Race Generation Faces Identity Crisis," *Los Angeles Times*, April 24, 1988, VI.
30. Wilson, "Blood Quantum," 108–10, 115–18, 122–25; Montgomery, *Identity Politics*, 1–25; Owens, *Mixedblood*, 18, 33–50, 53–66, 173, 215, 217.
31. Turner, "Reconsidering the Relationship," 133, 137–42.
32. Lee, "Racial Classifications," 75–94; Chew, Eggebeen, and Uhlenberg, "American Children," 56–85; Waters, "Multiple Ethnicities," 23–40; Perlmann and Waters, *The New Race Question* includes many chapters by demographers.
33. Prewitt, *What Is "Your" Race?*, 132.
34. Daniel et al., "Emerging Paradigms," 17.
35. DaCosta, *Making Multiracials*, 21–192; Daniel, *More Than Black?*, 93–154; K. Williams, *Mark One or More*, x, 1–64; K. Williams, "Recursive Outcomes," 88, 90, 102.
36. Political scientist Kim M. Williams contended that the multiracial movement, despite its small size, set in motion a process that has amplified and been amplified by broader structural and cultural changes in how people in the United States perceive race ("Recursive Outcomes," 90). Indeed, the size of active membership is not the final determinant of what constitutes a social movement, which is defined by sustained interaction with elites, opponents, and authorities by ordinary people through various contentious displays, performances, and campaigns making collective claims. Tilly, *Social Movements*, 3–4; Tarrow, *Power in Movement*, 24.
37. Exceptions include Nobles's *Shades of Citizenship* (2000) and Williams's *Mark One or More* (2008), although their work appeared after the early and mid-1990s.
38. Exceptions include Daniel's "Beyond Black and White" (1992) and Nakashima's "Voices from the Movement" (1996).
39. Niemonen, "Race Relations," 15, 20.
40. Daniel, "Sociology of Multiracial Identity," 112n5. Daniel's findings are also based on his conversations with faculty at the University of California and observations of public behavior that were dismissive of, if not hostile toward, public presentations he and others made on the topic of multiraciality in the

early 1990s. Of approximately 396 books published between 1989 and 2005 on the topic of multiracial identities, mixed-race experiences, and related topics in terms of U.S. racial formation, only 10 were written by sociologists. Riley, "Appendix A," 67–76. An examination of over forty standard U.S. sociology undergraduate textbooks published in the 1990s also reveals a noticeable absence of the topic.

41. Using the search terms "race AND (United States) AND (mixed race)," Daniel found one hundred relevant results; using "race AND (United States) AND (multiracial)," he found sixty-five relevant articles, most of them duplicates of titles found under "mixed race."

42. American Sociological Association, ASA Annual Meetings. Yet Daniel's observations of public behavior found there was still considerable controversy, conflict, and even acrimony surrounding multiracial identity displayed by attendees at sessions and panels of the ASA and Pacific Sociological Association annual meetings well into the late 1990s and early 2000s.

43. Omi published a journal article titled "Racial Identity and the State" (1997) that contains a brief discussion of multiraciality and the census debate. The third edition of *Racial Formation in the United States*, published in 2014, devotes considerable attention to the multiracial phenomenon.

44. Kinefuchi and Orbe, "Situating Oneself," 70–90; Thompson and Scurich, "When Does Absence," e18–e19.

45. Waters, "Multiple Ethnicities," 23–40.

46. Daniel, *Race and Multiraciality*, 163–64, McKibben, *Shades*, 92; Rockquemore, Brunsma, and Delgado, "Racing," 16–20.

47. Caballero and Aspinall, *Mixed Race*, 5, 140, 273; Park, "Human Migration," 881–93; Stonequist, *Marginal Man*, 10–11, 24–27; Rockquemore, Brunsma, and Delgado, "Racing," 16–17.

48. Nakashima, "Invisible Monster," 164.

49. Stonequist, *Marginal Man*, 10–11, 24–27; Park, Introduction, v, xvii–xviii; Daniel, *Race and Multiraciality*, 164.

50. Park, "Human Migration," 881–93; Stonequist, *Marginal Man*, 10–11, 24–27; Marotta, "Civilisation, Culture," 413–33; Marotta, "Idea of the In-Between," 179–99; Goldberg, "Robert Park's Marginal Man," 199–217; Antonovsky, "Toward a Refinement," 57–62; Gist and Dworkin, Introduction, 1–23; Goldberg, "Qualification," 52–58; Green, "Re-examination," 167–71; Kerchhoff and McCormick, "Marginal Status," 48–55; Wright and Wright, "Plea for Further," 361–68.

51. Hall, "Please Choose," 250–64; Taylor-Gibbs, "Identity and Marginality," 265–78; Taylor-Gibbs and Hines, "Negotiating Ethnic Identity," 223–38.

52. Hall, "Please Choose," 250–64.
53. Root, "Within, Between," 3–11; Williams-León and Nakashima, "Reconfiguring Race," 3–10; Wright and Wright, "Plea for Further," 361–68; Poston, "Biracial Identity," 152–55; Rockquemore, Brunsma, and Delgado, "Racing," 16–20; Goldberg, "Robert Park's Marginal Man," 199–217; Root, "Resolving 'Other' Status," 185–205; Wijeyesinghe, "Intersectional Model," 81–105.
54. Turner, *Forest of Symbols*, 93–111. Liminality (from the Latin *limen*, meaning "boundary or threshold") is typically associated with the initiation rites of adolescence to adulthood in parts of Africa, Latin America, and the Pacific. Liminality emerges from social rupture or discontinuity (pilgrimages, carnivals, religious conversions, life transitions, and holidays), and although not always neat and tidy, it is transformative and generative. Similar dynamics can be observed in individuals who are members of two or more racially or culturally distinct groups, or in practices, cultures, frames for knowing the world, and modes of communication. Hall, "Please Choose," 250–64.
55. Daniel, *More Than Black?*, 106–7, 113–14, 214; Root, "Resolving Other Status," 185–205; Williams-León and Nakashima, "Reconfiguring Race," 3–10; Adler, "Beyond Cultural Identity," 23–40; Antonovsky, "Toward Refinement," 57–67; Goldberg, "Qualification," 52–58; Green, "Re-examination," 167–71; Kerckhoff and McCormick, "Marginal Status," 48–55; Park, "Human Migration," 881–93; Poston, "Biracial Identity," 152–55; Wright and Wright, "Plea for Further Refinement," 361–68.
56. Obama, *Dreams*, xv, 23–25, 30–33. In the media Obama is generally referred to as Black or African American but less frequently as multiracial or biracial. Yet individuals have displayed varying responses, in terms of how he is viewed racially. Data on these attitudes were collected for Mark Williams by Zogby International in a November 2006 internet poll of 2,155 people. Individuals were told Obama's parents' background and then were asked to identify his race. Obama was identified as Black by 66 percent of African Americans, 9 percent of Latinas/os, 8 percent of whites, and 8 percent of Asian Americans. He was designated with multiracial identifiers by 88 percent of Latinas/os, 80 percent of whites, 77 percent of Asian Americans, and 34 percent of African Americans. Most respondents designated Obama with multiracial identifiers. Small percentages responded with "white," "none of the above," and "not sure." Blacks upheld the one-drop rule. BBS News, "Williams/Zogby Poll: Americans' Attitudes Changing towards Multiracial Candidates," February 12, 2007, http://web.archive.org/web/20070212084428/http://bbsnews.net/article.php/20061222014017231; M. Williams, "Identity Survey 11/1/06 thru 11/2/06." Indeed, Obama has never said he *identifies* as

multiracial, although he has referred to his interracial parentage. This was underscored when he checked only the "Black, African American, or Negro" box on the 2010 census race question, although since 2000 respondents have been allowed to check more than one box. Daniel and Kelekay, "From *Loving v. Virginia*," 650.

57. In the media Obama has more typically been described as African American or Black than as biracial. Harris is frequently described as African American and South Asian. This is largely due to her dual-minority background, the two distinct heritages of which do not as easily cancel each other out as does Black over white, which is more normative in U.S. racial formation. Harris's partial Asianness may also be highlighted because it is somewhat novel compared to Obama's half-whiteness.
58. Washington, *Blasian Invasion*, 32, 43, 71–76, 82–86.
59. Daniel, *More Than Black?*, 93–113; Rockquemore and Brunsma, *Beyond Black*, 40–52; Anzaldúa, *Borderlands*, 77–91; Renn, *Mixed Race*, 67–93; Wallace, *Relative/Outsider*, 121–25, 147–52; DaCosta, *Making Multiracials*, 138–43.
60. Daniel, Foreword, ix.
61. Lee and Bean, *Diversity Paradox*, 21, 101, 103, 104–10; Phinney and Alipuria, "At the Interface," 139–58; Sarah Townsend et al., "Being Mixed," 91–96.
62. Lee and Bean, *Diversity Paradox*, 21, 101, 103, 104–10; Mass, "Interracial Japanese Americans," 265–78; Spickard, "What Must I Be?," 44–45; Rockquemore and Arend, "Opting for White," 50, 55, 60.
63. Jiménez, "Negotiating Ethnic Boundaries," 75–97; Jiménez, "New Third Generation," 1040–79.
64. Miyawaki, "Part-Latinos," 289–306.
65. Christophe et al., "Examining Multiracial Pride," 22–38.
66. Bratter, "Will 'Multiracial' Survive," 821–49.
67. Masuoka, *Multiracial Identity*, 3, 5, 8, 73, 79; Khanna, "If You're Half Black," 96–117; Rockquemore and Brunsma, *Beyond Black*, 45–46; Roth, "End of One-Drop Rule," 35–36, 59–64.
68. Khanna, "If You're Half Black," 96–117; Khanna, *Biracial in America*, 51, 92, 102, 118–29, 131–46, 170; Korgen, *Black to Biracial*, 87; Rockquemore and Laszloffy, *Raising Biracial Children*, 7, 20–22, 118–21; Rockquemore and Arend, "Opting for White," 50, 55, 60.
69. Daniel, *Race and Multiraciality*, 116; Hoskins, *Asian American*, 54, 102–3, 139–41; Lee and Bean, *Diversity Paradox*, 108–10; Strmic-Pawl, *Multiracialism*, 26, 89–102, 118, 123–25.
70. Hoskins, *Asian American*, 4, 102–3, 139–41; Romo, "Between Black and Brown," 3–5, 7–21.

71. Hoskins, *Asian American*, 4, 102–3, 139–41.
72. Feagin and Feagin, *Racial and Ethnic Relations*, 38.
73. Daniel, "Sociology of Multiracial Identity," 115; Newman, "Revisiting," 3, 5; Qian and Lichter, "Social Boundaries," 68–94.
74. Daniel, "Sociology of Multiracial Identity," 118; Emily Alpert, "More Americans Consider Themselves Multiracial," *Los Angeles Times*, June 12, 2013, https://www.latimes.com/local/la-xpm-2013-jun-12-la-me-multiracial-growth-20130613-story.html; Farley, "Identifying," 6–15; Masuoka, *Multiracial Identity*, 170–78; Newman, "Revisiting," 3, 5.
75. Song, *Multiracial Parents*, 33–52, 59–63, 150–56.
76. A comprehensive list of English-language publications on the topic of mixed race can be found on Steven F. Riley's website, Mixed Race Studies: Scholarly Perspectives on the Mixed Race Experience, accessed July 15, 2022, http://www.mixedracestudies.org/.
77. Ifekwunigwe, *"Mixed Race" Studies*, front matter. In appendix B of the inaugural issue of *the Journal of Critical Mixed Race Studies*, Riley compiled a partial list of publications, specifically books, that incorporate material on race and multiraciality during this period. Riley, "Appendix B," 77–97.
78. Omi and Winant, *Racial Formation*, 16.
79. West and Fenstermaker, "Doing Difference," 19.

2. Anglo-America and Latin America

1. Bender, *Angola*, 33–54; Cox, *Caste, Class, and Race*, 351–80; M. Harris, *Patterns*, 79–94.
2. Reséndez, *Other Slavery*, 113.
3. Frederickson, *White Supremacy*, 59–62.
4. Dyer, "Patterns," 311–12; Pascoe, *What Comes Naturally*, 19–29; Kennedy, *Interracial Intimacies*, 41–69; Spickard, *Mixed Blood*, 237; Tenzer, *Completely New Look*, 56–68.
5. Williamson, *New People*, 7, 38.
6. Du Bois, *Black Reconstruction*, 700.
7. While the term *mulatto* is most often seen as derogatory in terms of contemporary thinking, we use it for clarity purposes, as it was the racial classification used during the historical period discussed here to refer to mixed-race people of African and European descent.
8. Murray, *States' Laws*, 5–8, 19; Moran, *Interracial*, 17–28; Dyer, "Patterns," 309–33; Williamson, *New People*, 8–11; Hodes, *White Women*, 1–15.
9. Nash, *Red, White, and Black*, 282, 285; Frederickson, *White Supremacy*, 102–4.
10. Nash, *Red, White, and Black*, 252, 254, 264.

NOTES TO PAGES 37–39   275

11. Indigenous people had no previous contact with the Old World. Consequently, they were immunologically defenseless against diseases that spread to the New World and to which Europeans and Africans had comparatively greater resistance. The major pathogens included smallpox, measles, whooping cough, chicken pox, bubonic plague, typhus, and malaria. Even influenza could prove deadly. Nunn and Qian, "Columbian Exchange," 165.
12. Proctor, *Damned Notions*, 14–15. Slavery continued de facto in a thinly disguised form in the Spanish colonies via the encomienda system. The Crown provided a grant to a colonist (encomendero), conferring the right to demand tribute and forced labor from the Indigenous inhabitants. Indigenous peoples were subjected to torture, extreme abuse, and, in some cases, death if they resisted. Encomenderos were also mandated through these grants to convert Indigenous people to Christianity and endorse Spanish as their primary language. Reséndez, *The Other Slavery*, 35, 36, 61n32, 354; Menchaca, *Recovering History*, 52.
13. Lockhart and Schwartz, *Early Latin America*, 197–200.
14. Meyer, Sherman, and Deeds, *Course of Mexican History*, 186–87; Menchaca, *Recovering History*, 749, 763–64; Vaughn, "Afro-Mexico," 118; Palmer, *Slaves of the White God*, 28, 30, 39.
15. Bennett, *Africans in Colonial Mexico*, 1; Menchaca, *Recovering History*, 59–60; Proctor, *Damned Notions*, 14–15; Palmer, *Slaves of the White God*, 2–3; Silva, *Urban Slavery*, 107–43; Valdés, "Decline of Slavery," 169.
16. Mörner, *Race Mixture*, 25, 26, 36, 38; Cline, "Guadalupe and Castas," 225.
17. Mörner, *Race Mixture*, 40; Furtado, *Chica da Silva*, 65–68.
18. Furtado, *Chica da Silva*, 65–68; Mörner, *Race Mixture*, 26; Seed, *To Love*, 148; Nazzari, "Concubinage," 108–12.
19. Carrera, *Imagining Identity*, 118; Katzew, *Casta Painting*, 53; Menchaca, *Recovering History*, 56; Mörner, *Race Mixture*, 25–26, 29–31, 38, 40; Saether, "Bourbon Absolutism," 490–95; Menchaca, *Recovering History*, 53–57; Rout, *African Experience*, 140–42.
20. Shumway, *Case of Ugly Suitor*, 26.
21. Saether, "Bourbon Absolutism," 490–95.
22. Mörner, *Race Mixture*, 25–26, 29–31, 40.
23. Menchaca, *Recovering History*, 55, 62; McDonald, "Intimacy and Empire," 27–31; Furtado, *Chica da Silva*, 65–68 Mörner, *Race Mixture*, 25–27, 29–30, 38–40; Nazzari, "Concubinage," 108–12.
24. Mulattoes were of Spanish and African descent although could also encompass other multiracials of African descent. *Pardo* (literally "brown") typically referred to individuals of Spanish, African, and Indigenous descent.

However, the term sometimes included mulattoes, particularly in official contexts. Forbes, "Black Pioneers," 240; Lockhart and Schwartz, *Early Latin America*, 197–200.

25. Schwaller, *Géneros de Gente*, 88; Mörner, *Race Mixture*, 26–29, 38; Althouse, "Contested," 153, 155–56.
26. A Morisco, the progeny of a mulatto and a white, is a perfect case study of this difference. The Morisco is the equivalent in terms of white and African ancestry to the *castizo* in terms of white and Indigenous ancestry. They are both three-quarters white and, respectively, one-quarter African and Indigenous. The progeny of castizos and whites were considered to be a return to Spanish purity, whereas the offspring of Moriscos and whites resulted in an albino. In fact, attitudes toward albinos were not unlike the U.S. one-drop rule. Still, the social liabilities of African ancestry in some rare cases could potentially be mitigated in Spanish America through the purchase of certificates of whiteness. No such policy existed in Anglo-America. Chance, *Race and Class*, 176; Schwaller, *Géneros de Gente*, 47–48; Cline, "Guadalupe," 228–30; Katzew, *Casta Painting*, 192, 52; Martínez, *Genealogical Fictions*, 159.
27. Lewis, *Hall of Mirrors*, 5.
28. Cline, "Guadalupe," 222.
29. Guerrero, "Caste, Race, and Class," 4–5, 9, 12–13, 16; Miranda, "Racial and Cultural," 265–71; Vaughn, "Afro-Mexico," 117.
30. Lewis, *Hall of Mirrors*, 23, 37, 193, 204; Martínez et al., "Editorial," 1–8; Rodríguez-García, "Persistence of Racial Constructs," 6.
31. Berlin, *Slaves Without Masters*, 5–6, 111; Vinson, *Before Mestizaje*, 2–6, 7–45; Cohen and Greene, "Introduction," 1–23; Klein, "Nineteenth-Century," 84–133, 309–34; Klein, *African Slavery*, 232; Hoetink, *Slavery*, 108; Russell-Wood, "Colonial Brazil," 84–133, 309–34.

3. Louisiana and the Gulf Coast

1. Anglo-America encompassed North Carolina and the colonies northward in New England and the mid-Atlantic colonies of New York, New Jersey, Pennsylvania, and Delaware. Latin North America included the lower Mississippi Valley and the Gulf Coast—particularly in Louisiana and the Gulf Ports of Mobile, Pensacola, and Natchez, as well as Saint Augustine—and English settlement in South Carolina (and to a lesser extent, Georgia). Although South Carolina was settled by the English, the early colonists were from the West Indies, specifically Barbados and Bermuda, where mulattoes were socially differentiated from, and positioned somewhat higher than, Blacks, who were a majority. Blacks were an estimated 70.6 percent of the

population on the eve of the American Revolution. Foner, *Black Americans*, 203–5; Williamson, *New People*, 14–16, 34–36, 40.

Between 1790 and 1810 the numbers of Free Coloreds grew to a total of 4,500, in part attributable to refugees fleeing the Haitian revolution. Berlin, *Slaves Without Masters*, 48.

Georgia's demographics were not conducive to extensive miscegenation compared to other regions of the Lower South. Yet by 1800 Georgia's small Free Colored population of 400 grew substantially to 1,800, in part, again, attributable to refugees fleeing the revolution in Haiti. Berlin, *Slaves Without Masters*, 36, 48.

Local whites, particularly in Savannah, encouraged the development of a status and privileges for Free Coloreds, like they did in Charleston, that was intermediate to whites and the mass of Black slaves, if for no other reason than as a strategy to draw them away from any dangerous liaison with the latter that could potentially challenge the dominant position of the former. Berlin, *Slaves Without Masters*, 196, 214; Williamson, *New People*, 27.

2. Berlin, *Slaves Without Masters*, 109; Williamson, *New People*, 14–15.
3. Domínguez, *White by Definition*, 24; Hanger, *Bounded Lives*, 7; Hazzard-Gordon, "Sexism and Racism," 14–25; Rankin, "Impact of the Civil War," 381.
4. Aslakson maintains that some of these *plaçage* relationships actually hovered between common-law marriage and concubinage. The Quadroon Balls were public dances open to young free women of color and white men. They were not necessarily the highly romanticized gateway to plaçage that is often portrayed in the popular imagination. Aslakson, "'Quadroon-Plaçage' Myth," 709–34.
5. Foner, *Black Americans*, 406–30; Rankin, "Impact of the Civil War," 379–416; Ulentin, "Free Women of Color," 25; Gould, "In Enjoyment of Their Liberty," 330–31; Hanger, "Coping in a Complex World," 226; Ribianszky, "She Appeared to be Mistress," 230, 232–35, 343; Hazzard-Gordon, "Sexism and Racism," 15.
6. Berlin, *Slaves Without Masters*, 130–32; Garvin, "The Free Negro," 1–17; Landers, *Black Society*, 1–28, 229–53; Thomas, "The Free Negro," 335–37; Williamson, *New People*, 22–23.
7. Mills, *Forgotten People*, 78.
8. Domínguez, *White by Definition*, 24; *Bounded Lives*, 7; Hazzard-Gordon, "Sexism and Racism," 14–25; Rankin, "Impact of the Civil War," 381
9. Berlin, *Slaves Without Masters*, 98–99, 104–17, 144, 163; Domínguez, *White by Definition*, 23–24; Haskins, *Creoles of Color*, 32–33; Johnson, "Colonial New

Orleans," 52–53; Rankin, "Impact of the Civil War," 380–82; Sterkx, *Free Negro*, 94.

10. Domínguez, *White by Definition*, 28–50, 113–15, 134–40; Berlin, *Slaves Without Masters*, 278.
11. Treaty between the United States of America and the French Republic . . . , April 30, 1803 (Louisiana Purchase Treaty).
12. Domínguez, *White by Definition*, 113–15; Logsdon and Bell, "Americanization," 189–261.
13. Treaty of Amity, Settlement, and Limits . . . , February 19, 1819 (Adams-Onís Treaty).
14. Smith, "Persistent Borderland," 8, 196, 222; Gould, "Free Creoles," 28–50, 40–44.
15. Haskins, *Creoles of Color*, 50; Rankin, "Impact of the Civil War," 386–87.
16. Domínguez, *White by Definition*, 30.
17. Lincoln's Emancipation Proclamation was a military measure to end slavery only in the states in rebellion that were under federal control. Congress passed the Thirteenth Amendment (1865) to ensure that slavery was permanently abolished throughout the United States. The Fourteenth Amendment (1868) grants all persons born or naturalized in the United States citizenship and equal protection under the laws. The Fifteenth Amendment (1870) gives all male citizens the right to vote. The Civil Rights Acts of 1866 and 1875 declared respectively that all persons born in the United States were citizens and provided everyone the right to equal treatment in public places and transportation. Myrdal, *American Dilemma*, xix.
18. Logsdon and Bell, "Americanization," 204.
19. Haskins, *Creoles of Color*, 61.
20. Olsen, *Thin Disguise*, 81–85; C. Harris, "Whiteness as Property," 1710, 1746–50.
21. Olsen, *Thin Disguise*, 81–85; C. Harris, "Whiteness as Property," 1710, 1746–50; Brook, *Plessy v. Ferguson*, 77–96, 98–138.
22. Others have argued the Citizens' Committee was more self-serving and less committed to the rights and needs of the Black masses. Rather, it was primarily concerned about the restrictions that segregation imposed on multiracials, that is, Creoles of color, who had historically enjoyed an elevated status in New Orleans and Louisiana. Dineen-Wimberly, *Allure of Blackness*, 36; Ingham and Feldman, *African-American Business Leaders*, 35.
23. Plessy v. Ferguson, 163 U.S. 537 (1896).
24. Davis, *Who Is Black?*, 8–9, 15, 52–53; Olsen, *Thin Disguise*, 112.
25. Ringer, *We the People*, 246.

26. Southern states adopted an "understanding clause," or a "grandfather clause," allowing individuals who could not pass the literacy test to register to vote if they could demonstrate they understood the meaning of a specific text in the state constitution to the satisfaction of the registrar or were descended from someone eligible to vote in 1867, the year before African Americans attained the franchise. A poll tax was a fee that had to be paid to vote. It was enacted in southern states between 1889 and 1910 and disenfranchised many poor whites as well as Blacks.
27. Daniel, *More Than Black?*, 82.
28. Daniel, *More Than Black?*, 19, 82; Haskins, *Creoles*, 64; Dugar, "I Am What I Say I Am," 12–14.
29. Daniel, *More Than Black?*, 82.

4. Black Identity Construction

1. Davis, *Who Is Black?*, 55.
2. Daniel, *More Than Black?*, 55–60.
3. Mathews, "Question of Color," 318.
4. Davis, *Who Is Black?*, 174, 190.
5. Myrdal, *American Dilemma*, 135; Williamson, *New People*, 120–21.
6. Opie, "Eating, Dancing," 79–109.
7. G. Hutchinson, *Harlem Renaissance*, 1–28.
8. Du Bois, *Souls of Black Folk*, 8; Gaines, *Uplifting the Race*, 9–10.
9. Nash, *Forbidden Love*, 141–45.
10. Zack, *Race and Mixed Race*, 99–101.
11. Past individual experiences mostly remain unknown and unreported. Yet there have been cases of notoriety in which individuals sought to embrace both their African American and European American backgrounds. Notable examples include Jean Toomer (1894–1967), a prominent writer of the Harlem Renaissance; Philippa Duke Schuyler (1931–67), daughter of Harlem Renaissance journalist George Schuyer; and Josephine Cogdell, a European American dancer and artist who was also the heiress of a Texas rancher granddaughter of slave owners. Several groups for interracial families (the Manasseh Societies, Penguin Clubs, Club Miscegenation) that emerged between the 1890s and 1940s also helped multiracials affirm their Black and white backgrounds. Daniel, *More Than Black?*, 96. The identities of Jean Toomer and Philippa Schuyler, and those supported by these early organizations, prefigured multiracial identities that emerged in the decades following the removal of the last antimiscegenation laws in the 1967 *Loving* decision.

12. Brown v. Board of Education, 347 U.S. 483 (1954).
13. Ringer, *We the People*, 425; Fuchs, *Kaleidoscope*, 159–68; Ringer, *We the People*, 327–39.
14. McKee, *Sociology and the Race Problem*, 222–55.
15. Select multiracials have been rewarded through what Carl Degler refers to as the "mulatto escape hatch," an informal window of opportunity by which exceptional individuals with "visibly" African phenotypical traits were allowed token vertical mobility, token inclusion, and the rank of situational "whiteness." Degler, *Neither Black nor White*, 140, 196–99. The escape hatch has broader implications: it has also allowed millions of individuals with African ancestry but phenotypically white features to self-identify and become socially designated as white. In the United States the one-drop rule can transform the identity of an individual who appears otherwise white into *Black*, subjecting them to the accompanying social indignities. In Latin America, in contrast, the escape hatch allows such individuals to completely escape Blackness and its social liabilities. It has thus served as a form of social control by co-opting into silence many individuals with the sociocultural capital to serve as voices in antiracist struggle. Daniel, *Race and Multiraciality*, x, 192.
16. Other communities of color began articulating similar logic, including advocacy for "Brown Power" among Latinas/os, "Red Power" among Native Americans, and "Yellow Power" among Asian Americans. For more on the "Brown Power" movement, see chapter 6.
17. Ringer, *We the People*, 531; Carmichael and Hamilton, *Black Power*, 5–32.
18. Omi and Winant, *Racial Formation*, 101–4.
19. The goal is to achieve equality of similarity without advocating assimilation that levels differences, to encourage unity without perpetuating uniformity, and to build new kinds of community without promoting conformity. Higham, *Send These to Me*, 242–46.
20. Affirmative action was initiated by the administration of President Lyndon B. Johnson (1963–69) as a compensatory measure to move beyond the achievement of equal opportunity of individuals through civil rights legislation to achieve equal outcome for Blacks as a group through social engineering in areas of systematic underrepresentation such as employment, education, housing, political representation, public services, and so on as a result of past purposeful discrimination and continuing racially biased attitudes and policies. Although affirmative action represented the culmination of Black protest, it was not until the militancy of the late 1960s that Blacks were able to exert the political pressure necessary for its implementation.

Subsequently, affirmative action was extended to other racial minorities and women. Daniel, *Race and Multiraciality*, 147.

5. California and the Southwest

1. The "Southwest" refers to the territories where Spanish settlements were founded in New Mexico, Texas, Arizona, and California, rather than the entire North American region claimed by Spain, which includes Nevada, Utah, parts of Colorado, and small sections of Oklahoma, Kansas, and Wyoming.
2. This included individuals, often referred to as neophytes, who typically had been converted to Christianity, were baptized, and had some understanding of the faith. They frequently had varying degrees of familiarity with and proficiency in the Spanish language. This culturally adaptive behavior came about largely through violence, coercion, and forced assimilation. Guerrero, "Caste, Race, and Class," 5, 13.
3. Taylor, *Search of the Racial Frontier*, 32–34; Chavez-Garcia, *Negotiating Conquest*, 4–6, 7; Casas, *Married to a Daughter*, 47; Pérez, *Colonial Intimacies*, 136–38; Forbes, "Black Pioneers," 234–36; Weber, *Spanish Frontier*, 237–30; Dobyns, *Spanish Colonial Tucson*, 137–38, Heath and Nunn, "Africans and Discrimination," 52–53; Chipman, *Spanish Texas*, 188–89; McDonald, "Intimacy and Empire," 147–48; Salomon, *Pío Pico*, 10.
4. Forbes, "Black Pioneers," 234–36.
5. Forbes, "Black Pioneers," 236, 242; Goode, *California's Black Pioneers*, 10–16.
6. Vinson, *Before Mestizaje*, 2–3; Miranda, "Racial and Cultural Dimensions," 266–68, 270–73.
7. Pérez, *Colonial Intimacies*, 9, 23–24; Miranda, "Racial and Cultural Dimensions," 265–66; Taylor, *Search of the Racial Frontier*, 36; Haney-López, *Racism on Trial*, 56; Forbes, "Black Pioneers," 244; Haney-López, *Racism on Trial*, 57, 65; Taylor, *Search of the Racial Frontier*, 36.
8. Goode, *California's Black Pioneers*, 22; Almaguer, *Racial Faultlines*, 47; Forbes, "Black Pioneers," 234–36.
9. Hurtado, *Intimate Frontiers*, 50; Haney-López, *Racism on Trial*, 57; Dysart, "Mexican Women," 371.
10. Orenstein, "Void of Vagueness," 376; Almaguer, *Racial Faultlines*, 58; Goode, *California's Black Pioneers*, 70.
11. Pérez, *Colonial Intimacies*, 11, 101, 121, 131, 160, 162, 197, 209–13.
12. Reséndez, *The Other Slavery*, 3, 7, 66, 221, 236, 306, 313, 320.
13. Treaty between the United States of America and the Mexican Republic . . . , February 2, 1848 (Treaty of Guadalupe Hidalgo).
14. Almaguer, *Racial Faultlines*, 1–74.

15. Almaguer, *Racial Faultlines*, 1–74; Forbes, "Black Pioneers," 244.
16. Davis, *Who Is Black?*, 174, 190.
17. Horseman, *Race and Manifest Destiny*, 219–48.
18. Farnham, *Life, Adventures, and Travels*, 413.
19. Browne, "Report of Debates." With the discovery of gold in 1848, southern slave owners saw a new opportunity to profit by working their slaves in the goldfields. Consequently, the number of African American slaves entering California soared. By 1852 there were approximately 2,200 African Americans in California, the majority of them slaves. Goode, *California's Black Pioneers*, 58–59.
20. Browne, "Report of Debates."
21. Salomon, *Pío Pico*, 115–16; Almaguer, *Racial Faultlines*, 1–74, 132.
22. Hurtado, *Intimate Frontiers*, 70; Almaguer, *Racial Faultlines*, 54.
23. Gross, "Texas Mexicans," 197.
24. Chavez-Garcia, *Negotiating Conquest*, 4–6, 7; Casas, *Married to a Daughter*, 47; Gross, *What Blood Won't Tell*, 256; Gross, "Texas Mexicans," 197; Montejano, *Anglos and Mexicans*, 235–52.
25. Jeff Wheelwright, "Sex, God, and DNA," *The Atlantic*, February 24, 2012, https://www.theatlantic.com/national/archive/2012/02/sex-god-and-dna-the-creation-of-new-mexicans/253406/; Montejano, *Anglos and Mexicans*, 83–88; Almaguer, *Racial Faultlines*, 58.
26. Orenstein, "Void of Vagueness," 369; Almaguer, *Racial Faultlines*, 58; Gross, "Texas Mexicans," 254, 281; Gómez, *Manifest Destinies*, 62, 64.
27. Takaki, *Different Mirror*, 155–76; Haney-López, *Racism on Trial*, 57.
28. Takaki, *Different Mirror*, 155–76.
29. Almaguer, *Racial Faultlines*, 66–68.
30. Takaki, *Different Mirror*, 155–76.
31. Foley, *Mexicans in the Making of America*, 36; Gómez, *Manifest Destinies*, 150; K. Johnson, *How Did You Get to Be Mexican?*, 56.
32. Mason, *Census of 1790*, 4; Forbes, "Black Pioneers," 30–33; Foley, *Mexicans in the Making of America*, 36.

6. Mexican American Identity

1. Fuchs, *Kaleidoscope*, 137–39; Aragon, "Difference," 22; Fox and Guglielmo, "Defining," 331–34.
2. Montejano, *Anglos and Mexicans*, 114, 168, 235–49.
3. Gross, "Texas Mexicans," 198; Montejano, *Anglos and Mexicans*, 235–54; Fuchs, *Kaleidoscope*, 139; Orozco, *No Mexicans*, 17, 30, 77, 87, 152; Sheridan, "'Another White Race,'" 112; Telles and Sue, *Durable Ethnicity*, 238.

NOTES TO PAGES 69–72

4. Bender, *Greasers and Gringos*, 120; Orozco, *No Mexicans*, 17, 30.
5. García, *White but Not Equal*, 7; Aragon, "Difference," 19, 22; Fox and Guglielmo, "Defining," 331–34.
6. LULAC is the largest and oldest Latina/o civil rights organization.
7. G. Rodríguez, *Mongrels*, 157–58.
8. Sánchez, *Becoming Mexican American*, 254.
9. Foley, "Over the Rainbow," 140–41; Foley, "Becoming Hispanic," 54; Macias, *Mestizo*, ix, 19, 47; Acuña, *Occupied America*, 190–91, 231–32; G. Rodríguez, *Mongrels*, 175–76.
10. Foley, "Becoming Hispanic," 54–59, 62–64; Sheridan, "'Another White Race,'" 126; Steptoe, *Houston Bound*, 131; G. Rodríguez, *Mongrels*, 175–76.
11. The American GI Forum (GIF), a congressionally chartered Hispanic veterans and civil rights organization founded in 1948, was one such similar organization.
12. Acuña, *Occupied America*, 190–91, 231–32; Gratton and Merchant, "La Raza," 544; Sheridan, "'Another White Race,'" 126; Steptoe, *Houston Bound*, 131; Chávez, "*¡Mi Raza Primero!*," 2; Foley, "Becoming Hispanic," 64–66. George I. Sánchez, a prominent activist and professor of education at the University of Texas from the 1930s to the 1950s, provided a more nuanced framing. He regarded Mexican Americans as white but also held that they were a minority group that experienced systematic and racialized oppression. Blanton, "George I. Sánchez," 574.
13. Foley, *White Scourge*, 210.
14. Fuchs, *Kaleidoscope*, 138; Gratton and Merchant, "La Raza," 546; Ortiz and Telles, "Racial Identity," 4.
15. Foley, *White Scourge*, 206–8.
16. Carrigan and Webb, "Lynching," 411–32; Telles and Ortiz, *Generations of Exclusion*, 39, 78, 101–2.
17. Gratton and Merchant, "La Raza," 539.
18. Barrera, *Race and Class*, 100–103; Jewell, "'We Have in This City,'" 2–7, 12; Foley, *White Scourge*, 2010–11; Aragon, "Difference," 19, 22; Fox and Guglielmo, "Defining," 331–34.
19. Mendez v. Westminster [sic] School District of Orange County et al., 64 F.Supp. 544 (S.D. 1946) aff'd, 161 F.2d 774 (9th Cir. 1947).
20. Valencia, "Mexican American Struggle," 389.
21. Foley, "Over the Rainbow," 144.
22. Brown v. Board of Education, 347 U.S. 483 (1954).
23. Hernandez v. Texas, 347 U.S. 475 (1954).

24. García, *White but Not Equal*, 40, 47, 75–76, 98; Sheridan, "'Another White Race,'" 109.
25. Chávez, *"¡Mi Raza Primero!,"* 5, 34, 42; Haney-López, *Racism on Trial*, 206, 303.
26. Simmen and Bauerle, "Chicano," 225–27.
27. Haney-López, *Racism on Trial*, 206–10.
28. Castro v. Superior Court, 1970. 9 Cal. App. 3d 675.
29. Montez v. Superior Court, 1970. 10 Cal. App. 3d.
30. Haney-López, *Racism on Trial*, 241–49.
31. Gonzales, *I Am Joaquín*, 1.
32. Vasconcelos, *Raza cósmica*, x–xvi, 72–74; Manrique, "Dreaming," 10–11; García, *Chicanismo*, 72.
33. Manrique, "Dreaming," 10–11. Although Asians were considerably smaller in numbers, Asians also formed part of the racial makeup of the slave population in colonial Mexico. Their numbers are difficult to estimate with accuracy. However, at least six hundred Asians per year entered Mexico during the seventeenth century. Typically, these Asian slaves arrived in the Manila galleons from the Philippines, China, Japan, and Portuguese India and were grouped together and categorized as *chinos*. Seijas, *Asian*, 1, 2, 49, 89, 229; Manrique, "Dreaming," 9.
34. Haney-López, *Racism on Trial*, 211–17, 167, 249.
35. Afro-Mexican Americans can include individuals born in United States who are multigenerational Mexican Americans or Chicanas/os with African ancestry. It can also encompass multigenerational individuals born in the United States who are descendants of Afro-Mexican immigrants.
36. Hernández, "Afro-Americans," 1537–47.
37. Hernández, "Afro-Americans," 1549–50; Lewis, "Little Mexican," 1000–1004.
38. Lewis, "Little Mexican," 1001.
39. Still, during the first half of the nineteenth century, Mexico provided safe passage, protection, and freedom for African Americans escaping from slavery in the United States. This helped serve as roadblock to U.S. proslavery imperialist dreams and also contributed to the major sectional controversy over the future of slavery in the United States. Baumgartner, *South to Freedom*, 12–13.
40. Hernández, "Afro-Americans," 1537–51.
41. Hernández, "Afro-Americans," 1543; Stevenson, *Both Black and Mexican*, 5, 14–15.
42. Zamora, *Racial Baggage*, 4, 11.
43. David Argen, "'We Exist. We're Here,'" *The Guardian*, March 19, 2020, https://

www.theguardian.com/world/2020/mar/19/afro-mexicans-census-history-identity; Lewis, "Little Mexican," 996.
44. Instituto Nacional de Estadística y Geografía, 2020.
45. Argen, "'We Exist. We're Here.'"
46. Landry and Maclean, *Spivak Reader*, 7, 54–71, 159, 204, 295.
47. Spivak envisioned strategic essentialism as a temporary phenomenon, which differentiates it from hypodescent and the monoracial imperative, which have been of a considerably longer duration. While at times "strategic," they are based on long-standing hegemonic essentialist beliefs.
48. Blackwell, "Contested Histories," 53, 68, 139. Also, the gendered division of political work was a reflection not only of male privilege but also of the ways in which Chicanas were disregarded as real political actors and relegated to the kitchens and mimeographing rooms of the movement. Chicanas were in charge of developing, typing up, and mimeographing position papers; doing all the fund-raising, cooking, and organizing events; and doing the office work, the cleanup work, and the majority of the organizational tasks. Notwithstanding the pivotal nature of this labor to the actual functioning of the political movement, it was considered women's work and devalued.
49. Pérez, *Decolonial Imaginary*, xvi, 10, 20, 22–28; Pérez-Torres, *Mestizaje*, 15–24.
50. Lipsitz, "Noises in the Blood," 32–35.
51. Anzaldúa, *Borderlands*, 63, 84.
52. Bhabha, *Location*, 28, 207–8.
53. Sandoval, *Methodology*, 72.
54. G. Rodríguez, *Mongrels*, x–xii. Machado, Sánchez, and Bacalski-Martínez pointed out that Chicanismo advocates also failed to acknowledge that Mexican American mestizaje not only included the Spanish but also the Anglo-American in terms of cultural contributions as well as interracial intimacy. This was a "fifth root," so to speak, if one thinks of the African dimension as the third root and the Asian one as a fourth root. One might also include the contribution of cultural exchange and miscegenation between Russian colonizers and Indigenous people during the first half of the nineteenth century in Colony Ross, the colonial maritime fur trading settlement in the greater San Francisco Bay Area. Lightfoot, *Indians, Missionaries, and Merchants*, 1–29.
55. Vigil, *Indians to Chicanos*, 263–65, 288.
56. The question of whether Mexican Americans and Latina/o constitute a race or an ethnicity is also attributable to the fact that race and ethnicity are erroneously viewed as critically different from each other. In fact, ethnicity

is not simply shared culture. It can also encompass shared ancestry or origin (real or imagined) and thus may serve as the basis of common geno-phenotypical (colloquially racial) traits.

57. Melville, "Hispanic Ethnicity," 90. Latina/o is a more recent development.
58. U.S. Bureau of the Census, 1970 and 1980; U.S. OMB 1997, 36909–13; Lee, "Racial Classifications," 80; Telles and Ortiz, *Generations of Exclusion*, 214.
59. From 1910 to 1980, this appeared as "Other"; in 1990 as "Other Race"; beginning in 2000 as "Some Other Race." https://www.census.gov/data-tools/demo/race/mread_1790_2010.html. Berkowitz, "Puerto Rico Focus Groups," 2–3, 23, 32; Hirschman, Alba, and Farley, "Meaning and Measurement," 381–83.
60. Tafoya, "Latinos and Racial Identification," 3.
61. Lee, "Racial Classifications," 83; U.S. OMB 1997, 36911.
62. Grieco and Cassidy, "Race and Hispanic Origin," 6.
63. Humes, Jones, and Ramirez, "Overview of Race," 6; Grieco and Cassidy, "Race and Hispanic Origin," 3; Ennis, Ríos-Vargas, and Albert, "Hispanic Population," 14.
64. There are various possible explanations for this flight from whiteness. It may, in part, reflect the perceived racially hostile climate and toxic whiteness that grew considerably during the Trump administration (2017–21).
65. U.S. Bureau of the Census, 2020; Thomas López, "MASC Analysis of Census 2020: Latinos Make Up a Majority of the Multiracial Population," accessed August 23, 2021, https://mailchi.mp/7430797217bc/august-events-for-the-mixed-race-community-in-socal-5631813?e=414939f104.
66. Tafoya, "Shades of Belonging," 5, 7, 8, 21.
67. Tafoya, "Shades of Belonging," 2, 3; Telles and Ortiz, *Generations of Exclusion*, 236.
68. Dowling, *Mexican Americans*, 5, 20. White identification for some was not based on color or assimilation into the ostensibly European American mainstream. In fact, most of the "white" Mexican Americans in Dowling's study spoke Spanish, identified strongly with their cultural background, reported incidents of discrimination, and were not lighter skinned than those who chose "some other race." Dowling concluded that a white identification was a strategy used to combat discrimination, particularly along the border in Texas, where there is considerable Spanish-language maintenance, high immigrant populations, and many low-income individuals.
69. Lewis, "Little Mexican," 1003–5, 1008–10.
70. Dowling, *Mexican Americans*, 5, 20.
71. Tran and Peterson, "'American' as Proxy," 345–46, 348–49, 351–52.
72. Humes, Jones, and Ramirez, "Overview of Race," 16, 17.

73. Lopez and Krogstad, "Mexican."
74. Humes, Jones, and Ramirez, "Overview of Race," 16; Logan and Turner, "Hispanics in the United States," 1, 3; Ennis, Ríos-Vargas, and Albert, "Hispanic Population," 2, 4, 15.
75. Humes, Jones, and Ramirez, "Overview of Race," 5, 6.
76. Ennis, Ríos-Vargas, and Albert, "Hispanic Population," 2. The Census Bureau projects that Hispanics will be 29 percent of the U.S. population by 2050. Passel and Cohn, "U.S. Population Projections."
77. Lopez and Krogstad, "'Mexican.'"
78. Logan, "How Race Counts," 2003.
79. Arredondo et al., "Introduction," 1–18; Pérez-Torres, *Mestizaje*, xii, 7.
80. Pérez, *Decolonial Imaginary*, 25, 79; Pérez-Torres, *Mestizaje*, 3–12, 33–82.
81. Aragon, "Difference," 19, 22; Fox and Guglielmo, "Defining," 331–34.

7. Multiracial Identities

1. Loving v. Virginia, 388 U.S. 1.
2. Precedent refers to a court decision considered to be an authority for deciding subsequent cases involving identical or similar facts or similar legal issues. Precedent requires courts to apply the law in the same manner to cases with the same facts. That was not the case with previous legal judgements before *Loving*.
3. Perez v. Sharp, 198 P.2d 17 (Cal. 1948).
4. Pascoe, *What Comes Naturally*, 205–45; Moran, *Interracial*, 84–88.
5. Lenhardt, *"Perez v. Sharp,"* 74; Pascoe, *What Comes Naturally*, 205–45; Moran, *Interracial*, 84–88.
6. Lenhardt, *"Perez v. Sharp,"* 75; Maillard and Villazor, "Introduction," 2; Volpp, "American Mestizo Filipinos," 68; Maillard and Villazor, "Introduction," 2; Pascoe, *What Comes Naturally*, 205–45; Moran, *Interracial*, 6, 84–88.
7. Moran, *"Loving* and Legacy," 239–81.
8. Lubin, *Romance*, ix–xxi, 66–95, 151–59; Moran, *Interracial*, 239, 249–50.
9. See chapter 8 for a discussion of Jeter's Native American identity.
10. An Act to Preserve Racial Integrity, ch. 371, § 5099a, 1924 Va. Acts 534.
11. Cashin, *Loving*, 2–4, 116–18.
12. Civil Rights Act of 1964 [Public Law 88-352; 78 Stat. 241].
13. Voting Rights Act of 1965 [Public Law 89-110]; Fair Housing Act of 1968 [Public Law 90-284; 82 Stat. 73].
14. Immigration and Nationality Act of 1965 [Public Law 89-236].
15. This has particularly been true historically of marriages between Black men and white women, although Black men are more likely than Black women

to outmarry. Hodes, *White Women, Black Men*, 44–46; Passel, Wang, and Taylor, *Marrying Out*, 11.

16. Frey, *Diversity*, 195, 196; Passel, Wang, and Taylor, *Marrying Out*, 4, 9; R. Spencer, *Reproducing Race*, 105–8; Steven F. Riley, "Don't Pass on Context: The Importance of Academic Discourses in Contemporary Discussions on the Multiracial Experience," *Mixed Race Studies* (blog), June 11, 2011, http://www.mixedracestudies.org/wordpress/?p=14196.

17. Billingsley, *Climbing*, 247; Lee and Bean, "America's Changing," 228; Pascoe, *What Comes Naturally*, 295–96; Romano, *Race Mixing*, 3; Root, *Love's Revolution*, 179–88; Sanjek, "Intermarriage," 105; U.S. Bureau of the Census, "1960 Census of Population"; U.S. Bureau of the Census, *1970 Census*; U.S. Bureau of the Census, *Questionnaire Reference Book*.

18. Frey, *Diversity*, 195; Passel, Wang, and Taylor, *Marrying Out*, 4, 9.

19. Frey, *Diversity*, 125, 195, 196.

20. Frey, *Diversity*, 192–200; Tanya K. Hernández, "Interracial Marriage and Latino/a Racial Identity," *Huffington Post* (blog), May 19, 2017, http://www.huffingtonpost.com/entry/interracial-marriage-and-latinoa-racial-identity_us_591f310fe4b07617ae4cbba8.

21. Frey, *Diversity*, 192–200; Daniel and Kelekay, "From *Loving*," 666.

22. Rico, Kreider, and Anderson, "Growth in Interracial"; Livingston and Brown, "Intermarriage in the U.S.," 6.

23. Daniel and Kelekay, "From *Loving*," 666.

24. Frederickson, "Positive Emotions," 218–26; Watson and Naragon, "Positive Affectivity," 207–15.

25. Root was not suggesting these were the first biracials in U.S. history. Rather, she coined this term to describe the growing number of multiracial offspring born following the *Loving* decision.

26. DaCosta, *Making Multiracials*, 21–46; Daniel, *More Than Black?*, 125–54; K. Williams, *Mark One or More*, 1–64.

27. Daniel, "Sociology of Multiracial Identity," 110; Nash, "Hidden History," 959–60.

28. Childs, *Navigating Interracial*, 2–4; Childs, *Fade to Black and White*, 7, 9, 33, 36, 42, 56; Rodriguez-Garcia, Solana-Solana, and Lubbers, "Preference and Prejudice," 521, 523, 534, 539–41.

29. See the "happy hapa" stereotype described in Kina and Dariotis, *War Baby / Love Child*, 13–14. See also Thornton, "Policing the Borderlands," 105–27; Daniel et al., "Emerging Paradigms," 19; Hollinger, *Postethnic America*, 21, 42, 182; R. Spencer, *Reproducing Race*, 3, 183–212; R. Spencer, "'Only the News,'" 164–78; McNeil, *Sex and Race*, 92–93, 105; McKibbin, "Current

State," 140, 161–90; G. Carter, *United States*, 140, 161–90; Squires, *Dispatches*, 168–81; DaCosta, *Making Multiracials*, 123–24; Joseph, *Transcending Blackness*, ix–36, 155–72

30. Daniel et al., "Emerging Paradigms," 99n43.
31. DaCosta, *Making Multiracials*, 1–20; Daniel, *More Than Black?*, 122–25, 128–51; K. Williams, *Mark One or More*, 4, 14–16; K. Williams, "Recursive Outcomes," 88–93.
32. Lee, "Racial Classifications," 75–94; Chew, Eggebeen, and Uhlenberg, "American Children," 56–85; Waters, "Multiple Ethnicities," 23–40. Perlmann and Waters, *New Race Question* includes many chapters by demographers.
33. For an insider's perspective on the U.S. multiracial movement, see chapter 7 in Daniel's *More Than Black?* and chapter 8 in his *Race and Multiraciality*. See also Nobles, *Shades*; R. Spencer, *Spurious Issues*; K. Williams, *Mark One or More*; and DaCosta, *Making Multiracials*.
34. K. Williams, *Mark One or More*, 4, 14–16; K. Williams, "Recursive Outcomes," 88–107.
35. K. Williams, "Recursive Outcomes," 88–89, 99, 102. Pew research data (2015) indicate many individuals acknowledge their multiracial backgrounds on forms but do not identify as multiracial. Consequently, a more detailed study of these 2020 census data would be needed to determine how to interpret the significant growth in the numbers of two or more race individuals along those lines. That said, these changes could be attributed to a number of factors, including demographic change since 2010. This may also be attributable to increasing numbers of individuals shifting from a white identification, possibly triggered by a desire to distance themselves from the toxic whiteness associated with the years of the Trump administration. These changes may also be due to the improvements to the design of the two separate questions for race and ethnicity, in addition to the data processing, and coding, which enabled a more thorough and accurate depiction of how people prefer to self-identify Jones et al., "Improved Race and Ethnicity."
36. Jones and Smith, "Two or More Races," 1; Jones, "We the People," 1–4, 7; Jones and Bullock, "Two or More Population," 1.
37. Humes, Jones, and Ramirez, "Overview of Race," 8–10. In 2010 Native American white individuals composed the fourth largest group, although considerably less empirical research has been devoted to them. Many claim a Native American white background but do not actually identify as multiracial. Cohn, "American Indian and White." However, there is a great deal of research on "mixed-bloods" and the historical Native American experience.
38. Jones et al., "Improved Race and Ethnicity."

39. Humes, Jones, and Ramirez, "Overview of Race," 17.
40. Lopez and Krogstad, "'Mexican,' 'Hispanic,' 'Latin American.'"
41. Humes, Jones, and Ramirez, "Overview of Race," 16; Rastogi et al., "Black Population," 3; Jones et al., "Improved Race and Ethnicity."
42. Daniel, "Black and White Identity," 128–30; Daniel, *More Than Black?*, 1.
43. Bradshaw, "Beauty and the Beast," 77–88; C. Hall, "Please Choose One," 250–64; Pauker et al., "Review of Multiracial Malleability," 2–11; Root, "Resolving 'Other' Status," 185–205; Sims, "Reevaluation," 570–81; Wallace, *Relative/Outsider*, 40–94; Wijeyesinghe, "Intersectional Model," 83–103.
44. Adler, "Beyond Cultural Identity," 23–40; Brown, "Biracial Identity," 319–37; Brunsma, Delgado, and Rockquemore, "Liminality," 486; Pauker et al., "Review of Multiracial Malleability," 2–11; Poston, "Biracial Identity," 153–55; Daniel, "Black and White Identity," 135–36; Root, "Resolving 'Other' Status," 185–201; Renn, *Mixed Race Students*, 67–93; Rockquemore and Brunsma, *Beyond Black*, 41–48; Wilton, Sanchez, and Garcia, "Stigma of Privilege," 41–56; Daniel, *More Than Black?*, 93–111; Gaither, "'Mixed' Results," 114–17; Korgen, *Black to Biracial*, 25–55; Wardle, "Are You Sensitive," 55–57; Wijeyesinghe, "Intersectional Model," 86.
45. Daniel, *More Than Black?*, 93–111.
46. Daniel, "Black and White Identity," 136, 137.
47. Elam, *Souls of Mixed Folk*, xiii–xx, 1–15, 22–56; Sexton, *Amalgamation Schemes*, 43–82, 191–226, 227–58; J. M. Spencer, *New Colored People*, xi–xiv, 3–14, 91–170; R. Spencer, *Spurious Issues*, 129–85.
48. Stonequist, *Marginal Man*, 184.
49. Daniel, *More Than Black?*, 75–84.
50. Daniel, *More Than Black?*, 85–88; Daniel, *Race and Multiraciality*, 126, 129.
51. On November 2, 2021, the U.S. House of Representatives passed the Lumbee Recognition Act (H.R.2758).
52. Daniel, *More Than Black?*, 88–89; Puckett, "Melungeon Identity Movement," 135–36.
53. Survey research indicates that educational attainment, occupational opportunities, and family income among African-descent Americans, for example, increases considerably with lighter skin regardless of one's identification. Similar patterns have been documented among other groups (e.g., Latina/os). Telles and Murguía, "Phenotypic Discrimination," 682–94. Hughes and Hertel conclude that skin color continues to operate as a "diffuse status characteristic" although hair texture, eye color, and nose and lip shape are also important. Hughes and Hertel, "Significance of Color," 1116; Hagiwara, Kashy, and Cesario, "Independent Effects," 892–97.

Other scholars, by contrast, hold that European Americans may consciously express a preference for individuals of color who more closely approximate their phenotypical norms. European Americans, even if only unconsciously, often select individuals of color who more closely approximate them in physical appearance, believing they are making impartial decisions based on competence or other criteria. See, for example, Allen, Telles, and Hunter, "Skin Color," 129–79; Keith and Herring, "Skin Tone," 760–77; Monk, "Skin Tone," 1113–336; Rondilla and Spickard, *Is Lighter Better?*, 1–17, 79–101, 105–16; Viglione, Hannon, and DeFina, "Impact of Light Skin," 250–57; Wade, Romano, and Blue, "Effect," 2550–56; Weaver, "Recognizing Our Past," 1–13; Thompson and Keith, "Blacker the Berry," 336–57; Dupree-Wilson, "Phenotypic Proximity," 528–46.

54. R. Hall, *Discrimination Among Oppressed*, vii–26; Gómez, "Brown Outs," 193–204. Similar to the results in the Clarks' doll studies of African American children in the 1950s, doll studies in the 1990s, the early 2000s, and as recently as 2021 showed a preference for the white, rather than the Black, doll. The Clark data were key evidence in the 1954 *Brown* case to advance integration due to the deleterious impact prejudice, discrimination, and particularly segregation had in terms of fostering a sense of inferiority among African American children.

55. Daniel, "Multiracial Identities in the United States," 14–16; Tara Bahrampour and Ted Mellnik, "Census Data Shows Widening Diversity: Number of White People Falls for First Time," *Washington Post*, August 12, 2021, https://www.washingtonpost.com/dc-md-va/2021/08/12/census-data-race-ethnicity-neighborhoods/.

56. Buggs, "Dating in the Time," 538–49; Daniel, *More Than Black?*, 8, 106–11, 189–90; Daniel, "Sociology of Multiracial Identity," 112; K. Jackson, "Living the Multiracial Experience," 42–58; Wijeyesinghe, "Intersectional Model," 81–103; Johnston-Guerrero and Wijeyesinghe, "Insights," 3–16.

8. "Dual Minority"

1. Jiménez, "Negotiating Ethnic Boundaries," 76; Salgado de Snyder, Lopez, and Padilla, "Ethnic Identity," 277; Williams-León and Nakashima, "Reconfiguring Race," 3–12; Castañeda-Liles, "Multiracial Reference Group," xv, 3; Spickard et al., "Introduction," 4.
2. Kwan and Speirs, *Mixing It Up*, 32–57.
3. C. Ortiz, "Parental Racial Socialization," 89–91, 100.
4. Jiménez, "Multiethnic Mexican Americans," 173.

5. This varies considerably regionally in the United States. In New York, for instance, there is affirmative action for Italian American and Irish Americans who, respectively, identify heavily with Italian and Irish backgrounds.
6. Castañeda-Liles, "Multiracial Reference Group," 162.
7. Flagg, "'Was Blind,'" 953, 969.
8. Flagg, "'Was Blind,'" 953, 969.
9. Flagg, "'Was Blind,'" 953, 969.
10. Carbado and Harris, "New Racial Preferences," 1169.
11. Flagg, "'Was Blind,'" 953, 969. Of course, not all whites experience the same privilege, power, and prestige of whiteness, given that privilege is refracted through the prism of gender, sexual orientation, class, and other types of social difference. Carbado and Harris, "New Racial Preferences," 1171.
12. Doane, "Rethinking Whiteness Studies," 3–20; Flagg, "'Was Blind,'" 629–31; Frankenberg, *White Women*, 71–102, 103–39; Castañeda-Liles, "Multiracial Reference Group," 162.
13. Lewis, "'What Group?,'" 624–42.
14. Washington, *Blasian Invasion*, 10.
15. Rondilla, Guevarra, and Spickard, *Red and Yellow* provides the first, most extensive, and insightful study of dual-minority multiracials along these lines. Spickard et al., "Introduction," 11–18; Sharma, "What We Learn," 219–30.
16. Spickard, Guevarra, and Rondilla, "Introduction," 8.
17. DaCosta, *Making Multiracials*, 143; Newman, "Revisiting the Marginal Man," 26–27.
18. Leonard, *Making Ethnic Choices*, 13, 205, 214; Lipsitz, *Possessive Investment*, 4.
19. Leonard, *Making Ethnic Choices*, 132, 134.
20. Guevarra, *Becoming Mexipino*, 8–10.
21. Guevarra, "Burritos and Bagoong," 80.
22. Leonard, *Making Ethnic Choices*, 13, 132, 134, 205.
23. Almaguer, *Faultlines*, 1, 4, 8, 46.
24. Lowen, *Mississippi Chinese*, viii–ix, 10.
25. Loewen, *Mississippi Chinese*, 4.
26. Loewen, *Mississippi Chinese*, 135–53.
27. The term *multiracial* appeared, as early as 1980, as a definition of someone with more than one racial background in Hall's groundbreaking doctoral dissertation "The Ethnic Identity of Racially Mixed People: A Study of Black-Japanese." This definition and terminology gained widespread usage in the late 1980s among activists in the multiracial movement, particularly the membership of the AMEA and affiliated organizations, A Place for US National (APN), and Project RACE in the 1990s.

28. Thornton, "Multiethnic Identity," 138.
29. Mukoyama, "Effects of Heritage Combination," 68–70.
30. M. Carter, "Being Blakanese," 202, 204.
31. DeBonis, *Children of the Enemy*, 1–18.
32. Pulido, *Black, Brown, Yellow*, 47.
33. DeBonis, *Children of the Enemy*, 1–18, 32, 89, 93, 94, 115.
34. Randolph, "I'm Black and Korean," 87–92; Stickmon, "Blackapina," 33–44; Hodges, "Realizing Blacknpinay," 53–63.
35. Root, "Factors," 69.
36. Randolph, "I'm Black and Korean," 90.
37. Stickmon, "Blackapina," 44.
38. Washington, *Blasian Invasion*, 6.
39. Washington, *Blasian Invasion*, 49–67.
40. Washington, *Blasian Invasion*, 69–89.
41. Washington, *Blasian Invasion*, 10.
42. Washington, *Blasian Invasion*, 14.
43. Kachun, "From Forgotten Founder," 249–50.
44. Oliver Velez, "Black History Month: The Afro-Indigenous," *Daily Kos*, February 2, 2020, https://www.dailykos.com/stories/2020/2/2/1913216/-Black-History-Month-The-Afro-Indigenous-Native-Americans-with-African-ancestry; Forbes, "Black Africans and Native Americans," 220.
45. Rountree, *Pocahontas's People*, 205, 212, 222–23, 233–34, 275–76; Feller, *Being Indigenous*, 1–6, 13, 25. The Rappahannock, along with other Indigenous groups in Virginia—the Chickahominy, Eastern Chickahominy, Upper Mattaponi, the Monacan, and the Nansemond—gained federal recognition in 2018.
46. Coleman, "Tell the Court," 67–80; Forbes, "Black Africans and Native Americans," 199–206; Feller, *Indigenous in Jim Crow*, 2.
47. Mildred Loving's primary identity was Native American, but she sometimes stated that she was Black and Native American. That was the case in the letter she wrote to Attorney General Robert F. Kennedy asking for assistance. The Justice Department put her in touch with lawyers from the American Civil Liberties Union. Cashin, *Loving*, 25, 111.
48. Coleman, "Tell the Judge," 72.
49. Coleman, "Tell the Court," 7; Cashin, *Loving*, 96.
50. Coleman, "Tell the Court," 74–75; Feller, *Indigenous in Jim Crow*, 4, 6, 163. Individuals of one-sixteenth or less Indigenous ancestry were considered white and exempted from these restrictions. This exception was made because there were prominent whites in Virginia who claimed to be descendants

of John Rolfe and Pocahontas, the Native American woman belonging to the Powhatan people who was notable for her association with the colonial settlement at Jamestown. Maillard, "Pocahontas Exception," 354.

51. Coleman, "Tell the Court," 74–75; Cashin, *Loving*, 24–25; Coleman, *That the Blood*, 161.
52. Coleman, "Tell the Court," 67–80; Feller, *Indigenous in Jim Crow*, 12, 49, 86.
53. Coleman, "Tell the Court," 74–76.
54. Katz, *Black Indians*, 254; Perdue, *Slavery and the Evolution*, 207; Earchiel Johnson, "Slaves of Tribe," *People's World*, November 29, 2017, https://peoplesworld.org/article/slaves-of-the-tribe-the-hidden-history-of-the-freedmen/.
55. Krauthamer, *Black Slaves, Indian Masters*, 2, 13, 29, 46; Johnson, "Slaves of Tribe"; Adams, *Education for Extinction*, 21–32.
56. Sturm, *Blood Politics*, 61–64; Strum, "Blood, Politics," 223–57.
57. Johnson, "Slaves of Tribe."
58. Johnson, "Slaves of Tribe"; Roberts, "Federal Court"; Sturm, *Blood Politics*, 78–95, 169–205; Miles, *Ties That Bind*, 194.
59. Alaina E. Roberts, "A Federal Court Has Ruled Blood Cannot Determine Tribal Citizenship. Here's Why That Matters," *Washington Post*, September 7, 2017, https://www.washingtonpost.com/news/made-by-history/wp/2017/09/07/a-federal-court-has-ruled-blood-cannot-determine-tribal-citizenship-heres-why-that-matters/; Miles, *Ties That Bind*, 195.
60. Sturm, *Blood Politics*, 186–90.
61. Roberts, "Federal Court."
62. S. Miller, "Seminoles and Africans," 23–47.
63. Sturm, *Blood Politics*, 69.
64. Brooks, *Confounding*, 145.
65. Sturm, *Blood Politics*, 68–71.
66. Sturm, *Blood Politics*, 69.
67. Sturm, *Blood Politics*, 70–71; Miles, *Ties That Bind*, 51, 56–57, 100–128.
68. Naylor, *African Cherokees*, 28–29.
69. Littlefield, *Africans and Seminoles*, 6–14, 203.
70. Mulroy, *Seminole Freedman*, 136–37.
71. Bateman, "We're Still Here," 235.
72. Buick, *Child of the Fire*, 96–98, 133, 209–13.
73. Cannon, *Black-Native*, 79, 78.
74. Cannon, *Black-Native*, 133–53.
75. Cooper, "For African Americans."
76. Maillard, "We Are Black Indians," 85. Dineen-Wimberly has examined similar

phenomena among the Makah Reservation in Neah Bay, Washington. See "Being Mixed Race," 109.
77. Comas-Díaz, "LatiNegra," 167–90.
78. For a further discussion, see the introduction.
79. Smith and Moore, "Intraracial Diversity," 25.
80. Smith and Moore, "Intraracial Diversity," 25.
81. Smith and Moore, "Intraracial Diversity," 26.
82. Diaz, "Race Doesn't Exist," 56.
83. Bettie, *Women without Class*, 4, 5, 7.
84. Logan, "How Race Counts," 3–4, 11; Nicholson, Pantoja, and Segura, "Race Matters," 7.
85. DaCosta, *Making Multiracials*, 44, 61, 77, 126, 144; Newman, "Revisiting the Marginal Man," 37.
86. The term *Hapa* was originally used in Hawai'i as a somewhat derogatory term to refer to multiracials of white (Haole) and Native Hawaiian descent, that is, Hapa Haoles. *Hapa* was originally a derogatory Hawaiian word for "half" and is now embraced as a term to refer to people of mixed-race Asian and Pacific Island heritage. Fulbeck, *Part Asian*, 2. Over time it came to encompass all multiracials, although those of African descent have not always been included in this expanded definition. Also, some individuals are critical of the term as being appropriated from Hawaiians when generically used to refer to all multiracials.
87. DaCosta, *Making Multiracials*, 143.
88. DaCosta, *Making Multiracials*, 143.
89. Hoskins, *Asian American*, 3; Strmic-Pawl, *Multiracialism*, 7, 27, 89, 123.
90. Treitler, *Ethnic Project*, 41, 44–45.
91. Root, "Factors Influencing," 67.

9. Racial Labels

1. Jones and Bullock, "Two or More Population," 11.
2. Park, Meyers, and Wei, "Multiracial Patterns," 2.
3. Wang, "Rise of Intermarriage," 9.
4. Waring and Purkayastha, "'I'm a Different Kind of Biracial,'" 13.
5. Daniel and Daniel, "Pre School," 471.
6. Davis, *Who Is Black?*, 4.
7. Hitlin, Elder, and Brown, "Racial Self-Categorization," 1303; Root, "Reconstructing Race," 141; Khanna, "If You're Half Black," 101–17.
8. Khanna, "If You're Half Black," 116.

9. Miyawaki, "Part-Latinos," 296.
10. Herman, "Forced to Choose," 744.
11. Harrison, "Racial Identification," 101–4; Herman, "Forced to Choose," 744; Tizard and Phoenix, "Identity," 1340.
12. Leonard, *Making Ethnic Choices*, 132, 205.
13. Binning et al., "Interpretation," 47.
14. Phinney, "When We Talk," 918; Stephan and Stephan, "Measurement," 542.
15. Newman and Daniel, "Colorblind," 21, 23.
16. McFarland, "Chicano Rap Roots," 946.
17. Rios, *Punished*, 30.
18. Hughes and Johnson, "Correlates," 981.
19. Herman, "Forced to Choose," 732.
20. Mohan and Chambers, "Two Researchers," 261.
21. Samuels, "Building Kinship," 31.
22. Samuels, "Building Kinship," 33.
23. Thompson, "Variables," 758.
24. McHale et al., "Mothers' and Fathers' Racial Socialization," 1398.
25. McHale et al., "Mothers' and Fathers' Racial Socialization," 1398.
26. Feinberg, "Internal," 96.
27. Hughes and Chen, "When and What," 208; Thornton et al., "Sociodemographic," 407.
28. Matthew Blotch, Shan Carter, and Alan McLean, "Mapping America: Every City, Every Block," Infographic, *New York Times*, accessed August 15, 2022, https://www.nytimes.com/projects/census/2010/explorer.html.
29. Sawyer, "Politics," 178.
30. Lopez-Aguado, "I Would Be," 217.
31. Cornell, "Variable," 266.
32. DaCosta, "All In," 21.
33. Menudo is a traditional Mexican soup made with beef stomach in a chili-based red broth. It is traditionally served on special occasions or with family.
34. García Coll et al., "Integrative," 1896, 1900, 1902–3; Harris and Simm, "Who Is Multiracial," 623; Turley, "When Do Neighborhoods Matter?," 61.
35. Jiménez, "Multiethnic," 163; Castañeda-Liles, "Multiracial Reference Group," 14, 162.

10. Defining Blaxicans

Some of the material in this chapter borrows from Romo, "'You're Not Black or Mexican Enough!'"

1. Daniel, *Race and Multiraciality*, 160.

2. Grusec and Hastings, *Handbook of Socialization*, 3–102.
3. García et al., "Code-Switching," 2353.
4. E. Anderson, *Code of the Street*, 36.
5. Rodriguez, Cargile, and Rich, "Reactions," 408.
6. Rothman and Rell, "Linguistic Analysis," 521–22.
7. WB is the Warner Brothers television network and broadcasted television sitcoms with all-Black casts, such as *Sister, Sister, The Wayans Bros.*, and *The Steve Harvey Show*. UPN stands for the United Paramount Network, a closely associated network that eventually merged with the WB.
8. Talmon-Chvaicer, *Hidden*, 2.
9. Kun and Pulido, *Black and Brown*, 390.
10. Cuevas, *Afro-Mexican Ancestors*, 130.
11. E. Rodríguez, *Celebrating Debutantes*, 26.
12. Davalos, "La Quinceañera," 108.
13. Davalos, "La Quinceañera," 122; E. Rodríguez, *Celebrating Debutantes*, 5.
14. Anderson, *Imagined*, 39, 182.
15. Daniel, *Race and Multiraciality*, 27.
16. Museus et al., "Multiracial Students' Experiences," 682–84, 692–95.
17. Leavitt et al., "'Frozen,'" 41.
18. Spickard, Guevarra, and Rondilla, "Introduction," 4.
19. Bonilla-Silva, *Racism*, 144–207.
20. Anzaldúa, *Borderlands*, 79.
21. Blea, *Researching Chicano Communities*, 1.
22. Anderson, *Imagined Communities*, 5, 6.
23. Jones and Bullock, "Two or More Population," 11.
24. According to the 2010 census, the West Coast, particularly Hawai'i and California, has the largest numerical majority and highest percentage of two or more races individuals. However, Hawai'i had a higher percentage of two or more race people (23.57 percent) in the population but a smaller numerical majority (320,629) than California. California had the greatest numerical majority (1,815,384), and 4.9 percent are two or more races in California compared to the rest of the United States, which was 2.9 percent. Jones and Bullock, "Two or More Population," 11. Similarly, in 2020 California had a larger "two or more races" population (5.8 million) but a smaller percentage (14.6 percent). Hawai'i had a larger percentage of "two or more races" population (25.3 percent) but a smaller number (259,343) than California, given its overall smaller population. Humes, Jones, and Ramirez, "Overview of Race," 6; Galdámez and Rios, "Multiracial and Multiethnic Growth"; Amanda Ulrich, "Census 2020," *Desert Sun*, August 8, 2020,

https://www.desertsun.com/story/news/2021/08/12/census-2020-california-population-grows-diversity/8112412002/; 2020 Census Redistricting Data (Public Law 94-171) Summary File.
25. Daniel et al., "Emerging Paradigms," en49, 37.
26. Park, Meyers, and Wei, "Multiracial Patterns," 2.
27. Newman and Daniel, "Colorblind," 22.
28. Park, Meyers, and Wei, "Multiracial Patterns," 1.
29. The "multiracial belt" around the Central Valley and greater Sacramento regions has the highest percent of multiracials in the center of the state. Newman and Daniel found that biracial adolescents in Northern California living in the "multiracial belt" are more accepted and even assumed to identify as multiracial. Indeed, a multiracial identification in California and Hawai'i is a normative part of the racial landscape in ways that do not appear to be duplicated elsewhere. Park, Meyers, and Wei, "Multiracial Patterns," 1; Newman and Daniel, "Colorblind."
30. Daniel, "Sociology of Multiracial Identity," 117.
31. Very few surveys, particularly those with large and diverse samples, have been conducted that include questions about group identity among multiracials. Some exceptions not mentioned in this study include Soojean Choi-Misailidis's unpublished dissertation, "Multiracial-Heritage Awareness and Personal Affiliation: Development and Validation of a New Measure to Assess Identity in People of Mixed-Race Descent" (Fordham University, 2003); Josef M. Castañeda-Liles's unpublished dissertation, "The Multiracial Reference Group Orientation Scale (MRGOS): A New Scale for Use with Mixed Race Populations" (University of California, Santa Barbara, 2012); Kelly F. Jackson's "Living the Multiracial Experience: Shifting Racial Expressions, Resisting Race, and Seeking Community" (published in *Qualitative Social Work* in 2010); and, more recently, Yoo et al. in "Construction and Initial Validation of the Multiracial Experiences Measure (MEM)" (published in *Journal of Counseling Psychology* in 2015). The question of groupness is part of these surveys, which in several cases draw data from samples consisting of at least three hundred multiracials in the United States.
32. Parker, Horowitz, Morin, and Lopez, "Multiracial in America," 7.
33. Cornell and Hartman, *Ethnicity and Race*, 75–106; Daniel, *More Than Black?*, 116.
34. Daniel, "Sociology of Multiracial Identity," 117; Johnston-Guerrero and Ford, "Draw Your Own Box?," 92; Spickard, *Race in Mind*, 352–54.
35. Pew, "Multiracial in America," 9.

36. Cornell and Hartman, *Ethnicity and Race*, 75–106; Daniel, "Sociology of Multiracial Identity," 117.
37. Daniel et al., "Emerging Paradigms," 21; Daniel, "Sociology of Multiracial Identity," 117; Jackson, "Living," 52; L. Jones, "Who Are We," 140–57.
38. Castañeda-Liles, *Multiracial Reference Group*, 57–62, 157–67; Daniel, *More Than Black?*, 112–16; Johnston-Guerrero and Ford, "Draw Your Own Box," 92; Newman and Daniel, "Colorblind," 22–33; Daniel, "Sociology of Multiracial Identity," 117; Pew, "Multiracial in America," 64–70; Spickard, *Race in Mind*, 352–54; Thornton, "Is Multiracial Status," 324–25.
39. Cornell and Hartman, *Ethnicity and Race*, 75–106; Daniel, *More Than Black?*, 114–16.
40. "Linked fate" refers to the joining of self-interests and racial group interests, the idea that the fate of individuals is linked to the overall well-being of their racial group. See Dawson, *Black Visions*, xii, 11, 82, 124; Davenport et al., "Racial Identity, Group Consciousness," 1–13; Pew, "Multiracial in America," 14–15.

11. Social Agency and Constraint

1. C. Ortiz, "Parental Racial Socialization," 89–103.
2. C. Ortiz, "Parental Racial Socialization," 89–103.
3. A. Harris, "Marginalization," 431.
4. Cruz-Jansen, "LatiNegras," 168–83.
5. Redding, California, has a population of 80.8 percent that mark "white alone." "QuickFacts: Redding City, California," United States Census Bureau (website), accessed July 30, 2023, https://www.census.gov/quickfacts/fact/table/reddingcitycalifornia/pst045222.
6. Collins, *Black Feminist Thought* (2000), 69.
7. Collins, *Black Feminist Thought* (2000), 69.
8. Warren and Twine, "White Americans," 207–8.
9. Newman and Daniel, "Colorblind," 22–33.
10. Sims, "Reevaluation," 578.
11. Psychiatrist Chester M. Pierce sought to unpack the mechanism of "subtle and stunning" daily racial offenses, known as *microaggressions*. Originally termed "offensive mechanisms," Pierce coined the word *microaggression* in 1970. Pierce, "Offensive Mechanisms," 272–82. His seminal description of the term *microaggressions* laid the groundwork for a reframing by counseling psychologist and scholar Derald Wing Sue, who popularized the study and understanding of racial microaggressions, which were defined as subtle,

daily, and unintentional racial slights committed against people of color because they are members of a racialized group. Yosso et al., "Critical Race Theory," 660–81; Nadal et al., "Microaggressions and the Multiracial Experience," 36–37; Constantine, "Racial Microaggressions," 2–13.
12. Nadal et al., "Microaggressions and the Multiracial Experience," 41, 43.
13. Newman and Daniel, "Colorblind," 22–23; Park, Meyers, and Wei, "Multiracial Patterns," 2.
14. Khanna, "If You're Half Black," 99–100, 102, 106–14.
15. Lewis, *Race in the Schoolyard*, 3–7, 11, 128–96; Bettie, *Women without Class*, 11, 12.
16. Herman, "Forced to Choose," 730.
17. Tajfel, *Differentiation*, 66, 74, 105–7, 206.
18. Shih et al., "Social Construction," 7.
19. Shih and Sanchez, "When Race Becomes," 2–10.
20. García Coll et al., "Integrative Model," 1901; Harris and Simm, "Who Is Multiracial?," 622; Turley, "When Do Neighborhoods Matter?," 62–64, 68–69, 73, 77.
21. Bettie, *Women without Class*, 48.
22. Glenn, *Unequal Freedom*, 6–17.

12. Race and Cultural Authenticity

Some of this analysis borrows from Romo, "'You're Not Black or Mexican Enough!'"

1. M. R. Jackson, "Profile," 434–38.
2. M. R. Jackson, "Profile," 437–38.
3. King O'Riain, *Pure Beauty*, 22.
4. Warikoo, "Racial Authenticity," 388–91, 395–401, 405–6.
5. Pierce, "Offensive Mechanism," 265–82.
6. Sue, *Microaggressions*, 3, 8.
7. Johnston and Nadal, "Multiracial Microaggressions," 123–26.
8. Dalmage, "Discovering Racial Borders," 99; Nadal et al., "Microaggressions and the Multiracial Experience," 36; Johnston and Nadal, "Multiracial Microaggressions," 123; Jackson et al., "Mixed Resilience," 212.
9. Dalmage, "Discovering Racial Borders," 94.
10. Nadal et al., "Microaggressions within Families," 192.
11. Rockquemore and Brunsma, *Beyond Black*; Sims and Joseph-Salisbury, "We Were All," 53–54, 56.
12. Telles and Sue, *Durable Ethnicity*, 169, 184; Lopez, *Language Maintenance*, 12–20.

13. Mason, "Annual Income, Hourly Wages," 819–20, 828–33; Ortiz and Arce, "Language Orientation," 127, 140–41.
14. Jiménez, "Multiethnic Mexican Americans," 176–77.
15. Bettie, *Women without Class*, 158, 215.
16. Telles, Sawyer, and Rivera-Salgado, Introduction, 4, 29; García, *Chicanismo*, 72.
17. Zamora, *Racial Baggage*, 5.
18. Zamora, *Racial Baggage*, 4.
19. Hernández, "Afro-Americans," 1537–51; Banks, "Mestizaje," 203–4; Vaughn, "Afro-Mexico," 118.
20. Arredondo et al., "Introduction," 1–18; Pérez-Torres, *Mestizaje*, xii, 7.
21. Hernández, "Afro-Americans," 1537–51.
22. Argen, "'We Exist. We're Here.'"
23. Root, "From Exotic," 20–29.
24. Nadal et al., "Microaggressions within Families," 192.
25. González, *Afro-Mexico*, 25; Thomas, *Cuban Zarzuela*, 42, 43, 50.
26. Corridos are a form of ballad or song, usually about oppression, peasant life, or history.
27. Dalmage, "Discovering Racial Borders," 99.
28. Collins, *Black Feminist Thought* (2000), 89.
29. Johnston and Nadal, "Multiracial Microaggressions," 124–39.
30. Johnston and Nadal, "Multiracial Microaggressions," 125.
31. Music Television and Black Entertainment Television, respectively.
32. Miller-Young, "Hip-Hop Honeys," 262.
33. Bettie, *Women without Class*, 46, 130.
34. Miller-Young, "Hip-Hop Honeys," 262, 278, 281.
35. Cohen, *Finding Afro-Mexico*, 154.
36. King O'Riain, *Pure Beauty*, 34.
37. A. Harris, "Marginalization," 431.
38. Anzaldúa, *Borderlands*, 79.
39. "Spanish" was the most frequent code used in the coding of interviews. A code is an analytical note that is assigned when reading through transcripts. We assigned a code whenever participants spoke about a specific topic, such as hair or Spanish.
40. Banks, *Hair Matters*, 7.
41. Patterson, *Slavery and Social Death*, 61.
42. Banks, *Hair Matters*, 150.
43. Hunter, *Race, Gender*, 7, 14, 94–95, 107, 116.
44. Lyman and Douglas, "Ethnicities," 351, 354, 361.

45. Craig, "Decline," 402.
46. Collins, *Black Feminist Thought* (1990), 78, 79–80, 90.
47. Craig, "Decline," 399.
48. Feagin and Vera, *White Racism*, 9–11.
49. Nadal et al., "Microaggressions within Families," 197.

13. Black and Brown Relations

1. U.S. Bureau of the Census, 2010.
2. Vaca, *Presumed Alliance*, 3, 69, 86, 97, 149, 174; Mindiola, Niemann, and Rodriguez, *Black-Brown Relations*, xi–xiii, 5, 16, 20–37, 65, 109–21; Zamora, "Mexican Illegality," 1901, 1906, 1910; Kun and Pulido, *Black and Brown*, 2–24; Martinez, *Neighborhood*, 8, 161–97; Telles, Sawyer, and Rivera-Salgado, "Introduction," 1–29.
3. Telles, Sawyer, and Rivera-Salgado, "Introduction," 2, 3, 13.
4. Martinez and Rios, "Conflict, Cooperation," 343, 360.
5. Zamora, "Framing Commonality," 299.
6. Pastor, "Keeping It Real," 1.
7. Daniel, "Sociology of Multiracial Identity," 106, 108.
8. Daniel, *More Than Black?*, 27, 189.
9. Gay, "Seeing the Difference," 982–85, 987–96.
10. Pulido, "Day without Immigrants," 5, 6.
11. Vigil, "Ethnic Succession," 325–26, 338–40.
12. "Bridging Black-Immigrant Divide," The Opportunity Agenda (website), last modified 2007, https://opportunityagenda.org/messaging_reports/bridging-the-black-immigrant-divide/.
13. Zamora and Osuji, "Mobilizing African Americans," 434–35.
14. Sawyer, "Politics in Los Angeles," 178. Special Order 40, implemented in 1979, prevents LAPD officers from questioning people to determine their immigration status. "Debate over Sanctuary Cities," CBS Los Angeles, November 14, 2016, https://www.cbsnews.com/losangeles/news/debate-over-sanctuary-cities-hits-home-with-man-whose-son-was-murdered/.
15. Melissa Pamer and Kennedy Ryan, "Jamiel Shaw Sr., Father of L.A. Teen Slain," KTLA, July 18, 2016, https://ktla.com/news/politics/jamiel-shaw-sr-father-of-l-a-teen-slain-by-undocumented-immigrant-gang-member-to-speak-at-rnc/. "Meet the Special Guests Attending President Donald J. Trump's Address to a Joint Session of Congress," Trump White House (website) archives, February 28, 2017, https://trumpwhitehouse.archives.gov/articles/meet-special-guests-attending-president-donald-j-trumps-address-joint-session-congress/.
16. Hutchinson, *Latino Challenge*, 6, 11, 52, 64, 114, 118, 121, 127.

NOTES TO PAGES 238–243

17. Hutchinson, *Latino Challenge*, 24–53, 64.
18. Glassner, *Culture of Fear*, 3–9, 17, 202, 208.
19. Alex Garcia, Diana Martinez, and Mike Terry, "Sylmar High School," *San Fernando Sun*, May 12, 2016, https://sanfernandosun.com/2016/05/12/sylmar-high-trying-to-recover-from-student-brawl/.
20. Vigil, "Ethnic Succession," 334. There is precedent to green-light fears against Black residents in the northeast San Fernando area and greater Los Angeles. See Quinones, "Race, Real Estate," 281.
21. Danny Jensen, "Danny Trejo Speaks Up," *LAist*, May 11, 2016, https://laist.com/news/machete-cuts-in.
22. Brittny Mejia and Veronica Rocha, "After Ugly Brawl," *Los Angeles Times*, May 12, 2016, https://www.latimes.com/local/lanow/la-me-ln-machete-actor-brawl-sylmar-high-school-20160512-story.html.
23. The following 2016–17 school year, only twenty Black students were enrolled at the school, according to first-hand accounts from students and "Sylmar Charter High School," National Center for Education Statistics (website), accessed September 14, 2020, https://nces.ed.gov/ccd/schoolsearch/school_detail.asp?Search=1&InstName=Sylmar+Charter+High+School&SchoolID=062271003385&SchoolType=1&SchoolType=2&SchoolType=3&SchoolType=4&SpecificSchlTypes=all&IncGrade=-1&LoGrade=-1&HiGrade=-1&ID=062271003385.
24. Pastor, "Keeping It Real," 33–34.
25. Telles, Sawyer, and Rivera-Salgado, "Introduction," 3–19.
26. "Demographics," City of Las Cruces (website), accessed September 10, 2020, https://www.lascruces.gov/1530/Demographics.
27. Telles, Sawyer, and Rivera-Salgado, "Introduction," 9.
28. "Most to Least Segregated Metro Regions in 2020 According to the 2020 Census Data," Othering and Belonging Institute (website), accessed December 11, 2023, https://belonging.berkeley.edu/most-least-segregated-metro-regions-2020.
29. Vasquez, "Blurred Borders," 52.
30. *Mayate* refers to a "Black dung beetle" and is a derogatory word referring to an African American or a dark-skinned person.
31. Telles, Sawyer, and Rivera-Salgado, "Introduction," 17.
32. Johnston and Nadal, "Multiracial Microaggressions," 125.
33. "Quick Facts: Los Angeles County, California," United States Census Bureau (website), accessed August 15, 2021, https://www.census.gov/quickfacts/losangelescountycalifornia.
34. Mindiola, Niemann, and Rodriguez, *Black-Brown Relations*, 28, 38, 74–77, 121–22.

35. Román and Flores, "Introduction," 1–2.
36. Mindiola, Niemann, and Rodriguez, *Black-Brown Relations*, 53.
37. Johnson, Farrell, and Guinn, "Immigration and Reform," 1087.
38. Kun and Pulido, *Black and Brown*, 17.
39. Miyawaki, "Expanding Boundaries," 996, 998, 1012–14.
40. Jordan and Spickard, "Historical Origins," 98–132.

Conclusion

1. Betancur, "Framing Discussion," 160–66.
2. King and DaCosta, "Changing Face," 237–38.
3. Vaca, *Presumed Alliance*, 2, 12, 48, 185; Betancur, "Framing Discussion," 159–69; Zamora, "Framing Commonality," 299–301; Martinez and Rios, "Conflict, Cooperation," 343–44; Vigil, "Ethnic Succession," 325.
4. Sawyer, "Politics in Los Angeles," 177; Zamora, "Framing Commonality," 300, 304–20; Hondagneu-Sotelo and Pastor, *South Central Dreams*, 1; Vigil, "Ethnic Succession," 330–32.
5. Johnson, *Spaces of Conflict*, 2–4.
6. Hondagneu-Sotelo and Pastor, *South Central Dreams*, 12, 25; Zamora, "Framing Commonality," 306, 314, 318; Dawson, *Black Visions*, xii, 11, 82, 124.
7. Jennifer Medina, "Latinos Back Black Lives," *New York Times*, July 3, 2020, https://www.nytimes.com/2020/07/03/us/politics/latinos-police-racism-black-lives-matter.html.
8. Mario Koran, "'We're Suffering,'" *The Guardian*, June 12, 2020, https://www.theguardian.com/world/2020/jun/12/latinos-police-brutality-protests-george-floyd; Foster-Frau, "Latinos Are Disproportionately Killed," *Washington Post*, June 2, 2020, https://www.washingtonpost.com/national/police-killings-latinos/2021/05/31/657bb7be-b4d4-11eb-a980-a60af976ed44_story.html; Russell Contreras, "Activists: Police Killings of Latinos," Associated Press, August 17, 2020, https://apnews.com/article/shootings-race-and-ethnicity-ca-state-wire-mexico-tx-state-wire-059f64f61b8d348611af6c6a00a71e4e; Gustavo Arellano, "What Will Make People Care?" *Los Angeles Times*, April 20, 2021, https://www.latimes.com/california/story/2021-04-20/latinos-police-shootings; Matt Kawahara and Anna Bauman, "Protesters Demand Justice," *San Francisco Chronicle*, June 9, 2020, https://www.sfchronicle.com/bayarea/article/Protesters-demand-justice-answers-in-killing-of-15326042.php; Sarah Moon and Cheri Mossburg, "Two LA County Sheriff's Deputies," CNN, December 12, 2020, https://www.cnn.com/2020/12/12/us/andres-guardado-deputies-relieved-of-duty/index.html; "Vallejo Cop Who fatally Shot Sean Monterrosa Violated Policy, Investigation Concludes," KTVU, December 3, 2021, https://www

NOTES TO PAGES 260–263

.ktvu.com/news/independent-investigation-of-fatal-vallejo-police-shooting-of-sean-monterrosa-concludes.

9. Emanuella Grinberg, "'Blaxicans' Photos Explore Angelenos Straddling Two Worlds," CNN, March 1, 2016, https://www.cnn.com/2016/03/01/living/blaxicans-of-los-angeles-photo-exhibit-feat/index.html; Julissa James, "A Pandemic, Protests, Identity: Being Both Black and Latino in 2020," *Los Angeles Times*, October 6, 2020, https://www.latimes.com/california/story/2020-10-06/being-both-black-and-latino-in-2020-pandemic-protests-and-identity.

10. Taylor, *From #BlackLivesMatter*, 75.

11. Bonilla-Silva, *Racism*, xii, 2, 16, 208, 82.

12. Daniel, *Race and Multiraciality*, 202, 215.

13. Gramsci, *Prison Notebooks*, 263; Omi and Winant, *Racial Formation*, 66–69, 84, 115, 148.

14. Lipsitz, *How Racism Takes Place*, 1–21.

15. Gramsci, *Prison Notebooks*, 263; Omi and Winant, *Racial Formation*, 66–69, 84, 115, 148.

16. Tesler, "Conditions Ripe," 110–23.

17. White backlash against affirmative action is largely based on claims of reverse discrimination ostensibly granting unfair advantages to less qualified people of color over more qualified whites. Legal challenges date back to the landmark *Regents of the University of California v. Bakke* decision, 438 U.S. 265 (1978). The Supreme Court ruled that allowing race as one of several factors determining admission was constitutional but designating a specific quota of seats for racial minorities was impermissible. Daniel, *Race and Multiraciality*, 219–33, 258–85; Adam Liptak, "Supreme Court Invalidates Key Part of Voting Rights Act," *New York Times*, June 25, 2013, http://www.nytimes.com/2013/06/26/us/supreme-court-ruling.html?pagewanted=all&_r=0.

18. Sarah Childress, "With Voting Rights Act Out, States Push Voter ID Laws," *Frontline*, June 26, 2013, https://www.pbs.org/wgbh/frontline/article/with-voting-rights-act-out-states-push-voter-id-laws/.

19. Hajnal, Lajevardi, and Nielson, "Voter Identification Laws," 363–78; Clarissa Hamlin, "'Sound the Death Knell': Judge Rules Texas Voter ID Law Is 'Intentionally Discriminatory,'" *Newsone*, April 10, 2017, https://newsone.com/3705050/federal-judge-nelva-gonzales-ramos-intentionally-discriminatory-texas-voter-id-law-ruling/.

20. John Eligon and Audra D. S. Burch, "After a Summer of Racial Reckoning, Race Is on the Ballot," *New York Times*, October 30, 2020, https://www.nytimes.com/2020/10/30/us/racial-justice-elections.html; Dunivin et al., "Black Lives Matter Protests," 1–11.

21. Erin Mansfield and Candy Woodall, "Republican Politicians All Over the Country Have Repeated the Great Replacement Theory," *USA Today*, May 29, 2022, https://www.usatoday.com/story/news/politics/2022/05/29/republicans-great-replacement-theory/9798199002/.

22. Law professor Derrick Bell, the intellectual father of the critical race theory movement, along with other principal legal scholars, maintained that the whole purpose of critical race theory (CRT) is to help facilitate a national collective understanding of and recking with racism by moving beyond the emphasis on microlevel individual acts and blame. The objective is to scrutinize macrolevel and mesolevel systems, policies, and institutions that maintain racial biases, which are embedded in and permeate U.S. laws, institutions, and social structures. Notwithstanding the formal removal of legalized racial discrimination, these biases continue to be the most insidious and pervasive ways in which our racialized social order is constructed, supported, and maintained. They have historically had and continue to have a disproportionately negative impact on people of color. CRT is rarely taught in K–12 public schools but has nevertheless become a lightning rod in districts across the nation—and a catalyst for conservative political candidates seeking to fire up their Republican base. Delgado and Stefancic, *Critical Race Theory*, 1–14; Sally Kohn, "Critical Race Theory and Loving America Are Not Mutually Exclusive. My Journey with CRT," *USA Today*, June 24, 2021, https://www.usatoday.com/story/opinion/voices/2021/06/24/learning-critical-race-theory-empowering-not-self-loathing/7775725002/; Rashawn Ray and Alexandra Gibbons, "Why Are States Banning Critical Race Theory?," *Brookings*, November 2021, https://www.brookings.edu/blog/fixgov/2021/07/02/why-are-states-banning-critical-race-theory/; Audrey Williams June and Brian O'Leary, "States Are Trying to Limit Talk About Race," *Chronicle of Higher Education*, August 12, 2021, https://www.chronicle.com/article/these-states-are-taking-aim-at-talking-about-race?cid2=gen_login_refresh&cid=gen_sign_in; Touré, "Expect to See More Republicans Using CRT as Racial Boogeyman to Activate White Voters," *Grio*, November 3, 2021, https://thegrio.com/2021/11/03/republicans-crt-critical-race-theory-white-voters/.

23. Ana Ceballos, "State University Faculty, Students to Be Surveyed on Beliefs," *Tampa Bay Times*, June 22, 2021, https://www.tampabay.com/news/florida-politics/2021/06/22/state-university-faculty-students-to-be-surveyed-on-beliefs/; Ted Millar, "Florida Joins the List of GOP-Led States Banning Critical Race Theory," *PoliticusUSA*, June 13, 2021, https://www.politicususa.com/2021/06/13/tm-florida-joins-list-gop-led-states-banning-critical-race-theory.html?utm

_source=rss&utm_medium=rss&utm_campaign=tm-florida-joins-list-gop-led-states-banning-critical-race-theory; Sofia Andrade, "Chilling New Florida Law Will Survey University Students and Faculty About Their Political Beliefs," *Slate*, June 24, 2021, https://slate.com/technology/2021/06/florida-survey-university-students-faculty-political-beliefs.html.

24. Elizabeth A. Harris and Alexandra Alter, "Book Ban Efforts Spread Across the U.S.," *New York Times*, February 8, 2022, https://www.nytimes.com/2022/01/30/books/book-ban-us-schools.html.

25. Seung Mung Kim and Marianna Sotomayor, "Race Hovered Over Ketanji Brown Jackson's Confirmation Hearing," *Washington Post*, March 24, 2022, https://www.washingtonpost.com/politics/2022/03/24/race-jackson-confirmation-hearing/.

26. Boykin, *Race Against Time*, 5–11, 34–43, 269. Bahrampour and Mellnik, "Census Data Shows." Republicans have become a minority party, composed of a majority of European Americans. Republicans have leads among whites—particularly white men. Democrats hold advantages among Blacks, Asian Americans, and Latinas/os. Since 1992 the Republican Party has lost the popular vote, except in 2004. Still, the way electoral votes are counted privileges smaller, whiter, and predominantly Republican-leaning states. This can tip the scales in the favor of Republican candidates in presidential elections. Still, the electorate is getting older, more so among Republicans than among Democrats. Party affiliation of voters between the ages of eighteen and twenty-four, one of the most racially diverse cohorts in U.S. history, is heavily Democratic at 60 percent. Abigail Johnson Hess, "The 2020 Election Shows Gen Z's Voting Power for Years to Come," CNBC, November 18, 2020, https://www.cnbc.com/2020/11/18/the-2020-election-shows-gen-zs-voting-power-for-years-to-come.html.

27. Childs, *Navigating Interracial Borders*, 2; Childs, *Fade to Black and White*, 36, 56; Rodríguez-Garcia, Solana-Solana, and Lubbers, "Preference and Prejudice," 521–23, 539–41; Kina and Dariotis, *War Baby / Love Child*, 13–14; Thornton, "Policing the Borderlands," 105–27; Daniel, *More Than Black?*, 178–79; Hollinger, *Postethnic America*, 21, 42, 182; R. Spencer, *Reproducing Race*, 3, 183–212; R. Spencer, "'Only the News,'" 163–78; McNeil, *Sex and Race*, 92–93, 105; McKibbin, "Current State," 192–93; Carter, *United States*, 140, 161–90; Squires, *Dispatches*, 168–81; DaCosta, *Making Multiracials*, 123–24; Joseph, *Transcending Blackness*, ix–36, 155–72.

28. Buggs, "Dating in the Time," 538–49; Daniel, *More Than Black?*, 8, 106–11, 189–90; Daniel, "Sociology of Multiracial Identity," 112; K. Jackson, "Living the

Multiracial Experience," 42–58; Wijeyesinghe, "Intersectional Model," 81–103; Johnston-Guerrero and Wijeyesinghe, "Insights on Multiracial Knowledge," 3–16.

29. Daniel, *More Than Black?*, 8, 189–90; J. M. Spencer, *New Colored People*, xi–xiv, 3–14, 91–170; R. Spencer, *Spurious Issues*, 129–85; Warren and Sue, "Comparative Racisms," 34–51; Mahtani, *Mixed Race Amnesia*, 4, 6.

30. Daniel et al., "Emerging Paradigms," 24; Jolivétte, "Critical Mixed Race Studies," 24–28; T. Williams et al., "Being Different Together," 395–78; Zack, *Race and Mixed Race*, 99.

31. Johnston-Guerrero and Wijeyesinghe, "Insights on Multiracial Knowledge," 46.

Bibliography

Acuña, Rodolfo. *Occupied America: A History of Chicanos*. 8th ed. New York: Pearson, 2015.

Adams, David Wallace. *Education for Extinction: American Indians and the Boarding School Experience, 1875–1928*. Lawrence: University Press of Kansas, 2020.

Adler, Peter S. "Beyond Cultural Identity: Reflections on Cultural and Multicultural Man." In *Topics in Cultural Learning*, vol. 2, edited by Robert W. Brislin, 23–40. Honolulu: East-West Center, 1974.

Alba, Richard. *Blurring of the Color Line: The New Chance for a More Integrated America*. Harvard University Press, 2009.

———. *The Great Demographic Illusion: Majority, Minority, and the Expanding American Mainstream*. Princeton NJ: Princeton University Press, 2020.

Alcoff, Linda Martin. *Visible Identities: Race, Gender, and the Self*. New York: Oxford University Press, 2006.

Allen, Walter, Edward E. Telles, and Margaret L. Hunter. "Skin Color, Income, and Education: A Comparison of African Americans and Mexican Americans." *National Journal of Sociology* 13, no. 1 (2000): 129–80.

Almaguer, Tomás. *Racial Faultlines: The Historical Origins of White Supremacy in California*. Berkeley: University of California Press, 1994.

Althouse, Aaron P. "Contested Mestizos, Alleged Mulattos: Racial Identity and Caste Hierarchy in Eighteenth-Century Pátzcuaro, Mexico." *The Americas* 62, no. 2 (October 2005): 151–75. https://doi.org/10.1353/tam.2005.0155.

American Sociological Association. ASA Annual Meetings. https://www.asanet.org/news-events/meetings/previous-annual-meetings.

Anderson, Benedict. *Imagined Communities: Reflections on the Origins and Spread of Nationalism*. New York: Verso, 1983.

Anderson, Elijah. *Code of the Street: Decency, Violence, and the Moral Life of the Inner City*. New York: W. W. Norton, 1999.

Antonovsky, Aaron. "Toward a Refinement of the 'Marginal Man' Concept." *Social Forces* 35, no. 1 (1956): 57–62. https://doi.org/10.2307/2573115.

Anzaldúa, Gloria. *Borderlands/La Frontera: The New Mestiza*. San Francisco: Aunt Lute Books, 1999.

Aragon, Margarita. "The Difference That 'One Drop' Makes: Mexican and African Americans, Mixedness and Racial Categorization in the Early twentieth Century." *Subjectivity* 7, no. 1 (2014): 18–36. https://doi.org/10.1057/sub.2014.1.

Arredondo, Gabriela F., Aída Hurtado, Norma Klahn, Olga Nájera-Ramírez, and Patricia Zavella. "Introduction: Chicana Feminisms at the Crossroads: Disruptions in Dialogue." In *Chicana Feminisms: A Critical Reader*, edited by Gabriela F. Arredondo, Aída Hurtado, Norma Klahn, Olga Nájera-Ramírez, and Patricia Zavella, 1–18. Durham NC: Duke University Press, 2003.

Aslakson, Kenneth. "The 'Quadroon-Plaçage' Myth of Antebellum New Orleans: Anglo-American (Mis)interpretations of a French-Caribbean Phenomenon." *Journal of Social History* 45, no. 3 (Spring 2012): 709–34. https://doi.org/10.1093/jsh/shr059.

Banks, Ingrid. *Hair Matters: Beauty, Power, and Black Women's Consciousness*. New York: New York University Press, 2000.

Banks, Taunya Lovell. "Mestizaje and the Mexican Mestizo Self: No Hay Sangre Negra, So There Is No Blackness." *Southern California Interdisciplinary Law Journal* 15 (2006): 199–234. https://digitalcommons.law.umaryland.edu/cgi/viewcontent.cgi?article=1029&context=fac_pubs.

Banton, Michael. *Racial Theories*. 2nd ed. Cambridge, UK: Cambridge University Press, 1998.

Barrera, Antonio. *Race and Class in the Southwest: A Theory of Racial Inequality*. Notre Dame IN: University of Notre Dame Press, 1979.

Bateman, Rebecca B. "We're Still Here: History, Kinship, and Group Identity among the Freedman of Oklahoma." PhD diss., John Hopkins University, 1990.

Baumgartner, Alice L. *South to Freedom: Runaway Slaves to Mexico and the Road to Civil War*. New York: Basic Books, 2020.

Bell, Caryn Cosé. *Revolution, Romanticism, and the Afro-Creole Protest Tradition in Louisiana, 1718–1868*. Baton Rouge: Louisiana State University Press, 1997.

Bender, Gerald. *Angola Under the Portuguese*. Berkeley: University of California Press, 1978.

Bender, Steven W. *Greasers and Gringos: Latinos, Law, and the American Imagination*. New York: New York University Press, 2003.

Bennett, Herman L. *Africans in Colonial Mexico: Absolutism, Christianity, and Afro-Creole Consciousness, 1570–1640*. Bloomington: Indiana University Press, 2003.

Berkowitz, Susan. "Puerto Rico Focus Groups on the Census 2000 Race and Ethnicity Questions." *Census*, July 17, 2001. https://www2.census.gov/programs-surveys/decennial/2000/program-management/5-review/txe-program/B_13.pdf.

Berlin, Ira. *Slaves Without Masters: The Free Negro in the Ante-bellum South*. New York: Random House Books, 1970.
Betancur, John J. "Framing the Discussion of African American-Latino Relations: A Review and Analysis." In *Neither Enemies nor Friends: Latinos, Blacks, Afro-Latinos*, edited by Anani Dzidzienyo and Suzanne Oboler, 159–72. New York: Palgrave Macmillan, 2005.
Bettie, Julie. *Women without Class: Girls, Race, and Identity*. Berkeley: University of California Press, 2003.
Bhabha, Homi. *Location of Culture*. New York: Routledge, 1994.
Billingsley, Andrew. *Climbing Jacob's Ladder: The Enduring Legacy of African American Families*. New York: Simon and Schuster, 1993.
Binning, Kevin R., Miguel M. Unzueta, Yuen J. Huo, and Ludwin E. Molina. "The Interpretation of Multiracial Status and Its Relation to Social Engagement and Psychological Well-Being." *Journal of Social Issues* 65, no. 1 (January 2009): 35–49. https://doi.org/10.1111/j.1540-4560.2008.01586.x.
Blackwell, Maylei. "Contested Histories: *Las Hijas de Cuauhtémoc*, Chicana Feminisms, and the Print Culture in the Chicano Movement, 1968–1973." In *Chicana Feminisms: A Critical Reader*, edited by Gabriela F. Arredondo, Aída Hurtado, Norma Klahn, Olga Nájera-Ramírez, and Patricia Zavella, 59–89. Durham NC: Duke University Press, 2003.
Blanton, Carlos K. "George I. Sánchez, Ideology, and Whiteness." *Journal of Southern History* 72, no. 3 (August 2006): 569–604. https://doi.org/10.2307/27649149.
Blauner, Robert. *Racial Oppression in America*. New York: Harper and Row, 1972.
Blea, Irene I. *Researching Chicano Communities: Social-Historical, Physical, Psychological, and Spiritual Space*. Westport CT: Praeger, 1995.
Bonilla-Silva, Eduardo. *Racism Without Racists: Color-Blind Racism and the Persistence of Racial Inequality in the United States*. New York: Rowman and Littlefield, 2021.
Bourdieu, Pierre. *Outline of a Theory of Practice*. Cambridge, UK: Cambridge University Press, 1977.
Boykin, Keith. *Race Against Time: The Politics of a Darkening America*. New York: Bold Type Books, 2021.
Bradshaw, Carla. "Beauty and the Beast." In *Racially Mixed People in America*, edited by Maria P. P. Root, 77–90. Newbury Park CA: Sage Publications, 1992.
Bratter, Jennifer. "Will 'Multiracial' Survive to the Next Generation? The Racial Classification of Children of Multiracial Parents." *Social Forces* 86, no. 2 (2007): 821–49. https://doi.org/10.1093/sf/86.2.821.
Brook, Thomas, ed. *Plessy v. Ferguson: A Brief History with Documents*. Boston: Bedford/St. Martin's Press, 1997.

Brooks, James F. *Confounding the Color Line: The Indian-Black Experience in North America*. Lincoln: University of Nebraska Press, 2002.

Brown, Phillip. "Biracial Identity and Social Marginality." *Child Adolescent Social Work* 7, no. 4 (1990): 319–37. https://doi.org/10.1007/BF00757029.

Browne, J. Ross. "Report of the Debates in the Convention of California, on the Formation of the State Constitution, in September and October, 1849." Washington DC: Printed by J. T. Towers, 1850. https://digitalcommons.csumb.edu /hornbeck_usa_3_d/18/?utm_source=digitalcommons.csumb.edu%2Fhornbeck _usa_3_d%2F18&utm_medium=PDF&utm_campaign=PDFCoverPages.

Brunsma, David, Daniel Delgado, and Kerry Anne Rockquemore. "Liminality in the Multiracial Experience: Towards a Concept of Identity Matrix." *Identities* 20, no. 5 (2013): 481–502. https://doi.org/10.1080/1070289X.2013.827576.

Buggs, Shantel Gabriel. "Dating in the Time of #BlackLivesMatter: Exploring Mixed-Race Women's Discourses of Race and Racism." *Sociology of Race and Ethnicity* 3, no. 2 (2017): 538–51. https://doi.org/10.1080/1070289X.2013.827576.

Buick, Kirsten Pai. *Child of the Fire: Mary Edmonia Lewis and the Problem of Art History's Black and Indian Subject*. Durham NC: Duke University Press, 2010.

Caballero, Chamion, and Peter J. Aspinall. *Mixed Race in Britain in the Twentieth Century*. New York: Palgrave Macmillan, 2015.

Cannon, Sarita. *Black-Native: Autobiographical Acts Navigating the Minefields of Authenticity*. Lanham MD: Lexington Books, 2021.

Carbado, Devon W., and Cheryl I. Harris. "New Racial Preferences." *California Law Review* 96, no. 5 (2008): 1139–214. https://www.jstor.org/stable/20441045.

Carmichael, Stolkey, and Charles V. Hamilton. *Black Power: The Politics of Liberation*. New York: Random House, 1967.

Carrera, Magali M. *Imagining Identity in New Spain: Race, Lineage, and the Colonial Body in Portraiture and Casta Paintings*. Austin: University of Texas Press, 2003.

Carrigan, William D., and Clive Webb. "The Lynching of Persons of Mexican Origin or Descent in the United States, 1848 to 1928." *Journal of Social History* 37, no. 2 (Winter 2003): 411–38. https://doi.org/10.1353/jsh.2003.0169.

Carter, Greg. *The United States of the United Races: A Utopian History of Racial Mixing*. New York: New York University Press, 2013.

Carter, Mitzi U. "On Being Blakanese." In *What Are You? Voices of Mixed-Race Young People*, edited by Pearl. F. Gaskins, 201–5. New York: Henry Holt, 1999.

Casas, María Raquél. *Married to a Daughter of the Land: Spanish Mexican Women and Interethnic Marriage in California. 1820–1880*. Reno: University of Nevada Press, 2007.

Cashin, Sheryll. *Loving: Interracial Intimacy in America and the Threat to White Supremacy*. Boston: Beacon Press, 2017.

Castañeda-Liles, Josef M. "The Multiracial Reference Group Orientation Scale (MRGOS): A New Scale for Use with Mixed Race Populations." PhD diss., University of California, Santa Barbara, 2012.

Chance, John K. *Race and Class in Colonial Oaxaca*. Stanford: Stanford University Press, 1978.

Chávez, Ernesto. *"¡Mi Raza Primero!" (My People First!): Nationalism, Identity, and Insurgency in the Chicano Movement in Los Angeles, 1966–1978*. Berkeley: University of California Press, 2002.

Chavez-Garcia, Miroslava. *Negotiating Conquest: Gender and Power in California, 1770s to 1880s*. Tucson: University of Arizona Press, 2004.

Cheeseboro, Anthony Q. "Conflict and Continuity: E. Franklin Frazier, Oliver C. Cox, and the Chicago School of Sociology." *Journal of the Illinois State Historical Society* 92, no. 2 (1999): 50–172. https://www.jstor.org/stable/40193213.

Chew, Kenneth S. Y., David J. Eggebeen, and Peter R. Uhlenberg. "American Children in Multiracial Households." *Sociological Perspectives* 32, no. 1 (1989): 56–85. https://doi.org/10.2307/1389008.

Childs, Erica C. *Fade to Black and White: Interracial Images in Popular Culture*. Lanham MD: Rowman & Littlefield, 2009.

———. *Navigating Interracial Borders: Black-White Couples and Their Social Worlds*. Piscataway NJ: Rutgers University Press, 2005.

Chipman, Donald E. *Spanish Texas, 1519–1821*. Austin: University of Texas Press, 1991.

Choi-Misailidis, Soojean. "Multiracial-Heritage Awareness and Personal Affiliation: Development and Validation of a New Measure to Assess Identity in People of Mixed Race Descent." PhD diss., Fordham University, 2003.

Christophe, N. Keita, Annabelle L. Atkin, Gabriela L. Stein, and Michele Chan. "Examining Multiracial Pride, Identity-Based Challenges and Discrimination: An Exploratory Investigation Among Biracial Emerging Adults." *Race and Social Problems* 14 (March 2, 2022): 22–38. https://doi.org/10.1007/s12552-021-09325-4.

Cline, Sarah. "Guadalupe and the Castas: The Power of a Singular Colonial Painting." *Mexican Studies/Estudios Mexicanos* 31, no. 2 (2015): 218–47. https://doi.org/10.1525/mex.2015.31.2.218.

Cohen, David W., and Jack P. Greene. Introduction to *Neither Slave nor Free: The Freemen of African Descent in the Slave Societies of the New World*, edited by David. W. Cohen and Jack P. Greene, 1–23. Baltimore MD: Johns Hopkins University Press, 1972.

Cohen, Theodore W. *Finding Afro-Mexico: Race and Nation after the Revolution*. New York: Cambridge University Press, 2020.

Cohn, D'Vera. "American Indian and White, but Not 'Multiracial.'" Pew Research Center. June 11, 2015. https://www.pewresearch.org/short-reads/2015/06/11/american-indian-and-white-but-not-multiracial/.

Coleman, Arica L. "'Tell the Court I Love My [Indian] Wife': Interrogating Race and Self-Identity in *Loving v. Virginia*." *Souls: A Critical Journal of Black Politics, Culture, and Society* 8, no. 1 (2006): 67–80. https://doi.org/10.1080/10999940500516983.

———. *That the Blood Stay Pure: African Americans, Native Americans, and the Predicament of Race and Identity in Virginia*. Bloomington: Indiana University Press, 2013.

Colker, Ruth. *Hybrid: Bisexuals, Multiracials, and Other Misfits Under American Law*. New York: New York University Press, 1996.

Collins, Patricia Hill. *Black Feminist Thought: Knowledge, Consciousness, and the Politics of Empowerment*. New York: Routledge, 2000.

———. *Black Feminist Thought: Knowledge, Consciousness, and the Politics of Empowerment*. Boston: Unwin Hyman, 1990.

Comas-Días, Lilliana. "LatiNegra: Mental Health Issues of African Latinas." In *The Multiracial Experience: Racial Borders as the New Frontier*, edited by Maria P. P. Root, 167–90. Thousand Oaks CA: Sage Publications, 1996.

Constantine, Madonna G. "Racial Microaggressions Against African American Clients in Cross-Racial Counseling Relationships." *Journal of Counseling Psychology* 54, no. 1 (January 2007): 1–16. https://doi.org/10.1037/0022-0167.54.1.1.

Cornell, Stephan. "The Variable Ties That Bind: Content and Circumstances in Ethnic Processes." *Racial and Ethnic Studies* 19, no. 2 (April 1996): 265–89. https://doi.org/10.1080/01419870.1996.9993910.

Cornell, Stephen, and David Hartmann. *Ethnicity and Race: Making Identities in a Changing World*. Thousand Oaks CA: Pine Forge Press, 1998.

Cox, Oliver. *Caste, Class, and Race: A Study in Social Dynamics*. New York: Monthly Review Press, 1948.

Craig, Maxine. "The Decline of the Conk; or, How to Read a Process." *Fashion Theory: The Journal of Dress, Body, and Culture* 1, no. 4 (November 1997): 399–419.

Cruz-Jansen, Marta I. "LatiNegras: Desired Women-Undesirable Mothers, Daughters, Sisters and Wives." *Frontiers: A Journal of Women Studies* 22, no. 3 (September 2001):168–83. https://doi.org/10.2307/3347247.

Cuevas, Marco Polo Hernández. *Afro-Mexican Ancestors and the Nation They Constructed*. New York: Edwin Mellen, 2015.

DaCosta, Kimberley M. "All in the Family: The Familial Roots of Racial Division." In *The Politics of Multiracialism*, edited by Heather M. Dalmage, 19–42. Albany NY: SUNY, 2004.

———. *Making Multiracials: State, Family, and Market in the Redrawing of the Color Line*. Stanford CA: Stanford University Press, 2007.

Dalmage, Heather M. "Discovering Racial Borders." In *Race in an Era of Change: A Reader*, edited by Heather M. Dalmage and Barbara Katz Rothman, 94–103. New York: Oxford University Press, 2011.

Daniel, G. Reginald. "Beyond Black and White: The New Multiracial Consciousness." In *Racially Mixed people in America*, edited by Maria P. P. Root, 333–41. Newbury Park CA: Sage Publications, 1992.

———. "Black and White Identity in the New Millennium: Unsevering the Ties That Bind." In *The Multiracial Experience: Racial Borders as the New Frontier*, edited by Maria P. P. Root, 121–39. Thousand Oaks CA: Sage Publications, 1996.

———. Foreword to *Multiracial Experiences in Higher Education: Contesting Knowledge, Honoring Voice, and Innovating Practice*, edited by Marc P. Johnston-Guerrero and Charmaine L. Wijeyesinghe, ix–xix. New York: Routledge, 2023.

———. *More Than Black? Multiracial Identity and the New Racial Order*. Philadelphia: Temple University Press, 2001.

———. "Multiracial Identities in the United States: Towards the Brazilian of South African Paths?" *Social Sciences* 11, no. 204 (2022): 1-24. https://doi.org/10.3390/socsci11050204.

———. *Race and Multiraciality in Brazil and the United States: Converging Paths?* University Park: Pennsylvania State University Press, 2006.

———. "Sociology of Multiracial Identity in the Late 1980s and Early 1990s: The Failure of a Perspective." *Ethnic and Cultural Studies* 8, no. 2 (2021): 106–25. http://dx.doi.org/10.29333/ejecs/643.

Daniel, G. Reginald, and Jasmine Kelekay. "From *Loving v. Virginia* to Barack Obama: The Symbolic Tie That Binds." *Creighton Law Review* 50, no. 3 (January 2017): 641–68. https://dspace2.creighton.edu/xmlui/bitstream/handle/10504/113307/cre_50-3.pdf?sequence=1&isAllowed=y.

Daniel, G. Reginald, and J Sterphone. "Hypodescent." In *Routledge Encyclopedia of Race and Racism*, edited by John Solomos. New York: Routledge Press, forthcoming.

Daniel, G. Reginald, Laura Kina, Wei Ming Dariotis, and Camilla Fojas. "Emerging Paradigms in Critical Mixed Race Studies." *Journal of Critical Mixed Race Studies* 1, no. 1 (2014): 1–65. https://doi.org/10.5070/C811013868.

Daniel, Jerlean E., and Jack J. Daniel. "Pre School Children's Selection of Race-Related Personal Names." *Journal of Black Studies* 28, no. 4 (March 1998): 471–90. https://doi.org/10.1177/002193479802800403.

Davalos, Karen M. "La Quinceañera: Making Gender and Ethnic Identities." *Frontiers: A Journal of Women Studies* 16, no. 3 (January 1996): 101–27. https://doi.org/10.2307/3346805.

Davenport, Lauren D. "The Role of Class, Gender, and Religion in Biracial Americans' Racial Labeling Decisions." *American Sociological Review* 81, no. 1 (January 2016): 57–84. https://doi.org/10.1177/0003122415623286.

Davenport, Lauren D., Shanto Iyengar, and Sean J. Westwood. "Racial Identity, Group Consciousness, and Attitudes: A Framework for Assessing Multiracial Self-Classification." *American Journal of Political Science* (October 2021). https://doi.org/10.1111/ajps.12674.

Davis, F. James. *Who Is Black? One Nation's Definition*. University Park: Pennsylvania State University Press, 1991.

Dawson, Michael C. *Black Visions: The Roots of Contemporary African-American Political Ideologies*. Chicago: University of Chicago Press, 2001.

DeBonis, Steve. *Children of the Enemy: Oral Histories of Vietnamese Amerasians and Their Mothers*. Jefferson NC: McFarland, 1995.

Degler, Carl N. *Neither Black nor White: Slavery and Race Relations in Brazil and the United States*. New York: Macmillan, 1971.

Delgado, Richard, and Jean Stefancic. *Critical Race Theory: An Introduction*. 4th ed. New York: New York University Press, 2023.

Diaz, Monina. "Race Doesn't Exist." In *What Are You? Voices of Mixed-Race Young People*, edited by Pearl F. Gaskins, 53–58. New York: Henry Holt, 1999.

Dineen-Wimberly, Ingrid. *The Allure of Blackness among Mixed-Race Americans, 1862–1916*. Lincoln: University of Nebraska Press, 2019.

———. "Being Mixed Race in the Makah Nation Redeeming the Existence of African Native Americans." In *Red and Yellow, Black and Brown: Decentering Whiteness in Mixed Race Studies*, edited by Joanne L. Rondilla, Rudy P. Guevarra Jr., and Paul Spickard, 109–26. New Brunswick NJ: Rutgers University Press, 2017.

Doane, Ashely W. "Rethinking Whiteness Studies." In *White Out: The Continuing Significance of Racism*, edited by Doane and Eduardo Bonilla-Silva, 3–20. New York: Routledge, 2003.

Dobyns, Henry F. *Spanish Colonial Tucson: A Demographic History*. Tucson: University of Arizona Press, 1976.

Domínguez, Virginia R. *White by Definition: Social Classification in Creole Louisiana*. New Brunswick NJ: Rutgers University Press, 1986.

Dowling, Julie A. *Mexican Americans and the Question of Race*. Austin: University of Texas Press, 2014.

Du Bois, W. E. B. *Black Reconstruction in America*. New York: Free Press, 1998.

———. *The Souls of Black Folk*. Oxford: Oxford University Press, 2007.
Dugar, Nikki. "I Am What I Say I Am: Racial and Cultural Identity among Creoles of Color in New Orleans." PhD diss., University of New Orleans, 2009. https://scholarworks.uno.edu/td/945/.
Dunivan, Zachary Okun, Harry Yaojun Yan, Jelani Ince, and Fabio Rojas. "Black Lives Matter Protests Shift Public Discourse." *Proceedings of the National Academy of Sciences* 119, no. 10 (2022): 1–11. https://doi.org/10.1073/pnas.2117320119.
Dupree-Wilson, Teisha. "Phenotypic Proximity: Colorism and Intraracial Discrimination among Blacks in the United States and Brazil, 1928 to 1988." *Journal of Black Studies* 52, no. 5 (2021): 528–46. https://doi.org/10.1177/00219347211021088.
Dyer, Kenneth Frank. "Patterns of Gene Flow Between Negroes and Whites in the U.S." *Journal of Biosocial Science* 8, no. 4 (October 1976): 309–33. https://doi.org/10.1017/S002193200001083X.
Dystart, Jane. "Mexican Women in San Antonio. 1830–1860: The Assimilation Process." *Western Historical Quarterly* 7, no. 4 (1976): 365–75. https://doi.org/10.2307/968057.
Elam, Michelle. *The Souls of Mixed Folk: Race, Politics, and Aesthetics in the New Millennium*. Stanford CA: Stanford University Press, 2011.
Ennis, Sharon, Merarys Ríos-Vargas, and Nora G. Albert. "The Hispanic Population: 2010." C2010BR-04. U.S. Bureau of the Census. May 2001. https://www.census.gov/history/pdf/c2010br-04-092020.pdf.
Farley, Reynolds. "Identifying with Multiple Races: A Social Movement that Succeeded but Failed?" PSC Research Report, no. 01-491. 2001. https://www.psc.isr.umich.edu/pubs/rr01-4910a0e.pdf?i=89131672318526222804066938 9&f=rr01-491.pdf.
Farnham, Thomas J. *Life, Adventures, and Travels in California*. 2nd ed. New York: Nafis and Cornish, 1849.
Feagin, Joe, and Clairece Booher Feagin. *Racial and Ethnic Relations*. 9th ed. Saddle River NJ: Prentice Hall, 2012.
Feagin, Joe, and Hernán Vera. *White Racism*. New York: Routledge, 1995.
Feinberg, Mark. E. "The Internal Structure and Ecological Context of Coparenting: A Framework for Research and Intervention." *Parenting: Science and Practice* 3, no. 2 (January 2003): 95–131. https://doi.org/10.1207/S15327922PAR0302_01.
Feller, Laura J. *Being Indigenous in Jim Crow Virginia: Powhatan People and the Color Line*. Norman: University of Oklahoma Press, 2022.
Flagg, Barbara J. "'Was Blind, but Now I See': White Race Consciousness and the Requirement of Discriminatory Intent." *Michigan Law Review* 91, no. 5 (1993): 953–1017. https://repository.law.umich.edu/mlr/vol91/iss5/5.

Foley, Neil. "Becoming Hispanic: Mexican Americans and Whiteness." In *White Privilege: Essential Readings on the Other Side of Racism*, edited by Paula Rothenberg, 49–59. New York: Worth, 2002.

———. *Mexicans in the Making of America*. Cambridge MA: Harvard University Press, 2014.

———. "Over the Rainbow: *Hernandez v. Texas*, *Brown v. Board of Education*, and *Black v. Brown*." *Chicana/o Latina/o Law Review* 25, no. 1 (2005): 139–52. https://doi.org/10.5070/C7251021158.

———. *The White Scourge: Mexicans, Black, and Poor Whites in Texas Cotton Culture*. Berkeley: University of California Press, 1997.

Foner, Philip S. *History of Black Americans: From Africa to the Emergence of the Cotton Kingdom*. Vol. 1. Westport CT: Greenwood Press, 1975.

Forbes, Jack D. "Black Africans and Native Americans: Color, Race, and Caste in the Evolution of Red-Black Peoples." *Journal of American History* 77, no. 1 (June 1990): 276–77. https://doi.org/10.2307/2078670.

———. "Black Pioneers: The Spanish-Speaking Afroamericans of the Southwest." *Phylon* 27, no. 3 (3rd Qtr., 1966): 233–46. https://doi.org/10.2307/274264.

———. "Manipulation of Race, Caste, and Identity: Classifying Afro-Americans, Native Americans, and Red-Black People." *Journal of Ethnic Studies* 17, no. 4 (Winter 1990): 1–51. https://www.proquest.com/docview/1300558499?pq-origsite=gscholar&fromopenview=true&imgSeq=1.

Fox, Cybelle, and Thomas A. Guglielmo. "Defining America's Racial Boundaries: Blacks, Mexicans, and European Immigrants, 1890–1945." *American Journal of Sociology* 118, no. 2 (September 2012): 327–79. https://doi.org/10.1086/666383.

Frankenberg, Ruth. *White Women, Race Matters: The Social Construction of Whiteness*. New York: Routledge, 1993.

Frederickson, Barbara L. "The Role of *Positive Emotions* in Positive Psychology: The Broaden-and-Build Theory of Positive Emotions." *American Psychologist* 56, no. 3 (2001): 218–26. https://doi.org/10.1037//0003-066x.56.3.218.

Fredrickson, George M. *White Supremacy: A Comparative Study of American and South African History*. New York: Oxford University Press, 1981.

Frey, William H. *Diversity Explosion: How New Racial Demographics Are Remaking America*. Washington DC: Brookings Institution Press.

Fuchs, Lawrence H. *The American Kaleidoscope: Race, Ethnicity, and the Civic Culture*. Hanover DE: Wesleyan Press, 1990.

Fulbeck, Kip. *Part Asian 100% Hapa*. San Francisco: Chronicle, 2006.

Furtado, Júnia Ferreira. *Chica da Silva: A Brazilian Slave of the Eighteenth Century; New Approaches to the Americas*. New York: Cambridge University Press, 2008.

Gaines, Kevin K. *Uplifting the Race: Black Leadership, Politics, and Culture in the Twentieth Century*. Chapel Hill: University of North Carolina Press, 1996.

Gaither, Sarah E. "'Mixed' Results Multiracial Research and Identity Explorations." *Current Directions in Psychological Science* 24, no. 2 (2015): 114–19. https://doi.org/10.1177/0963721414558115.

Galdámez, Misael, and Michael Rios. "Multiracial and Multiethnic Growth in California: An Analysis of 2020 Census Data." UCLA Latino Policy & Politics Institute. August 19, 2021. https://latino.ucla.edu/research/multiracial-and-multiethnic-growth-in-california-an-analysis-of-2020-census-data/.

Gans, Herbert J. "Symbolic Ethnicity: The Future of Ethnic Groups and Cultures in America." *Ethnic and Racial Studies* 2, no. 1 (January 1979): 1–20. https://doi.org/10.1080/01419870.1979.9993248.

———. "'Whitening' and the Changing American Racial Hierarchy." *Du Bois Review* 9, no. 2 (2012): 267–79. https://doi.org/10.1017/S1742058X12000288.

García, Ignacio M. *Chicanismo: The Forging of a Militant Ethos among Mexican Americans*. Tucson: University of Arizona Press, 1997.

———. *White but Not Equal: Mexican Americans, Jury Discrimination, and the Supreme Court*. Tucson: University of Arizona Press, 2008.

García, Paula B., Lori Leibold, Emily Buss, Lauren Calandruccio, and Barbara Vasquez. "Code-Switching in Highly Proficient Spanish/English Bilingual Adults: Impact on Masked Word Recognition." *Journal of Speech, Language, and Hearing Research* 61, no. 9 (September 2018): 2353–62. https://doi.org/10.1044/2018_JSLHR-H-17-0399.

García Coll, Cynthia, Gontran Lamberty, Renee Jenkins, Harriet P. McAdoo, Keith Crnic, Barbara H. Wasik, and Heidi V. García. "An Integrative Model for the Study of Developmental Competencies in Minority Children." *Child Development* 67, no. 5 (October 1996): 1891–914. https://pubmed.ncbi.nlm.nih.gov/9022222/.

Garvin, Russell. "The Free Negro in Florida Before the Civil War." *Florida Historical Quarterly* 46, no. 1 (July 1967): 1–17. https://www.jstor.org/stable/30140212.

Gay, Claudine. "Seeing the Difference: The Effect of Economic Disparity on Black Attitudes Towards Latinos." *American Journal of Political Science* 50, no. 4 (September 2006): 982–97.

Gines, Kathryn T. "Introduction: Critical Philosophy of Race Beyond the Black/White Binary." *Critical Philosophy of Race* 1, no. 1 (2013): 28–37. https://doi.org/10.5325/critphilrace.1.1.0028.

Gist, Noel P., and Anthony G. Dworkin. Introduction to *The Blending of Races: Marginality and Identity in World Perspective*, edited by Noel P. Gist and Anthony G. Dworkin, 1–23. Hoboken NJ: Wiley-Interscience Publication, 1972.

Glassner, Barry. *The Culture of Fear: Why Americans are Afraid of the Wrong Things: Crime, Drugs, Minorities, Teen Moms, Killer Kids, Mutant Microbes, Plane Crashes, Road Rage and So Much More.* New York: Basic Books, 2010.

Glenn, Evelyn Nakano. *Unequal Freedom: How Race and Gender Shaped American Citizenship and Labor.* Cambridge MA: Harvard University Press, 2002.

Goldberg, Chad Allen. "Robert Park's Marginal Man: The Career of a Concept in American Sociology." *Laboratorium* 4, no. 2 (2012): 199–217. https://www.soclabo.org/index.php/laboratorium/article/view/4.

Goldberg, Milton M. "A Qualification of the Marginal Man Theory." *American Sociological Review* 6, no. 1 (1941): 52–58. http://www.jstor.org/stable/2086343.

Gómez, Christina. "Brown Outs: The Role of Skin Color and Latinas." In *Racism in the 21st Century: An Empirical Analysis of Skin Color*, edited by Ronald E. Hall, 193–204. New York: Springer, 2008.

Gómez, Laura E. *Manifest Destinies: The Making of the Mexican American Race.* 2nd ed. New York: New York University Press, 2018.

Gonzales, Rodolfo. *I Am Joaquín.* New York: Bantam Books, 1967.

González, Anita. *Afro-Mexico: Dancing Between Myth and Reality.* Austin: University of Texas Press, 2010.

Goode, Kenneth G. *California's Black Pioneers: A Brief Historical Survey.* Santa Barbara CA: McNally and Loftin, 1973.

Gordon, Milton. *Assimilation in American Life: The Role of Race, Religion and National Origins.* New York: Oxford University Press, 1964.

Gould, Virginia Meacham. "The Free Creoles of Color of the Antebellum Gulf Ports of Mobile and Pensacola: A Struggle for the Common Ground." In *Creoles of Color of the Gulf South*, edited by James H. Dorman, 28–50. Nashville: University of Tennessee, 1996.

———. "In Enjoyment of Their Liberty: The Free Women of Color of the Gulf Ports of New Orleans, Mobile, and Pensacola, 1769–1860." PhD diss., Emory University, 1992.

Gramsci, Antonio. *Selections from the Prison Notebooks.* Translated and edited by Quentin Hoare and Geoffrey Nowell Smith. New York: International Publishers, 1971.

Gratton, Brian, and Emily Klancher Merchant. "La Raza: Mexicans in the United States Census." *Journal of Policy History* 28, no. 4 (2016): 537–67. https://doi.org/10.1017/S0898030616000257.

Green, Arnold W. "A Re-examination of the Marginal Man Concept." *Social Forces* 26, no. 2 (1947): 167–71. https://doi.org/10.2307/2571773.

Grieco, Elizabeth M., and Rachel C. Cassidy. "Overview of Race and Hispanic Origin: Census 2000 Brief." C2KBR/01-1. U.S. Bureau of the Census. March

2001. https://www2.census.gov/library/publications/decennial/2000/briefs/c2kbr01-01.pdf.

Gross, Ariela J. 2003. "Texas Mexicans and the Politics of Whiteness." *Law and History Review* 21, no. 1 (2003): 195–205. https://doi.org/10.2307/3595072.

———. *What Blood Won't Tell: A History of Race on Trial in America*. Cambridge MA: Harvard University Press, 2008.

Grusec, Joan, and Paul D. Hastings. *Handbook of Socialization: Theory and Research*. New York: Guilford Press, 2007.

Guerrero, Vladimir. "Caste, Race, and Class in Spanish California." *Southern California Quarterly* 92, no. 1 (2010): 1–18. https://doi.org/10.2307/41172505.

Guevarra, Rudy P. *Becoming Mexipino: Multiethnic Identities and Communities in San Diego*. New Brunswick NJ: Rutgers University Press, 2012.

———. "Burritos and Bagoong: Mexipinos and Multiethnic Identity in San Diego, California." In *Crossing Lines: Race and Mixed Race Across the Geohistorical Divide*, edited by Marc Coronado, Rudy P. Guevarra Jr., Jeffrey Moniz, and Laura F. Szanto, 72–96. Lanham MD: AltaMira Press, 2003.

Gunz, Philipp, Fred L. Bookstein, Philipp Mitteroecker, Andrea Stadlmayr, Horst Seidler, and Gerhard W. Weber. "Early Modern Human Diversity Suggests Subdivided Population Structure and a Complex Out-of-Africa Scenario." *PNAS* 106, no. 15 (2009): 6094–98. https://doi.org/10.1073/pnas.0808160106.

Hagiwara, Nao, Deborah A. Kashy, and Joseph Cesario. "The Independent Effects of Skin Tone and Facial Features on Whites' Affective Reactions to Blacks." *Journal of Experimental Social Psychology* 48, no. 4 (2012): 892–98. https://doi.org/10.1016/j.jesp.2012.02.001.

Hajnal, Zoltan, Nazita Lajevardi, and Lindsay Nielson. "Voter Identification Laws and the Suppression of Minority." *Journal of Politics* 79, no. 2 (January 5, 2017): 363–78. http://dx.doi.org/10.1086/688343.

Hall, Christine C. Iijima. "The Ethnic Identity of Racially Mixed People: A Study of Black Japanese." PhD diss., University of California Los Angeles, 1980.

———. "Please Choose One: Ethnic Identity Choices for Biracial Individuals." In *Racially Mixed People in America*, edited by Maria P. P. Root, 250–64. Newbury Park CA: Sage Publications.

Hall, Ronald E. *Discrimination Among Oppressed Populations*. Lewiston NY: Edwin Mellen Press, 2003.

Haney-López, Ian F. *Racism on Trial: The Chicano Fight for Justice*. Cambridge MA: Belknap Press of Harvard University, 2003.

Hanger, Kimberly S. *Bounded Lives, Bounded Places: Free Black Society in Colonial New Orleans, 1769–1803*. Durham NC: Duke University Press. 1997.

———. "Coping in a Complex World Free Black Women in Colonial New Orleans." In *The Devil's Lane: Sex and Race in the Early South*, edited by Catherine Clinton and Michele Gillespie, Michele, 218–31. New York: Oxford University Press, 1997.

Harris, Angelique. "Marginalization by the Marginalized: Race, Homophobia, Heterosexism, and 'the Problem of the 21st Century.'" *Journal of Gay and Lesbian Social Services* 21, no. 4 (October 2009): 430–48. https://doi.org/10.1080/10538720903163171.

Harris, Cheryl I. "Whiteness as Property." *Harvard Law Review* 106, no. 8 (June 1993): 1707–91. https://doi.org/10.2307/1341787.

Harris, David, and Jeremiah Simm. "Who Is Multiracial: Assessing the Complexity of Lived Race." *American Sociological Review* 67, no. 4 (August 2002): 614–27. https://doi.org/10.2307/3088948.

Harris, Jessica C. "Multiracial Campus Professionals' Experiences with Racial Authenticity." *Equity and Excellence in Education* 52, no. 1 (2019): 1–15. https://doi.org/10.1080/10665684.2019.1631232.

Harris, Marvin. *Patterns of Race in the Americas*. New York: W. W. Norton, 1964.

Harrison, Patricia Maria. "Racial Identification and Self-Concept Issues in Biracial (Black-White) Adolescent Girls." PhD. diss, Columbia University, 1997.

Harwood, Robin L., Axel Schoelmerich, and Pamela A. Schulze. "Homogeneity and Heterogeneity in Cultural Belief Systems." In *New Directions for Child and Adolescent Development: Variability in the Social Construction of the Child*, edited by Sara Harkness, Catherine Raeff, and Charles M. Super, 41–57. San Francisco: Jossey-Bass, 2000.

Haskins, James. *Creoles of Color of New Orleans*. New York: Thomas Y. Crowell, 1975.

Hazzard-Gordon, Katrina. "The Interaction of Sexism and Racism in the Old South: The New Orleans Bals Du Cordon Bleu." *Minority Voices*, 2nd series, 6, no. 1 (Fall 1989): 14–25.

Heath, Jim F., and Frederick M. Nunn. "Africans and Discrimination in Colonial New Mexico." In *African American History in New Mexico: Portraits from Five Hundred Years*, edited by Bruce A. Glasrud, 44–57. Albuquerque: University of New Mexico Press, 2013.

Herman, Melissa. "Forced to Choose: Some Determinants of Racial Identification in Multiracial Adolescents." *Child Development* 75, no. 3 (May 2004): 730–48. https://doi.org/10.1111/j.1467-8624.2004.00703.x.

Hernández, Tanya Katerí. "Afro-Americans and the Chicano Movement: The Unknown Story." Review of *Racism on Trial* by Ian F. Haney López. *California Law Review* 92 (October 2004): 1537–51. https://doi.org/10.2307/3481424.

Higham, John. *Send These to Me: Jews and Other Immigrants in Urban America*. New York: Atheneum, 1975.

Hirschman, Charles, Richard Alba, and Reynolds Farley. "The Meaning and Measurement of Race in the U.S. Census: Glimpses into the Future." *Demography* 37, no. 3 (August 2000): 381–83. https://doi.org/10.2307/2648049.

Hitlin, Steven, Glen H. Elder Jr., and J. Scott Brown. "Racial Self-Categorization in Adolescence: Multiracial Development and Social Pathways." *Child Development* 77, no. 5 (September 2006): 1298–308. https://doi.org/10.1111/j.1467-8624.2006.00935.x.

Hodes, Martha. *White Women, Black Men: Illicit Sex in the Nineteenth-Century South*. New Haven CT: Yale University Press., 1997.

Hodges, Teresa. "Realizing Blacknpinay: Negotiating Notions of Authenticity in Janet Stickmon's *Crushing Soft Rubies*." *Asian American Literature: Discourses and Pedagogies* 3 (2012): 53–63. https://scholarworks.sjsu.edu/aaldp/vol3/iss1/7/.

Hoetink, Hartimus. *Slavery and Race Relations in the Americas: Comparative Notes on Their Nature and Nexus*. New York: Harper and Row, 1973.

Hollinger, David A. *Postethnic America: Beyond Multiculturalism*. New York: Basic Books, 2000.

Hondagneu-Sotelo, Pierrette, and Manual Pastor. *South Central Dreams: Finding Home and Building Community in South L.A.* New York: New York University Press, 2021.

Horseman, Reginald. *Race and Manifest Destiny: The Origins of American Racial Anglo-Saxonism*. Cambridge MA: Harvard University Press, 1981.

Horton, John. "Order and Conflict Theories of Social Problems as Competing Ideologies." *American Journal of Sociology* 7, no. 6 (1966): 701–13. https://doi.org/10.1086/224226.

Hoskins, Bruce C. *Asian American Racial Realities in Black and White*. Boulder CO: Lynne Rienner Publishers, 2011.

Hughes, Diane, and Deborah Johnson. "Correlates in Children's Experiences of Parents' Racial Socialization Behaviors." *Journal of Marriage and Family* 63, no. 4 (November 2001): 981–95. https://doi.org/10.1111/j.1741-3737.2001.00981.x.

Hughes, Diane, and Lisa Chen. "When and What Parents Tell Children about Race: An Examination of Race Related Socialization among African American Families." *Applied Developmental Science* 1, no. 4 (1997): 200–214. https://doi.org/10.1207/s1532480xads0104_4.

Hughes, Michael, and Bradley R. Hertel. "The Significance of Color Remains: A Study of Life Chances, Mate Selection, and Ethnic Consciousness among Black Americans." *Social Forces* 68, no, 4 (1990): 1105–20. https://doi.org/10.2307/2579136.

Humes, Karen R., Nicholas A. Jones, and Roberto R. Ramirez. "Overview of Race and Hispanic Origin." *2010 Census Briefs.* C2010BR-02. U.S. Bureau of the Census. March 2011. https://www.census.gov/content/dam/Census/library/publications/2011/dec/c2010br-02.pdf.

Hunter, Margaret L. *Race, Gender, and the Politics of Skin Tone.* New York: Routledge, 2005.

Hurtado, Albert L. *Intimate Frontiers: Sex, Gender, and Culture in Old California.* Albuquerque: University of New Mexico Press, 1999.

Hutchinson, Earl Ofri. *The Latino Challenge to Black America: Towards a Conversation Between African Americans and Hispanics.* Chicago: Middle Passage Press, 2007.

Hutchinson, George. *The Harlem Renaissance in Black and White.* Cambridge MA: Harvard University Press, 1995.

Ifekwunigwe, Jayne O., ed. *"Mixed Race" Studies: A Reader.* London: Routledge, 2004.

Ingham, John N., and Lynne B. Feldman. *African-American Business Leaders: A Biographical Dictionary.* Westport CT: Greenwood, 1994.

Instituto Nacional de Estadística y Geografía (INEGI). Censo de Población y Vivienda 2020. Aguascalientes, Mexico, 2020. https://www.inegi.org.mx/.

Jackson, Kelly F. "Living the Multiracial Experience: Shifting Racial Expressions, Resisting Race, and Seeking Community." *Qualitative Social Work* 11, no. 1 (2010): 42–60. https://doi.org/10.1177/1473325010375646.

Jackson, Kelly F., Thera Wolven, and Kimberly Aguilera. "Mixed Resilience: A Study of Multiethnic Mexican American Stress and Coping in Arizona." *Family Relations* 62, no. 1 (February 2013): 212–25. https://doi.org/10.1111/j.1741-3729.2012.00755.x.

Jackson, María Rosario. "Profile of an Afro-Latina: Black, Mexican, Both." In *The Afro-Latin@ Reader: History and Culture in the United States*, edited by Miriam Jiménez Román and Juan Flores, 434–38. Durham NC: Duke University Press, 2010.

Jewell, Joseph O. "'We Have in This City Many Good Mexican Citizens': The Race-Class Intersection and Racial Boundary Shifting in Late Nineteenth-Century San Antonio." *Sociology of Race and Ethnicity* 2, no. 2 (2015): 186–99. https://doi.org/10.1177/2332649215614868.

Jiménez, Tomás R. "Multiethnic Mexican Americans in Demographic and Ethnographic Perspectives." In *Crossing Lines: Race and Mixed Race Across the Geohistorical Divide*, edited by Marc Coronado, Rudy P. Guevarra Jr., Jeffrey Moniz, and Laura F. Szanto, 161–88. Lanham MD: AltaMira, 2003.

———. "Negotiating Ethnic Boundaries Multiethnic Mexican Americans and Ethnic Identity in the United States." *Ethnicities* 4, no. 1 (2004): 75–97. https://doi.org/10.1177/1468796804040329.

Jiménez, Tomás R., Julie Park, and Juan Pedroza. "The New Third Generation: Post-1965 Immigration and the Next Chapter in the Long Story of Assimilation." *International Migration Review* 52, no. 4 (Winter 2018): 1040–79. https://doi.org/10.1111/imre.12343.

Johnson, Gaye Theresa. *Spaces of Conflict, Sounds of Solidarity: Music, Race, and Spatial Entitlement in Los Angeles*. Berkeley: University of California Press, 2013.

Johnson, James H., Jr., Walter C. Farrell Jr., and Chandra Guinn. "Immigration and Reform and the Browning of America: Tensions, Conflicts and Community Instability in Metropolitan Los Angeles." *International Migration Review* 31, no. 4 (Winter 1997): 1055–95. https://doi.org/10.2307/2547424.

Johnson, Jerah. "Colonial New Orleans: A Fragment of the Eighteenth-Century French Ethos." In *Creole New Orleans: Race and Americanization*, edited by Arnold R. Hirsch and Joseph Logsdon, 12–57. Baton Rouge: Louisiana State University Press, 1992.

Johnson, Kevin R. *How Did You Get to Be Mexican? A White/Brown Man's Search for Identity*. Philadelphia: Temple University Press, 1999.

Johnston, Marc P., and Kevin L. Nadal. "Multiracial Microaggressions: Exposing Monoracism in Everyday Life and Clinical Practice." In *Microaggressions and Marginality: Manifestation, Dynamics, and Impact*, edited by Derald Wing Sue, 123–44. Hoboken NJ: Wiley and Sons, 2010.

Johnston-Guerrero, Marc, and Charmaine Wijeyesinghe. "Insights on Multiracial Knowledge." In *Multiracial Experiences in Higher Education: Contesting Knowledge, Honoring Voice, and Innovating Practice*, edited by Marc Johnston-Guerrero and Charmaine L. Wijeyesinghe, 3–16. Sterling VA: Stylus, 2021.

Johnston-Guerrero, Marc, and Karly Sarita Ford. "Draw Your Own Box? Further Complicating Racial Data for Multiracial/Two or More Races College Students." In *Measuring Race: Why Disaggregating Data Matters for Addressing Educational Inequality*, edited by Robert T. Teranishi, Bach Mai Dolly Nguyen, Cynthia M. Alcantar, and Edward R. Curammeng, 84–102. New York: Teachers College Press, 2015.

Jolivétte, Andrew J. "Critical Mixed-Race Studies: The Intersections of Identity and Social Justice." In *Sociologists in Action: Sociology, Social Change, and Social Justice*, edited by Kathleen O. Korgen, Jonathan M. White, and Shelley K. White, 24–28. Thousand Oaks CA: Pine Forge Press, 2011.

Jones, Lisa A. "Who Are We? Producing Group Identity Through Everyday Practices of Conflict and Discourse." *Sociological Perspectives* 54, no. 2 (2011): 139–62. https://doi.org/10.1525/sop.2011.54.2.139.

Jones, Nicholas A. "We the People of More Than One Race in the United States." Census 2000 Special Reports CENSR-22. U.S. Bureau of the Census. April 2005. http://www.sreenimeka.com/pdf/censr-22.pdf.

Jones, Nicholas A., and Amy Symens Smith. "The Two or More Races Population: 2000." Census 2000 Brief. C2KBR/01-6. U.S. Bureau of the Census. November 2001. https://www2.census.gov/library/publications/decennial/2000/briefs/c2kbr01-06.pdf.

Jones, Nicholas A., and Jungmiwha Bullock. "The Two or More Population: 2010." *2010 Census Briefs*. C2010BR-13. U.S. Bureau of the Census. September 2012. https://www2.census.gov/library/publications/cen2010/briefs/c2010br-13.pdf.

Jones, Nicholas A., Rachel Marks, Roberto Ramirez, and Merarys Ríos-Vargas. "Improved Race and Ethnicity Measures Reveal U.S. Population Is Much More Multiracial." U.S. Bureau of the Census. August 12, 2001. https://www.census.gov/library/stories/2021/08/improved-race-ethnicity-measures-reveal-united-states-population-much-more-multiracial.html.

Jones, Rett S. "The End of Africanity? The Assault on Blackness." *Western Journal of Black Studies* 18, no. 4 (1994): 201–10. https://eric.ed.gov/?q=End+of+Africanity.

Jordan, Winthrop D., and Paul Spickard. "Historical Origins of the One-Drop Rule in the United States." *Journal of Critical Mixed Race Studies* 1, no. 1 (2014): 98–132. https://doi.org/10.5070/C811013867.

Joseph, Ralina L. *Transcending Blackness: From the New Millennium Mulatta to the Exceptional Multiracial*. Durham NC: Duke University Press, 2012.

Kachun, Mitch. "From Forgotten Founder to Indispensable Icon: Crispus Attucks, Black Citizenship, and Collective Memory, 1770–1865." *Journal of the Early Republic* 29, no. 2 (Summer 2009): 249–86. https://doi.org/10.1353/JER.0.0072.

Katz, William Loren. *Black Indians: A Hidden Heritage*. New York: Atheneum Books, 1986.

Katzew, Ilona. *Casta Painting: Images of Race in Eighteenth-Century Mexico*. New Haven CT: Yale University Press, 2004.

Keith, Verna M., and Herring, Cedric. "Skin Tone and Stratification in the Black Community." *American Journal of Sociology* 97, no. 3 (1991): 760–78. https://doi.org/10.1086/229819.

Kennedy, Randall. *Interracial Intimacies: Sex, Marriage, Identity, and Adoption*. New York: Pantheon, 2003.

Kerckhoff, Allen C., and Thomas C. McCormick. "Marginal Status and Marginal Personality." *Social Forces* 34, no. 1 (1995): 48–55. https://doi.org/10.2307/2574259.

Khanna, Nikki. *Biracial in America: Forming and Performing Racial Identity*. Lanham MD: Lexington Books, 2011.

———. "If You're Half Black, You're Just Black: Reflected Appraisals and the Persistence of the One-Drop Rule." *Sociological Quarterly* 51, no. 1 (2010): 96–121. https://doi.org/10.1111/j.1533-8525.2009.01162.x.

Kim, Claire Jean. "The Racial Triangulation of Asian Americans." *Politics and Society* 27, no. 1 (March 1999): 105–38. https://doi.org/10.1177/0032329299027001005.

Kina, Laura, and Wei Ming Dariotis. *War Baby / Love Child: Mixed Race Asian American Art*. Seattle: University of Washington Press, 2013.

Kinefuchi, Etsuko, and Mark P. Orbe. "Situating Oneself in a Racialized World: Understanding Student Reactions to Crash Through Standpoint Theory and Context-Positionality Frames." *Journal of International and Intercultural Communication* 1, no. 1 (2008): 70–90. https://doi.org/10.1080/17513050701742909.

King, Rebecca Chiyoko, and Kimberly M. DaCosta. "Changing Face, Changing Race: The Remaking of Race in the Japanese American and African American Communities." In *The Multiracial Experience: Racial Borders as the New Frontier*, edited by Maria P. P. Root, 227–44. Thousand Oaks CA: Sage Publications, 1996.

King O'Riain, Rebecca C. *Pure Beauty: Judging Race in Japanese American Beauty Pageants*. Minneapolis: University of Minnesota Press, 2006.

Klein, Herbert S. *African Slavery in Latin America and the Caribbean*. New York: Oxford University Press, 1986.

———. "Nineteenth-Century Brazil." In *Neither Slave nor Free: The Freemen of African Descent in the Slave Societies of the New World*, edited by David. W. Cohen and Jack P. Greene, 309–34. Baltimore MD: Johns Hopkins University Press, 1972.

Korgen, Kathleen. *From Black to Biracial: Transforming Identity Among Americans*. Westport CT: Praeger, 1998.

Krauthamer, Barbara. *Black Slaves, Indian Masters: Slavery, Emancipation, and Citizenship in the Native American South*. Chapel Hill: University of North Carolina Press, 2013.

Kun, Josh, and Laura Pulido. *Black and Brown in Los Angeles: Beyond Conflict and Coalition*. Berkeley: University of California Press, 2014.

Kwan, SanSan, and Kenneth Speirs. *Mixing It Up: Multiracial Subjects*. Austin: University of Texas Press, 2004.

Ladner, Joyce. Introduction to *The Death of White Sociology*, edited by Joyce Ladner, xix–xxix. New York: Vintage Books, 1973.

Landers, Jane. *Black Society in Spanish Florida*. Urbana: University of Illinois Press, 1999.

Landry, Donna, and Gerald Maclean, eds. *The Spivak Reader: Selected Works of Gayatri Chakravorty Spivak*. New York: Routledge, 1995.

Leavitt, Peter A., Rebecca Covarrubias, Yvonne A. Perez, and Stephanie A. Fryberg. "'Frozen in Time': The Impact of Native American Media Representations on Identity and Self-Understanding." *Journal of Social Issues* 71, no. 1 (March 2015): 39–53. https://doi.org/10.1111/josi.12095.

Lee, Jennifer, and Frank D. Bean. "America's Changing Colorlines: Immigration, Race/Ethnicity, and Multiracial Identification." *Annual Review of Sociology* 30, no. 1 (August 2004): 221–42.

———. *The Diversity Paradox: Immigration and the Color Line in Twenty-First Century America*. New York: Russell Sage Foundation, 2010.

Lee, Sharon M. "Racial Classifications in the U.S. Census." *Ethnic and Racial Studies* 16, no. 1 (1993): 75–94. https://doi.org/10.1080/01419870.1993.9993773.

Lenhardt, Robin A. "*Perez v. Sharp* and the Limits of Loving." In *Loving v. Virginia in a Postracial World: Rethinking Race, Sex, and Marriage*, edited by Kevin Noble Maillard and Rose Cuison Villazor, 73–88 Cambridge, UK: Cambridge University Press, 2012.

Leonard, Karen I. *Making Ethnic Choices: California's Punjabi Mexican Americans*. Philadelphia: Temple University Press, 1992.

Lewis, Amanda E. *Race in the Schoolyard: Negotiating the Color Line in Classrooms and Communities*. New Brunswick NJ: Rutgers University Press, 2003.

———. "'What Group?': Studying Whites and Whiteness in the Era of 'Color-Blindness.'" *Sociological Theory* 22, no. 4 (December 2004): 623–46. https://doi.org/10.1111/j.0735-2751.2004.00237.x.

Lewis, Laura A. *Hall of Mirrors: Power, Witchcraft, and Caste in Colonial Mexico*. Durham NC: Duke University Press, 2003.

———. "That Little Mexican Part of Me: Race, Place and Transnationalism among U.S. African-Descent Mexicans." *Ethnic and Racial Studies* 43, no. 6 (2020): 995–1012. https://doi.org/10.1080/01419870.2019.1626016.

Lightfoot, Kent G. *Indians, Missionaries, and Merchants: The Legacy of Colonial Encounters on the California Frontiers*. New Brunswick NJ: Rutgers University Press, 2005.

Lipsitz, George. *How Racism Takes Place*. Philadelphia: Temple University Press, 2011.

———. "Noises in the Blood: Culture, Conflict, and Mixed Race Identities." In *Crossing Lines: Race and Mixed Race Across the Geohistorical Divide*, edited by Marc Coronado, Rudy P. Guevarra Jr., Jeffrey Moniz, and Laura Furlan Szanto, 32–35. Lanham MD: AltaMira Press, 2003.

———. *The Possessive Investment in Whiteness: How White People Profit from Identity Politics*. Philadelphia: Temple University Press, 1998.

Littlefield, Daniel F., Jr. *Africans and Seminoles: From Removal to Emancipation*. Jackson: University Press of Mississippi, 2004.

Livingston, Gretchen, and Anna Brown. "Intermarriage in the U.S. 50 Years After *Loving v. Virginia*." Pew Research Center. May 18, 2017. https://www.pewresearch.org/social-trends/2017/05/18/intermarriage-in-the-u-s-50-years-after-loving-v-virginia/.

Lockhart, James, and Stuart B. Schwartz. *Early Latin America: A History of Colonial Spanish America and Brazil*. New York: Cambridge University Press, 1987.

Loewen, James W. *The Mississippi Chinese: Between Black and White*. Long Grove IL: Waveland Press, 1988.

Logan, John R. "How Race Counts for Hispanic Americans." Lewis Mumford Center, University at Albany. July 14, 2003. https://files.eric.ed.gov/fulltext/ED479962.pdf.

Logan, John R., and Richard N. Turner. "Hispanics in the United States: Not Only Mexicans." Russell Sage Foundation. January 2013. https://s4.ad.brown.edu/Projects/Diversity/Data/Report/report03202013.pdf.

Logsdon, Joseph, and Caryn Cosé Bell. "The Americanization of Black New Orleans, 1850–1900." In *Creole New Orleans*, edited by Arnold R. Hirsch and Joseph Logsdon, 201–61. Baton Rouge: Louisiana State University Press, 1992.

Lopez, David. *Language Maintenance and Shift in the U.S. Today: The Basic Patterns and their Implications*. Los Alamitos CA: National Center for Bilingual Research, 1982.

Lopez, Mark Hugo, and Jens Manual Krogstad. "'Mexican,' 'Hispanic,' 'Latin American' Top the List of Race Write-ins on the 2010 Census." Pew Research Center. April 4, 2014. http://pewrsr.ch/1i7iiW6.

Lopez-Aguado, Patrick. "'I Would Be a Bulldog': Tracing the Spillover of Carceral Identity." *Social Problems* 63, no. 2 (May 2016): 203–21. https://doi.org/10.1093/socpro/spw001.

Lubin, Alex. *Romance and Rights: The Politics of Interracial Intimacy, 1945–1954*. Jackson: University Press of Mississippi, 2005.

Lyman, Stanford M., and William A. Douglas. "Ethnicities: Strategies of Collective and Individuals Impression Management." *Social Research* 40, no. 2 (Summer 1973): 344–65. http://www.jstor.org/stable/40970142.

Macias, Thomas. *Mestizo in America: Generations of Mexican Ethnicity in the Suburban Southwest*. Tucson: University of Arizona Press, 2006.

Mahtani, Minelle. *Mixed Race Amnesia: Resisting the Romantization of Multiraciality*. Vancouver: UBC Press, 2014.

Maillard, Kevin. "The Pocahontas Exception: The Exemption of American Indian Ancestry From Racial Purity Law." *Michigan Journal of Race and Law* 12, no. 2 (2007): 351–86.

———. "We Are Black Indians." In *What Are You? Voices of Mixed-Race Young People*, edited by Pearl F. Gaskins, 81–86. New York: Henry Holt, 1999.

Maillard, Kevin Noble, and Rose Cuison Villazor. "Introduction—*Loving v. Virginia* in a Post-Racial World." In *Loving v. Virginia in a Postracial World: Rethinking Race, Sex, and Marriage*, edited by Kevin Noble Maillard and Rose Cuison Villazor, 1–10. Cambridge, UK: Cambridge University Press, 2012.

Manrique, Linnete. "Dreaming of a Cosmic Race: José Vasconcelos and the Politics of Race in Mexico, 1920s–1930s." *Cogent Arts and Humanities* 3, no. 1 (2018): 1–13. http://dx.doi.org/10.1080/23311983.2016.1218316.

Marotta, Vince P. "Civilisation, Culture, and the Hybrid Self in the Work of Robert Ezra Park." *Journal of Intercultural Studies* 27, no. 4 (2007): 413–33. https://doi.org/10.1080/07256860600936911.

———. "The Hybrid Self and the Ambivalence of Boundaries." *Social Identities* 14, no. 3 (2008): 295–312. https://doi.org/10.1080/13504630802088052.

———. "The Idea of the In-Between Subject." In *Intercultural Relations in a Global World*, edited by Michele Lobo, Vince Marotta, and Nicole Oke, 179–99. Champaign IL: Common Ground Publishing, 2011.

Martinez, Cid G. *The Neighborhood Has Its Own Rules: Latinos and African Americans in South Los Angeles*. New York: New York University Press, 2016.

Martinez, Cid G., and Victor M. Rios. "Conflict, Cooperation, and Avoidance." In *Just Neighbors? Research on African American and Latino Relations in the United States*, edited by Edward Telles, Mark Q. Sawyer, and Gaspar Rivera-Salgado, 343–62. New York: Russell Sage Foundation, 2011.

Martinez, Cynthia M. "African American-Latino Relations in Houston: An Interview with Tatcho Mindiola, Jr." *Harvard Journal of African American Public Policy* 13 (2007): 71–78.

Martínez, María Elena. *Genealogical Fictions: Limpieza de Sangre, Religion, and Gender in Colonial Mexico*. Stanford CA: Stanford University Press, 2008.

Mason, Patrick L. "Annual Income, Hourly Wages, and Identity among Mexican Americans and other Latinos." *Industrial Relations* 43, no. 4 (October 2004): 817–34. https://doi.org/10.1111/j.0019-8676.2004.00363.x.

Mason, William M. *The Census of 1790: A Demographic History of Colonial California*. Santa Barbara CA: Ballena Press Anthropological Papers, 1998.

Mass, Amy Iwasaki. "Interracial Japanese Americans: The Best of Both Worlds or the End of the Japanese American Community?" In *Racially Mixed People in America*, edited by Maria P. P. Root, 265–78. Newbury Park CA: Sage Publications, 1992.

Masuoka, Natalie. *Multiracial Identity and Racial Politics in the United States*. New York: Oxford University Press, 2017.

Matthews, Thomas G. "The Question of Color in Puerto Rico." In *Slavery and Race Relations in Latin America*, edited by Robert Brent Toplin, 299–323. Westport CT: Greenwood Press, 1974.

McDonald, Dedra S. "Intimacy and Empire: Indian-African Interaction in Spanish Colonial New Mexico, 1500–1800." *American Indian Quarterly* 22, no. 1/2 (1998): 134–56. http://www.jstor.org/stable/1185114.

McFarland, Pancho. "Chicano Rap Roots: Black-Brown Cultural Exchange and the Making of a Genre." *Callaloo* 29, no. 3 (2006): 939–55. https://www.jstor.org/stable/4488380.

McHale, Susan M., Ann C. Crouter, Ji-Yeon Kim, Linda M. Burton, Kelly D. Davis, Aryn M. Dotterer, and Dena P. Swanson. "Mothers' and Fathers' Racial Socialization in African American Families: Implications for Youth." *Child Development* 77, no. 5 (September 2006): 1387–402. https://doi.org/10.1111/j.1467-8624.2006.00942.x.

McKee, James B. *Sociology and the Race Problem: The Failure of a Perspective*. Urbana: University of Illinois Press, 1993.

McKibbin, Molly Littlewood. "The Current State of Multiracial Discourse." *Journal of Critical Mixed Race Studies* 1, no. 1 (2014): 183–202. https://doi.org/10.5070/C811012861.

———. *Shades of Gray: Writing the New American Multiracialism*. Lincoln: University of Nebraska Press, 2018.

McNeil, Daniel. *Sex and Race in the Black Atlantic: Mulatto Devils and Multiracial Messiahs*. New York: Routledge, 2010.

Melville, Margarita B. "Hispanic Ethnicity, Race and Class." In *Handbook of Hispanic Cultures in the United States: Anthropology*, edited by Thomas Weaver, 90. Houston: Arte Publico, University of Houston Press, 1994.

Menchaca, Martha. *Recovering History Constructing Race: The Indian, Black and White Roots of Mexican Americans*. Austin: University of Texas Press, 2001.

Meyer, Michael C., William L. Sherman, and Susan M. Deeds. *The Course of Mexican History*. New York: Oxford University Press, 2007.

Miles, Tiya. *Ties That Bind: The Story of An Afro-Cherokee Family in Slavery and Freedom*. Los Angeles: University of California Press, 2005.

———. "Uncle Tom Was an Indian: Tracing the Red in Black Slavery." In *Confounding the Color Line: The Indian-Black Experience in North America*, edited by James F. Brooks, 121–44. Lincoln: University of Nebraska Press, 2002.

Miller, Susan A. "Seminoles and Africans under Seminole Law: Sources and Discourses of Tribal Sovereignty and 'Black Indian' Entitlement." *Wicazo Sa Review* 20, no. 1 (Spring, 2005): 23–47. https://doi.org/10.1353/wic.2005.0011.

Miller-Young, Mireille. "Hip-Hop Honeys and Da Hustlaz: Black Sexualities and the New Hip-Hop Pornography." *Meridians: Feminism, Race, Transnationalism* 8, no. 1 (December 2008): 261–92.

Mills, Gary B. *Forgotten People: Cane River's Creoles of Color.* Baton Rouge: Louisiana State University Press, 1997.

Mindiola, Tatcho, Jr., Yolanda Flores Niemann, and Nestor Rodriguez. *Black-Brown Relations and Stereotypes.* Austin: University of Texas Press, 2002.

Miranda, Gloria E. "Racial and Cultural Dimensions of 'Gente de Razón' in Spanish and Mexican California." *Southern California Quarterly* 70, no. 3 (1988): 265–78. https://doi.org/10.2307/41171310.

Miyawaki, Michael Hajime. "Expanding Boundaries of Whiteness? A Look at the Marital Patterns of Part-White Multiracial Groups." *Sociological Forum* 30, no. 4 (December 2015): 995–1016. https://doi.org/10.1111/socf.12205.

———. "Part-Latinos and Racial Reporting in the Census: An Issue of Question Format?" *Sociology of Race and Ethnicity* 2, no. 3 (July 2016): 289–306. https://doi.org/10.1177/2332649215613531.

Mohan, Erica, and Terah V. Chambers. "Two Researchers Reflect on Navigating Multiracial Identities in the Research Situation." *International Journal of Qualitative Studies in Education* 23, no. 3 (May 2010): 259–81. https://doi.org/10.1080/09518390903196609.

Monk, Ellis. "Skin Tone Stratification Among Black Americans, 2001–2003." *Social Forces* 92, no. 4 (2014): 1313–37. https://doi.org/10.1093/sf/sou007.

Montejano, David. *Anglos and Mexicans in the Making of Texts, 1836–1986.* Austin: University of Texas Press, 1987.

Montgomery, Michelle R. *Identity Politics of Difference: The Mixed-Race American Experience.* Boulder: University Press of Colorado, 2017.

Moran, Rachel F. *Interracial Intimacy: The Regulation of Race and Romance.* Chicago: University of Chicago Press, 2001.

———. "*Loving* and the Legacy of Unintended Consequences." *Wisconsin Law Review* 2 (2007): 239–81. https://repository.law.wisc.edu/s/uwlaw/media/36564.

Morgan, David L., and Richard A. Krueger. "When to Use Focus Groups and Why." In *Successful Focus Groups Advancing the State of the Art*, edited by David L. Morgan, 3–19. Newbury Park CA: Sage, 1993.

Mörner, Magnus. *Race Mixture in the History of Latin America.* Boston: Little, Brown, 1967.

Mukoyama, Tammy Hiroko-Josefa. "Effects of Heritage Combination on Ethnic Identity, Self Esteem, and Adjustment Among American Biethnic Adults." PhD diss., California School of Professional Psychology, Berkeley, 1998.
Mulroy, Kevin. *The Seminole Freedman: A History*. Norman: University of Oklahoma Press, 2007.
Murray, Pauli. *States' Laws on Race and Color*. Athens: University of Georgia Press, 1997.
Museus, Samuel D., Susan A. Lambe Sariñana, April L. Yee, and Thomas E. Robinson. "A Qualitative Analysis of Multiracial Students' Experiences with Prejudice and Discrimination in College." *Journal of College Student Development* 57, no. 6 (2016): 680–97. https://doi.org/10.1353/csd.2016.0068.
Myrdal, Gunnar. *An American Dilemma: The Negro Problem and Modern Democracy*. New York: Harper and Brothers, 1944.
Nadal, Kevin L., Julie Sriken, Kristen C. Davidoff, Yinglee Wong, and Kathryn McLean. "Microaggressions within Families: Experiences of Multiracial People." *National Council on Family Relations* 62, no. 1 (February 2013): 190–201.
Nadal, Kevin L., Yinglee Wong, Katie Griffin, Julie Sriken, Vivian Vargas, Michelle Wideman, and Ajayi Kolawole. "Microaggressions and the Multiracial Experience." *International Journal of Humanities and Social Science* 7, no. 1 (January 2011): 36–44. http://www.ijhssnet.com/journals/Vol._1_No._7_%5BSpecial_Issue_June_2011%5D/6.pdf.
Nagle, Jill. "Framing Radical Bisexuality: Toward a Gender Agenda." In *Bisexual Politics: Theories, Queries and Visions*, edited by Naomi Tucker, 305–14. Binghamton NY: Haworth Press, 1995.
Nakashima, Cynthia L. "An Invisible Monster: The Creation and Denial of Mixed-Race People in America." In *Racially Mixed People in America*, edited by Maria P. P. Root, 162–80. Newbury Park CA: Sage Publications: 1992.
———. "Voices from the Movement: Approaches to Multiraciality." In *The Multiracial Experience: Racial Borders as the New Frontier*, edited by Maria P. P. Root, 79–100. Thousand Oaks CA: Sage Publications, 1996.
Nash, Gary B. *Forbidden Love: The Hidden History of Mixed-Race America*. New York: Henry Holt, 1999.
———. "The Hidden History of Mestizo America." *Journal of American History* 82, no. 3 (December 1995): 941–96. https://doi.org/10.2307/2945107.
———. *Red, White, and Black: The Peoples of Early America*. 2nd ed. Englewood Cliffs NJ: Prentice Hall, 1982.
Naylor, Celia E. *African Cherokees in Indian Territory: From Chattel to Citizens*. Chapel Hill: University of North Carolina Press, 2008.

Nazzari, Muriel. "Concubinage in Colonial Brazil: The Inequalities of Race, Class, and Gender." *Journal of Family History* 21, no. 2 (1996): 107–24. https://doi.org/10.1177/036319909602100201.

Newbeck, Phyl. *Virginia Hasn't Always Been for Lovers: Interracial Marriage Bans and the Case of Richard and Mildred Loving.* Carbondale: Southern Illinois University Press, 2004.

Newman, Alyssa M. "Revisiting the Marginal Man: Bridging Immigration Scholarship and Mixed-Race Studies." *Sociology of Race and Ethnicity* 7, no. 1 (July 2021): 26–40. https://doi.org/10.1177/2332649220933302.

Newman, Alyssa M., and G. Reginald Daniel. "Colorblind Ideology Multiculturalism, and Collective Identity Formation among Mixed Race Adolescents in Northern California." In *Adolescent Identity and Schooling: Diverse Perspectives*, edited by Cynthia Hudley, 22–33. New York: Routledge, 2015.

Nicholson, Stephen P., Adrian D. Pantoja, and Gary M. Segura. "Race Matters: Latino Racial Identities and Political Beliefs." Presentation at the Annual Meeting of the American Political Science Association, Washington DC, August 31–September 4, 2005. https://escholarship.org/uc/item/39g3f25h.

Niemonen, Jack. "The Race Relations Problematic in American Sociology: A Case Study and Critique." *American Sociologist* 28, no. 1 (1997): 15–54. https://doi.org/10.1007/s12108-997-1025-0.

Nobles, Melissa. *Shades of Citizenship: Race and the Census in Modern Politics.* Stanford CA: Stanford University Press, 2000.

Nunn, Nathan, and Nancy Qian. "Columbian Exchange." *Journal of Economic Perspectives* 24, no. 2 (Spring 2010): 163–88. http://dx.doi.org/10.1257/jep.24.2.163.

Obama, Barack. *Dreams from My Father: A Story of Race and Inheritance.* New York: Random House, 1995.

O'Brien, Eileen. *The Racial Middle: Latinos and Asian Americans Living Beyond the Racial Divide.* New York: New York University Press, 2008.

O'Hare, B. C. "Parents' Race and Racial Classification of Children." *National Network of State Polls Newsletter* 35 (Winter 1999): 1–8.

Olsen, Otto H. *The Thin Disguise: The Turning Point in Negro History—Plessy v. Ferguson, A Documentary Presentation (1864–1896).* New York: Humanities Press, 1967.

Olson, Steve. *Mapping Human History: Discovering the Past Through Our Genes.* New York: Houghton Mifflin, 2002.

Omi, Michael. "Racial Identity and the State: The Dilemmas of Classification." *Law and Inequality: A Journal of Theory and Practice* 15, no. 1 (1997): 7–22. https://scholarship.law.umn.edu/lawineq/vol15/iss1/2.

Omi, Michael, and Howard Winant. *Racial Formation in the United States from the 1960s to the 1990s.* 2nd ed. New York: Routledge, 1994.

Opie, Frederick Douglass. "Eating, Dancing, and Courting in New York Black and Latino Relations, 1930–1970." *Journal of Social History* 42, no. 1 (Fall 2008): 79–109.

Orenstein, Dara. "Void of Vagueness: Mexicans and the Collapse of Miscegenation Law in California." *Pacific Historical Review* 74, no. 3 (2005): 367–408. https://doi.org/10.1525/phr.2005.74.3.367.

Orozco, Cynthia. *No Mexicans, Women, or Dogs Allowed: The Rise of the Mexican American Civil Rights Movement.* Austin: University of Texas Press, 2009.

Ortiz, Cristina M. "Parental Racial Socialization: A Glimpse into the Racial Socialization Process as It Occurs in a Dual-Minority Multiracial Family." In *Red and Yellow, Black and Brown: Decentering Whiteness in Mixed Race Studies*, edited by Joanne L. Rondilla, Rudy P. Guevarra Jr., and Paul Spickard, 88–105. New Brunswick NJ: Rutgers University Press, 2017.

Ortiz, Vilma, and Carlos Arce. "Language Orientation and Mental Health Status among Persons of Mexican Descent." *Hispanic Journal of Behavioral Sciences* 6, no. 2 (June 1984): 127–43. https://doi.org/10.1177/07399863840062004.

Ortiz, Vilma, and Edward E. Telles. "Racial Identity and Racial Treatment of Mexican Americans." *Race and Social Problems* 4, no. 1 (April 2012): 1–28. https://doi.org/10.1007/s12552-012-9064-8.

Owens, Louis. *Mixedblood Messages: Literature, Film, Family, Place.* Norman: University of Oklahoma Press, 1998.

Palmer, Colin A. *Slaves of the White God: Blacks in Mexico, 1570–1650.* Cambridge MA: Harvard University Press, 1976.

Park, Julie, Dowell Meyers, and Liang Wei. "Multiracial Patterns in California by County." Public Research Report No. 2001-3. Race Contours 2000 Study. Population Dynamics Group, University of Southern California School of Policy, Planning and Development. 2001. https://sites.usc.edu/popdynamics/race-and-ethnicity/.

Park, Robert E. "Human Migration and the Marginal Man." *American Journal of Sociology* 33, no. 6 (1928): 881–93. https://doi.org/10.1086/214592.

———. Introduction to *The Marginal Man: A Study in Personality and Culture Conflict*, edited by Everett V. Stonequist, xiii–xviii. C. Scribner's Sons, 1937.

Parker, Kim, Juliana Menasce Horowitz, Rich Morin, and Mark Hugo Lopez. "Multiracial in America: Proud, Diverse, and Growing in Numbers." Pew Research Center. June 11, 2015. https://www.pewsocialtrends.org/2015/06/11/multiracial-in-america/.

Pascoe, Peggy. *Doing What Comes Naturally: Miscegenation Law and the Making of Race in America*. New York: Oxford University Press, 2009.

Passel, Jeffrey S., and D'Vera Cohn. "U.S. Population Projections: 2005–2050." Pew Research Center, February 11, 2008. https://www.pewresearch.org/hispanic/2008/02/11/us-population-projections-2005-2050/.

Passel, Jeffrey S., Wendy Wang, and Paul Taylor. "Marrying Out: One-in-Seven New U.S. Marriages is Interracial or Interethnic." Pew Research Center. June 4, 2010. http://www.pewsocialtrends.org/2010/06/04/marrying-out/.

Pastor, Manuel. "Keeping It Real: Demographic Change, Economic Conflict, and Interethnic Organizing for Social Justice in Los Angeles." In *Black and Brown in Los Angeles: Beyond Conflict and Coalition*, edited by Josh Kun and Laura Pulido, 33–66. Berkeley: University of California Press, 2014.

Patterson, Orlando. *Slavery and Social Death: A Comparative Study*. Cambridge MA: Harvard University Press, 1982.

Pauker, Kristin, Chanel Meyers, Diana T. Sanchez, Sarah E. Gaither, and Danielle M. "A Review of Multiracial Malleability: Identity, Categorization, and Shifting Racial Attitudes." *Social and Personality Psychology Compass* 12, no. 6 (2018): 1–15. https://doi.org/10.1111/spc3.12392.

Perdue, Theda. *Slavery and the Evolution of Cherokee Society, 1540–1866*. Knoxville: University of Tennessee Press, 1987.

Perea, Juan. F. "The Black/White Binary Paradigm of Race: The Normal Science of American Racial Thought." *California Law Review* 85, no. 5 (1997): 127–72. https://doi.org/10.15779/Z38MF05.

Pérez, Emma. *The Decolonial Imaginary: Writing Chicanas into History*. Bloomington: Indiana University Press, 1999.

Pérez, Erika. *Colonial Intimacies Interethnic Kinship, Sexuality, and Marriage in Southern California, 1769–1885*. Norman: University of Oklahoma Press, 2018.

Pérez-Torres, Rafael. *Mestizaje: Critical Use of Race in Chicano Culture*. Minneapolis: University of Minnesota Press. 2006.

Perlmann, Joel, and Mary C. Waters, eds. *The New Race Question: How the Census Counts Multiracial Individuals*. New York: Russell Sage Foundation, 2002.

Phinney, Jean S. "When We Talk About American Ethnic Groups, What Do We Mean?" *American Psychologist* 51, no. 9 (September 1996): 918–27. https://doi.org/10.1037/0003-066X.51.9.918.

Phinney, Jean S., and Linda L Alipuria. "At the Interface of Cultures: Multiethnic/Multiracial High School and College Students." *Journal of Social Psychology* 136, no. 2 (1996): 139–58. https://doi.org/10.1080/00224545.1996.9713988.

Pierce, Chester M. "Offensive Mechanisms." In *The Black Seventies*, edited by Floyd B. Barbour, 265–82. Boston: Porter Sargent Publisher, 1970.

Poston, W. S. Carlos. "The Biracial Identity Development Model: A Needed Addition." *Journal of Counseling & Development* 69, no. 2 (1990): 152–55. https://doi.org/10.1002/j.1556-6676.1990.tb01477.x.

Prewitt, Kenneth. *What Is "Your" Race? The Census and Our Flawed Efforts to Classify Americans*. Princeton NJ: Princeton University Press, 2013.

Proctor, Frank T. *Damned Notions of Liberty: Slavery, Culture, and Power in Colonial Mexico, 1640–1769*. Albuquerque: University of New Mexico Press, 2010.

Puckett, Anita. "The Melungeon Identity Movement and the Construction of Appalachian Whiteness." *Journal of Linguistic Anthropology* 11, no. 1 (2001): 131–46. https://doi.org/10.1525/jlin.2001.11.1.131.

Pulido, Laura. *Black, Brown, Yellow and Left: Radical Activism in Los Angeles*. Berkeley: University of California Press, 2006. https://doi.org/10.1111/j.1467-8330.2007.00502.x.

———. "A Day Without Immigrants: The Racial and Class Politics of Immigrant Exclusion." *Antipode: A Radical Journal of Geography* 39, no. 1 (2007): 1–7.

Qian, Zhenchao, and Daniel T. Lichter. "Social Boundaries and Marital Assimilation: Interpreting Trends in Racial and Ethnic Intermarriage." *American Sociological Review* 72, no. 1 (2007): 68–94. https://doi.org/10.1177/000312240707200104.

Quinones, Sam. "Race, Real Estate, and the Mexican Mafia." In *Black and Brown in Los Angeles: Beyond Conflict and Coalition*, edited by Josh Kun and Laura Pulido, 261–97. Berkeley: University of California Press, 2014.

Randolph, Donna Maketa. "I'm Black and Korean." In *What Are You? Voices of Mixed-Race Young People*, edited by Pearl F. Gaskins, 87–92. New York: Henry Holt, 1999.

Rankin, David C. "The Impact of the Civil War on the Free Colored Community of New Orleans." *Perspectives in American History* 11 (August 1975): 379–416.

Rastogi, Sonya, Tallese D. Johnson, Elizabeth M. Hoeffel, and Malcolm P. Drewery Jr. "The Black Population: 2010." *2010 Census Briefs*. C2010BR-06. U.S. Bureau of the Census. April 2005. https://www.census.gov/content/dam/Census/library/publications/2011/dec/c2010br-06.pdf.

Renn, Kristen A. *Mixed Race Students in College: The Ecology of Race, Identity, and Community on Campus*. Albany: State University of New York Press, 2004.

Reséndez, Andrés. *The Other Slavery: The Uncovered Story of Indian Enslavement in America*. Boston: Houghton Mifflin Harcourt, 2016.

Ribianszky, Nicole S. "She Appeared to Be Mistress of Her Own Actions: Free From Control of Anyone: Property-Holding Free Women of Color in Natchez, Mississippi, 1779–1865." *Journal of Mississippi History* 67, no. 3 (Fall 2005): 217–46. https://www.academia.edu/2647886/_She_Appeared_to_be_Mistress_of

_Her_Own_Actions_Free_From_the_Control_of_Anyone_Property_Holding_Free_Women_of_Color_in_Natchez_Mississippi_1779_1865_.

Rico, Brittany, Rose M. Kreider, and Lydia Anderson. "Growth in Interracial and Interethnic Married-Couple Households." U.S. Bureau of the Census. July 9, 2018. https://www.census.gov/library/stories/2018/07/interracial-marriages.html.

Riley, Steven F. "Appendix A: Publications from 1989 to 2004." *Journal of Critical Mixed Race Studies* 1, no. 1 (2014): 66–76. https://doi.org/10.5070/C811021382.

———. "Appendix B: Publications from 2005 to 2013." *Journal of Critical Mixed Race Studies* 1, no. 1 (2014): 77–97. https://doi.org/10.5070/C811021383.

Ringer, Benjamin B. *We the People and Others: Duality and America's Treatment of Its Racial Minorities*. Abingdon VA: Routledge Kegan & Paul, 1983.

Rios, Victor. *Punished: Policing the Lives of Black and Latino Boys*. New York: New York University Press, 2011.

Roberts, Robert E. T. "Black-White Intermarriage in the United States." In *Inside the Mixed Marriage: Accounts of Changing Attitudes, Patterns, and Perceptions of Cross-Cultural and Interracial Marriages*, edited by Walton R. Johnson and Michael C. Warren, 25–79. Lanham MD: University Press of America, 1994.

Rockquemore, Kerry A., and David L. Brunsma. *Beyond Black: Biracial Identity in America*. Thousand Oaks CA: Sage, 2002.

Rockquemore, Kerry A., and Patricia Arend. "Opting for White: Choice, Fluidity, and Black Identity Construction in Post-Civil Rights America." *Race and Society* 5, no. 1 (December 2003): 51–66. https://doi.org/10.1016/j.racsoc.2003.12.004.

Rockquemore, Kerry A., and Tracey Laszloffy. *Raising Biracial Children*. Lanham MD: AltaMira Press, 2005.

Rockquemore, Kerry A., David L. Brunsma, and Daniel J. Delgado. "Racing to Theory or Retheorizing Race? Understanding the Struggle to Build a Multiracial Identity Theory." *Journal of Social Issues* 65, no. 1 (January 2009): 13–34. https://doi.org/10.1111/j.1540-4560.2008.01585.x.

Rodríguez, Clara E. *Puerto Ricans: Born in the U.S.A.* Boston: Unwin Hyman, 1989.

———. "Race, Culture, and Latino 'Otherness' in the 1980 Census." *Social Science Quarterly* 73, no. 4 (1992): 930–37.

Rodríguez, Evelyn I. *Celebrating Debutantes and Quinceañeras: Coming of Age in American Ethnic Communities*. Philadelphia: Temple University Press, 2013.

Rodríguez, Gregory. *Mongrels, Bastards, Orphans, and Vagabonds: Mexican Immigration and the Future of Race in America*. New York: Random House, 2007.

Rodríguez, José I., Aaron Castelan Cargile, and Marc D. Rich. "Reactions to African-American Vernacular English: Do More Phonological Feature Matter?" *Western Journal of Black Studies* 28, no. 3 (September 2004): 407–14.

https://www.researchgate.net/publication/281526521_Reactions_to_African_American_Vernacular_English_Do_More_Phonological_Features_Matter.

Rodríguez-García, Dan. "Intermarriage and Integration Revisited: International Experiences and Cross-Disciplinary Approaches." *Annals of the American Academy of Political and Social Science* 662, no. 1 (2015): 8–36. https://doi.org/10.1177/0002716215601397.

Rodríguez-García, Dan, Miguel Solana-Solana, and Miranda J. Lubbers. "Preference and Prejudice: Does Intermarriage Erode Negative Ethno-Racial Attitudes Between Groups in Spain?" *Ethnicities* 16, no. 4 (2016): 521–46. https://doi.org/10.1177/1468796816638404.

Román, Miriam Jiménez, and Juan Flores. Introduction to *Afro-Latin@ Reader: History and Culture in the United States*, 1–18. Durham NC: Duke University Press, 2010.

Romano, Renee Christine. *Race Mixing: Black-White Marriage in Postwar America*. Cambridge MA: Harvard University Press, 2003.

Romo, Rebecca. "Between Black and Brown: Blaxican (Black-Mexican) Multiracial identity in California." *Journal of Black Studies* 42, no. 3 (2011): 402–26. https://doi.org/10.1177/0021934710376172.

———. "Blaxican Identity: An Exploratory Study of Multiracial Blacks/Chicanas/os in California." Master's thesis, University of California, Santa Barbara, California, 2007.

———. "'You're Not Black or Mexican Enough!': Policing Racial/Ethnic Authenticity among Blaxicans in the United States." In *Red and Yellow, Black and Brown: Decentering Whiteness in Mixed Race Studies*, edited by Joanne L. Rondilla, Rudy P. Guevarra Jr., and Paul Spickard, 127–44. New Brunswick NJ: Rutgers University Press, 2017.

Rondilla, Joanne L., and Paul Spickard. *Is Lighter Better? Skin Tone Discrimination among Asian Americans*. Lanham MD: Rowman and Littlefield, 2007.

Rondilla, Joanne L., Rudy P. Guevarra Jr., and Paul Spickard. *Red and Yellow, Black and Brown: Decentering Whiteness in Mixed Race Studies*. New Brunswick NJ: Rutgers University Press, 2017.

Root, Maria P. P. "Factors Influencing the Variation in Racial and Ethnic Identity of Mixed-Heritage Persons of Asian Ancestry." In *The Sum of Our Parts: Mixed-Heritage Asian Americans*, edited by Teresa Williams-Leon and Cynthia L. Nakashima, 61–70. Philadelphia: Temple University Press, 2001.

———. "From Exotic to a Dime a Dozen." *Women and Therapy* 27, no. 1–2 (January 2004): 19–31. https://doi.org/10.1300/J015v27n01_02.

———. *Love's Revolution: Interracial Marriage*. Philadelphia: Temple University Press, 2001.

———. *The Multiracial Experience: Racial Borders as the New Frontier.* Thousand Oaks CA: Sage Publications, 1996.

———, ed. *Racially Mixed People in America.* Newbury Park CA: Sage Publications, 1992.

———. "Reconstructing Race, Rethinking Ethnicity." In *Comprehensive Clinical Psychology: Vol. 10. Sociocultural and Individual Differences*, edited by Alan S. Bellack and Michel Hersen, 141–60. New York: Elsevier, 2001.

———. "Resolving 'Other' Status: Identity Development of Biracial Individuals." In *Complexity and Diversity in Feminist Theory and Therapy*, edited by Laura S. Brown and Maria P. P. Root, 185–205. New York: Routledge, 1990.

———. "Within, Between, and Beyond Race." In *Racially Mixed People in America*, edited by Maria P. P. Root, 3–11. Newbury Park CA: Sage Publications, 1992.

Roque Ramírez, Horacio N. "Borderlands, Diasporas, and Transnational Crossing: Teaching LGBT Latina and Latino Histories." *OAH Magazine of History* (March 2006): 39–42.

Roth, Wendy D. "The End of One-Drop Rule: Labeling of Multiracial Children in Black Intermarriages." *Sociological Forum* 20, no. 1 (March 2005): 35–67. https://doi.org/10.1007/s11206-005-1897-0.

Rothman, Janson, and Amy Beth Rell. "A Linguistic Analysis of Spanglish: Relating Language to Identity." *Linguistics and the Human Sciences* 1, no. 3 (2005): 515–36. https://doi.org/10.1558/lhs.2005.1.3.515.

Rountree, Helen C. *Pocahontas's People: The Powhatan Indians of Virginia through Four Centuries.* Norman: University of Oklahoma Press, 1990.

Rout, Leslie B., Jr. *The African Experience in Spanish America.* Princeton NJ: Markus Wiener, 1976.

Russell-Wood, Anthony John R. "Colonial Brazil." In *Neither Slave nor Free: The Freemen of African Descent in the Slave Societies of the New World*, edited by David W. Cohen and Jack P. Greene, 84–133. Baltimore MD: Johns Hopkins University Press, 1972.

Saether, Steiner A. "Bourbon Absolutism in Late Colonial Spanish America." *The Americas* 59, no. 4 (April 2003): 494–95. http://www.jstor.org/stable/1008567.

Salgado de Snyder, Nelly, Cynthia M. Lopez, and Amado M. Padilla. "Ethnic Identity and Cultural Awareness Among the Offspring of Mexican Interethnic Marriages." *Journal of Early Adolescence* 2, no. 3 (August 1982): 277–82. https://doi.org/10.1177/027243168200200310.

Salomon, Carlos Manuel. *Pío Pico: The Last Governor of Mexican California.* Norman: University Press of Oklahoma, 2010.

Samuels, Gina Miranda. "Building Kinship and Community: Relational Processes of Bicultural Identity Among Multiracial Adoptees." *Family Processes* 49, no. 1 (March 2010): 26–42. https://doi.org/10.1111/j.1545-5300.2010.01306.x.

Sánchez, George J. *Becoming Mexican American: Ethnicity, Culture, and Identity in Chicano Los Angeles, 1900–1945*. New York: Oxford University Press, 1993.

Sandoval, Chela. *Methodology of the Oppressed*. Minneapolis: University of Minnesota Press, 2000.

Sanjek, Roger. "Intermarriage and the Future of Races." In *Race*, edited by Steven Gregory and Roger Sanjek, 103–30. New Brunswick NJ: Rutgers University Press, 1994.

Sawyer, Mark Q. "Politics in Los Angeles." In *Just Neighbors? Research on African American and Latino Relations in the United States*, edited by Edward Telles, Mark Q. Sawyer, and Gaspar Rivera-Salgado, 177–98. New York: Russell Sage Foundation, 2011.

Schwaller, Robert C. *Géneros de Gente in Early Mexico: Defining Racial Difference*. Norman: University of Oklahoma Press, 2016.

Seed, Patricia. *To Love, Honor, and Obey in Colonial Mexico: Conflicts over Marriage Choice, 1574–1821*. Stanford CA: Stanford University Press, 1988.

Seijas, Tatiana. *Asian Slaves in Colonial Mexico: From Chinos to Indians*. New York: Cambridge University Press, 2014.

Sexton, Jared. *Amalgamation Schemes: AntiBlackness and the Critique of Multiracialism*. Minneapolis: University of Minnesota Press, 2008.

Sharma, Nitasha Tamar. "Epilogue: Expanding the Terrain of Mixed Race Studies What We Learn from the Study of Non-White Multiracials." In *Red and Yellow, Black and Brown: Decentering Whiteness in Mixed Race Studies*, edited by Joanne L. Rondilla, Rudy P. Guevarra Jr., and Paul Spickard, 219–30. New Brunswick NJ: Rutgers University Press, 2017.

Sheridan, Clare. "'Another White Race': Mexican Americans and the Paradox of Whiteness in Jury Selection." *Law and History Review* 21, no. 1 (2003): 109–44. https://doi.org/10.2307/3595070.

Shih, Margaret, and Diana T. Sanchez. "When Race Becomes Even More Complex: Toward Understanding the Landscape of Multiracial Identity and Experiences." *Journal of Social Issues* 65, no. 1 (March 2009): 1–11. https://doi.org/10.1111/j.1540-4560.2008.01584.x.

Shih, Margaret, Courtney Bonam, Diana Sanchez, and Courtney Peck. "The Social Construction of Race: Biracial Identity and Susceptibility to Stereotypes." *Cultural Diversity and Ethnic Minority Psychology* 13, no. 2 (March 2007): 123–33. https://doi.org/10.1037/1099-9809.13.2.125.

Shumway, Jeffrey M. *The Case of the Ugly Suitor and Other Histories of Love, Gender, and Nation in Bueno Aires*. Lincoln: University of Nebraska Press, 2005.

Silva, Pablo Miguel Sierra. *Urban Slavery in Colonial Mexico: Puebla de los Ángeles, 1531–1706*. New York: Cambridge University Press, 2018.

Simmen, Edward A., and Richard F. Bauerle. "Chicano: Origin and Meaning." *American Speech* 44, no. 3 (Autumn 1969): 225–30. https://doi.org/10.2307/454588.

Simone, T. Maliqalim. *About Face: Race in Postmodern America*. New York: Autonomedia, 1989.

Sims, Jennifer P. "Reevaluation of the Influence on Appearance and Reflected Appraisals for Mixed Race Identity: The Role of Consistent Inconsistent Racial Perception." *Sociology of Race and Ethnicity* 2, no. 4 (October 2016): 569–83. https://doi.org/10.1177/2332649216634740.

Sims, Jennifer P., and Remi Joseph-Salisbury. "'We Were All Just the Black Kids': Black Mixed-Race Men and the Importance of Adolescent Peer Groups for Identity Development." *Social Currents* 6, no. 1 (February 2019): 51–66. https://doi.org/10.1177/2329496518797840.

Smedley, Audrey. *Race in North America: Origin and Evolution of a World View*. Boulder CO: West View Press, 1993.

Smith, Michelle René. "Alain Locke: Culture and the Plurality of Black Life." PhD diss., Cornell University, 2009.

Smith, Phillip Matthew. "Persistent Borderland: Freedom and Citizenship in Territorial Florida." PhD diss., Texas A&M University, 2007.

Smith, Sandra, and Mignon R. Moore. "Intraracial Diversity and Relations Among African Americans: Closeness Among Black Students at a Predominantly White University." *American Journal of Sociology* 106, no. 1 (July 2000): 1–39. https://doi.org/10.1086/303112.

Smith, William, Tara J. Yosso, and Daniel Solórzano. "Challenging Racial Battle Fatigue on Historically White Campuses: A Critical Race Examination of Race-Related Stress." In *Faculty of Color: Teaching in Predominately White Colleges and Universities*, edited by Christine A. Stanley, 299–327. Bolton MA: Anker Publishing, 2006. Reprinted in *Covert Racism: Theories, Institutions, and Experiences*, edited by Rodney D. Coates. Boston: Brill, 2011.

Song, Miri. "Is Intermarriage a Good Indicator of Integration?" *Journal of Ethnic and Migration Studies* 35, no. 2 (2009): 331–48. https://doi.org/10.1080/13691830802586476.

———. *Multiracial Parents: Mixed Families, Generational Change, and the Future of Race*. New York: New York University Press, 2017.

Spencer, Jon Michael. *The New Colored People: The Mixed-Race Movement in America*. New York: New York University Press, 1997.

Spencer, Rainer. "'Only the News They Want to Print': Mainstream Media and Critical Mixed-Race Studies." *Journal of Critical Mixed Race Studies* 1, no. 1 (2014): 162–82. https://doi.org/10.5070/C811013098.

———. *Reproducing Race: The Paradox of Generation Mix*. Boulder CO: Lynne Rienner, 2011.

———. *Spurious Issues: Race and Multiracial Identity Politics in the United States*. Boulder CO: Westview Press, 1999.

Spickard, Paul. *Mixed Blood: Intermarriage and Ethnic Identity in Twentieth-Century America*. Madison: University of Wisconsin Press, 1989.

———. *Race in Mind: Critical Essays*. With Jeffrey Moniz and Ingrid Dineen-Wimberly. Notre Dame IN: University of Notre Dame Press, 2016.

———. "What Must I Be? Asian Americans and the Question of Multiethnic Identity." *Amerasia Journal* 23, no. 1 (February 13, 1997): 43–60. https://doi.org/10.17953/amer.23.1.j2427w767v758k55.

Spickard, Paul, Rudy P. Guevarra Jr., and Joanne Rondilla. "Introduction: About Mixed Race, Not about Whiteness." In *Red and Yellow, Black and Brown: Decentering Whiteness in Mixed Race Studies*, edited by Joanne L Rondilla, Rudy P. Guevarra Jr., and Paul Spickard, 11–18. New Brunswick NJ: Rutgers University Press, 2017.

Squires, Catherine R. *Dispatches from the Color Line: The Press and Multiracial America*. Albany NY: SUNY Press, 2007.

Steinberg, Stephen. *Race Relations: A Critique*. Stanford CA: Stanford University Press, 2007.

Stephan, Cookie W., and Walter G. Stephan. "The Measurement of Racial and Ethnic Identity." *International Journal of Intercultural Relations* 24, no. 5 (September 2000): 541–52. https://doi.org/10.1016/S0147-1767(00)00016-X.

Steptoe, Tyina L. *Houston Bound: Culture and Color in a Jim Crow City*. Berkeley: University of California Press, 2016.

Sterkx, Henry E. *The Free Negro in Antebellum Louisiana*. New York: Associated University Press, 1972.

Stevenson, Alva Moore. *Both Black and Mexican: The Thornton Family of Nogales, Arizona*. Saarbrücken, Germany: LAP LAMBERT Academic Publishing, 2012.

Stickmon, Janet C. Mendoza. "Blackapina." In *Red and Yellow, Black and Brown: Decentering Whiteness in Mixed Race Studies*, edited by Joanne L. Rondilla, Rudy P. Guevarra Jr., and Paul Spickard, 33–46. New Brunswick NJ: Rutgers University Press, 2017.

Stonequist, Everett V. *The Marginal Man: A Study in Personality and Culture Conflict*. New York: Russell & Russell, 1937.

Strmic-Pawl, Hephzibah V. *Multiracialism and Its Discontents: A Comparative Analysis of Asian-White and Black-White Multiracials*. Lanham MD: Lexington Books, 2016.

Strum, Circe. "Blood, Politics, Racial Classification, and Cherokee National Identity: The Trials and Tribulations of the Cherokee Freedman." In *Confounding the Color Line: The Indian-Black Experience in North America*, edited by James F. Brooks, 223–57. Lincoln: University of Nebraska Press, 2002.

———. *Blood Politics: Race, Culture, and Identity in the Cherokee Nation of Oklahoma*. Berkeley: University of California Press, 2002.

Sue, Derald Wing. *Microaggressions and Marginality: Manifestation, Dynamics, and Impact*. Hoboken NJ: John Wiley and Sons, 2010.

Tafoya, Sonya M. "Latinos and Racial Identification in California." *California Counts* 4, no. 4 (May 2003): 1–16. https://www.ppic.org/publication/latinos-and-racial-identification-in-california/.

———. "Shades of Belonging." Pew Research Center. December 6, 2004. https://www.pewresearch.org/hispanic/2004/12/06/shades-of-belonging/.

Tafoya, Sonya M., Hans Johnson, and Laura E. Hill. *Who Chooses to Choose Two: Multiracial Identification and Census 2000*. New York: Russell Sage Foundation, 2004.

Tajfel, Henri. *Differentiation Between Social Groups: Studies In the Social Psychology of Intergroup Relations*. New York: Academic Press, 1978.

Takaki, Ronald. *A Different Mirror: A History of Multicultural America*. New York: Little, Brown, 2008.

Talmon-Chvaicer, Maya. *The Hidden History of Capoeira: A Collision of Cultures in the Brazilian Battle Dance*. Austin: University of Texas Press, 2008.

Tarrow, Sidney. *Power in Movement: Social Movements and Contentious Politics*. 3rd ed. Cambridge, UK: Cambridge University Press, 2011.

Taylor, Keeanga-Yamahatta. *From #BlackLivesMatter to Black Liberation*. Chicago: Haymarket Books, 2016.

Taylor, Quintard. *In Search of the Racial Frontier: African Americans in the American West 1528–1990*. New York: Norton, 1998.

Taylor-Gibbs, Jewelle. "Identity and Marginality: Issues in the Treatment of Biracial Adolescents." *American Journal of Orthopsychiatry* 57, no. 2 (1987): 265–78. https://doi.org/10.1111/j.1939-0025.1987.tb03537.x.

Taylor-Gibbs, Jewelle, and Anne Hines. "Negotiating Ethnic Identity." In *Racially Mixed People in America*, edited by Maria P. P. Root, 223–38. Newbury Park CA: Sage Publications, 1992.

Telles, Edward E., and Christina A. Sue. *Durable Ethnicity: Mexican Americans and the Ethnic Core*. New York: Oxford University Press, 2020.

Telles, Edward E., and Edward Murguía. "Phenotypic Discrimination and Income Differences Among Mexican Americans." *Social Science Quarterly* 71, no. 4 (December 1, 1990): 682–96. https://www.proquest.com/docview/1291645963 ?accountid=14522&imgSeq=1.

Telles, Edward E., and Vilma Ortiz. *Generations of Exclusion: Mexican Americans, Assimilation, and Race*. New York: Russell Sage Foundation, 2007.

Telles, Edward E., Gaspar Rivera-Salgado, Mark Q. Sawyer, and Sylvia Zamora. Introduction to *Just Neighbors? Research on African American and Latino Relations in the United States*, 1–33. New York: Russell Sage Foundation, 2011.

Tenzer, Lawrence Raymond. *A Completely New Look at Interracial Sexuality: Public Opinion and Select Commentaries*. Manahawkin NJ: Scholars Pub House, 1991.

Tesler, Michael. "The Conditions Ripe for Racial Spillover Effects." *Advances in Political Psychology* 36, no. s1 (February 20, 2015): 101–17. https://doi.org/10 .1111/pops.12246.

Thomas, David Y. "The Free Negro in Florida Before 1865." *South Atlantic Quarterly* 10, no. 4 (October 1911): 335–37.

Thomas, Susan. *Cuban Zarzuela: Performing Race and Gender on Havana's Lyric Stage*. Urbana: University of Illinois Press, 2009.

Thompson, Maxine, and Verna M. Keith. "The Blacker the Berry: Gender, Skin Tone, Self Esteem, and Self-Efficacy." *Gender and Society* 15, no. 3 (June 2001): 336–57. https://doi.org/10.1177/089124301015003002.

Thompson, Vetta Sanders. "Variables Affecting Racial Identity Salience among African Americans." *Journal of Social Psychology* 139, no. 6 (January 2000): 748–61. https://doi.org/10.1080/00224549909598254.

Thompson, William C., and Nicholas Scurich. "When Does Absence of Evidence Constitute Evidence of Absence?" *Forensic Science International* 291 (2018): e18–e19. https://doi.org/10.1016/j.forsciint.2018.08.040.

Thornton, Michael C. "Is Multiracial Status Unique? The Personal and Social Experience." In *Racially Mixed People in America*, edited by Maria P. P. Root, 321–25. Newbury Park CA: Sage Publications, 1992.

———. "Policing the Borderlands: White- and Black-American Newspaper Perceptions of Multiracial Heritage and the Idea of Race, 1996–2006." *Journal of Social Issues* 65, no. 1 (January 2009): 105–27. https://doi.org/10.1111/j.1540 -4560.2008.01590.x.

———. "A Social History of Multiethnic Identity: The Case of Black Japanese Americans." PhD diss., University of Michigan, 1983.

Thornton, Michael C., Linda M. Chatters, Robert J. Taylor, and Walter R. Allen. "Sociodemographic and Environmental Correlates of Racial Socialization by Black Parents." *Child Development* 61, no. 2 (April 1990): 401–9. https://doi.org/10.1111/j.1467-8624.1990.tb02786.x.

Tilly, Charles. *Social Movements, 1768–2004*. Boulder CO: Paradigm, 2004.

Tizard, Barbara, and Ann Phoenix. "The Identity of Mixed Parentage Adolescents." *Journal of Child Psychology and Psychiatry and Allied Disciplines* 36, no. 8 (November 1995): 1399–410. https://doi.org/10.1111/j.1469-7610.1995.tb01671.x.

Tobias, Philip V. "The Meaning of Race." In *Race and Social Difference*, edited by Paul Baxter and Basil Sansom, 19–43. London: Penguin Books, 1972.

Torres, Max S. Hering, Maria Elena Martinez, and David Nirenberg. "Editorial." In *Race and Blood in the Iberian World*, edited by Max S. Hering Torres, Maria Elena Martinez, and David Nirenberg, 1–8. Berlin: LIT Verlag, 2012.

Townsend, Sarah S. M., Stephanie A, Fryberg, Clara Wilkins, and Hazel Rose Markus. "Being Mixed: Who Claims a Biracial Identity?" *Cultural Diversity and Ethnic Minority Psychology* 18, no. 1 (2012): 91–96. https://doi.org/10.1037/a0026845.

Tran, Nellie, and Susan E. Peterson. "'American' as Proxy for 'Whiteness': Racial Color-Blindness in Everyday Life." *Women and Therapy* 38, no. 3–4 (2015): 341–55. https://doi.org/10.1080/02703149.2015.1059216.

Treaty between the United States of America and the French Republic ceding the province of Louisiana to the United States. U.S.-Fr. April 30, 1803. *Records Relating to Treaties with Foreign Countries, 1789–2000*. https://catalog.archives.gov/id/306462.

Treaty between the United States of America and the Mexican Republic. Peace, friendship, limits, and settlement. U.S.-MX. February 2, 1848. *Perfected Treaties 1778–1945*. PDF. https://www.loc.gov/item/18014905/.

Treaty of Amity, Settlement, and Limits between the United States of America and His Catholic Majesty. February 19, 1819, 8 Stat. 252.

Treitler, Vilna Bashi. *Ethnic Project: Transforming Racial Fiction into Ethnic Factions*. Stanford CA: Stanford University Press, 2013.

Turley, Ruth N. L. "When Do Neighborhoods Matter? The Role of Race and Neighborhood Peers." *Social Science Research* 32, no. 1 (March 2003): 61–79.

Turner, Jessie. "Reconsidering the Relationship Between New Mestizaje and New Multiraciality as Mixed-Race Identity Models." *Journal of Critical Mixed Race Studies* 1, no. 1 (2014): 133–48. https://doi.org/10.5070/C811021378.

Turner, Victor. *The Forest of Symbols: Aspects of Ndembu Ritual*. Ithaca NY: Cornell University Press, 1967.

Ulentin, Ann. "Free Women of Color and Slaveholding in New Orleans, 1810–1830." Master's thesis, Louisiana State University, 2007.

U.S. Bureau of the Census. "1960 Census of Population: Supplementary Reports: Population Characteristics of Selected Ethnic Groups in the Five Southwestern States." July 1968. https://www.census.gov/library/publications/1968/dec/population-pc-s1-55.html.

———. *1970 Census. General Coding Procedures III-III-A-Attachment C-1*. Washington DC: Government Printing Office, 1970.

———. *1990 Census Alphabetical Race and American Indian Tribe Code List (Outside Data Users)*. April. Washington DC: Government Printing Office, 1992.

———. *Questionnaire Reference Book. 20th Decennial Census—1980*. Form D-561. May. Washington DC: Government Printing Office, 1980.

———. "Race and Ethnicity in the United States: 2010 Census and 2020 Census." August 12, 2021. https://www.census.gov/library/visualizations/interactive/race-and-ethnicity-in-the-united-state-2010-and-2020-census.html.

———. "Redistricting File (Public Law 94-171) Dataset." August 12, 2021. 2020 Census. https://www.census.gov/data/datasets/2020/dec/2020-census-redistricting-summary-file-dataset.html.

U.S. Congress. House. Subcommittee on Census, Statistics and Postal Personnel. *Review of Federal Measurements of Race and Ethnicity*. 103rd Cong., 1st sess., Serial No. 103-7 (April 14; June 30; July 29; November 3, 1993). Washington DC: Government Printing Office.

U.S. Office of Management and Budget. "Recommendations from the Interagency Committee for Review of the Racial and Ethnic Standards to the Office of Management and Budget Concerning Changes to the Standards for the Classification of Federal Data on Race and Ethnicity; Notice." *Federal Register* 62, no. 131 (July 9, 1997).

Vaca, Nicolás C. *The Presumed Alliance: The Unspoken Conflict Between Latinos and Blacks and What It Means for America*. New York: HarperCollins, 2004.

Valdés, Dennis N. "The Decline of Slavery in Mexico." *Americas* 75, no. 1 (2018): 167–94. https://muse.jhu.edu/article/714749.

Valencia, Richard R. "The Mexican American Struggle for Equal Educational Opportunity in *Mendez v. Westminster*: Helping to Pave the Way for *Brown v. Board of Education*." *Teachers College Record* 107, no. 3 (March 2005): 389–423. https://doi.org/10.1111/j.1467-9620.2005.00481.x.

Vasconcelos, José. *La raza cósmica*. Mexico D.F.: Espasa Calpe, S.A, 1925.

Vasquez, Jessica M. "Blurred Borders for Some but Not 'Others': Racialization, 'Flexible Ethnicity,' Gender, and Third-Generation Mexican American Identity." *Sociological Perspectives* 53, no. 1 (March 2010): 45–72. https://doi.org/10.1525/sop.2010.53.1.45.

Vaughn, Bobby. "Afro-Mexico: Blacks, Indígenas, Politics, and the Greater Diaspora." In *Neither Enemies nor Friends: Latinos, Blacks, Afro Latinos*, edited by Anani Dzidzienyo and Suzanne Oboler, 117–36. New York: Palgrave Macmillan, 2005.

Vélez-Ibáñez, Carlos G. "Through the Eyes of an Anthropologist." In *The Chicanos: As We See Ourselves*, edited by Arnulfo Trejo, 37–48. Tucson: University of Arizona Press, 1979.

Vigil, James Diego. "Ethnic Succession and Ethnic Conflict." In *Just Neighbors? Research on African American and Latino Relations in the United States*, edited by Edward Telles, Mark Q. Sawyer, Gaspar Rivera-Salgado, 325–42. New York: Russell Sage Foundation, 2011.

———. *From Indians to Chicanos: The Dynamics of Mexican-American Culture*. 3rd ed. Long Grove IL: Waveland, 1998.

Viglione, Jill, Lance Hannon, and Robert DeFina. "The Impact of Light Skin on Prison Time for Black Female Offenders." *Social Science Journal* 48, no. 1 (2011): 250–58. https://doi.org/10.1016/j.soscij.2010.08.003.

Vinson, Ben, III. *Before Mestizaje: The Frontiers of Race and Caste in Colonial Mexico*. New York: Cambridge University Press, 2018.

Volpp, Leti. "American Mestizo Filipinos and Antimiscegenation Laws in California." In *Loving v. Virginia in a Postracial World: Rethinking Race, Sex, and Marriage*, edited by Kevin Noble Maillard and Rose Cuison Villazor, 59–72. Cambridge, UK: Cambridge University Press, 2012.

Wade, T. Joel., Melanie Judkins Romano, and Leslie Blue. "The Effect of African American Skin Color on Hiring Practices." *Journal of Applied Social Psychology* 34, no. 12 (2004): 2550–58. https://doi.org/10.1111/j.1559-1816.2004.tb01991.x.

Wallace, Kendra R. *Relative/Outsider: The Art and Politics of Identity among Mixed Heritage Students*. Westport CT: Ablex, 2001.

Wang, Wendy. "The Rise of Intermarriage: Rates, Characteristics Vary by Race and Gender." Pew Research Center, Social and Demographic Trends Project. February 16, 2012. http://www.pewsocialtrends.org/2012/02/16/the-rise-of-intermarriage/.

Wardle, Francis. "Are You Sensitive to Interracial Children's Special Identity Needs?" *Young Children* 4, no. 2 (January 1987): 53–59. https://www.jstor.org/stable/42725878.

Warikoo, Natasha Kumar. "Racial Authenticity among Second Generation Youth in Multiethnic New York and London." *Poetics* 36, no. 6 (December 2007): 388–408. https://doi.org/10.1016/j.poetic.2007.09.001.

Waring, Chandra D. L., and Bandana Purkayastha. "'I'm a Different Kind of

Biracial': How Black/White Biracial Americans with Immigrant Parents Negotiate Race." *Social Identities* 23, no. 5 (2017): 614–30.
Warren, Jonathan, and Christina A. Sue. "Comparative Racisms: What Anti-Racists Can Learn from Latin America." *Ethnicities* 11, no. 1 (2011): 32–58. https://doi.org/10.1177/1468796810388699.
Warren, Jonathan W., and France Winddance Twine. "White Americans, the New Minority? Non-Blacks and the Ever-Expanding Boundaries of Whiteness." *Journal of Black Studies* 28, no. 2 (November 1997): 200–218. https://doi.org/10.1177/002193479702800204.
Washington, Myra S. *Blasian Invasion: Race Mixing in the Celebrity Industrial Complex*. Jackson: University Press of Mississippi, 2017.
Waters, Mary C. "Multiple Ethnicities and Identity Choices: Some Implications for Race and Ethnic Relations in the United States." In *We Are a People: Narrative and Multiplicity in Ethnic Identity*, edited by Paul Spickard and W. Jeffrey Burroughs, 23–40. Philadelphia: Temple University Press, 2000.
Watson, David, and Kristin Naragon. "Positive Affectivity: The Disposition to Experience Positive Emotional States." In *Oxford Handbook of Positive Psychology*, 2nd ed., edited by C. R. Snyder and Shane J. Lopez, 207–15. New York: Oxford University Press, 2009.
Weaver, Hilary N. "Recognizing Our Past and Moving Toward Our Future: Decolonizing Attitudes about Skin Color and Native Americans." *Journal of Indigenous Social Development* 4, no. 1 (2015): 1–15. http://hdl.handle.net/10125/37627.
Weber, David J. *The Spanish Frontier in North America*. New Haven CT: Yale University Press, 1992.
West, Candice, and Sarah Fenstermaker. "Doing Difference." *Gender and Society* 9, no. 1 (February 1995): 8–37. http://www.jstor.org/stable/189596.
Wijeyesinghe, Charmaine L. "The Intersectional Model of Multiracial Identity: Integrating Multiracial Identity Theories and Intersectional Perspectives on Social Identity." In *New Perspectives on Racial Identity Development: Integrating Emerging Frameworks*, 2nd ed., edited by Charmaine L. Wijeyesinghe and Bailey W. Jackson, 81–107. New York: New York University Press, 2012.
Wilber, Ken. *Integral Psychology: Consciousness, Spirit, Psychology, Therapy*. Boston: Shambhala, 2000.
Williams, Kim M. *Mark One or More: Civil Rights in Multiracial America*. Ann Arbor: University of Michigan Press, 2008.
———. "Recursive Outcomes of the Multiracial Movement and the End of American Racial Categories." *Studies in American Political Development* 31, no. 1 (April 2017): 88–107. https://doi.org/10.1017/S0898588X17000074.

Williams, Teresa K., Cynthia L. Nakashima, George Kitahara Kich, and G. Reginald Daniel. "Being Different Together in the University Classroom: Multiracial Identity as Transgressive Education." In *The Multiracial Experience: Racial Borders as the New Frontier*, edited by Maria P. P. Root, 359–79. Thousand Oaks CA: Sage Publications, 1996.

Williams-León, Teresa K., and Cynthia L. Nakashima. "Reconfiguring Race, Rearticulating Ethnicity." In *The Sum of Our Parts: Mixed-Heritage Asian Americans*, edited by Teresa Williams-León and Cynthia L. Nakashima, 3–10. Philadelphia: Temple University Press, 2001.

Williamson, Joel. *New People: Mulattoes and Miscegenation in the United States*. New York: New York University Press, 1984.

Wilson, Carter A. *Racism: From Slavery to Advanced Capitalism*. Thousand Oaks CA: Sage Publications, 1996.

Wilson, Terry. "Blood Quantum: Native American Mixed Bloods." In *Racially Mixed People in America*, edited by Maria P. P. Root, 3–11. Newberry Park CA: Sage Publications, 1992.

Wilton, Leigh S., Diana T. Sanchez, and Julie A. Garcia. "The Stigma of Privilege: Racial Identity and Stigma Consciousness among Biracial Individuals." *Race and Social Problems* 5, no. 1 (2013): 41–56. https://doi.org/10.1007/s12552-012-9083-5.

Wright, Roy Dean, and Susan N. Wright. "A Plea for a Further Refinement of the Marginal Man." *Phylon* 33, no. 4 (1972): 361–68. https://www.jstor.org/stable/273681.

Yoo, Hyung Chol, Kelly F. Jackson, Rudy P. Guevarra, Matthew J. Miller, and Blair Harrington. "Construction and Initial Validation of the Multiracial Experience Measure (MEM)." *Journal of Counseling Psychology* 63, no. 2 (2016): 198–209. https://doi.org/10.1037/cou0000117.

Yosso, Tara, William A. Smith, Miguel Ceja, and Daniel Solórzano. "Critical Race Theory: Racial Microaggressions, and Campus Racial Climate for Latina/o Undergraduates." *Harvard Educational Review* 79, no. 4 (December 2009): 659–90. https://doi.org/10.17763/haer.79.4.m6867014157m707l.

Zack, Naomi. *Race and Mixed Race*. Philadelphia: Temple University Press, 1993.

Zamora, Sylvia. "Framing Commonality in a Multiracial, Multiethnic Coalition." In *Just Neighbors? Research on African American and Latino Relations in the United States*, edited by Edward Telles, Mark Q. Sawyer, and Gaspar Rivera-Salgado, 299–322. New York: Russell Sage Foundation, 2011.

———. "Mexican Illegality, Black Citizenship, and White Power: Immigrant Perceptions of the U.S. Socioracial Hierarchy." *Journal of Ethnic and Migration Studies* 44, no. 11 (2018): 1897–914. https://doi.org/10.1080/1369183X.2017.1352466.

———. *Racial Baggage: Mexican Immigrants and Race Across the Border*. Stanford CA: Stanford University Press, 2022.

Zamora, Sylvia, and Chinyere Osuji. "Mobilizing African Americans for Immigrant Rights: Framing Strategies in Two Multi-Racial Coalitions." *Latino Studies* 12, no. 3 (September 2014): 424–48. https://doi.org/10.1057/lst.2014.47.

Index

ACLU. *See* American Civil Liberties Union (ACLU)
"acting Black," 174, 222, 224
"acting white," 217, 222
Adams-Onís Treaty of 1819, 46–47
adolescence, racial identity formation in, 126
adoption: into Native American tribes, 110; transracial, 133–34
affirmative action, 60, 262–63, 280n20, 292n5, 305n17
Africa: food of, 163; origins of humans in, 2, 267n3
African American, term of, 9. *See also* Black Americans
African American identity. *See* Black identity
African American vernacular English, 157
African descent, term of, 9–10
African diaspora, 2
African slaves. *See* slaves, African
Afro-Brazilians, 160
Afro-Latinos, 177–78
afromestizos, 75
AfroMex, 125. *See also* Blaxican(s)
Afro-Mexican Americans, 5, 74, 284n35
Afro-Mexicans, 74–76; Black identity of, 74; vs. Black Latinos, 112; vs.
Blaxicans, 5, 129; Chicano identity of, 74–76; colonial population of, 37; invisibility of, 177–78; in Mexican census, 75, 214; term of, 5, 125
Akwid (musical group), 162
Alabama, racial order of, 44, 46–47
Albert Bennett (pseudonym), 132t, 153, 240–41
albinos, 276n26
Allen, Robert L., 58
alliances, Black-Brown. *See* Black-Brown alliances
Alta California, 62
AMEA. *See* Association of MultiEthnic Americans (AMEA)
American Civil Liberties Union (ACLU), 85, 293n47
American creed, 48, 49, 56–57
American Dilemma, 57
American identity, whiteness in, 79–80
American Journal of Sociology, 23
American Revolution, 104
American Sociological Association (ASA), 24
American Sociological Review, 23
ancestry: in ethnicity, 8; vs. identity, multiraciality in, 1, 130; notions of race based on, 2–3; in racial formation theory, 7; in racial identities,

ancestry (*continued*)
3–6; "What are you?" questions about, 196–200
Anderson, Benedict, 184
Andrea Avila (pseudonym): on authenticity policing, 230–31; on Black-Brown relations, 237, 242, 256–57; on community of Blaxicans, 181–82; on diversity of Blaxican experiences, 122–23; on invisibility of Blaxicans, 176–77; parents and identity of, 136t; strategies for identity expression by, 153, 158–59
Anglo-America: binary racial order of, 10, 33–36; definition of, 276n1; interracial relationships in, 35–36; ternary racial order of, 10, 43–46
Anglo-Americans, term of, 10. *See also* white Americans
anti-Black racism. *See* racism
anticolonialism, 76–77
antiessentialism, 76
antimiscegenation laws: Black white couples as target of, 18, 36, 86, 269n12; in colonial Anglo-America, 35–36; Mexican Americans' exemption from, 66; of Native American tribes, 109, 110; one-drop rule in, 35–36; overturning of, 83–85; in Virginia, 36, 85, 105
Antonio Tijerina (pseudonym), 127–30, 148t, 154, 170, 201–2
Anzaldúa, Gloria, 76, 180, 223
appearances. *See* phenotypes (physical appearance)
ASA. *See* American Sociological Association (ASA)
Asian Americans in interracial relationships, 22, 87, 101

Asian American studies, 22
Asian Black multiracials, 29, 100–104, 114–15
Asian Mexican multiracials, 18, 98–100
Asian slaves in colonial Mexico, 284n33
Asian white multiracials, 27, 90, 114–15
Aslakson, Kenneth, 277n4
assimilation: as goal of integration, 58, 82, 262; vs. integrative pluralism, 59, 280n19; of Mexican Americans, 69–70, 72–73; of Native Americans, 106; and Talented Tenth, 54
Association of MultiEthnic Americans (AMEA), 89, 292n27
Attucks, Crispus, 104
authenticity: of Black Americans, 216–17; of Black Asians, 102; of Black Latinos, 113; of Black Native Americans, 111; of Blaxicans, 149–52
authenticity policing: Black, 216–18; of Blaxicans, 209–32; definition of, 210–11; gender in, 212, 214–15, 220, 228–31; goals of, 211; Mexican, 212–16; overlapping Black and Mexican, 218–26; phenotype in, 213, 217–18, 226–31

baby boom, biracial, 87, 288n25
Bacalski-Martínez, Roberto R., 77, 285n54
backlash, white, 262–63, 305n17
balancing, multiracial, 151–56, 174
Banks, Ingrid, 226
Baptist religion, 167–69
Bean, Frank D., 27, 28
beauty standards, 226, 228–30

INDEX

Bell, Derrick, 306n22
Biden, Joe, 263
Biltmore Six case, 73
binary racial order: of Anglo-America, 10, 33–36; of California and Southwest, 67, 80–81; in dual-minority multiracial identities, 98; of Louisiana and Gulf Coast, 47; origins and history of, 17–18; in sociology, 17. *See also* one-drop rule
biological determinism, 2, 6, 53, 64, 262
biracial, term of, 9. *See also* multiracial, term of
Black: "acting," 174, 222, 224; term of, 9, 59
Black Americans: anti-Mexican sentiment among, 230, 242–48; authenticity markers of, 216–17; authenticity policing by, 218–26; colorism among, 52–53, 92; controlling images of, 194, 217; food of, 162–66; Great Migration of, 54, 56; masculinity in, 103; as mostly multiracial by 1920s, 53; multigenerational multiraciality of, 4, 129–30; phenotypes of, 53, 226–30; stereotypes of, 103, 135, 138, 194, 202; term of, 9; "What are you?" questions asked by, 199–200. *See also* Blaxican(s); one-drop rule
Black and Brown in Los Angeles (Kun and Pulido), 253–54
Blackapina identity, 102–3
Black Asian multiracials, 29, 100–104, 114–15
Black Brazilians, 160
Black-Brown alliances, 251–60; Blaxicans' sense of responsibility for building, 255–60; both/neither identity in, 255–57; counternarratives about, 252–60; as focus of scholarship, 233, 252–54
Black-Brown divide, 233–50; in Blaxican identity, 240–45; in Blaxicans' families, 245–50; counternarratives to, 252–60; as focus of scholarship, 233; issue of immigration in, 235–38; media coverage of, 234–40, 252
Black Chicanas, 125. *See also* Blaxican(s)
Black dual-minority multiracials: Black Asians as, 29, 100–104, 114–15; Black Latinos as, 112–14; Black Native Americans as, 104–11; marginalization of, 98, 114–15. *See also* Blaxican(s)
Black exceptionalism, 115
Black hair, 226, 228–29
Black identity: of African Americans, 11, 20, 52–60, 81–82, 216–17; of Afro-Mexicans, 74; of Black Latinos, 112–13; of Black white multiracials, 28, 124; of Blasians, 103–4; of Chicanos, 74, 75. *See also* one-drop rule
Black Latino multiracials, 112–14. *See also* Blaxican(s)
Black liberation, 217
Black Lives Matter, 259–60, 263
Black masculinity, 103
Black Muslims, 59
Black nationalism, 16, 58, 82
Black Native American multiracials, 104–11
Blackness: in civil rights movement, 60; "commonsense" definitions of, 3, 18, 49; controlling images in ideas about, 194, 217; legal definitions of,

Blackness (*continued*)
49; paranoia about invisible, 53.
See also one-drop rule
Black Panthers, 58, 254, 257
Black Power, 16, 58–60
Black pride, 16, 53, 58–60
Black racism, 230
Black separatism, 58
Blacksicans, 125. *See also* Blaxican(s)
Black studies, 21–22, 171–72, 175
Black vernacular English, 157
Black white binary. *See* binary racial order; one-drop rule
Black white couples: in colonial America, 34–36, 43–44; statistics on, 86–87; as target of antimiscegenation laws, 18, 36, 86, 269n12
Black white multiracials: baby boom of, 87, 288n25; Black identity of, 28, 124; and both racial and cultural identity, 121; census data on, 89–90; as focus of scholarship, 96
Black women: controlling images of, 194, 217; phenotypes of, 217, 226–30
Blakanese identity, 102
Blasian identity, 103–4. *See also* Black Asian multiracials
Blasian Invasion (Washington), 103–4
Blatina identity, 113
Blauner, Robert, 15–16, 58
Blaxican(s): vs. Afro-Mexicans, 5, 129; community of, 131, 178–85; demographics of study participants, 120–21, 121t; diversity of experiences of, 122–23; as first-generation multiracials, 5, 129, 149–50; in interracial relationships, 246–50; other terms for, 125; term of, 10, 123–31. *See also* parents of Blaxicans

Blaxicana, 125–26
Blaxican authenticity. *See* authenticity
Blaxican community, 131, 178–85
Blaxican identity: in borderlands space, 6, 119, 180, 212, 223; as both/neither identity, 169, 231–32, 255–57; cultural strategies for expressing, 156–69; as designation of choice, 125–31; first-generation status of, 5, 129, 149–50; as form of resistance to monoraciality, 3–5, 122, 247, 255; future of, 188; invisibility of, 176–78; marginalization of, 177, 206, 223; as new form of identity, 130–31; as public vs. internalized identity, 123–24; racial strategies for expressing, 152–56; shared understandings of, 149–52; shifting between Black and Mexican elements in, 150; shifts over lifetime in, 124, 126; whiteness in, lack of, 195; work involved in claiming, 209–10, 225–26. *See also specific aspects and influences*
Blaxican phenotypes: authenticity policing based on, 213, 217–18, 226–31; in expressions of Blaxican identity, 152–56, 226; vs. Mexican phenotypes, 212–13; vs. white multiracial phenotypes, 124–25
blood purity, 40–41
blood quantum, 108, 110
blue-vein societies, 52–53, 92
body language, 211, 241
Bond, Julian, 58
Bonilla-Silva, Eduardo, 261
book bans, 264
borderism, 211

INDEX 357

borderlands space, Blaxican identities in, 6, 119, 180, 212, 223
border patrolling, 211
both/and identity, 91, 256
both/neither identity: Blaxicans' approach to, 169, 231–32, 255–57; multiracials' embrace of, 91; work involved in claiming, 210
boundary crossing, 211, 234, 246–47
Boykin, Keith, 264
Bracero Program, 70
Bratter, Jennifer, 28, 29
Brazil: Black Brazilians in, 160; interracial relationships in, 170; ternary racial order of, 170
Brazilian identity, 170
Brooks, James F., 109
Brown, Michael, 259
Brown Berets, 254, 257
Brown-Black relations. *See* Black-Brown alliances; Black-Brown divide
Brown identity, 74–75, 206
"browning," 53
Brown Power, 280n16
Brown v. Board of Education, 57, 72, 84, 85, 269n25
Butler, Henrietta, 58

California: Afro-Mexicans in, 74; antimiscegenation laws in, 83–84; Blaxican identity in, 185–86; gangs in, 143–44, 233; gold in, 282n19; immigration to, 62–63; Mexican Asians in, 98–100; multiracial identity in, 185–86, 197, 298n29; prisons of, 143; racial composition of, 61–62, 66, 185, 297n24; racial order of, history of, 11, 61–67; segregation in, 68, 71, 143; slaves in, 63–65, 282n19. *See also specific locations*
Californios, 62–67
Cannon, Sarita, 111
capital: racial, 261–62; sociocultural, 15, 280n15
capoeira, 160
carceral identities, 143–44
Carmichael, Stokely, 58
Carter, Mitzi Uehara, 102
caste system in Latin America, 39–40
castizos, 40, 276n26
Castro v. Superior Court, 73
Catholicism: in Blaxican identity, 166–69; purity of blood in, 40–41
Caucasian Race Resolution of 1943 (Texas), 70
censorship, book, 264
census, Mexican, 75, 214
census, U.S.: of 1890, 53; of 1930, 70; of 1940, 70, 78; of 1980, 78; of 1990, 22–23, 89; of 2000, 22, 24, 78–80, 89, 185; of 2010, 24, 78–80, 89–90, 297n24; of 2020, 79, 90; Blaxicans in, 124; definitions of race in, 23; Hispanic category of, 77–80; Hispanics' answers to questions on, 77–80, 90, 114; interracial marriage in, 86; Latinos in, 78–80; on majority-minority multiracials, 89–90; Mexican Americans in, 70, 78–80; mulattoes vs. Blacks in, 53; multiple boxes allowed on, 22–23, 89–90, 273n56; multiracial movement's effects on, 22–23, 88–89; of multiracial population of California, 185, 297n24; in rise of scholarship on multiraciality, 24
Census Bureau, U.S., 287n76

Cherokees, 106–11
Chicana/o identity, 72–82; of Afro-Mexicans, 74–76; Black identity and, 74, 75; gender in, 76, 285n48; *mestizaje* in, 73–77, 81; race vs. ethnicity in, 77–79; strategic essentialism in, 76; term of, 9, 73
Chicana/o studies, 22, 171–72, 175
Chicanas, Black, 125. *See also* Blaxican(s)
Chicanismo, 73–77
Chicano movement, 73–77
Chicano nationalism, 82
Chicanozaje, 77
Chickasaws, 106–9
Chinese Black multiracials, 100–101
Chinese immigrants, 100–101
chinos, 284n33
Choctaws, 106–9
Christianity: in Blaxican identity, 166–69; purity of blood in, 40–41
Christmas, 142, 164, 166
cities, Black migration to, 54
Citizens' Committee, 48–49, 278n22
citizenship, tribal, 108–9
citizenship, U.S.: in Adams-Onís Treaty, 46–47; in Louisiana Purchase, 46; for Mexican Americans, 63–64, 65–66; for Native Americans, 108; in Reconstruction, 48–49, 278n17
Civil Rights Act of 1866, 278n17
Civil Rights Act of 1875, 278n17
Civil Rights Act of 1964, 85, 269n25
civil rights movement: acceptance of one-drop rule in, 57–58, 60; Black identity in, 57–58, 60; Creoles in, 92; growth in interracial marriages after, 21; immigrant rights as next struggle in, 236; integration as goal of, 57, 82; interracial marriage as issue in, 84; sociologists' failure to anticipate, 15–17
Civil War, American, 47
Claudio Holmes (pseudonym), 132t, 134
Cline, Sarah, 38, 40
CMRS. *See* critical mixed race studies (CMRS)
code-switching in Blaxican identity, 157–59
Cody, Radmilla, 111
coerced labor, 34
Cogdell, Josephine, 279n11
Coleman, Arica L., 106
collective subjectivity in Blaxican identity, 169, 184–88
colleges: affirmative action in admissions to, 262–63, 305n17; in Blaxican identity, 171–76; intellectual diversity at, 264
Collins, Patricia Hill, 229–30
colonialism: internal, 59; origins of concept of race in, 1–2; in Third World, 58. *See also specific locations*
colorblind ideology, 79–80, 261
colorblind racism, 261–62
Colored, term of, 59
colorism: in authenticity policing, 227; among Black Americans, 52–53, 92; in Mexico, 75, 192–93, 207; in Vietnam, 102
color line, 211
coming-of-age ceremonies, 167
Comité des Citoyens, 48–49, 278n22
community, Blaxicans' sense of, 131, 178–85
Concreet, 260

concubinage in colonial era, 35, 36, 38, 44
Congressional Hearings on Racial Census Categories, 89
Congressional Hispanic Caucus, 78
Connecticut, Native Americans in, 104
consciousness: double, 55; mestiza, 76–77; postcolonial, 76–77
controlling images, 194, 217
conversos, 41
cooperation, Black-Brown. *See* Black-Brown alliances
coparenting in Blaxican identity, 141–48, 141t, 147t
counternarratives to Black-Brown divide, 252–60
Creeks, 106–10
Creoles: definitions of, 46, 47; multiracial identity of, 92–93; in racial order, 46–51
The Crisis (magazine), 53–54
critical legal studies, 31
critical mixed race studies (CMRS), 29–32
Critical Mixed Race Studies Association, 30
Critical Mixed Race Studies conferences, 30
critical multiraciality, 265–66
critical race theory (CRT), 31, 306n22
CRT. *See* critical race theory (CRT)
cryptomelanism, 53
Cullen, Countee, 54
cultural authenticity. *See* authenticity
cultural crossfaders, 162
cultural identities: of Black Americans, 55; and Blaxican identity, 123, 132, 151; definition of, 131; vs. racial identities, 131, 151

cultural integration, 16–17, 58
cultural socialization, 132, 140–42, 148. *See also* parents
cultural strategies for expressing Blaxican identity, 156–69
cultural traditions in Blaxican identity, 166–69
culture: in ethnicity, 8–9; transmission of, 250. *See also specific cultures*
Curtis Sandoval (pseudonym), 136t

DaCosta, Kimberly M., 114
Dalmage, Heather, 211
dance in Blaxican identity, 135, 159–61, 220–22
Dan Gonzales (pseudonym): on Black-Brown divide, 247–48; on Blaxican community, 182–83; parents and identity of, 142t, 160–61; strategies for identity expression by, 160–61, 166
Daniel, G. Reginald, 23, 185, 197, 270n40, 271nn41–42, 298n29
Davenport, Lauren D., 187
Davis, F. James, 18
Davis, Sylvester, 83–84
Dawes Act. *See* General Allotment Act of 1887
Dawes Commission, 108
Dawes Roll, 108
Debra Gibbons (pseudonym), 141t, 142, 170–71, 199
Degler, Carl, 280n15
Delinquent Habits (musical group), 126
Demitrius Hunter (pseudonym), 142t
Democratic Party, 307n26
demographics of study participants, 120–21, 121t

Desire Campbell (pseudonym): on authenticity policing, 215–16; on Black-Brown divide, 240; on choice of Blaxican identity, 125–26; parents and identity of, 141t, 142, 144–46; strategies for identity expression by, 156, 165
Día de los Muertos, 142
Diaz, Manuel, 260
Diaz, Monina, 113
divide. *See* Black-Brown divide
double consciousness, 55
Douglass, William A., 227
Dowling, Julie A., 79–80
doxa, 4
dual-minority multiracials, 11–12, 96–115; Black Asians as, 29, 100–104, 114–15; Black Latinos as, 112–14; Black Native Americans as, 104–11; gaps in scholarship on, 31, 96; hypodescent rules applied to, 18–19; invisibility of, in popular culture, 176–77; marginalization of, 98, 114–15; Mexican Asians as, 18, 98–100; in racial hierarchy, 18–19, 98; racism experienced by, 98, 113–15; vs. white multiracials, experiences of, 96–98; whiteness in identity of, lack of, 98; work involved in identity claims of, 209–10. *See also specific groups*
dual oppression, 258–59
Du Bois, W. E. B., 53–55
due process, 84

East LA Thirteen case, 73
Eduardo Tijerina (pseudonym): on Black-Brown alliances, 257–58; on Black-Brown divide, 235–37; on choice of Blaxican identity, 127–29; on neighborhood influences, 204–5, 208; parents and identity of, 147t; on social clubs, 173–74; strategies for identity expression by, 161–62; on "What are you?" questions, 196–97
education. *See* colleges; schools
either/or identity: and Black-Brown divide, 235, 238, 242, 244, 247; Blaxicans' approach to, 169, 256–57; multiracials' rejection of, 91
elections. *See* presidential elections
Eli Maciel (pseudonym), 136t, 137–38, 244–45
elite: Black, 52–55, 92; in colonial Latin America, 39–40; in colonial Southwest, 62–65; controlling images created by, 194
Eliza Montes (pseudonym), 132t, 134–35, 214–15
Emancipation Proclamation, 278n17
encomienda system, 275n12
English language in code-switching, 157–59
entitlement, spatial, 253
epidemics, 37, 275n11
equal protection clause, 71–73, 84, 85
Erica Donald (pseudonym): on authenticity policing, 218–20, 228–29; on Black-Brown alliances, 258; on Blaxican community, 178–82; on choice of Blaxican identity, 128–29; on invisibility of Blaxicans, 177–78; parents and identity of, 136t; on social clubs, 174–75; strategies for identity expression by, 156, 165–66
Españoles, 39, 62
Espinoza, Pedro, 238
essentialism, strategic, 76, 285n47

ethnic cues, 227
ethnicity: culture in, 8–9; definition of, 8; Hispanic as, 77–80; vs. race, 8, 267n20, 285n56; terms for, 8–10
ethnic studies: in Blaxican identity, 171–72, 175; in critical mixed race studies, 31; history of field of, 21–24
ethnic succession, 237
Eugenics, 105
European Americans, term of, 10. *See also* white Americans
European colonialism, origins of concept of race in, 1–2. *See also specific locations*
European descent, term of, 10
European identity, 97, 292n5
European immigrants, 16, 34–37, 267n20
evolution, human, 2, 267n3
exceptionalism, Black, 115
excluded middle, law of the, 4
exoticization, 196, 214–15

Facebook groups, 182–83
facial morphology, 2. *See also* phenotypes (physical appearance)
Fair Housing Act of 1968, 85–86, 269n25
families, Black-Brown divide in, 245–50. *See also* parents
Farnham, Thomas Jefferson, 64
favoritism, 231
feminists, Chicana, 76
Fenstermaker, Sarah, 32
Fernando Thomas (pseudonym), 142t, 161, 163–64
Fifteenth Amendment, 48–50, 278n17
Filipino Black multiracials, 102–3
Filipino Mexican multiracials, 18, 99

first-generation multiracials: Blaxicans as, 5, 129, 149–50; Loving Generation as, 87, 149; multiracial identity of, 90; as target of hypodescent, 18
Five Civilized Tribes, 106–10
Flagg, Barbara, 97
flexibility in identities, 18, 27–28
Florida, racial order of, 44, 46–47
Floyd, George, 259, 263
folklórico, 160, 220–22
food in Blaxican identity, 162–66
Fourteenth Amendment, 48–50, 71–73, 84, 85, 278n17
France, Louisiana under, 43–46
fraternities in Blaxican identity, 172–76
Free Coloreds: in Anglo-America, 35; in Latin America, 41–42; in Louisiana and Gulf Coast, 44–47, 277n1
freedmen, 107–10
Frey, William, 86–87

Gaby Porter (pseudonym): on Black-Brown divide, 235, 245–46; on choice of Blaxican identity, 126–27, 130–31; on neighborhood influences, 205–6, 208; parents and identity of, 148t; strategies for identity expression by, 159, 168–69; on "What are you?" questions, 197
Galarza, Ernesto, 77
Gallegos, Herman, 77
gangs, 143–44, 233, 237, 239
Garner, Eric, 259
Garvey, Marcus, 55
gender: in authenticity policing, 212, 214–15, 220, 228–31; in Blasian identity, 103; in Chicano movement, 76,

gender (continued)
  285n48; in cultural socialization,
    140, 141–42, 148
gender discrimination in Mexico, 192
gender ratio, colonial, 34, 37, 43
General Allotment Act of 1887, 107–8
genetics in concept of race, 2–3
genotypes, 2–3, 8
gente de razón, 40, 62
gente sin razón, 40, 62
Georgia, colonial, 277n1
Gerardo Jones (pseudonym), 142t, 154
GI Forum (GIF), 283n11
Glassner, Barry, 238
global perspective on race in Blaxican identity, 169–71, 206–7
Goldberg, David Theo, 7
gold in California, 282n19
"good hair," 217, 229–30
Gramsci, Antonio, 262
grandfather clauses, 50, 279n26
Great Migration, 54, 56
Great Replacement theory, 263
Gross, Ariela, 65
groupness, sense of, 187–88
Guadalupe Hidalgo, Treaty of, 64, 65–66
Guardado, Andrés, 259–60
Guevarra, Rudy P., Jr., 99
Gulf Coast, racial order of, 10–11, 43–51

hair: in authenticity policing, 226–31; Black, 226, 228–29; in Blaxican identity, 152–56, 226; "good," 217, 229–30; mixed, 153; as racial trait, 2. *See also* phenotypes (physical appearance)
Haitian revolution, 45, 277n1

Hall, Christine C. I., 101, 292n27
Hapas, 114, 295n86
Harlem Renaissance, 53–55, 58, 59
Harris, Kamala, 26, 273n57
Harris, Mavin, 268n11
Hawai'i: multiracial identity in, 298n29; Native Hawaiians in, 295n86; racial composition of, 297n24
Hayes, Rutherford B., 48
Hayes-Tilden Compromise of 1877, 48
Heaton, Zak, 103
hegemony, white, 95, 195, 262
Hendrix, Jimi, 111
Herman, Melissa, 200
Hernandez, Pete, 72
Hernández, Tanya Katerí, 74, 75
Hernandez v. Texas, 72
Hertel, Bradley R., 290n53
higher education. *See* colleges
hip-hop music, 126, 140, 220
Hispanic as racial vs. ethnic category, 77–80
Hispanicized Indigenous people, 61–62
Hispanics: answers to census questions by, 77–80, 90, 114; as percentage of U.S. population, 233, 287n76; term of, 9, 78. *See also* Latinas/os
Hodges, Teresa, 102
Hondagneu-Sotelo, Pierrette, 254
Hoskins, Bruce C., 27, 28–29
housing segregation, 240–42, 251–52
Houston, Charles Hamilton, 56
Houston, Velina Hasu, 101
Hughes, Langston, 54
Hughes, Michael, 290n53
human genome, 2
humans, origins and evolution of, 2, 267n3
Hunter, Margaret L., 227

Hurston, Zora Neale, 54
hybrid degeneracy, 24
hypodescent: applicability of, to non-Black dual minorities, 18–19; vs. monoraciality, 20; origins and meaning of, 17–19, 268n11. *See also* one-drop rule

identities. *See specific identities*
Ifekwunigwe, Jayne, 30
images, controlling, 194, 217
imagined communities, 184
immigration: in Black-Brown divide, 235–38; in Great Replacement theory, 263; in growth of interracial marriage, 86; and immigrant rights, 235–38. *See also specific locations*
Immigration and Nationality Act of 1965, 86, 270n25
included middle, law of the, 91, 235, 244
indentured servitude, 34–36
Indian Removal Act of 1830, 107
Indian Territory, 107, 110
Indigenous people: enslavement of, 37, 63, 275n12; epidemics among, 37, 275n11; Hispanicized, 61–62; in racial order of Latin America, 37–41, 275n12; in racial order of Southwest, 61–63. *See also* Native American(s)
individualism, 261, 262
Instagram, 183
integration, racial: assimilation and, 58, 82, 262; vs. cultural integration, 16–17, 58; as goal of civil rights movement, 57, 82; in order-functionalist paradigm, 15; in power-conflict paradigm, 16–17; selective, 94–95, 261–62, 265. *See also* segregation
integrative multiracial identity, 91
integrative pluralism, 59–60, 280n19
intellectual diversity, 264
interethnic discrimination, 211
intergenerational transfer of multiracial identities, 23, 28–29, 188
intergroup prejudice, Black and Mexican American, 193–96, 242–49
internal colonialism, 59
internalized identities vs. public identities, 123–24
internal miscegenation, 53
internet, Blaxican community on, 180–85
interracial relationships: as civil rights movement issue, 84; gaps in scholarship on children of, 25–27; legalization of, 83–85; in rise of multiracial identities, 11, 83–87; social changes in growth of, 21, 86–87; statistics on racial composition of, 86–87. *See also* antimiscegenation laws; *and specific groups and locations*
intragroup authenticity policing. *See* authenticity policing
intragroup marginalization, 192, 223
intraracial discrimination, 211
invisibility: of Blackness, 53; of Blaxican identity, 176–78; of Native Americans, 176
Irish Americans, 292n5
Italian Americans, 292n5

Jackie Jones (pseudonym), 136t, 194, 249–50

Jackson, Andrew, 107
Jackson, Ketanji Brown, 264
Jackson, María Rosario, 209
James Ramsey (pseudonym), 142–44, 142t, 150, 154–55, 162
Japanese Black multiracials, 101–2, 114–15
Jenny Griffin (pseudonym), 142t, 243–44, 248–49
Jermaine Wallace (pseudonym), 142t
Jesus Sanchez (pseudonym), 132t, 190
Jeter, Musie Byrd, 105
Jeter, Theoliver, 105
Jewish people, 40–41
Jim Crow segregation laws: Creoles under, 50–51; and Harlem Renaissance, 53–55; in monoracial Black identity, 11, 52–58; one-drop rule in, 52–53; overturning of, 56–57
Jiménez, Tomás, 37–38
John Jackson (pseudonym), 142t, 190, 206–8
Johnson, Dwayne "The Rock," 103
Johnson, Elaine, 114–15
Johnson, Gaye Theresa, 253
Johnson, James Weldon, 54
Johnson, Lyman, 58
Johnson, Lyndon B., 78, 280n20
Johnston, Marc P., 20
Johnston-Guerrero, Marc P., 217, 265
Jones, Rhett S., 20
Jordan, Winthrop D., 18, 250
Journal of Critical Mixed Race Studies, 30, 274n77
Julia Miramar (pseudonym), 127, 147t, 152, 192
jurors, 72, 73

Justice Department, U.S., 293n47
Kemo the Blaxican, 126
Kennedy, Robert F., 293n47
Khanna, Nikki, 123–24, 199
Kidd, May Street, 57
King O'Riain, Rebecca C., 210
kin networks, 145
knowledge, multiracial, 265
Korean Black multiracials, 102
Kun, Josh, 6, 162, 253–54

labor market, Black-Brown competition in, 251–52
Ladner, Joyce, 15–16
land: of Mexicans in Southwest, 65–66, 68; of Native Americans, 106–8
LAPD. *See* Los Angeles Police Department (LAPD)
la Raza, 73–74
Las Posadas, 142, 166
Latin America: vs. Anglo-America, 33; Indigenous people in, 37–41, 275n12; interracial relationships in, 37–39; mulatto escape hatch in, 58, 280n15; slaves in, 37, 39–42, 275n12; ternary racial order of, 37–42
Latin American identity, 69
Latin Americans, term of, 69
Latinas/os: census responses of, 78–80; Hispanic identity of, 78; in interracial relationships, 87; as percentage of U.S. population, 233, 287n76; race vs. ethnicity in identity of, 78; term of, 9, 214. *See also specific groups*
Latinidad, 169
"Latin" North America, 276n1. *See also specific locations*

Latino-Black alliances. *See* Black-Brown alliances
Latino-Black divide. *See* Black-Brown divide
Latino Black multiracials, 112–14. *See also* Blaxican(s)
Latino white multiracials, 27–28
LaTrice Johnson (pseudonym): on authenticity policing, 224–25; on learning about racism, 193–94; neighborhood influences on, 208; parents and identity of, 120, 129, 136–37, 136t; on social clubs, 172–73; strategies for identity expression by, 159, 161, 166
League of United Latin American Citizens (LULAC), 69–72, 81
Lee, Jennifer, 27, 28
Legal Defense and Education Fund, NAACP, 56–57
legal-political realm vs. social realm, 49, 56–57
legal studies, critical, 31
Leonard, Karen Isaken, 98, 125
Lewis, Laura A., 40
Lewis, Mary Edmonia, 111
Lewis Cole (pseudonym), 136t
liminality, 26–27, 55, 186, 272n54
Lincoln, Abraham, 278n17
linked fate, 187, 254, 299n40
Lipsitz, George, 19
literacy tests, 50, 279n26
Littlefield, Daniel F., Jr., 110
loan words, 157
Loewen, James W., 100
Logan, John R., 114
Lopez-Aguado, Patrick, 143
Loraine Fisher (pseudonym), 136t

Los Angeles: Black-Brown alliances in, 253–54; Black-Brown divide in, 237–44; racial composition of, 62, 253
Los Angeles Police Department (LAPD), 238, 302n14
Louisiana: Creoles in, 46–51, 92–93; interracial relationships in, 43–44; racial order of, 10–11, 43–51; Reconstruction in, 48–50; U.S. acquisition of, 45–46
Louisiana Purchase, 45–46
Louisiana Supreme Court, 47
Loving, Mildred, 85, 105–6, 293n47
Loving, Richard Perry, 85
Loving Generation, 22, 87–90, 149
Loving v. Virginia, 83–87; context of, 83–85; in growth of interracial marriage, 86–87; Loving Generation after, 22, 87–90; Native American ancestry in, 105–6; in post–civil rights era, 269n25
Lower South, 43, 276n1
loyalty, symbolic, 231–32
LULAC. *See* League of United Latin American Citizens (LULAC)
Lumbee, 93, 290n51
Lyman, Stanford M., 227
lynchings, 71

Machado, Manuel A., Jr., 77, 285n54
macroaggressions, 19
Maillard, Kevin, 111
maize, 163
majordomos, 61
majority-minority multiracials, 89–90, 96–97. *See also* white multiracials

manifest destiny, 64
Margery Samson (pseudonym), 136t
marginality, history of scholarship on, 24–26
marginalization: of Black dual-minority multiracials, 98, 114–15; of Blaxicans, 177, 206, 223; intragroup, 192, 223
marginal man thesis, 25
maroons, 110
marriage. *See* antimiscegenation laws; interracial relationships
Marshall, Thurgood, 56, 58
Martinez, Cid G., 233
Maryland, antimiscegenation laws in, 36
masculinity, Black, 103
Mashpee Wampanoag Tribe, 111
Massachusetts, Native Americans in, 104
matrilineal descent, 109–10
Matthews, Thomas, 53
mayate, 242, 244–45, 303n30
McGill, Charlotte, 58
McKee, James B., 15
McKinley, Geron, 260
media coverage: of Barack Obama's identity, 272n56, 273n57; of Black-Brown divide, 234–40, 252; invisibility of Blaxican identity in, 176
Melungeons, 93
Mendez v. Westminster, 71–72
meritocracy, 261
meso-aggressions, 19
mestiza consciousness, 76–77
mestizaje: in Chicana/o studies, 22; in Mexican American identity, 73–77, 81, 178

mestizos: and mestizo privilege, 213; in Mexican American identity, 73–77, 81, 178; in racial order of Latin America, 39–40; term of, 39
metaracial identity, 91
methodology, 120–22
Metoyers, 51
MexiBlack, 125. *See also* Blaxican(s)
Mexican(s): anti-Blackness among, 192–94; authenticity markers of, 212–13; authenticity policing by, 212–16, 218–26; colorism among, 75, 192–93, 207; multiracial ancestry of, 130; phenotype of, 212–13; in racial order of Southwest, 63–67; term of, 9, 68–69
Mexican American(s): anti-Blackness among, 192–94, 244–49; authenticity policing by, 212–16, 218–26; in interracial relationships, 65–66; multigenerational multiraciality of, 4, 129–30; non-Black dual-minority, 18; phenotypes of, 153, 212–13, 227; as race vs. ethnicity, 78–80, 121, 285n56; in racial order of Southwest, 63–67, 69–70; racism against, 70–72, 189–96; segregation of, 68–72; stereotypes of, 138, 202; term of, 9, 69. *See also* Blaxican(s)
Mexican American identity, 68–82; vs. Black identity, 81–82; as Chicana/o, 72–82; *mestizaje* in, 73–77, 81, 178; as monoracial, 77, 80–81, 213; race vs. ethnicity in, 78–80, 121; as white, 65–72, 79, 286n68
Mexican American War, 63–64, 65–66
Mexican Asian multiracials, 18, 98–100

Mexican Black multiracials. *See* Blaxican(s)
Mexican-Black relations. *See* Black-Brown alliances; Black-Brown divide
Mexican culture, transmission of, 250
Mexican-descent Americans, term of, 9. *See also* Mexican American(s)
Mexican food, 162–66
Mexicanos, 71
Mexican Revolution, 70
Mexicans of African descent. *See* Afro-Mexicans
Mexico: on Bracero Program, 70; end of slavery in, 63; racial composition of, 75; racial order of Southwest under, 62–63; slaves in, 37, 284n33; on U.S. census classifications, 70. *See also* Afro-Mexicans; Mexican(s)
Mexipinos, 18, 99
Meyers, Dowell, 185
microaggressions: definition of, 19, 196, 299n11; multiracial, 200, 202–3, 211, 215, 217, 230
middle: law of the excluded, 4; law of the included, 91, 235, 244; racial, 17, 99, 130
military, U.S., 101, 102
Mindiola, Tatcho, Jr., 243, 245
miscegenation. *See* antimiscegenation laws; interracial relationships
Mississippi, Black Asians in, 100–101
Miss Navajo Nation, 111
Mixed Blood (Spickard), 30
mixed-blood category, 22, 111
mixed hair, 153
mixed race, term of, 9. *See also* multiracial, term of
mixed race identities. *See* multiracial identities

mixed race studies, 29–32
"Mixed Race" Studies (Ifekwunigwe), 30
Miyawaki, Michael, 27, 124
mongrelization, 64
Monica Bell (pseudonym), 136t, 160, 220–23
monological paradigm, 4–5
monoracial identities: of Black Americans, 11, 20, 52–60, 81–82; Blaxican identities as rejection of, 5; of Mexican Americans, 77, 80–81, 213
monoracial imperative: Blaxican identity as resistance to, 3–5, 122, 247, 255; definition of, 3; in dual-minority multiracial identities, 98; vs. hypodescent, 20; origins and history of, 17–21; sociologists' acceptance of, 17
monoracial privilege, 19–20, 198
monoracism, 20, 211, 218, 242–43
Montejano, David, 68
Monterey Constitutional Convention, 64–65
Monterrosa, Sean, 259–60
Montez v. Superior Court, 73
Montoya, Joseph, 78
Moore, Mignon, 112–13
Moors, 221
Morehouse, Henry L., 53–54
Moriscos, 41, 276n26
Mörner, Magnus, 38
Mukoyama, Tammy Hiroko-Josefa, 101–2
mulattoes: exoticization of, 215; as indentured servants, 36; in racial order of Anglo-America, 35–36; in racial order of Latin America, 39–40; term of, 36, 274n7, 275n24; in U.S. census, 53

mulatto escape hatch, 58, 280n15
multiculturalism, 22
multicultural social clubs, 172–76
multiethnic, term of, 8–9, 101
multigenerational multiraciality, 4–5, 31, 90, 129–30
multiple passing, 99
multiracial, term of, 8–9, 292n27
multiracial balancing, 151–56, 174
multiracial belt, 185, 197, 298n29
multiracial identities, 83–95; complexity of, 91–92; intergenerational transfer of, 23, 28–29, 188; interracial marriage in rise of, 11, 83–87; vs. multiracial ancestry, 1, 130; multiracial movement in rise of, 88–89; public vs. internalized, 123–24; resistance to white adjacency in, 92–95; shifts over lifetime in, 90–91, 124; sociological research on, 21–32, 270n40, 271n41; work involved in claiming, 209–10. *See also specific identities*
multiracial individuals (multiracials): as percentage of U.S. population, 89; as solution to racism, 88, 264–65; terminology for, 8–9. *See also specific groups and locations*
multiraciality: in ancestry vs. identity, 1, 130; critical, 265–66; multigenerational, 4–5, 31, 90, 129–30
multiracial knowledge, 265
multiracial movement, 22–23, 30, 88–89, 185, 270n36
multiracial mythology, 25
music: in Black-Brown alliances, 253–54; in Blaxican identity, 126, 140, 146–47, 159–62, 220
Myrdal, Gunnar, 48, 57

mythology: of end of racism, 261–62; multiracial, 25

NAACP. *See* National Association for the Advancement of Colored People (NAACP)
Nadal, Kevin L., 20, 217, 231
Nakashima, Cynthia L., 25
names, personal: cultural aspects of, 121–22, 245–46; pseudonyms used for, 121–22
National Association for the Advancement of Colored People (NAACP), 53, 56–57, 60, 72, 82
National Hispanic Week, 78
nationalism: Black, 16, 58, 82; Chicano, 82
National Urban League, 57, 60
Nation of Islam, 59
Native American(s), 104–11; coerced labor of, 34; federal definitions of, 104, 108–9; federal recognition of tribes of, 105, 293n45; in interracial relationships, 105–6, 109–10, 269n12; invisibility of, in popular culture, 176; mixed-blood category of, 22, 111; racial classification of, on government forms, 105, 108; in racial order of California, 65; in racial order of Virginia, 106; slaves of, 106, 107, 109; tribal citizenship of, 108–9; U.S. citizenship of, 108
Native American Black multiracials, 104–11
Native American studies, 22
Native American white multiracials, 90, 106, 108, 289n37
Native Hawaiians, 295n86
Navajo Nation, 111

INDEX

Naylor, Celia E., 109–10
Negro, term of, 59, 245
"Negro Problem," 17, 48
neighborhoods: Blaxican, 128; in Blaxican identity formation, 200–208; residential segregation in, 240–42, 251–52
neophytes, 281n2
Newman, Alyssa M., 185, 197, 298n29
New Mexico, 61, 65, 71, 78
New Negro Movement, 53–55
New Orleans, racial order in, 45–47, 51
new racism, 262
news media. *See* media coverage
New York, Native Americans in, 104
New York Times, 259
Nicole Hodges (pseudonym), 136t, 192–93
Niemonen, Jack, 23
Nipmuc, 104
Norteños, 143–44
North, Black migration to, 54, 56
N-word, 193, 245

Obama, Barack: others' views on identity of, 272n56, 273n57; self-identification of, 26, 119, 272n56; white backlash during presidency of, 262–63
O'Brien, Eileen, 17
Oklahoma, 107
old-fashioned racism, 262
Omi, Michael, 6, 24, 262, 271n43
one-drop rule: acceptance of, in civil rights movement, 57–58, 60; in anti-miscegenation laws, 35–36; Blasian identity as challenge to, 103–4; Blaxican identity as resistance to, 3–5, 122; in colonial Anglo-America, 35; definition of, 3, 268n11; global perspective on, 169–71; in Jim Crow segregation, 52–53; in legal definitions of Blackness, 49; in monoracial Black identity, 52–53, 57–58, 60; vs. mulatto escape hatch, 280n15; origins and history of, 18–21, 58; phenotype as replacement for, 261–62; sociologists' acceptance of, 17; in U.S. state laws, 52; in "What are you?" questions, 199–200
oppression, dual, 258–59
order-functionalist paradigm, 15, 29
Osuji, Chinyere, 237
"other" racial category, 78, 127
outmarriage. *See* interracial relationships

palenques, 37
pan-Africanist movement, 55
pardos, 39, 275n24
parents: in Black Latinos' identity, 112–13; white, of multiracials, 97
parents of Blaxicans, 131–48; learning about race and racism from, 189–96; monoracial identity of, 5, 129; musical tastes of, 146–47, 160–62; overview of influence of, 131–32, 189; single Black, 132–35, 132t; single Mexican or Mexican American, 135–41, 136t; in two-parent households, 141–48, 141t, 147t
Park, Julie, 185
Park, Robert E., 25, 26
passing: multiple, 99; for white, 51, 53, 92
Pastor, Manuel, 239, 254
Paterson, Susan E., 79–80

369

Patterson, Orlando, 226
peer influences on Blaxican identity, 196–200
Pequot, 104
Perea, Juan, 17
Perez, Andrea, 83–84
Perez v. Sharp, 83–84
personal names: cultural aspects of, 121–22, 245–46; pseudonyms used for, 121–22
Peters, Morgan James, 111
Pew Research, 186, 187
phenotypes (physical appearance): of Black Americans, 53, 226–30; in ethnic cues, 227; in ethnicity, 8; in Latin American caste system, 40; of Mexican Americans, 153, 212–13, 227; of Mexicans, 212–13; in mulatto escape hatch, 280n15; in racial formation theory, 7; "racial traits" in, 2–3; as replacement for one-drop rule, 261–62. *See also* Blaxican phenotypes
Pierce, Chester M., 299n11
plaçage, 43–44, 277n4
A Place for US National (APN), 292n27
Plessy, Hommeré A., 48–50
Plessy v. Ferguson, 48–50, 56, 72
pluralism, integrative, 59–60, 280n19
pluralistic multiracial identity, 91
Pocahontas, 294n50
police violence, 259–60
political mobilization: multiracial, 23; against police violence, 259–60
poll taxes, 50, 71, 279n26
popular culture: Black culture in, 219; invisibility of Blaxican identity in, 176; invisibility of dual-minority multiracials in, 176–77; invisibility of Native Americans in, 176; visibility of white multiracials in, 177
population, U.S.: Latinos as percentage of, 233, 287n76; multiracials as percentage of, 89
postcolonial consciousness, 76–77
Powell, Adam Clayton, 57
power-conflict paradigm, 16–17, 29
power dynamics: in authenticity policing, 211–12, 231; in "What are you?" questions, 198
prejudice, intergroup, 193–96, 242–49. *See also* racism
presidential elections: of 1876, 48; of 2020, 263; Republican losses in, 307n26
press coverage. *See* media coverage
prisons, 143–44
privilege: mestizo, 213; monoracial, 19–20, 198; white, 19, 97
Project RACE, 89, 292n27
pseudonyms, 121–22
public identities vs. internalized identities, 123–24
Puerto Rican Black multiracials, 113
Puerto Rico, 113, 170
Pulido, Laura, 6, 253–54
Punjabi Mexicans, 18, 98–100, 125
purity: of blood, 40–41; white racial, 36
Purkayastha, Bandana, 121

Quadroon Balls, 44, 277n4
quinceañeras, 166–67

race: Blaxicans learning from parents about, 189–96; definitions of, used in academia, 23; vs. ethnicity,

INDEX 371

8, 267n20, 285n56; global perspective on, 169–71, 206–7; as kin network, 145; origins of concept of, 1–3; school curricula on topic of, 263–64, 306n22; social construction of, 6, 202; terminology for, 8–10; white privilege of not thinking about, 97
racelessness, 75, 88
race problem, 17
race studies, 10
race suicide fears, 53, 64
race work, 210
Rachel Mabley (pseudonym): on authenticity policing, 229–30; parents and identity of, 141t, 142; strategies for identity expression by, 157–58, 160, 162–63, 167
racial authenticity. *See* authenticity
racial capital, 261–62
racial categories: arbitrary nature of, in segregation, 49; Hispanic, 77–80; "other," 78, 127; in racial formation theory, 7; in Virginia law, 105, 293n50; white as default in, 79, 97, 210
racial creed, 56–57
racial epithets, 125, 192, 203
racial extinction, 64–65
Racial Formation in the United States (Omi and Winant), 24, 271n43
racial formation theory, 6–8, 31–32
racial hierarchies. *See* racial order
racial identities: in adolescence, 126; vs. cultural identities, 131, 151; flexibility in, 18, 27–28; racial ancestry in, 3–6; "What are you?" questions about, 196–200. *See also specific identities*

racial integration. *See* integration, racial; segregation
Racial Integrity Act of 1924 (Virginia), 85, 105
Racially Mixed People in America (Root), 23, 30
racial middle, 17, 99, 130
racial order: definition of, 7; dual-minority multiracials in, 18–19, 98; in racial formation theory, 7–8. *See also* binary racial order; ternary racial order; *and specific locations*
racial power, 198
racial purity, white, 36
racial reckoning, 263
racial segregation. *See* integration, racial; segregation
racial self-designation. *See specific identities*
racial socialization, 87, 131–32. *See also* parents
racial state, 7–8, 77–78, 84
racial strategies for expressing Blaxican identity, 152–56
racial subjectivity of sociologists, 15–17, 24
"racial traits," 2–3
racism: during Barack Obama's presidency, 262–63; Blaxicans learning from parents about, 189–96; civil rights movement's approach to, 57; dual-minority multiracials' experience of, 98, 113–15; institutionalization of, in European colonialism, 2; intergroup, between Black and Mexican Americans, 193–96, 242–49; against Mexican Americans, 70–72, 189–96; multiracials as solution to, 88, 264–65; myth of end

racism (*continued*)
 of, 261–62; old-fashioned vs. new, 262; of sociologists, 16; term of, 59. *See also specific forms*
radical *mestizaje*, 77
Randolph, Maketa, 102–3
Rappahannock, 104–5, 293n45
Reconstruction, 48–50, 57, 278n17
Reconstruction Amendments, 48–50, 278n17
recruitment, 231
Red Power, 280n16
Regents of the University of California v. Bakke, 305n17
religion in Blaxican identity, 166–69
reproductive agency, 157–59
Republican Party, 263–64, 306n22, 307n26
residential segregation, 240–42, 251–52
resistant agency, 157–59
reverse discrimination, 305n17
Rice, Tamir, 259
Riley, Steven F., 274n77
Rios, Victor, 128, 233
Rodriguez, Gregory, 77
Rodriguez, Santos, 260
Rolfe, John, 294n50
Romo, Rebecca, 28–29, 214
Ron Salazar (pseudonym), 148t
Root, Maria P. P., 23, 30, 87, 102, 115, 288n25
Royal Pragmatic on Marriage, 38
rural areas, Black migration out of, 54

Sabrina Johnston (pseudonym): on learning about racism, 191–92; neighborhood influences on, 203–4, 208; parents and identity of, 132t, 133; on social clubs, 174; strategies for identity expression by, 168
Saether, Steinar A., 38
Salgado, Erik, 259–60
Samora, Julian, 77
Samuels, Gina Miranda, 133–34
Sánchez, Federico A., 77, 285n54
Sánchez, George I., 283n12
Sandoval, Chela, 77
San Francisco, racial composition of, 62
schools: in Blaxican identity, 196, 200–204; end of segregation in, 57, 72; fighting in, 238–39, 243–44; race in curricula of, 263–64, 306n22; segregation of Mexican Americans in, 68, 71–72. *See also* colleges
Schuyler, Philippa Duke, 279n11
scientific racism, 6, 24, 53, 64
SCLC. *See* Southern Christian Leadership Conference (SCLC)
Sebastiano Flores (pseudonym), 136t, 139–40, 258–59
Second Reconstruction, 57
segregation: Jim Crow, 11, 50–58; in Louisiana, 48–49; of Mexican Americans, 68–72; in monoracial Black identity, 11, 52–60; overturning of laws enforcing, 56–57; in prisons, 143; problems with racial definitions in, 49; residential, 240–42, 251–52; school, 57, 68, 71–72; Supreme Court on, 49–50, 56–57, 72. *See also* integration, racial
selective integration, 94–95, 261–62, 265
Selena Fernandez (pseudonym), 132t, 171–72

INDEX

self-identification. *See* racial identities; *and specific identities*
Seminoles, 106–11
Seminole Wars, 110
"separate but equal" doctrine, 49, 56
Separate Car Act of 1890 (Louisiana), 48
separatism, Black, 58
sexism in Mexico, 192
Shaw, Jamiel, Jr., 238
Sheila Ramirez (pseudonym), 136t
Shinnecock, 104
Siena College, 259
Simmons, Kimora Lee, 103
single parents of Blaxicans: Black, 132–35, 132t; Mexican or Mexican American, 135–41, 136t
Sistema de Castas, 39
skin color: in authenticity policing of Blaxicans, 226–31; in Blaxican identity, 152–56; as racial trait, 2; and social mobility, 94, 290n53. *See also* colorism; phenotypes (physical appearance)
slavery, end of: in Mexico, 63; in United States, 278n17
slaves: Asian, 284n33; Indigenous, 37, 63, 275n12; Native American, 34
slaves, African: in California, 63–65, 282n19; hair and skin color of, 226; legal status of, 34–35; Native American adoption of, 110; Native American owners of, 106, 107, 109; in racial order of Anglo-America, 34–36; in racial order of Latin America, 37, 39–42, 275n12; in racial order of Louisiana, 44–47; in racial order of Southwest, 63–65
Smith, Sandra, 112–13

social class in Blaxican identity, 200–201, 206
social clubs in Blaxican identity, 172–76
social construction of race, 6, 202
social engineering, 60, 280n20
Social Forces (journal), 23
socialization: cultural, 132, 140–42, 148; racial, 87, 131–32. *See also* parents
social media, Blaxican community on, 182–85
social mobility: in Latin America, 40; and skin color, 94, 290n53; in Southwest, 62, 69
social movements, definition of, 270n36. *See also specific movements*
Social Problems (journal), 23
social realm vs. legal-political realm, 49, 56–57
social science, 21–24
Sociedad de Castas, 39
sociocultural capital, 15, 280n15
Sociological Abstracts (journal), 23
sociology, 10, 15–32; critical mixed race studies in, 29–32; ethnic studies in, 21–24; failure to anticipate civil rights movement in, 15–17; history of multiracial identity scholarship in, 21–32, 270n40, 271n41; liminality in, 26–27; marginality in, 24–26; order-functional paradigm in, 15, 29; power-conflict paradigm in, 16–17, 29; racial subjectivity in, 15–17, 24
Song, Miri, 29, 187–88
sororities in Blaxican identity, 172–76
soul food, 163–64
soundscapes, 253

South, U.S.: Black migration out of, 54, 56; Lower, 43, 276n1. *See also* Jim Crow segregation laws; *and specific locations*
South Carolina, colonial, 276n1
South Central Dreams (Hondagneu-Sotelo and Pastor), 254
Southern Christian Leadership Conference (SCLC), 57, 60
Southwest, U.S.: definition of, 281n1; interracial relationships in, 61, 65; Mexican American identity in, 70–71, 80–81; racial order in, 11, 61–70, 80; segregation in, 68. *See also specific locations*
Spaces of Conflict, Sounds of Solidarity (Johnson), 253
Spain: Latin America under, 37–40; Louisiana under, 45–46; Southwest under, 61–62
Spanglish, 157–58
Spanish America. *See* Latin America
Spanish clubs, 172
Spanish identity in California, 65, 67
Spanish language: in authenticity policing, 212, 216, 224–25; in Black-Brown divide, 243; in Blaxican identity formation, 205; in California history, 63; in code-switching, 157–59; expression of Blaxican identity through, 159–61; as marker of Mexican authenticity, 212
spatial entitlement, 253
Spickard, Paul, 29–30
spigger, term of, 125
Spivak, Gayatari, 76, 285n47
state, racial, 7–8, 77–78, 84
State Department, U.S., 70
Steinberg, Stephen, 15–16

stereotypes: of Black Americans, 103, 135, 138, 194, 202; in Black-Brown divide, 238; in controlling images, 194; of Mexican Americans, 138, 202
Stevenson, Coke, 70
Stickmon, Janet, 102
Stonequist, Everett V., 25
strategic antiessentialism, 76
strategic essentialism, 76, 285n47
Strum, Circe Dawn, 109
subjectivity: collective, in Blaxican identity, 169, 184–88; racial, of sociologists, 15–17, 24
succession, ethnic, 237
Sue, Derald Wing, 299n11
suicide, race, 53, 64
Supreme Court, Louisiana, 47
Supreme Court, U.S.: on affirmative action, 262–63, 305n17; on interracial marriage, 84–85; Ketanji Brown Jackson's confirmation hearings for, 264; on nationality in Fourteenth Amendment, 72; on segregation, 49–50, 56–57, 72; "separate but equal" doctrine of, 49, 56; on voting rights, 50, 263. *See also specific cases*
Sureños, 143–44
Suzanna Williams (pseudonym), 136t

Tabb, William K., 58
Tafoya, Sonya, 79
Talented Tenth, 54
Talia Ramos (pseudonym): on authenticity policing, 217–18; on Black-Brown divide, 246–47; on learning about racism, 190–91; parents and identity of, 136t, 138–39, 146; school influences on, 202–3; strategies for identity expression by,

159–60, 163–64, 167–68; on "What are you?" questions, 198
Taylor, Breonna, 259
ternary racial order: of Brazil, 170; of California and Southwest, 61–64, 67, 80; of Latin America, 10, 33, 37–42; of Louisiana and Gulf Coast, 10, 43–47
Terrance Williams (pseudonym), 136t
Tesler, Michael, 262
Texas: racial order of, 65; racism against Mexican Americans in, 70–71; segregation of Mexican Americans in, 68
Texas Republic, 65
third root, 75, 285n54
Third World, colonialism in, 58
Thirteenth Amendment, 48–50, 278n17
Thornton, Michael C., 101
TikTok, 183
Tilden, Samuel, 48
Toledo, Adam, 260
Toomer, Jean, 54, 279n11
Townsend, Sarah S. M., 27
Trail of Tears, 107
Tran, Nellie, 79–80
transgender theory, 104
transracial adoption, 133–34
travel, global perspective on race through, 169–71, 206–7
Treitler, Bashi, 115
Trejo, Danny, 239
triracial isolates, 93
Truman, Harry S., 56
Trump, Donald, 238, 263, 264, 286n64, 289n35
Turner, Jessie, 22
Twine, France Winddance, 195

understanding clauses, 50, 279n26

Vaca, Nicolás, 252
Valenzuela, Antonio, 259–60
Vanessa Solis (pseudonym), 142t, 147, 160
Vasconcelos, José, 73–74
Vélez-Ibáñez, Carlos G., 77
vernacular English, African American, 157
Vietnamese Black multiracials, 102
Vigil, James Diego, 77, 237
violence: police, 259–60; school, 238–39, 243–44
Virginia: antimiscegenation laws in, 36, 85, 105; Native Americans in, 104–6, 293n45; one-drop rule in, 52, 105; racial categories in, 105, 293n50
visibility. See invisibility
voter fraud, 263
voting rights, 50, 85–86, 263, 279n26
Voting Rights Act of 1965, 85–86, 263, 269n25

Wampanoag, 104, 111
Ward, Hines, 103
Waring, Chandra, 121
Warren, Earl, 84, 85
Warren, Jonathan W., 195
Washington, Myra S., 103–4
Watts, 253
Wei, Liang, 185
West, Candice, 32
West, Cornel, 257–58
wetblack, term of, 125
"What are you?" questions, 196–200
white: "acting," 217, 222; passing for, 51, 53, 92; term of, 10
White, Walter, 57

white adjacency: of Creoles, 49; of Mexican Americans, 49; multiracials' resistance to, 92–95; of white multiracials, 27
white Americans: European identity of, 97, 292n5; in Harlem Renaissance, 54; in Republican Party, 307n26; term of, 10; "What are you?" questions by, 198
white Asian multiracials, 27, 90, 114–15
white backlash, 262–63, 305n17
white Black binary. *See* binary racial order
white Black couples. *See* Black white couples
white Black multiracials. *See* Black white multiracials
white domination, 41, 45, 58, 95, 262
white hegemony, 95, 195, 262
white identity: of Chinese immigrants, 100–101; as default identity, 79, 97, 210; dual-minority multiracials' lack of, 98; of Mexican Americans, 65–72, 79, 286n68; multiracials' resistance to, 92–95; white privilege of not thinking about, 97
white multiracials: census data on, 89–90; vs. dual-minority multiracials, 96–97; as focus of multiracial scholarship, 96, 177; racial identity of, 124, 148; visibility of, in popular culture, 177; white Asians as, 27, 90, 114–15; white Latinos as, 27–28; white Native Americans as, 90, 106, 108, 289n37. *See also* Black white multiracials
whiteness: in American identity, 79–80; certificates of, in colonial Latin America, 276n26; decentering, in dual-minority multiracial identities, 98; as default category, 79, 97, 210; illusion of complete, 3; of indentured servants, 35; as option only for non-Black groups, 195; in transracial adoption, 133–34; white privilege of not thinking about, 97
white parents: of multiracials, 97; transracial adoption by, 133–34
white privilege, 19, 97
white racial purity, 36
white racism. *See* racism
White Redemption, 48
white supremacy: during Barack Obama's presidency, 262–63; dual-minority multiracials' experience of, 98–99; institutionalization of, in European colonialism, 2; paranoia about passing for white in, 53; Reconstruction and, 49–50; in sociology, 16; whiteness of indentured servants in, 35
white women in colonial era, 34, 37
Wijeyesinghe, Charmaine L., 265
Williams, Kim M., 270n36
Williams, Mark, 272n56
Williamson, Joel, 53
Winant, Howard, 6, 24, 262, 271n43
women: beauty standards for, 226, 228–30; Black, phenotypes of, 217, 226–30; Blasian, 103; Blaxican, authenticity policing of, 212, 214–15, 220, 228–31; in cultural socialization, 140; Mexican, sexism against, 192; Mexican American, phenotypes of, 153, 227; role of, in cultural socialization, 140; white, in colonial era, 34, 37

Woods, Mario, 259
Woods, Tiger, 26, 103
World War I, 54, 56

X, Malcolm, 58

Yellow Power, 280n16
Young, Whitney, 57–58

Zahira Davis (pseudonym), 142, 142t, 161, 165, 174
zambos, 39
Zamora, Sylvia, 75, 237
Zogby International, 272n56

In the Borderlands and Transcultural Studies series

Indigenous Sacraments: Christian Rituals and Local Responses at the Fringes of Spanish America, 1529–1800
by Oriol Ambrogio Gali

The Storied Landscape of Iroquoia: History, Conquest, and Memory in the Native Northeast
by Chad Anderson

Country of the Cursed and the Driven: Slavery and the Texas Borderlands
by Paul Barba

How the West Was Drawn: Mapping, Indians, and the Construction of the Tran-Mississippi West
by David Bernstein

Chiricahua and Janos: Communities of Violence in the Southwestern Borderlands, 1680–1880
by Lance R. Blyth

The Borderland of Fear: Vincennes, Prophetstown, and the Invasion of the Miami Homeland
by Patrick Bottiger

Captives: How Stolen People Changed the World
by Catherine M. Cameron

The Allure of Blackness among Mixed-Race Americans, 1862–1916
by Ingrid Dineen-Wimberly

Intermarriage from Central Europe to Central Asia: Mixed Families in the Age of Extremes
edited and introduced by Adrienne Edgar and Benjamin Frommer

Words Like Birds: Sakha Language Discourses and Practices in the City
by Jenanne Ferguson

Transnational Crossroads: Remapping the Americas and the Pacific
edited by Camilla Fojas and Rudy P. Guevarra Jr.

Conquering Sickness: Race, Health, and Colonization in the Texas Borderlands
by Mark Allan Goldberg

Creek Internationalism in an Age of Revolution, 1763–1818
by James L. Hill

The Forgotten Diaspora: Mesoamerican Migrations and the Making of the U.S.-Mexico Borderlands
by Travis Jeffres

Globalizing Borderlands Studies in Europe and North America
edited and with an introduction by John W. I. Lee and Michael North

Of Corn and Catholicism: A History of Religion and Power in Pueblo Indian Patron Saint Feast Days
by Andrea Maria McComb Sanchez

Illicit Love: Interracial Sex and Marriage in the United States and Australia
by Ann McGrath

Shades of Gray: Writing the New American Multiracialism
by Molly Littlewood McKibbin

The Limits of Liberty: Mobility and the Making of the Eastern U.S.-Mexico Border
by James David Nichols

In Praise of the Ancestors: Names, Identity, and Memory in Africa and the Americas
by Susan Elizabeth Ramírez

Between Black and Brown: Blaxicans and Multiraciality in Comparative Historical Perspective
by Rebecca Romo, G. Reginald Daniel, and J Sterphone

Native Diasporas: Indigenous Identities and Settler Colonialism in the Americas
edited by Gregory D. Smithers and Brooke N. Newman

Shape Shifters: Journeys across Terrains of Race and Identity
edited by Lily Anne Y. Welty Tamai, Ingrid Dineen-Wimberly, and Paul Spickard

Scars of War: The Politics of Paternity and Responsibility for the Amerasians of Vietnam
by Sabrina Thomas

The Southern Exodus to Mexico: Migration across the Borderlands after the American Civil War
by Todd W. Wahlstrom

To order or obtain more information on these or other University of Nebraska Press titles, visit nebraskapress.unl.edu.

www.ingramcontent.com/pod-product-compliance
Lightning Source LLC
Chambersburg PA
CBHW031845220426
43663CB00006B/500